JENNIFER SERRAVALLO

300+
Strategies
with Learning
Progressions

The Reading Strategies Book 2.0

YOUR RESEARCH-BASED GUIDE TO DEVELOPING SKILLED READERS

HEINEMANN • PORTSMOUTH, NH

Heinemann
145 Maplewood Avenue, Suite 300
Portsmouth, NH 03801
www.heinemann.com

"Dedicated to Teachers" is a trademark of Greenwood Publishing Group, LLC.

The author and publisher wish to thank those who have generously given permission to reprint borrowed material:

page 8: Used with permission of Guilford Press, from "Connecting Early Language and Literacy to Later Reading (Dis)abilities: Evidence, Theory, and Practice" by H.S. Scarborough from *Handbook of Early Literacy Research* edited by S.B. Neuman and D.K. Dickinson, copyright © 2003; permission conveyed through Copyright Clearance Center.

page 9: Used with permission of John Wiley & Sons, from "The Science of Reading Progresses: Communicating Advances Beyond the Simple View of Reading" by Nell K. Duke and Kelly B. Cartwright from *Reading Research Quarterly* 56(S1) 2021 by the International Literacy Association, copyright 2021; permission conveyed through Copyright Clearance Center.

page 13: ©Copyright 2010. National Governors Association Center for Best Practices and Council of Chief State School Officers. All rights reserved.

page 60: Engagement Inventory from *Teaching Reading in Small Groups* by Jennifer Serravallo. Copyright © 2010 by Jennifer Serravallo. Published by Heinemann, Portsmouth, NH. Reprinted by permission of the publisher.

page 63: Reading Interest Survey from "'But There's Nothing Good to Read' (In the Library Media Center)" by Denice Hildebrandt, originally appearing in *Media Spectrum: The Journal for Library Media Specialists in Michigan* (vol. 28, no. 3, pp. 34–37, Fall 2001). Reprinted by permission of the author.

page 121: Adapted from *Letter Lessons and First Words: Phonics Foundations That Work* by Heidi Anne Mesmer. Copyright © 2019 by Heidi Anne Mesmer. Published by Heinemann, Portsmouth, NH. Reprinted by permission of the publisher.

See page 463 for image credits.

Library of Congress Control Number: 2022947911
ISBN-13: 978-0-325-13267-9

Editor: Katie Wood Ray
Production: Denise Botelho, Victoria Merecki
Cover and interior designs: Suzanne Heiser
Composition: Gina Poirier Design
Cover image: Mark Airs / Ikon Images
Illustrations: Many of the charts were provided by Merridy Gnagey and Tiffany Abbott Fuller
Manufacturing: Val Cooper

Printed in the United States of America on acid-free paper.

1 2 3 4 5   BB   26 25 24 23 22 PO4500863885

Contents

Acknowledgments

My first and deepest thanks go to my editor, my writing soul mate, Katie Wood Ray. Thank you for making time each week (during your retirement!) to lend your wisdom and writing chops to this project. I could not have done this level of re-visioning without you as a thought partner. I appreciate every time we had a 30-plus-minute conversation over a single word to make sure we had *just the right one*, every time you found ways to make huge cuts without losing the core meaning, every time you called me on my tendency to use passive voice. I appreciate every one of the many, many passes to make each chapter just a *little bit better*. I'm so, so grateful to you. Thank you.

One of the biggest tasks in this new edition was to lean on research more heavily than ever before, and I knew to do it well I needed help. I needed a research assistant—someone who would be deeply familiar with research related to the content I was writing about, have access to the studies we needed, and have the knowledge to help me evaluate the quality of studies we read and choose the best of the best. I asked several researchers for help, and Rachael Gabriel came through for me (thank you, Rachael!) by introducing me to the incredibly smart, deeply knowledgeable, passionate, hardest-working postdoc, Gabriel DellaVecchia. Gabe, thank you for every one of the many ways you helped with this project, from weighing in on which strategies to cut from the first edition, to finding hundreds and hundreds of relevant studies for us to read, to giving guidance on possible revisions for those strategies that remained, to providing research citations throughout. I learned so much from our weekly meetings and all you wrote and shared. I never want to write another book without a research assistant (*ahem,* *Gabe*) again!

And speaking of researchers, I want to thank Drs. Linneah Ehri and Maryanne Wolf for being readers of an earlier version of the Accuracy chapter. Your feedback was invaluable. Thanks also to Sandra Maddox and Angie Neal for your collaboration, insights, and feedback during the revision of that chapter.

Thank you to Merridy Gnagey and Tiffany Fuller for lending your artistry, creativity, and skill by stepping in as illustrators for this book. By my count, there are more than **180** new charts throughout this book that you lovingly hand-created at your dining room table or desk, in between family obligations, across many months. You both have such a talent for translating ideas into teacher- and student-friendly, classroom-ready visuals.

Thanks to my team at Heinemann—Roderick Spelman for your constant and consistent support and helping to make sure I had what I needed to do this book and do it well; Sarah Fournier, Denise Botelho, and Victoria Merecki for your critical roles in production, making sure we were on schedule and the book was on point; Suzanne Heiser for yet another gorgeous design that kept all the elements teachers have grown to love while still updating the look and feel in a fresh, modern way; Cindy Black, my incredible copy editor, who read this giant book with such detail and care; Alicia Mitchell, Eric Chalek, and Pam Smith for your marketing and sales savvy; and Brett Whitmarsh and Erika McCaffrey for your ideas and support with getting my message out there.

Finally, thank you to my children, Lola and Vivian, not only for helping to identify the best children's literature and informational books, which I used as a text set to replace all the lesson language examples throughout the book (you two have great tastes!), but also for sharing me with educators and kids around the world. I hope you grow up to find a career that you love as much as I love mine.

◎ Strategy Basics

Strategies are deliberate, intentional, purposeful actions a learner can take to accomplish a specific task or become skilled (Afflerbach, Pearson, & Paris, 2008; Manoli & Papadopoulou, 2012). Strategies make something a reader is attempting doable, actionable, and visible through a step-by-step procedure. Strategies offer a temporary scaffold to support a student's independent practice. Eventually, after the reader develops automaticity, the need for the strategy fades away. Strategies are a means to an end, not an end unto themselves (Duke, 2014b).

Researchers, practitioners, and theorists use the terms *skill* and *strategy* differently (e.g., Afflerbach, Pearson, & Paris, 2008; Beers, 2002; Harris & Hodges, 1995; Harvey & Goudvis, 2007; Keene & Zimmermann, 2007; Sinatra, Brown, & Reynolds, 2002; Taberski, 2000; Wiggins, 2013), with some using the word *strategy* to refer to a set of seven processes specific to comprehension (e.g., determining importance, visualizing, activating prior knowledge, and so on). In this book, you'll see those processes referred to as *skills*. As for strategies, you will find hundreds of them in this book that will support not only reading comprehension but also other important reading goals such as engagement, reading with accuracy, conversing about books, and more.

What Is the Research Base for Strategy Instruction?

The rationale for using strategies in the classroom is supported by an enormous research base (e.g., Alexander, Graham, & Harris, 1998; Chiu, 1998; Dignath & Büttner, 2008; Donker et al., 2014; Georgiou & Das, 2018; Haller, Child, & Walberg, 1988; Hattie, Biggs, & Purdie, 1996; Ho & Lau, 2018; Pressley & Afflerbach, 1995; Weinstein, Husman, & Dierking, 2000). Strategy instruction has been demonstrated to positively impact *all* students, no matter their age, socioeconomic background, or gifted designation or if they have a learning disability (Berkeley, Scruggs, & Mastropieri, 2010; Donker et al., 2014; Okkinga et al., 2018; Shanahan et al., 2010). Children who learn to use strategies are more *self-regulated*, actively working to use what they know to be successful and engaged with reading, which ultimately enhances their learning and overall performance (Duke & Cartwright, 2021; Zimmerman, 1986, 2002).

Reading strategies have been shown to improve all areas of reading including, but not limited to, student's motivation and engagement (see McBreen & Savage, 2021), word-level reading (see Steacy et al., 2016), vocabulary acquisition (see Wright & Cervetti, 2017), comprehension (see Samuelstuen & Bråten, 2005), fluency (see Stevens, Walker, & Vaughn, 2017), and more.

Strategies offer *procedural* knowledge (i.e., "how-to"), which a learner can apply with intention and purpose, aligned to a reading goal (Alexander, Graham, & Harris, 1998). Research has shown even more effective results when strategies students learn are coupled with *conditional* knowledge (i.e., knowing *when* to apply them [Donker et al., 2014]), when they are meaningfully tied to students' goals, and when learners have agency and choice in their use (Allen & Hancock, 2008; Mason, 2004).

Throughout the literature on strategies, researchers tend to organize them into three main types: *cognitive*, *metacognitive*, and *management* (e.g., Boekaerts 1997; de Boer et al., 2018; Mayer, 2008; Pressley, 2002a; Weinstein & Mayer, 1986). The three hundred–plus strategies in this book address all categories and subtypes (see chart on page 2).

Key Ideas from the Research

Strategies:

- provide **actionable steps**.

- are a **means to an end** (skills, goals), not an end in and of themselves.

- offer a **temporary scaffold**. As readers become increasingly automatic, conscious attention to a strategy fades.

- can **support readers' improvement in all areas of reading**—from motivation to decoding to fluency to comprehension and more.

- **benefit all students**—no matter their age, developmental level, or abilities.

- **support active self-regulation**, a key to learning and performance.

Types of Strategies, Definitions, and Examples

Type of Strategy	Definition	Examples	Example Strategies from This Book
Cognitive (see Brown & Palincsar, 1989; Mayer, 2008; Pintrich et al., 1991; Weinstein, Husman, & Dierking, 2000)	*Strategies used to increase understanding and make learning more meaningful*	Rehearsal strategies such as repeating information to remember it	**9.5** Read, Cover, Remember, Retell
		Elaboration strategies such as building connections between information and summarizing and paraphrasing	**5.16** Summarize with "Uh-oh . . . UH-OH . . . Phew!"
		Organization strategies such as drawing graphs or pictures to remember information or to represent relationships	**8.14** Consider Structure: Problem/Solution
Metacognitive (see Schraw & Dennison, 1994; Veenman, Van Hout-Wolters, & Afflerbach, 2006; Zimmerman, 2002)	*Strategies that activate and regulate cognition and help learners to monitor and control their learning*	Planning strategies such as setting goals, making a plan for learning time, deciding an order in which to approach a set of tasks	**2.9** Read with a Purpose in Mind
		Monitoring strategies such as checking on one's learning/comprehension and taking action to correct misunderstandings, such as rereading	**3.9** Check In with Yourself, Reread, Fix Up
		Evaluating strategies such as analyzing whether and how much was learned	**7.25** Analyze the Development of Theme
Management (see Palincsar & Brown, 1984; Pintrich, 2000)	*Strategies used to manage context to improve learning*	Management of effort strategies such as staying focused on the task(s) despite distractions or challenges	**2.17** Consider Mind over Matter
		Management of peers and others strategies such as working with peers or teachers in cooperation or collaboration to learn	**12.11** Reflect and Set Goals for a Conversation
		Management of the environment strategies such as using materials appropriately during learning, setting up a learning environment to be successful	**2.14** Choose Your Reading Environment

When Do I Teach Strategies?

Strategies are helpful any time you want students to get better at their reading, writing about reading, or conversation about reading. Strategies simply suggest to children *how to do it*, whether the *it* is reading with more stamina, decoding a word, reading with expression, figuring out the main idea, and so on. Teaching strategies means teaching explicitly, and that's good teaching for all children (e.g., Donker et al., 2014; Ehri, 2020; Shanahan et al., 2010; Williams, 2005).

During Your ELA/Literacy Block

If you teach reading as a subject area, reading strategies can help. Whether your students are all reading the same book, they're split into book clubs or literature circles, or they're all reading books they've chosen independently; whether you call your literacy time "balanced" or "comprehensive" or "structured"; whether you read novels together as a class, run a reading workshop, or teach using a core program; no matter who published your curriculum or how the lessons are organized—strategies have an important place. Also, it's a misconception that children *learn to read* until third grade and then they *read to learn* thereafter. Students of all ages continue to learn to read with increasing insight, depth, and engagement; can consistently add to their vocabulary knowledge; and can improve their conversations and writing about reading (e.g., Pearson, Moje, & Greenleaf, 2010; Shanahan & Shanahan, 2012). Strategies belong in every literacy classroom, from preschool through high school . . . and beyond!

During Whole-Class, Small-Group, or One-on-One Instruction

Strategies offer students a how-to that helps the learning click more quickly and makes what you're teaching transferrable. If you're teaching a lesson to the whole class, before sending students off for independent practice, add a strategy to your demonstration to give students the steps they need to repeat what you showed them when they are working on their own. When you read aloud to your students, plan stopping places to think aloud and model strategies. If you find a small group of students in need of the same support, pull them together and offer a strategy with some guided practice. When students are in a book club, listen in to their conversation and consider if they could benefit from a strategy to deepen comprehension or conversation skills. When you're working with students one on one, quickly assess and then offer a strategy for what they can try next.

During Content Studies

During content studies you undoubtedly have knowledge-based goals and are explicitly teaching children information and vocabulary aligned to them. However, if children are reading (or writing or speaking about) texts during any part of your lessons, chances are they can learn to read, write, and speak with more care and comprehension by learning reading strategies along the way. If you teach some lessons focused on *what* you want students to know, and other lessons focused on *how* students access that knowledge from texts, they will learn even more content (Cervetti et al., 2012; Guthrie et al., 2004; Romance & Vitale, 2001).

Why Are There Three Hundred-Plus Strategies?

Students make the most progress when teaching is responsive to their needs; with the valuable instructional minutes we have, we should offer students strategies to help them stretch and grow beyond what they can already do (Anderson, Graham, & Harris, 1998; Glaser, 1984). In any given classroom, students are likely to have a wide range of abilities and interests and needs, their needs will shift as the year progresses, and the types of texts and genres they will read will vary (Fitzgerald, 2016; Tobin, 2008). To teach responsively, teachers need a massive toolbox of strategies and ideas, and the ability to be flexible and nimble.

Similarly, readers who have several ways to get at the same skill benefit because they can be flexible and nimble based on text type, reading situation, and more (Cartwright, 2006; Gnaedinger, Hund, & Hesson-McInnis, 2016). For this reason, in each chapter you'll find suites of strategies that build the same skill(s) or support readers in similar situations.

You may be excited about the hundreds of strategies in this book—but resist the urge to teach too many at once, or even throughout the year! In your weekly planning, you may select a few strategies to use for whole-class instruction (while guiding children through a read-aloud text, during science or social studies instruction to help them learn information from their textbook, during reading time to understand how to jot about their reading in meaningful ways), others to use with different small groups or targeted one-on-one instruction. But be careful not to teach too many all at once, or you risk burdening your students with a heavy cognitive load that may result in *no* strategies being used (Chandler & Sweller, 1991). Also, for students who learn with one teacher for Tier 1 instruction and a different teacher for intervention, try to give them practice with the *same* strategies focused on the *same goal* in both places rather than overwhelm them with too much all at once.

◎ Navigate the Book

Although this book is filled with hundreds of ideas for instruction, you don't need to read it in order—or really, read it in its entirety—before using it effectively. The book is organized according to *goals* with one chapter for each of thirteen goals. Then, each chapter is organized according to *skill progressions* that move from more basic strategies to more sophisticated ones across the chapter. Each *strategy* is explored on its own page, with accompanying lesson language, teaching tips, research links, prompts, charts, and more. The book is designed so you can quickly flip and find what you need to teach responsively and with intention.

Understand the Goals That Focus Each Chapter

A *goal* is something to work toward. You can also think of a goal as a large category on which you focus instruction for an individual, group, or whole class. Having goals in mind helps us to choose relevant strategies, offer feedback tied to goals, and invite students to reflect according to success criteria—a collection of practices shown to have a strong positive effect on student growth and achievement (Fuchs, Fuchs, & Deno, 1985; Hattie, 2009; Schunk & Rice, 1989, 1991) and that correlate to stronger comprehension and motivation (Cartwright, 2015). *Process* goals (such as how to learn information or read with a clear purpose) have been shown to make a bigger positive difference than *product* goals (such as reading to answer a teacher's comprehension question), especially for children with reading comprehension difficulties (Cartwright, 2015; Pressley & Allington, 2014; Schunk & Rice, 1989, 1991).

Each chapter in this book focuses on one of thirteen equally important reading process goals. While it is critically important that children develop skills in all areas from the beginning and throughout their development (see Scarborough, 2001; National Reading Panel, 2000), I've arranged the thirteen goals in a "hierarchy of action" to help you decide what goal you might focus on during your targeted, individualized instruction when students need help with more than one. Focus is important so as not to overwhelm the learner with a heavy cognitive load (Chandler & Sweller, 1991). For example, if a reader could use support with reading words accurately *and* with inferring theme, during

Reading Goals: A Hierarchy of Action

Notice that the colors for each goal on the hierarchy graphic correspond to the color of each chapter.

small-group instruction I'd teach a few strategies over a few weeks focused on accuracy first, and then once I noticed they've made skill progress, I'd move on to a few weeks of strategies to support their understanding of theme.

In addition to the goal-focused strategies a reader is learning during small-group instruction, they are also working toward collective (class) goals aligned to grade-level standards. For example, a student working to improve their fluency may learn strategies connected to that goal during their targeted small-group and one-on-one instruction. At the same time, that student might be engaged with their whole class in a study focused around a few goals related to reading informational texts with more understanding, such as learning how to determine main ideas, key details, and the meaning of unknown vocabulary.

On the first few pages of each chapter, you will find a description of each goal, as well as information about how to assess to determine if students would benefit from that goal. The book is organized this way so you can quickly flip to the section you need to respond to student needs or to find strategies aligned to grade-level expectations or curriculum goals. You may want to read across the first few pages of all chapters to become familiar with the goals, the research support for the goal, and the skills that a reader will work on as part of the goal and to get suggestions for formative assessments to learn if your student(s) would benefit from working on that goal.

Over 35 years ago, Gough and Tunmer (1986) shared a theoretical framework they called The Simple View of Reading, based on scientific findings from educational research, proposing that *comprehension* (synonymous with "reading" in their definition) is the product of *word recognition* and *language comprehension*.

word recognition
the ability to transform print into spoken language

✕

language comprehension
the ability to understand spoken language

From Gough and Tunmer (1986).

=

reading comprehension

About 15 years later, Scarborough (2001) presented her theoretical framework known as Scarborough's Reading Rope or The Rope Model in which she unpacked the larger categories presented in the Simple View and specified strands within each that educators should assess and teach over time to develop skilled, automatic readers.

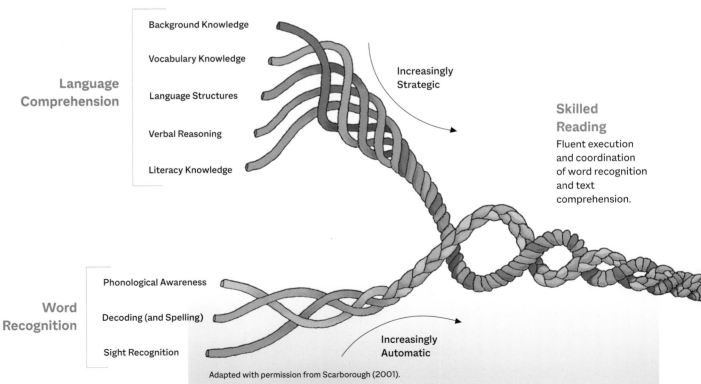

Language Comprehension
- Background Knowledge
- Vocabulary Knowledge
- Language Structures
- Verbal Reasoning
- Literacy Knowledge

Increasingly Strategic

Word Recognition
- Phonological Awareness
- Decoding (and Spelling)
- Sight Recognition

Increasingly Automatic

Skilled Reading
Fluent execution and coordination of word recognition and text comprehension.

Adapted with permission from Scarborough (2001).

Recently, Duke and Cartwright (2021) expanded upon these previous models in their Active View of Reading theoretical framework, which incorporates the findings of studies conducted in the 20 years since the publication of Scarborough's Rope. This framework includes two essential new categories: *active self-regulation* (including but not limited to motivation and engagement, metacognitive strategy use, and executive functioning skills) and *bridging processes* (including but not limited to reading fluency and print concepts). This new model also includes an expansion of the "language comprehension" category to include *theory of mind* and *cultural and content knowledge*.

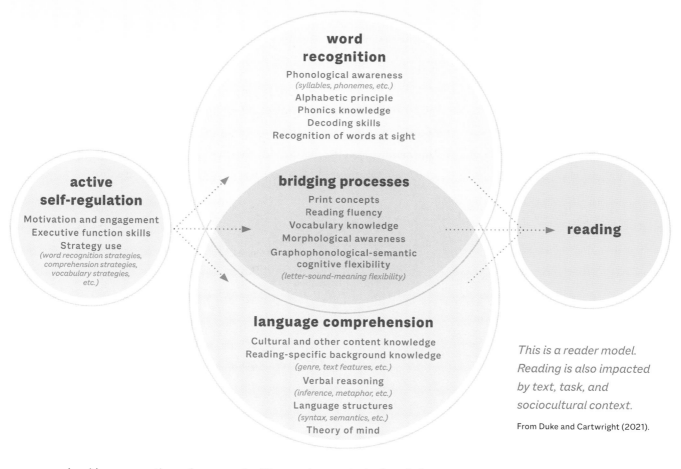

This is a reader model. Reading is also impacted by text, task, and sociocultural context.

From Duke and Cartwright (2021).

Looking across these frameworks, it's easy to conclude that defining reading and the reading process, and categorizing the goals that make up skilled reading, is a complex endeavor. You can complicate it even more if you add in the Five Pillars proposed by the National Reading Panel (2000) where you'll find "vocabulary" separate from "comprehension," and "phonological awareness" separate from "phonics," or if you compare the *Common Core State Standards for ELA* (CCSSO, 2010), which separate comprehension objectives into larger "literature" and "informational texts" categories, with theoretical models like the Simple View of Reading, Scarborough's Reading Rope, and the Active View of Reading, all of which consider "genre knowledge" to be a component of language comprehension.

The goal categories I use to organize the strategies in this book overlap with categories from many of these frameworks, with the addition of a couple of additional categories (writing about reading and conversation about reading), the inclusion of engagement and motivation (present also in the Active View framework), and a recognition of comprehension and language development opportunities for preconventional readers based on research by Sulzby and Teale (see, for example, Sulzby, 1991, 1996; Sulzby & Teale, 1991; Teale, 1987).

Hierarchy of Reading Goals Serravallo (2015, 2023)	Active View Duke and Cartwright (2021)	Rope Model Scarborough (2001)	Simple View Gough and Tunmer (1986)
Emergent Reading	Bridging Process (print concepts) and Language Comprehension	Language Comprehension	n/a
Engagement and Motivation	Active Self-Regulation	n/a	n/a
Accuracy	Word Recognition	Word Recognition	Word Recognition
Fluency	Bridging Process	n/a	n/a
Comprehension (e.g., Understanding Plot and Setting, Character, Main Idea, and so on)	Language Comprehension	Language Comprehension	Language Comprehension
Conversation	n/a	n/a	n/a
Writing About Reading	n/a	n/a	n/a

A comparison of goal categories in *The Reading Strategies Book 2.0* and categories from other well-known research-based theoretical frameworks.

Understand Skills and Skill Progressions Within Goals

Within each goal, there are several *skills* a reader might work on. Think of skills as proficiencies—something a reader is able to do. For example, if a student is working on a goal of comprehending character, they may be working to infer (reading between the lines to name traits and/or feelings) and also synthesize (putting together information across a book to determine how a character changes). At the beginning of each chapter, you'll see a collection of skills aligned to the goal; note that the skills are presented in no particular order. The example below comes from Chapter 4: Fluency.

Expression
The aspect of prosody that includes reading to match the meaning and/or feeling of the piece, changing pitch to match end- and midsentence punctuation, and changing intonation for dialogue.

Inferring
Using background knowledge together with details in the text to understand meaning that influences prosody (e.g., when reading character dialogue based on feelings, emphasizing important words, and so on).

Skills a reader might work on as part of this goal

Phrasing (also known as *parsing*)
The aspect of prosody that includes pausing after meaningful phrases and attending to midsentence punctuation.

Self-monitoring
Attending to one's own fluency (during oral and silent reading) and rereading to improve fluency as necessary.

Emphasis
The aspect of prosody that includes stressing words in the sentence to match the author's meaning, and paying attention to text treatments (for example: bold, italics, or all caps).

Pacing
Reading at a speed that matches the reader's natural rate of speech.

As readers become more proficient within a goal, and as they practice reading increasingly more complex texts, the work they do increases in sophistication, as shown by a skill *progression*. For example, in simple beginning books, a reader with a goal of fluency may work on phrasing, scooping up several words before pausing. Then, as their books become more complex with varied punctuation and dialogue, they will need to work on reading with expression and intonation. Then, as sentences become longer and authors use more midsentence punctuation (commas, em dashes, parentheses), they'll need to attend to this punctuation in order to achieve prosody.

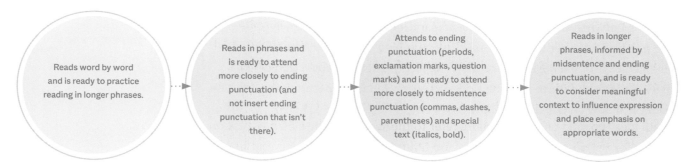

Reads word by word and is ready to practice reading in longer phrases.

Reads in phrases and is ready to attend more closely to ending punctuation (and not insert ending punctuation that isn't there).

Attends to ending punctuation (periods, exclamation marks, question marks) and is ready to attend more closely to midsentence punctuation (commas, dashes, parentheses) and special text (italics, bold).

Reads in longer phrases, informed by midsentence and ending punctuation, and is ready to consider meaningful context to influence expression and place emphasis on appropriate words.

Skill progressions will help you match what you notice from the assessments you give your students to specific strategies your students need to progress.

On the left of each chapter's progression, you'll find a conclusion you can draw from observing or assessing a student.

On the right, you'll find suggested strategies to help the student grow.

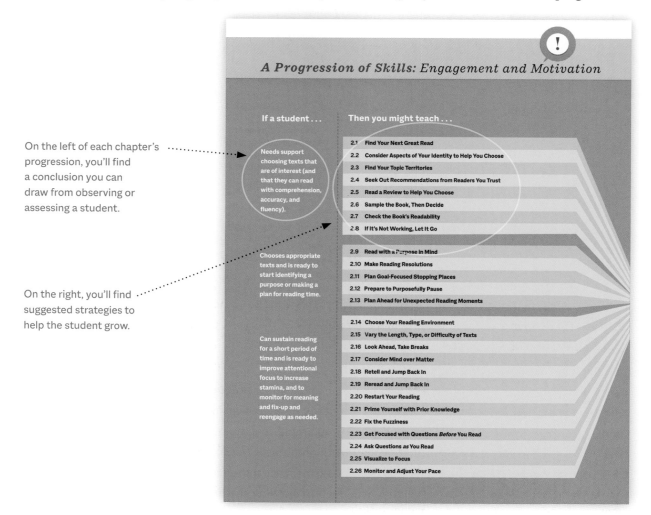

A Progression of Skills: Engagement and Motivation

If a student . . .

Needs support choosing texts that are of interest (and that they can read with comprehension, accuracy, and fluency).

Chooses appropriate texts and is ready to start identifying a purpose or making a plan for reading time.

Can sustain reading for a short period of time and is ready to improve attentional focus to increase stamina, and to monitor for meaning and fix-up and reengage as needed.

Then you might teach . . .

2.1 Find Your Next Great Read
2.2 Consider Aspects of Your Identity to Help You Choose
2.3 Find Your Topic Territories
2.4 Seek Out Recommendations from Readers You Trust
2.5 Read a Review to Help You Choose
2.6 Sample the Book, Then Decide
2.7 Check the Book's Readability
2.8 If It's Not Working, Let It Go

2.9 Read with a Purpose in Mind
2.10 Make Reading Resolutions
2.11 Plan Goal-Focused Stopping Places
2.12 Prepare to Purposefully Pause
2.13 Plan Ahead for Unexpected Reading Moments

2.14 Choose Your Reading Environment
2.15 Vary the Length, Type, or Difficulty of Texts
2.16 Look Ahead, Take Breaks
2.17 Consider Mind over Matter
2.18 Retell and Jump Back In
2.19 Reread and Jump Back In
2.20 Restart Your Reading
2.21 Prime Yourself with Prior Knowledge
2.22 Fix the Fuzziness
2.23 Get Focused with Questions *Before* You Read
2.24 Ask Questions *as* You Read
2.25 Visualize to Focus
2.26 Monitor and Adjust Your Pace

As students are working on a goal, learning strategies, and making progress over time, you can use these same progressions to monitor their growth and to make ongoing decisions about what to teach next.

You might also use the skill progressions to find strategies aligned to your grade-level standards. For example, if you are a fifth-grade teacher in a state that uses the Common Core State Standards and are teaching students to read informational texts, you might be looking for strategies to support Reading Information Standard 2: *Determine two or more main ideas of a text and explain how they are supported by key details; summarize the text.* For the "main idea" portion of that standard, refer to the section of the skill progression in Chapter 8: Comprehending Topics and Main Ideas that mentions multiple main ideas to find appropriate strategies.

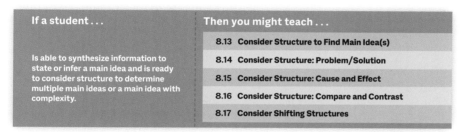

If a student...	Then you might teach...
Is able to synthesize information to state or infer a main idea and is ready to consider structure to determine multiple main ideas or a main idea with complexity.	8.13 Consider Structure to Find Main Idea(s)
	8.14 Consider Structure: Problem/Solution
	8.15 Consider Structure: Cause and Effect
	8.16 Consider Structure: Compare and Contrast
	8.17 Consider Shifting Structures

For the "key details" portion of the standard, turn to the skill progression for Chapter 9: Comprehending Key Details, and find the section with strategies to help students find relevant details aligned to a main idea.

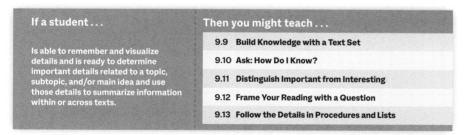

If a student...	Then you might teach...
Is able to remember and visualize details and is ready to determine important details related to a topic, subtopic, and/or main idea and use those details to summarize information within or across texts.	9.9 Build Knowledge with a Text Set
	9.10 Ask: How Do I Know?
	9.11 Distinguish Important from Interesting
	9.12 Frame Your Reading with a Question
	9.13 Follow the Details in Procedures and Lists

When using the skill progressions (or *any* skill progressions or standards for that matter), keep in mind that development is rarely perfectly linear, and it's unlikely that all children will develop skills in the same order or at the same rate. That said, skill progressions can help you pinpoint where a student is now and what might come next to find the most helpful strategies to use right away.

Explore the Strategy Page

Once you have identified goals for each of your readers and have used the skill progressions to find specific strategies within the chapter, you'll find each strategy on its own page with a familiar, repeated structure to help you easily find what you need to teach the strategy successfully.

11.14 Get Help from Cogn[ates]

Strategy If the word looks, or is pronounced, like a word you know from another language, think about what the word means in the other language. See if a similar meaning would fit in the context in which you encountered the English word.

Skills

- **analyzing**
- **inferring**
- **activating prior knowledge**

Teaching Tip This strategy would be best for [...] or who is studying another language. Be aware [...] Some are phonologically similar and orthograph[...] "perfect cognates" (e.g., *animal* [English]—*anim*[...] similar and orthographically similar (e.g., *accid*[...] Especially tricky are "false cognates" which are [...] or orthographically similar but not related in m[...] [English]—"foot" [Spanish]) or *recorder*, which [...] means "to remember or remind" in Spanish (R[...]

Progression

Is able to use context and prior knowledge to infer and is ready to learn to analyze word parts and apply a knowledge of grammar, morphology, and/or etymology.

●●●○○

Prompts

- Do you know a word in another language t[...]
- Think about what the word means in the o[...]
- What might this word mean in English?
- Think about how it's used here—does the w[...] word fit here?

Hat Tip

No More "Look Up the List" Vocabulary Instruction (Cobb & Blachowicz, 2014)

Research Link

[I]n a study of Spanish-English [b]ilingual kindergarteners and [fi]rst graders, researchers [f]ound that children who were [e]xposed to more Spanish knew [m]ore English cognates than [t]hose who received balanced [a]mounts of Spanish and [E]nglish or who were exposed [t]o more English (Pérez, Peña, & Bedore, 2010). A speaker of [t]wo (or more) languages has an expanded repertoire of linguistic resources, with particular word-learning benefits when languages have related origins.

Hey! That Sounds Just Like a Word I Know...

In English...	In Spanish...
Abuse	Abuso
Abbreviate	Abreviar
Accept	Aceptar
Majority	Mayoría
Realization	Realización

↓ ↓

"cognates" – there are hundreds + hund[...]

① THINK of a word you know in another language that looks +/or sounds like the word.

② THINK what does the word mean in the other language?

③ CHECK does the word in this book mean the [...]

374 THE READING STRATEGIES BOOK 2.0

11.15 *Use a Referen...*

Strategy If you can't figure out a wo[rd]... in the way of your understanding, find reference within or outside of the boo... appears to see how the word is being u... the context. Explain what the word m... being used.

Lesson Language *When you've fo... and you still can't figure out the wor... you may choose to look it up. You don't want to interrupt your reading on e...ry page to run to a reference, but if you find that not knowing the word interfere...with understanding what you're reading, or if you are just really curious about ...hat the word might mean, you may choose to find a definition. Whether you u...e an online dictionary, a printed dictionary, or a glossary within the text, the im...ortant thing to remember is that a simple definition is rarely enough to reall...help you understand the word. Always think about the context in which the wor...appears to make sure you're choosing the right definition (as we know man...words have multiple meanings!).*

Teaching Tip As standard dictionaries assume an adult audience, be sure to have children's dictionaries available, physically or online, for younger learners. ...or quick access with older learners, let them know they can type *define* plus any ...ord into Google, which displays definition(s) from the Oxford Dictionary, plus ...ther useful information, like audio pronunciations and synonyms. You might also ...onsider various browser extensions, such as Google Dictionary, which can display ...he definition of any word encountered online with a simple click. These and similar ...

...EALLY can't figure ...rd *(and you want to know its meaning)* ...OK IT UP!

choose the right definition. ✓

Teaching Tips are small bits of advice—about text types to use, modifications to consider, extensions to try, background knowledge, and so on—for teachers to keep in mind when planning.

Lesson Language is included with some of the lessons to show how I might explain or demonstrate a strategy to an individual, small group, or whole class. You don't always need to explain or demonstrate; some children will be able to get to work after only hearing the strategy. Adapt any and all language to make it your own: match what you say to the age and experiences of the readers you're teaching; use the books I chose, or use ones you know and love.

Skills

- building knowle[dge]
- self-monitoring
- synthesizing

Progression

Is confidently and independently using a va... of strategies to figure out... unfamiliar words and is r... supplement word learning... outside resources.

●●●●○

Skill Progression Callout in the margin reminds you when and for which readers this strategy might be most helpful, and the highlighted dots remind you of the stage of the progression.

Research Links offer empirical support for the strategy. In most cases, the link offers direct support for the strategy, other times for the skill, and occasionally a bit of related information that will be helpful to know when teaching the strategy.

Research Link

In a study using eye-tracking technology, researchers found that readers whose second language was English relied on dictionary use even when an unknown word was irrelevant and the meaning could be easily inferred (Prichard & Atkins, 2021). This underscores the importance of helping readers to consider when it's worth pausing their reading to turn to a resource.

...mprehending Vocabulary and Figurative Language

◎ Build Your Knowledge

Now that you understand how the book is organized to find what you need quickly and with purpose, here's some more information to help build your knowledge and support effective implementation of the strategies.

Lean on Research

As you saw in the annotated spread (pages 14–15), you'll find Research Links on every one of the 300+ strategy pages, often with multiple citations to peer-reviewed research. In addition, you'll find research cited throughout this Getting Started chapter and in the introductions to each of the thirteen goal-focused chapters. Altogether, you'll find *over 700* unique references to research from various journal types and disciplines including education, psychology, cognitive science, neuroscience, linguistics, and humanities; some from journals that are practitioner focused, others that are academic—as well as books and book chapters from academic presses. The citations provide an important evidence base for every suggestion and idea in this book.

The strategies in this book contain student-facing, step-by-step language that explains something found to be helpful or important in research. Note that crafting this language often involves a process of interpretation. For example, the first strategy in Chapter 2 offers a way for students to use online search tools to find reviews of books that might be of interest, while the research link summarizes findings from three separate studies that deal with the interconnection of choice, agency, and reading volume. In other words, the *specific strategy* may not have been studied, as the actual steps are my own invention. But the efficacy of the *general concept*, *idea*, or *skill* is something that has demonstrated positive outcomes in one or more studies. The links also often provide additional or related background information that will help you teach the strategy, and may pique your interest to learn more.

Most commonly, the research citations you'll find are empirical, drawing from either quantitative or qualitative studies, though sometimes they are theoretical. You'll notice a range of publication dates across the referenced studies. I used older studies when they are classic or heavily cited, when I'm referring to the original source of a term, or when a research area has gone dormant because it's been studied a lot and the findings are well replicated. When possible, I've chosen more recent studies.

I believe in the importance of making science-informed decisions in all areas of life—from following public health advice to crafting solutions to climate change. In education, I respect and appreciate research we have to inform our practice, and I believe we need to be aware of trends in research and make decisions that have the best chance of working for the most students. We all benefit from the systematic collection and analysis of data to deepen understandings and change literacy instructional practices for the better. However, it's important to note limitations of research as well.

First, researchers need funding and support to conduct studies, and funding sources sometimes have particular areas of interest that skew the range of topics that are examined during a particular period of time. In other words, just because something hasn't been studied doesn't mean it won't work; it may just mean nobody has funded a study to find out if it would.

Second, it's rare to find educational research that is directly replicated (where multiple independent research teams use the same question to guide their study in an attempt to come to the same findings), and many researchers have emphasized the importance of direct replication to ensure reliability of results (Irvine, 2021; Plucker & Makel, 2021; Simons, 2014). Without replication, practitioners and policy makers make decisions based on findings from singular or narrow sets of studies or generalize findings to contexts or populations that have not yet been studied.

Third, since studies in education are often conducted by university-affiliated researchers, the transfer and communication of promising approaches from academia to teachers in classrooms is not always direct or clear (Adams, 1990; Snow, Burns, & Griffin, 1998). Even if the transfer from academia to the classroom was direct and clear, an added challenge is that academic research is often locked behind paywalls, inaccessible to anyone except those with a university affiliation.

Finally, though we can and should learn from research, it's essential that we also trust the collective knowledge that comes from practice and value the experience and expertise that comes from working with classrooms of children every day, year after year.

Choose Texts with a Knowledge of Genres and Text Types

In the introduction to each chapter, you'll find a box titled "What Texts Might Students Use When Practicing Strategies from This Chapter?" to guide your text selection.

In some chapters, you'll find that you can use just about any text (e.g., Chapters 2, 3, 4). Conversely, in the cases of the comprehension chapters, you'll need to select strategies with the type of text the student is reading clearly in mind such as the example on page 18 from Chapter 10: Text Features. As Duke and

What Texts Might Students Use When Practicing Strategies from This Chapter?

Any text containing graphic features (maps, charts, tables, and so on), headings or subheadings, or visuals (photographs, illustrations), For example:

Informational picture books. Short texts that use both pictures and words to tell about a topic such as the Bill of Rights, the solar system, gorillas, and so on.

Articles. Short articles, such as those found in popular children's magazines.

Textbooks. Subject-area (science, history) course books.

Procedural/how-to texts. Texts written to teach the reader how to do or make something (e.g., recipes, craft books, owner's manuals, and so on), which often include lists of materials and explanatory steps.

Narrative nonfiction. Texts that teach about a person (e.g., biographies), or events (e.g., historical accounts), or books that teach about a topic but are organized chronologically, such as the story of bird migration.

Roberts (2010) point out, "The research suggests that the differences between comprehension of text in different genres are substantial. Rather than being a unitary construct, reading comprehension is best seen as a collection of processes that are substantially differentiated by genre" (p. 75).

For organizational purposes, rather than the more conventional division between *fiction* and *nonfiction*, I've decided to use Grabe's (2002) "macro-genres" of *narrative* and *expository*. Strategies in Chapters 5, 6, and 7 will work best in narrative texts that tell a story and have a plot, setting(s), character(s), and theme(s) that the reader needs to understand. Strategies in Chapters 8, 9, and 10 will work best in expository texts that tell about a topic or idea, have key details, and sometimes text features. In all texts, readers will need to infer the meaning of vocabulary and figurative language (Chapter 11).

Without a doubt, many stories contain moments of exposition, and many books about a topic include stories to elaborate on ideas. Also, certain genres are sometimes written as narratives and other times as expository texts (memoir, essay, poetry, articles, and so on). And then, there are some books that are clearly both. Think about literary nonfiction picture books like those in the Read and Wonder series from Candlewick Press. *One Tiny Turtle* (Davies, 2005), for example, tells a story about a sea turtle but also includes additional facts about sea turtles on each page and at the end. For books like these, you'll find strategies in all seven comprehension chapters that may be helpful. You can regard the turtle as a character and infer its traits, you can retell the story by thinking of the sequence of events as a plot, and you can learn key details from the information on the pages.

Most of the strategies in this book will work with text types within a broad category; most strategies that work with one type of narrative, for example, will work with any. There are a few exceptions: a strategy that helps a reader to understand a historical setting's impact on character, for example, is really best for a student reading historical fiction. In these cases, I've included a note somewhere on the strategy page.

Narrative: tells a story, moves through time	Expository: tells *about* a topic(s) or idea(s), moves through subtopics (parts, kinds, reasons, examples, and so on)

Genre/text type examples:
    Realistic fiction
    Graphic novels
    Plays
    Scripts
    Fantasy
    Mystery
    Historical fiction
    True accounts
    Personal narrative
    Biographies
    Historical accounts
    Wordless picture books
	Genre/text type examples:
	    Informational texts
	    Chemistry, biology, history textbook
	    How-to/procedural texts
	    Concept books
	    Profiles
	    List books
	    Persuasive
	    Op-Ed
	    Feature article
	    Alphabet books

Poetry
Memoir
Essay
Literary nonfiction
Blog
Article
Picture books
Chapter books

Examples of genres and text types

While it is critical for you, as the teacher, to understand text structures and genres, research also suggests it's critical for readers to have this knowledge. You'll see strategies throughout the comprehension chapters supporting this knowledge building (see, for example, Strategies 5.8, 5.15, 8.13) (Perfetti, 1994).

Select Mentor Texts

Mentor texts are children's literature you'll return to again and again to demonstrate strategies. You might keep them on hand for when you teach strategies to the whole class, tuck them under your arm to carry with you as you confer about the room, and/or store them in a bin at your small-group table for easy access. They will become your trusted co-teachers.

When you select mentor texts, it's helpful to keep a number of things in mind:

- **Engagement.** Choose texts you and your students will love: ones with well-developed characters, about interesting topics, that will move or amaze your students. Since you'll return to these texts again and again, make sure students will welcome each revisit!

- **Inclusivity.** Student success depends on the extent to which your teaching is relevant, identity-affirming, culturally responsive and sustaining, and inclusive (Ebarvia et al., 2020; España & Herrera, 2020; Hammond, 2015; Minor, 2018; Souto-Manning et al., 2018). Pay careful attention to who is represented in the texts you choose (and to the texts' authors and illustrators) to ensure that students see themselves reflected and that what you choose causes no harm (Bishop, 1990; Jones, 2020).

- **Alignment.** Take a close look at your curriculum plans for the year, the content studies you'll be engaged in, and the level of text complexity that is appropriate for the grade you teach. Consider which strategies you'll most likely need to demonstrate across the year, then curate a collection of texts that are well aligned to those strategies.

- **Accessibility.** If you want students to have access to your class mentor texts, consider choosing something that's available in both paper form and as digital text. Digital texts allow students to reference them at home, and depending on the format, they may be able to use the "read to me" feature if needed. You might also consider making an audiobook version available. (For more on accessibility considerations, see www.cast.org.)

- **Variety.** You'll want a collection that checks a lot of boxes so you can use them flexibly throughout the year: a variety of text types and genres, a variety of text lengths, different formats and styles, and texts about different topics to engage readers with different interests.

Before revising this book, I collected a stack of narrative and expository mentor texts with these tenets in mind, and you'll see them used across the book, again and again, to teach different strategies aligned to different goals. This repetition is intentional!

For the most part, the children's books I've included in the Lesson Language examples were published within the last ten years, though you'll see classic texts mentioned occasionally as well. Of course, my "stack" is larger than yours will be since this book covers strategies for grades K–8 and you'll likely be creating a collection for a single grade or a few grades. Still, I hope that you check out some of the excellent texts I've chosen and find your own when you prefer!

Create Curriculum

The strategies in this book, alone, are not a curriculum. Curriculum is a well-planned course of study, often organized into a series of units, where students practice skills and acquire content knowledge aligned to grade-level expectations. One use of the strategies in this book, however, is as starter dough to design your own curricular units or to enhance existing units with explicit strategies to support your predetermined learning objectives. To do this, you

Week 1	**Understanding Main Idea** 8.3 Look for Main Ideas in the Introduction	**Understanding Main Idea** 8.5 Clue in to Key Sentences	**Understanding Main Idea** 8.6 Name the *What* and *So What*	(Flex—reteach one of first three lessons with new example)	**Understanding Main Idea** 8.8 Survey the Text
Week 2	**Understanding Main Idea** 8.10 Sketch Each Chunk, Then Put the Pieces Together	**Understanding Main Idea** 8.13 Consider Structure to Find Main Idea(s)	**Identifying Key Details** 9.4 Monitor for Clicks and Clunks	**Identifying Key Details** 9.5 Read, Cover, Remember, Retell	(Flex—responsive small group based on observed needs)
Week 3	**Identifying Key Details** 9.6 Slow Down for Numbers	**Main Idea + Details = Summarizing** 9.9 Build Knowledge with a Text Set	**Main Idea + Details = Summarizing** 9.16 Summarize with Explanations	**Main Idea + Details = Summarizing** 9.17 Analyze the Development of an Idea with Details	**Celebrate!** (Invite a younger-grade class to learn about topics from student teachers.)

Example sequence of strategies focused on understanding main ideas and details in informational texts to summarize the most important information.

will need to identify your unit focus and the goals you have for your learners; design assessments to help you understand what students know before, during, and after the unit; choose mentor texts you'll use in demonstrations; and map out a flow of strategies that you'll teach aligned to goals over time. The example on the bottom of page 21 is one fourth-grade teacher's planned strategy sequence designed to support students with informational text comprehension in a content area unit.

Understand Effective Feedback

Guided by student goals, you'll articulate clear strategies for students to help unpack for them *how* to do what you are suggesting they try. Then, you'll guide, coach, and deliver feedback as you confer and work with small groups. Guided practice with feedback helps the learning stick (Hattie & Timperley, 2007).

On each strategy page you'll find suggested prompts that can help you during guided practice time. Of course, these are just examples; you should feel free to make your own. Keep the principles of effective feedback in mind to help you craft and deliver prompts to students as they practice (see box at left).

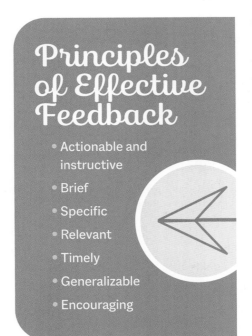

Principles of Effective Feedback

- Actionable and instructive
- Brief
- Specific
- Relevant
- Timely
- Generalizable
- Encouraging

Actionable and instructive feedback offers students a next step toward their goal, cues them to try something, or reinforces something they are doing well (Hattie, 2009). You're trying to help the student get from where they are to where they are aiming to be (Sadler, 1989).

As you offer feedback, try to be *brief*. The less you say, the more time and space students have to do the work. Also, too much teacher talk can take away student agency and can erode their confidence. Remember, productive struggle is a good thing; children won't always generate what they want to say immediately. They need processing time and the opportunity to grapple with the strategy. Occasionally, you need to say more to be clear or to remind students of a step or two of a strategy. If the moment calls for it, then by all means talk more. But if you can get away with saying less, do.

Aim to make your feedback *specific and relevant*: it should align to both the goal and strategy(ies) students are practicing during the lesson and be delivered with one thing to consider at a time, so as not to overwhelm the reader (Hammond, 2015; Schunk & Rice, 1991). Use words directly from the strategy in your feedback to ensure what you say to children during the guided practice aligns to what you told them you were practicing in the setup of the lesson. To help the feedback be as clear as it can, offer children clear "success criteria" in the form of a mentor text, exemplar piece of writing about reading, or skill progression descriptors (Hattie & Clarke, 2019).

Ensure *timely* delivery of your feedback (Hammond, 2015). While a child is practicing, offer prompts that course correct, nudge them along, or point out what they did well *in the moment*. When it's in the moment, you can also get feedback *from* students as they continue to practice, noticing what they understood and didn't understand. It turns out that research has found that children prefer immediate feedback, too (Hattie & Clarke, 2019).

Make sure your feedback is *generalizable*. While it is specific to the strategy, it should be generalizable enough to apply across contexts, and in other texts. The more applicable the feedback is, the more likely the student will be able to transfer and apply what you're saying the next time they are utilizing the same strategy.

Perhaps most importantly: student progress only happens when they are willing to receive the feedback from their teacher. The content and tone of feedback should communicate your belief that students are capable so that they have confidence to continue working (Kluger & DeNisi, 1996). Therefore, feedback should be *encouraging* and delivered in a low-stress, supportive environment where there is a strong relationship between teacher and student (Hammond, 2015; Howard, Milner-McCall, & Howard, 2020). This kind of feedback will influence a learner's "self-efficacy, [and] self-regulatory proficiencies" (Hattie, 2009).

The prompt examples in this book represent five common types of feedback you can use flexibly and responsively; different situations call for different types. In the table that follows, notice how the prompts align to the principles of effective feedback you just read about, and make note of the *why/when* for each.

Teachers receive feedback from students as well. In fact, this feedback is shown to be even more crucial to learning than feedback that teachers provide *to* students (Hattie & Clarke, 2019). Feedback *from* students is constant if you watch, listen, and explicitly ask children to tell you how the lesson went for them. If you are open to the feedback: noticing where there are misconceptions, what they do and don't understand, what is and is not engaging them, why they are making the errors they are, and so on, you can adapt both the strategies you offer as well as the methods you use to teach.

Type	Why/When?	Examples
Directive	To prompt the reader to do something specific.	• "Reread the paragraph, trying to picture the character's facial expressions." • "Check the beginning, middle, and end of that word."
Question	To prompt the reader to try something, to elicit information, or to get them to self-reflect.	• "What is this whole section mostly about?" • "Can you change your voice to sound like the character?"
Redirection	To point out what the reader is doing and how what I'm prompting for is different.	• "You told me the theme as one word. Can you ask yourself, 'So what about that?' and say it as a sentence?" • You found a detail to support the main idea from the section. Check the text features to find key details, too.
Compliment	To reinforce something the reader does that they should continue doing. To celebrate progress toward their goal.	• You noticed you read something incorrectly and went back to fix your error! • I noticed you thought about what was happening in the story to figure out what that word means.
Sentence Starter or Frame	To nudge the reader by offering some language that they can repeat, and then finish the sentence on their own.	• "In the beginning . . . middle . . ." • "My character __ so I think she is __."

Support Independence with Visual Anchor Charts and Tools

When someone provides visuals to accompany their written text or speech, the receiver is more likely to remember what they've read or heard (Kress, 2009; Mayer, 2005). The visuals included on each strategy page are there in part to help you remember the strategies so you can use them fluently and effortlessly with your students. I also hope they inspire you to create visuals whenever you're teaching, to increase the likelihood that your students will remember what *you* say.

The sample charts and tools across this book were created with some common principles in mind:

- They are clear and simple.
- Often, there isn't much text.

- They have icons, pictures, and/or color-coding.
- They are appropriate for the age and readability level of the students for whom they're intended.
- They have clear headings that tell you what the chart's about.

(For more on charts and tools see Martinelli and Mraz [2012] and Mraz and Martinelli [2014].)

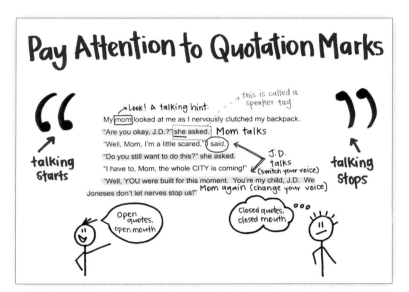

Exemplar charts often include an annotated piece of text, some student work with callouts, or a chart the class created together that can serve as an example of what the reader's own work might look like or what the reader might be looking for in their books when they practice the strategy. These are often crafted with students—the teacher may choose the piece of text ahead of time and then ask students to help them annotate as they work through the strategy.

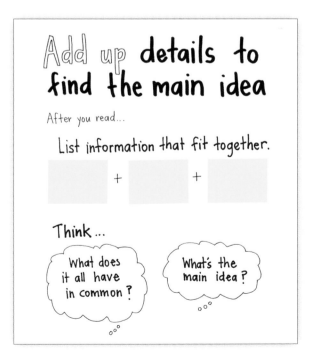

Process charts help remind students of the steps of the strategy with pictures, icons, and/or key words.

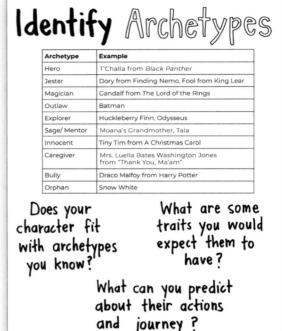

Tools are visuals made for individual students to keep in a folder, on a bookmark, in a book baggie, or stuck to a page in a notebook so they have their own differentiated "chart" to use when practicing independently. You may create a tool with the student or create it ahead of time and leave it with the student after a conference or small group.

Content charts offer students a reference for their work with a strategy, such as a list of character traits or rules for decoding.

Repertoire charts remind students of the strategies they're practicing and should be incorporating as part of a regular habit. Sometimes teachers combine summaries from a collection of individual charts or tools (e.g., four separate process charts) on one larger repertoire chart and "retire" the more detailed process chart.

Incorporate Strategy Instruction as Part of a Comprehensive Literacy Approach

Although this book covers thirteen goals and includes over three hundred strategies, it's still not everything you need in your reading instruction! Depending on the age and proficiency levels of the students you teach, you may also need some or all of the following elements to round out your comprehensive approach.

Phonics and Phonological Awareness Curriculum

Beginning readers need to develop an understanding of the alphabetic principle, develop attention to the sounds in spoken language, and build content knowledge around grapheme-phoneme relations (Connelly, Johnston, & Thompson, 2001; Ehri, Nunes, Stahl, & Willows, 2001; Ehri, Nunes, Willows, et al., 2001). Children deserve phonics and phonological awareness instruction that matches their needs, is assessment based, is well paced, is engaging, and that provides the amount of repetition each child needs to learn (Kilpatrick, 2015; Mesmer, 2019; Snow et al., 1998).

Although Chapter 3 is filled with strategy ideas to help students read with accuracy, those strategies are meant to complement, but not replace, phonics instruction; the strategies are meant to support students' *application* and *transfer* of what they know and understand about how words work to read the words accurately during their connected text reading.

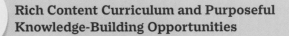

Rich Content Curriculum and Purposeful Knowledge-Building Opportunities

Knowledge is critical to both a reader's ability to understand text (Best, Floyd, & McNamara, 2008; Reutzel & Morgan, 1990), and read with accuracy and fluency (Priebe, Keenan, & Miller, 2012; Taft & Leslie, 1985). The amount of relevant knowledge a reader brings to a text also impacts their ability to be able to learn information and vocabulary *from* the text (Cervetti & Hiebert, 2015; Cervetti & Wright, 2020; Kintsch, 1986), and infer messages and deeper meanings (Graesser, Singer, & Trabasso, 1994).

Different kinds of knowledge support comprehension for readers of all ages and across text types (Cervetti & Wright, 2020). *Factual* (or *topic*) knowledge refers to whether the reader knows about information directly addressed in the text. *Domain-specific* is knowledge related to a disciplinary area (such as chemistry). *General* (or *world*) knowledge is knowledge in typical academic areas, such as the humanities. *Cultural* knowledge refers to the extent to which the reader's sociocultural background aligns with the themes and information in the text. *Vocabulary* knowledge is whether the reader understands the words in the text.

As teachers of reading, we should actively plan to support students' knowledge building from the very beginning, and knowledge building should continue every year they are in school (Rapp et al., 2007). We can intentionally plan units of study aligned to content standards, such as Next Generation Science Standards or the National Council for the Social Studies standards. We can also curate concept-rich text sets for students to read independently or with partners or in book clubs, and we can be intentional about developing conceptual understanding and deepening knowledge during daily read-aloud instruction (Cervetti & Hiebert, 2015; Tarchi, 2010).

Research is also clear that knowledge alone won't automatically yield strong comprehension; children need to know how to activate the knowledge and use other reading strategies and skills (e.g., summarizing, inferring) to integrate and mediate knowledge while reading and form a coherent mental model of the text (Cervetti & Wright, 2020; Cromley & Azevedo, 2007). So, although knowledge is critical, it's important students are learning the what, when, and how of strategies as well.

A Library Filled with Books and Protected Time for Children to Read

To get better at reading, children need to read a lot (Allington, 2014; Allington & McGill-Franzen, 2021; Krashen, 2004; Stanovich et al., 1996; Taylor, Frye, & Maruyama, 1990). That means they need reliable time each day in school to read, encouragement and support to read at home, and a wide variety of materials to choose from that they can and want to read. Ideally, you'll have a well-stocked, well-organized class-room library filled with an inclusive collection of narrative and expository texts that helps students both see themselves in the books they read and learn about the world (Bishop, 1990). A crucial component to student engagement is matching readers with high-quality texts by authors they want to read and about topics they are interested in exploring (Miller, 2009; Miller & Moss, 2013). Across the day and throughout the year, children should have experiences with texts that they can read with independence (Hiebert & Reutzel, 2010; Hiebert, 2015), and support with reading texts that are a stretch (Burns, 2007; Hall, Sabey, & McClellan, 2005); texts that help them build and develop content knowledge (see previous section); texts in a variety of lengths (e.g., short stories, picture books, novels) and formats (e.g., digital texts, paper texts). Experience with a wide range of texts and ample opportunity to read provides children not only with critical reading volume but also opportunities to practice and apply strategies across many contexts, critical for developing automaticity.

A Curriculum Aligned to Your Grade-Level Standards for Literacy

As mentioned earlier, the strategies in this book are not a curriculum, but they could be used to create your own curriculum or to augment, supplement, or revise existing curriculum. Look to your grade-level standards for English language arts and be sure that you are giving children explicit instruction and ample opportunity to practice grade-level appropriate strategies on grade-level texts alongside purposeful content and knowledge development.

Additional Strategies

Although the three hundred–plus strategies in this book cover a lot of ground, you will undoubtedly find opportunities to invent new strategies or reimagine what's here. For example, you can simplify complex strategies (e.g., a strategy to help a reader understand and track multiple plotlines can be simplified to help them track a single plot) or tweak a strategy based on the genre or text type (e.g., a strategy written to help a reader understand setting in historical fiction could be adapted to help a reader working to understand setting in a fantasy novel). You may find that there is something in your standards or curriculum that is not covered in this book. In this case, I hope the plentiful examples help you understand predictable ways to phrase strategies so you can create your own.

No matter what, remember that you and your reading experiences can be excellent resources. Find new strategies by reflecting on yourself as a reader—how do you stay engaged? Choose books? Figure out the meaning of unfamiliar words? Make a movie in your mind? Figure out what the map has to do with the surrounding text on the page? Articulate your process for your students, and you've just shared your own self-made strategy.

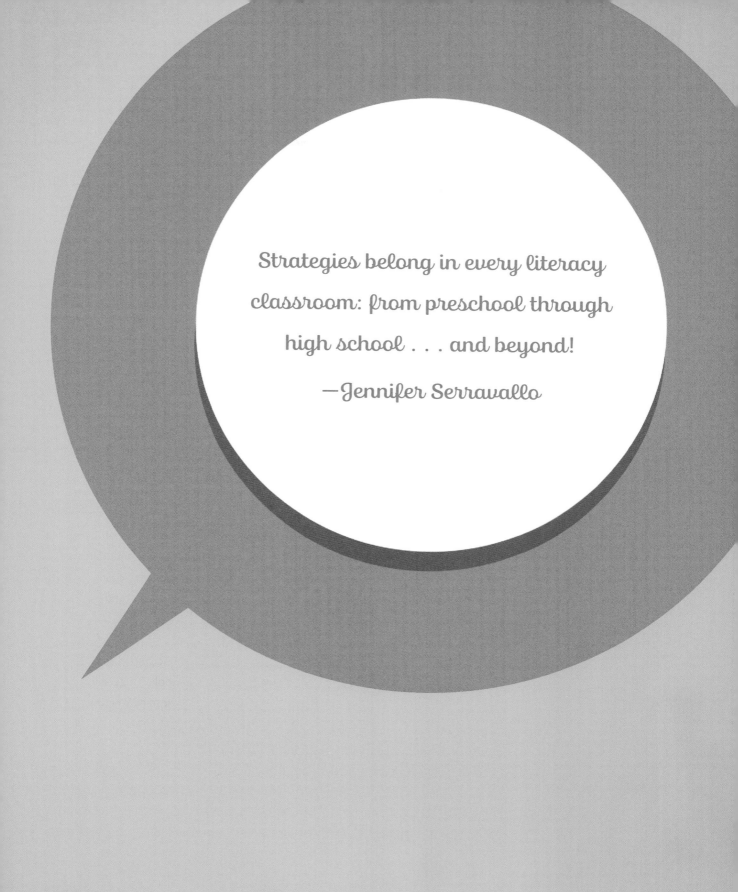

Strategies belong in every literacy classroom: from preschool through high school . . . and beyond!

—Jennifer Serravallo

Goal 1

Emergent Literacy and Language Development

◎ Why is this goal important?

Think back to the last time you watched a four- or five-year-old child sitting independently with a book. You may have noticed them "reading" the book—perhaps they were using some of the vocabulary they acquired as they listened to you read that same book aloud to them many times. Perhaps they were studying illustrations for details, and using those pictures to do higher level thinking such as inferring what the character might say or think, or synthesizing how an event from one page connects to an event from another. Perhaps they were studying photos in an informational text, excited to share something they learned with a friend or family member. Maybe they were tracing their finger over the enlarged letter on each page of an alphabet book, naming the things that begin with the letter pictured on the page.

Children who engage with texts in this way, who are not yet attending to words in a text, may be considered *pre-alphabetic* (Ehri & McCormick, 1998) or *emergent* readers (Mason & Allen, 1986; Paratore, Cassano, & Schickedanz, 2011; Sulzby & Teale, 1986). In the years before formal schooling, children may have some limited understanding of letters, but don't yet have enough phonics knowledge to connect the written symbols to sounds from language in conventional ways. They may be able to read some words that have become part of their sight word vocabulary (for example, brand names such as *Nike* on their sneakers, or words on common signs such as *STOP*); their own name or the names of family members; possibly even a few high-frequency words they've been taught (e.g., *me, the, to*). More often than not, they read these words by picking up clues from the environment (such as the name brand on the front of a sweatshirt) or about the look of the word rather than using *phonetic* knowledge (which is necessary for word learning, see Chapter 3).

The majority of researchers see emergent literacy as a continuum that has spurts and hesitations and may not be uniform (e.g., Mason & Allen, 1986; Paratore, Cassano, & Schickedanz, 2011). Young children may demonstrate skills in nonconventional ways, or partially conventional ways, before they learn conventional literacy (Yaden, Rowe, & MacGillivray, 2000). To develop into conventional readers, they will benefit from deepening their phonemic awareness (the knowledge that spoken words are made up of separate sounds), effective letter instruction (remembering the shape of each letter and some of the most common sounds each letter represents), systematic phonics instruction, and plenty of opportunities to write using invented spellings, which helps forge connections between letters (graphemes) and sounds (phonemes) (Mason & Allen, 1986; Paratore, Cassano, & Schickedanz, 2011; Sulzby & Teale, 1991; Teale, 1987; Yaden, Rowe, & MacGillivray, 2000). The majority of these activities need to be planned and led by a teacher.

What will also benefit readers at this stage are opportunities to spend time with texts independently and with reading partners to develop their book awareness and concepts of print, deepen vocabulary and language, begin to develop identities as readers based on the books they love to explore, and think about and beyond the text. The work of the early childhood researchers Elizabeth Sulzby and William Teale (see, for example, Sulzby, 1991, 1996; Sulzby & Teale, 1991; Teale, 1987) and well-regarded experts in early childhood literacy such as Kathy Collins and Matt Glover (see, for example, Collins, 2004, 2008; Collins & Glover, 2015; Ray & Glover, 2008) show us that students can engage with and enjoy books alone or with their peers, even *before* or *in tandem with* conventional teacher-led reading instruction.

In addition to the benefits to children, setting readers up to engage with books independently and with partners helps the *teacher* who is working to plan and coordinate responsive instruction to suit the varied needs of the twenty-plus children in their charge. When working with a small group, the rest of the class needs to be meaningfully engaged, and the strategies in this chapter are meant to help children do just that.

Book awareness and print concepts
Understanding how books work and how a reader reads them (e.g., identifying the cover, left to right/top to bottom orientation, knowing where the beginning and end are in a line of print, understanding punctuation).

Genre awareness
Understanding that there are different types of books and that readers read them differently based on genre.

Self-monitoring
Noticing when reading is making sense and revising when it doesn't.

Skills a reader might work on as part of this goal

Synthesizing
Developing an understanding of how pages in a book go together and using that knowledge to storytell from pictures or connect information across pages in a text.

Talking about books
Using "book language" to storytell or talk about books to develop language and vocabulary, as well as talking with peer(s) about what a reader is learning about or noticing in a text.

Determining importance
Slowing down to attend to details on a page.

Letter-sound knowledge
Learning what upper- and lowercase letters look like in print and developing an understanding that there are predictable relationships between written letters and spoken sounds (also known as the *alphabetic principle*).

Inferring
Coming up with thoughts and ideas based on what a reader notices in a book.

What Texts Might Students Use When Practicing Strategies from This Chapter?

The texts students engage with depend upon the purpose. For independent and peer work focused on language development and vocabulary (Strategies 1.1–1.14), you'll choose a variety of picture books: familiar storybooks, wordless picture books, informational picture books, concept books, and so on. When children are working on learning letters (Strategies 1.15–1.18), you'll choose alphabet books.

Familiar storybooks. Books that you have read aloud to students multiple times so they know them well. The books should have pictures that match the story closely (to help children remember it), some dialogue, and perhaps some repetition (e.g., *Knuffle Bunny*).

Wordless picture books. Books that tell stories through pictures with no or very few words (e.g., *Good Night, Gorilla*).

Informational picture books. Look for texts with engaging visual features that offer opportunities to learn content.

Concept books. A specific type of informational picture book where the whole book is focused on one concept such as opposites, colors, shapes, or numbers.

List books. Books about a topic that may offer information, description, and/or a series of things to appreciate about the topic.

Alphabet books. Look for books with upper- and lowercase letters and matching pictures to help reinforce knowledge of letters and connect those letter symbols to the first sound in each of the words represented in pictures or words.

◎ How do I know if this goal is right for my student?

Many of the suggestions for teaching in this chapter answer the question, "What might independent and partner time with books look like *before* children can decode most or any of the words in their books, or when children's book interests exceed their decoding ability?" Some of the strategies may also be helpful for emergent bilingual students to use with a partner as they work to develop receptive and expressive language, deepen vocabulary, and develop letter-sound knowledge in English.

To select strategies from the first part of this chapter, watch how students storytell or talk about a book using its pictures in both familiar and unfamiliar stories and informational texts, and/or administer a Concepts About Print assessment (Clay, 2017). To select strategies from the last portion of the chapter, administer a letter-sound identification assessment. Match your observations to the if–then chart on page 37.

◎ How do I support students as they work on skills to help their accuracy?

After watching students storytell or talk about a book from its pictures, and/or administering a letter-sound identification or Concepts About Print assessment, select strategies that you can model, that they can practice with you, and that they can use independently to increase their skills.

Although development is rarely perfectly linear, skill progressions can help us pinpoint where a student is now and what might come next. Use the if–then chart on page 37 to evaluate your students' reading and find strategies that will support their growth.

A Progression of Skills: Emergent Literacy and Language Development

If a student...

Then you might teach...

Needs support to develop book awareness, print concepts, and genre awareness.

1.1	Go Left to Right, Top to Bottom
1.2	Find the Parts (with a Partner)
1.3	Pause, Look Around the Page, Think
1.4	Notice the Type of Book to Decide How to Read It

In a story, alone or with a teacher/partner, labels and elaborates briefly on what's in pictures. Is ready to start elaborating with story language, including dialogue.

1.5	Notice, Think, Explain
1.6	Sound Like a Storyteller
1.7	Express the Emotions
1.8	Act It Out to Storytell It

In an informational text, alone or with a teacher/partner, labels and elaborates briefly on what's in pictures. Is ready to start elaborating with more content-specific language or more detailed information.

1.9	Talk Like an Expert
1.10	Say a Few Details
1.11	Pay Attention to the WHOLE and Teeny-Tiny Details

Is elaborating well on each individual page and is ready to start synthesizing pages, either alone or with a teacher/partner.

1.12	Connect Pages Like a Storyteller
1.13	Back Up, Revise
1.14	Connect the Information

Is paying attention to the print in books and is ready to develop letter-sound knowledge.

1.15	Match Letters as You Sing
1.16	Connect Letters in the Book to Letters in the World
1.17	Trace and Compare the Letters (Uppercase Versus Lowercase)
1.18	Match Letters and Sounds

Strategy Start with the front cover. Open the book. Look at everything on the left page (top to bottom), then look at everything on the right (top to bottom). Turn the page. Repeat.

Teaching Tip As you support children with developing their print concepts, you'll want to weave in mentions of book orientation and directionality throughout the day. For example, during your read-aloud or shared reading, you might think aloud, "Hm. Can anybody help me? Where should I start reading?" or "Here's the *front cover*. I know it's the front because . . ." and "Now that the book is open, should I start on this page (*pointing to left*) or this page (*pointing to right*)?" Shared and interactive writing offer other opportunities to think aloud and involve children in response. You might start a lesson with "Where should I start writing?" and point to the top of the paper, left side, right side and then reinforce by saying, "That's correct! Left to right, top to bottom."

Prompts
- Which side is the left and which is the right?
- Point to where you'll start reading. Now where will you go next?
- That's the back cover. You can tell this is the front cover because the book opens on the right.
- Remember, as you turn the page start on the left page then move to the right.

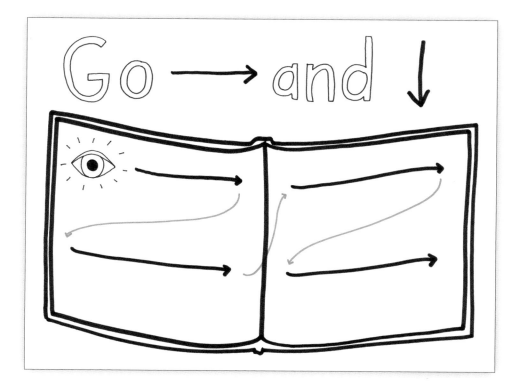

Skills
- **book awareness**
- **print concepts**

Progression

Needs support to develop book awareness, print concepts, and genre awareness.

● ○ ○ ○ ○

Research Link

In one study, preschoolers who had not yet started formal literacy instruction and who were identified as not being able to read simple words were able to correctly identify the horizontal and left-to-right nature of print in English (Treiman et al., 2007). This suggests that, even before students are able to decode, they are already learning about the orientation and direction of print.

Skills

- **book awareness**
- **print concepts**
- **talking about books**

Progression

Needs support to develop book awareness, print concepts, and genre awareness.

Strategy Find and name the parts of the book. Correct your partner if they make a mistake. Use the chart/checklist to help. Then start at the beginning and explore the book together.

Teaching Tip Using big books and other picture books you select for read-aloud, draw students' attention to the front and back covers, the words on the page and the pictures on the page, and where the sentences begin and end. This regular exposure and review will support their emerging understanding of print concepts. This strategy and recommended anchor chart can be used during peer reading time as well to help children apply what they've learned with more independence.

Prompts

- Which is the front cover and which is the back cover?
- Find the pictures. Find the words.
- What's the beginning of the sentence? Where's the end?
- What punctuation can you find?

Strategy Instead of zooming through your book, pause and stay for a while on each page. Look across the parts on the page. Think—what do you see? What do you wonder? When you've spent some time on the page, you can turn to the next one.

Lesson Language *When I get to a new book, I know that what's inside is filled with fun, interesting, cool, and beautiful things. I know I need to make sure I don't just rush through the whole thing, getting to the end soon after I've just begun! No, I need to slow down. Pointing around the page helps my eyes focus, and I'll often see something I may have otherwise overlooked. So, on each new page, I'm going to look around the page, saying what I see, and then I will pause to think or wonder about it. I only turn the page once I've noticed everything I can.*

Prompts
- Move your finger around the page. Tell me what you see.
- Not so fast! Stay on the page a moment.
- You went across the whole page and said sentences about what you saw!
- What can you (notice/say/think about __) before you turn the page?

Skills
- **inferring**
- **determining importance**

Progression

Needs support to develop book awareness, print concepts, and genre awareness.

Research Link

A series of studies revealed that when an adult uses thoughtful verbal and gestural supports to help young children maintain their attention as they share and talk about books, children comprehend better and acquire more language (Landry & Smith, 2006).

Notice the Type of Book to Decide How to Read It

Skill

- **genre awareness**

Progression

Needs support to develop book awareness, print concepts, and genre awareness.

● ○ ○ ○ ○

Research Link

Young children, even before they are able to decode, are able to differentiate between narrative and informational texts, changing their oral reading to match the genre (Duke & Purcell-Gates, 2003; Pappas, 1993). This allows them to make important connections between texts of various genres that they have encountered at home and at school.

Strategy Look quickly at the cover and flip through the inside pages of the book. As you look, decide what type of book it is. Is it a story? Is it going to teach you something? Go back to the beginning to explore the pages in order, storytelling or learning from the pictures.

Teaching Tip This strategy will help children to apply what you've taught them about text types and genres. If they need additional scaffolding, you might give them *only* one type of text for a few days and notice aloud with them how you can determine the type of book: "Oh, this book has photographs of real things. And so does this one. Both of these books are books that teach us about something." Or "This book has illustrations that someone drew. But it looks like they are all about different animals. This book will teach information." Or "There isn't one character that shows up on each of the pages. So even though it's illustrated, it's still an information book." Once children start to see similarities between several examples of the same text type, you could provide them with bins of mixed genre books to see if they can sort them.

Prompts

- What are you noticing about this book? So, what kind of book is it?
- You noticed the same character appears in most of the pictures in this book. So, is this a *story*, or a *book that will teach you about a topic*?
- I agree, the photographs make me think this is a book that will teach you about a topic.

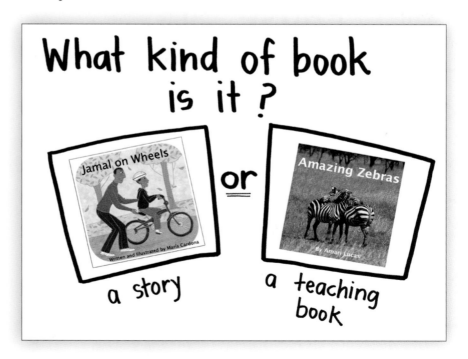

Notice, Think, Explain

Strategy Notice the details on the page. Say (to yourself or a partner) what you see. Then, have your own idea or thought about what you notice. Explain why you thought what you did, using details from the pictures.

Lesson Language *In books there is so much to think about as long as I spend some time on each page! Watch as I read and think about* Wave *(Lee, 2008). Even though the pictures are simple, there is still a lot to notice and think about!* (Model pointing to and around the picture.) *On this first page, I see a young girl at the edge of the sea. She seems to be leaning in. Oh! And there is a line of seagulls behind her.* (Point to your head.) *I'm thinking that because she's leaning in but still far away, she sort of wants to explore the water but is maybe a little nervous too. I think the seagulls might be curious about her.* (Point to the page.) *On the next page, I see her running away.* (Point to your head.) *I'm wondering if she's nervous or just being playful. And then on the next page* (point to page) *she's got her hands up and her face looks like she's growling.* (Point to head.) *I think she's trying to be in charge of the waves! Trying to scare them back away from her.*

Prompts
- What are you noticing on this page?
- What does it make you think? Wonder?
- Tell me how you got that idea.
- That's a clear explanation! It matches the pictures.

Skills
- **determining importance**
- **talking about books**
- **inferring**

Progression

In a story, alone or with a teacher/partner, labels and elaborates briefly on what's in pictures. Is ready to start elaborating with story language, including dialogue.

Hat Tip

I Am Reading: Nurturing Young Children's Meaning Making and Joyful Engagement with Any Book (Collins & Glover, 2015)

Research Link

Numerous studies demonstrate that supporting students with self-regulation, such as focusing on a page to think more deeply about its content, develops both executive functioning skills (such as inhibitory control and cognitive flexibility) and early literacy skills (Hanno, Jones, & McCoy, 2020).

Skills

- **genre awareness**
- **inferring**
- **talking about books**

Progression

In a story, alone or with a teacher/partner, labels and elaborates briefly on what's in pictures. Is ready to start elaborating with story language, including dialogue.

Hat Tip

I Am Reading: Nurturing Young Children's Meaning Making and Joyful Engagement with Any Book (Collins & Glover, 2015)

Research Link

In reviews of multiple studies (Arizpe, 2013; Dowhower, 1997), researchers have established that wordless picture books provide a context for readers to make sense of what they see by mentally filling in the gaps between images, recognize that stories have a sequence, and hypothesize about the connections between the illustrated moments. Repeated interactions with picture books acclimate young children to the conventions of narratives (Purcell-Gates, 1988).

Strategy On every page of a story, try to sound like a storyteller. Look carefully at the picture. Say what the character is *doing*. Say what the character is *saying*.

Teaching Tip You can set children up to practice this strategy in slightly different ways depending on the books they are using. If they are using books that have been read aloud to them several times, they may be trying to *remember* what the characters do and say and use that same story language. Alternatively, you can set children up with wordless picture books (or picture books with rich illustrations that have words, but which they won't yet be able to decode). In this case, they will be inferring what the characters *might* be doing or *might* say, similar to how children create storylines and dialogue when they play with dolls or figurines.

Prompts

- What do you think they might be saying?
- Look closely at the picture. What are they doing?
- Stop here. Say what they do and say.
- Say it like the character would.

Strategy Look closely at the character's face. Think about how the character is feeling. Think about how the character would talk. When you say the dialogue, sound like the character.

Teaching Tip There are several strategies in Chapter 4 to support prosody when reading dialogue (see Strategies 4.19, 4.20, 4.21). The difference here is that although children may not be decoding the words, they can still practice inferring character feelings and saying dialogue with expression to match the meaning they are making. This strategy can be helpful when children are working with books that are familiar or unfamiliar.

Prompts
- How did the character say that? Show me.
- Say it thinking about how the character is feeling.
- I could tell he sounded happy (or mad or sad) because of how you said that.
- Your voice matched the character's feeling on that page.

Skills
- **genre awareness**
- **inferring**
- **talking about books**

Progression

In a story, alone or with a teacher/partner, labels and elaborates briefly on what's in pictures. Is ready to start elaborating with story language, including dialogue.

Research Link

In a two-year study of young children's interactions with picture books, Arizpe and Styles (2016) established that, even before they are able to decode, young readers are able to identify different moods, emotions, and viewpoints in images and can articulate responses to what they see. Identifying emotions in pictures, and recognizing emotions of others as separate from their own, helps develop emotional literacy (Nikolajeva, 2017).

Skills

- **genre awareness**
- **inferring**
- **talking about books**

Progression

In a story, alone or with a teacher/partner, labels and elaborates briefly on what's in pictures. Is ready to start elaborating with story language, including dialogue.

●●○○○○

Research Link

In one small study, an adult read a folktale to preschool- and kindergarten-age children, then had one group reenact the story through pretend play using toys, while another group was asked to simply retell the story (Kim, 1999). The students encouraged to play act the story provided more elaborate narratives with more structure, indicating that pretend play supported recall and expression.

Strategy Decide with your partner who will play each character. Together, use your faces, bodies, and voices to bring the story to life: act like the characters, talk like the characters, move like the characters.

Teaching Tip I recommend Porcelli and Tyler's phenomenal book *A Quick Guide to Boosting English Acquisition in Choice Time, K–2* (2008) for all pre-K and K teachers who want to help bring story play to their choice time. In their book, the authors suggest ways to have students re-create, play with, and storytell familiar read-alouds when engaged in centers such as blocks, dramatic play, art, and more. This strategy idea is just one adapted from their book and would work well in choice time or even during partnership time in your regular reading workshop. Use familiar stories (books that have been read aloud to them many times), wordless picture books, or any narrative picture books with illustrations that suggest storytelling actions.

Prompts

- Show me with your face and body—what's the character doing now?
- Imagine the character in this part. Now talk like the character.
- You're really bringing the story to life with your words and with your actions!
- Your acting matches what's happening on the page! Explain what you're doing.

Strategy Talk like a topic expert when you're reading information. Study the picture. Think about the specific expert words you'd need to use to describe what you see. Use those words when you're exploring the book by yourself or with a partner.

Teaching Tip This strategy will only work if the child knows the vocabulary needed for the book, but doesn't use the vocabulary when reading independently or with a partner. For some readers, this strategy might work best when used with books that have already been read to them or in books that are connected in some way to class studies in science, social studies, or math. If a child has selected an unfamiliar text, you could, in a conference, introduce the vocabulary: "Oh, you notice that bird? That's called a *seagull*. The next time you read this, you can call it that."

Prompts
- I can see you're looking carefully at the details. Can you use a specific word there?
- What exactly is that called?
- Try to use the word an expert in __ would use for that.
- Now you're talking like an expert! The word __ is one an expert would use when talking about this topic.

Skills
- **genre awareness**
- **determining importance**
- **talking about books**

Progression

In an informational text, alone or with a teacher/partner, labels and elaborates briefly on what's in pictures. Is ready to start elaborating with more content-specific language or more detailed information.

Research Link

In an observational study of teachers and mothers reading with preschool-age children, researchers discovered that adults effectively shared lots of technical vocabulary through talk *about* the book. Rather than reading straight through the text, or only pausing to provide definitions for unknown words, the adults explored concepts with the children and often made connections to a child's prior experiences or existing knowledge (Torr & Scott, 2006).

Skills

- **determining importance**
- **talking about books**
- **genre awareness**

Progression

In an informational text, alone or with a teacher/partner, labels and elaborates briefly on what's in pictures. Is ready to start elaborating with more content-specific language or more detailed information.

● ● ● ○ ○

Research Link

Numerous studies over the decades have consistently indicated a strong reciprocal relationship between prior knowledge and comprehension: activating knowledge about what the child already knows about a subject helps them to both understand the text and construct new knowledge (Fielding & Pearson, 1994).

Strategy Point to something you see in an image on the page. Say a detail. Before you turn the page, look closely to see if you can say another, and another. Once you've said a few, go to the next image on the next page.

Lesson Language *Information book and concept book authors work with illustrators and photographers to teach their readers using pictures and words. Even if you can't yet read the words on the page, you can still learn a lot of information! Watch me as I explore the book* Shapes *by Shelley Rotner and Anne Woodhull (2019). On each page, I'm not just going to say one detail. I'm going to look closely to see if I can say a few. I need to look around the page and look closely at each image. Let's see . . . on this page I see a photo that is showing me that circles can be used to make a pattern on a shirt. As I look around to the next image, I see that some lollipops are shaped like a circle. There are more images to look at—I won't stop yet! Over here, I see marbles, peas in a pod, and a huge ball. They look like circles, but I know they are more like a sphere. Do you see how I didn't just say "I see circles" and moved on, but instead I spent time on the page and said a few details by looking around the whole page, at every image? I also tried to use specific words like* sphere *and* pattern *rather than* stuff *and* thing.

Prompts

- Spend a little more time on this page, with this image. Can you say another detail?
- I heard you say one, two, three details before moving on to another image.
- Did you just learn something new by studying that image?
- I can tell you taught your partner something, and your partner taught you something by staying on this page and saying a few details!

Pay Attention to the WHOLE and Teeny-Tiny Details

Strategy Pay attention to the WHOLE and the teeny-tiny details on the page. Moving your finger around the whole page, say what the page is mostly about. Then zoom in on small parts, saying at least one thing for each part you see.

Teaching Tip Readers can practice this strategy with any genre or text type. When reading informational text, this strategy will help students develop an understanding of main idea/topic and key details: that an informational text spread or section is often about one overarching idea (or topic) with multiple supporting details or facts. For some students, looking at the details first (see the previous strategy) and then putting them together to come up with a "whole" is more natural. Therefore, you could reword this strategy to ask students to list all the facts they can find on the page looking at each of the teeny-tiny details, and then ask, "What is the whole page mostly about?" and name the main topic. The best texts to practice this strategy with, whether you're going part to whole or whole to part, are ones where there are distinct subtopics (for example, a book about African animals with the first few pages about elephants, the next few pages about lions, the next few pages about zebras) rather than information books with a very narrow focus, such as Nic Bishop's *Frogs* (2008) where every page features . . . a frog!

Prompts
- Use your finger. Sweep it around the whole page.
- Say, "This whole page is about . . ."
- Now zoom in on a small part. Say what you're learning.
- Move your finger to another part. What else did you learn?

Skills
- **determining importance**
- **synthesizing**

Progression
In an informational text, alone or with a teacher/partner, labels and elaborates briefly on what's in pictures. Is ready to start elaborating with more content-specific language or more detailed information.

●●●○○

Research Link
In one small study, kindergartners were asked to read a wordless informational text at the very beginning of the year and again in December. Although the children started school with some knowledge of these kinds of texts, after only three months of regular exposure to them, the researchers noted an increase in the children's ability to read using the language typical of informational texts (Duke & Kays, 1998).

Skills

- **talking about books**
- **synthesizing**
- **genre awareness**

Progression

Is elaborating well on each individual page and is ready to start synthesizing pages, either alone or with a teacher/partner.

Research Link

In a classic study, Sulzby and colleagues (1985) observed as kindergarteners read from a favorite book, and then the researchers developed a classification scheme to describe emergent readings. They saw that at first, children tend to focus entirely on the pictures and share disconnected labels and comments. Over time, and with practice, children are able to compose a "story" that spans the entire book and connects the pages cohesively.

Strategy Use the words and phrases we often hear in stories to sound like a storyteller who is connecting the parts.

Lesson Language *Every page in the book connects to make one whole story. You can move from page to page connecting them as you go. Watch as I connect the pages from* A Visitor for Bear *(Becker, 2012).* (Touch page 1.) *"There was a sign on the door and it says 'NO!' So he doesn't want anyone to come inside."* (Touch the next page.) *"Later, the bear wanted breakfast, so he put on his apron in the kitchen."* (Touch the next page.) *"Suddenly, a mouse came to his door and he just said 'Get away! Don't you see my sign?' and then he shut the door."* (Touch the next page.) *"And then he went back to his kitchen and put a spoon and a cup on the table."* (Touch the next page.) *"After that, the mouse came back!"*

Teaching Tip This strategy may best be introduced in coaching conferences, and then you can encourage children to use the words and phrases independently as they storytell narrative picture books to themselves and with peers when partner reading. When sitting with a student who is reading across pages, you might simply offer words and phrases, as appropriate, when they transition from part to part or page to page: *once upon a time, happily ever after, after that, later that day, but that evening, the next morning, suddenly,* and so on.

Prompts

- How would the story start?
- What word might you use as you move from page to page?
- We're at the end! What word(s) would you use?
- Let's start the story again. Say, "Once upon a time . . ."

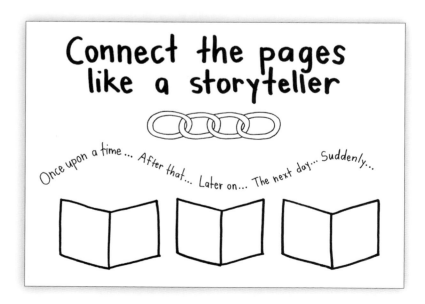

Strategy As you're storytelling you may realize "Wait! That doesn't make sense." When this happens, you can fix it—you can *revise* your storytelling. Back up and retell the story to match what the pictures show.

Teaching Tip This strategy is meant to support children's ability to understand how stories unfold, self-monitor their comprehension, and self-correct or revise when needed. When telling a story, their inference about what is happening on each page may make sense, but on subsequent pages, the meaning doesn't add up. For example, if a child is storytelling the Caldecott award-winning *Blackout* (Rocco, 2011) and gets to the page where all the lights go out, they might say, "And then all the lights in the whole city went out. The game she was playing turned off. She decided to go to bed." But then when the child turns the page and sees the character in the dark with a speech bubble that reads "MOM!" they need to back up and say, "Actually, all the lights went out and the game stopped and then . . . she got nervous in the dark all by herself and shouted for her mom!"

Prompts
- Hm. Does that follow what happened on the last page? Back up and tell this part again, knowing what happens next.
- Oh, so that's what happens next. What do you think happened on the page before?
- Make sure your pages connect.
- I notice you went back to change what happened on that page so it all would make sense.

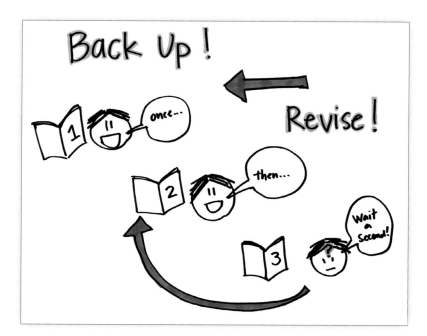

Skills
- **self-monitoring**
- **inferring**

Progression

Is elaborating well on each individual page and is ready to start synthesizing pages, either alone or with a teacher/partner.

Hat Tip

I Am Reading: Nurturing Young Children's Meaning Making and Joyful Engagement with Any Book (Collins & Glover, 2015)

Research Link

The process of reading without words is challenging and "misreadings" are inevitable (Graham, 1998). To construct a meaningful narrative, the reader must scan every image for clues and work hard to infer without any guidance from the printed text (Arizpe, 2013; Nodelman, 1988).

Skills

- **synthesizing**
- **determining importance**
- **genre awareness**

Progression

Is elaborating well on each individual page and is ready to start synthesizing pages, either alone or with a teacher/partner.

Research Link

In a small study of preschoolers reading stories and informational texts with adults, researchers noted that the children spontaneously used informational discourse (same, different, etc.) to describe and ask questions about classes and groups of objects (Shine & Roser, 1999). This talk was specific to informational books and was noticeably different than the way the children responded to other genres.

Strategy Use the cover to say what the whole book is mostly about. Learn from the first page. As you turn the page notice: "What's the same?" and "What's new or different?"

Lesson Language *Watch me think about how the pages in this information book connect. I'll notice what's the same and what's new or different on each spread in this book,* Farm *(Arlon, 2021). This is a book about farms—I see a tractor, a field of crops, a barn, pigs, and a duck, all on the front cover. I know all those things are at a farm. (Turn the page.) On these two pages I see ducks, chickens, turkeys, and geese and all other kinds of birds. Well, not all birds—just birds at the farm. So that's the same as the book—the book is about farms; this page is about birds at a farm. (Turn the page.) Oh, these pages aren't about birds anymore. Now I'm seeing cows and horses. Lots of cows! What's the same? This is still about farms, and specifically a kind of farm that has cows. It's different because instead of birds on the farm, it's about cows and horses on the farm. (Turn the page.) More cows! But I also see milk in all kinds of containers and cheese. So it's the same as the last page because it's still about cows and it's the same as all the pages because it's about a farm, but what's new is about how cows make milk and milk can get turned into cheese.*

Teaching Tip Questions may help children track the topic across the book (What's the same?) and also sense shifts and see connections in the subtopics (What's new or different?). For children who are not yet able to conceptualize categories of information, the questions may simply help them compare and contrast information within a text.

Prompts

- Think about how these pages connect.
- Say, "Another thing is . . ."
- How does what you learn on this page fit with what you learn on that page?
- How does the information on this page connect with the information on the next page?

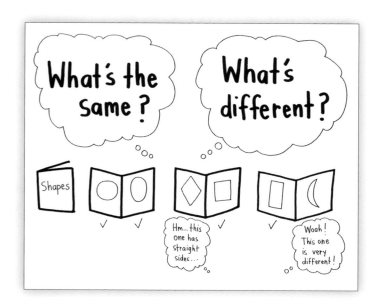

Strategy Flip through the pages of the alphabet book in order. As you sing the alphabet song (alone or with a partner), point under each letter as you go. Reread the book without singing to see if you can remember the name of each of the letters.

Lesson Language *We know there are 26 letters, and upper- and lowercase versions of each one. One way to help you remember what each letter looks like is to match the name of the letter with the letter in print. Alphabet books have the letters in order, and if you know your alphabet song—and I know you all do!—you can sing and match the letters in the book as you go. Will you sing with me as I turn the pages in this book and point under each letter on every page?*

Prompts:
- Point as you sing!
- Sing a little slower. Make sure you're pointing under each letter as you sing/say it.
- Now that you've sung the alphabet, go back to the start of the book to see if you can remember what each letter is called.
- Point to the letter. Say it.

Skill

- **letter-sound knowledge**

Progression

Is paying attention to the print in books and is ready to develop letter-sound knowledge.

Research Link

In a quasi-experimental study exploring the relationship between music and reading acquisition, children who participated in a "songs group" increased their letter-sound knowledge, among gains in other early literacy skills, compared with their peers in a control group (Walton, 2014).

Connect Letters in the Book to Letters in the World

Skill

- **letter-sound knowledge**

Progression

Is paying attention to the print in books and is ready to develop letter-sound knowledge.

Research Link

Children learning to read and write in English can typically recite the alphabet before the age of 4, but often need up to 2 years to learn the shapes of those letters (Honig, 2001). According to a review of research by Adams (1990), the ability to quickly and accurately name and recognize the shapes of letters is one of the strongest predictors of later decoding ability.

Strategy Find a letter in your alphabet book. Match the letter in your book to the letter somewhere in the classroom, on index cards, or in another book. "Write" the letter with your finger.

Lesson Language *The letters of the alphabet you're learning are in your alphabet books, and they are also in the world! Look around the classroom—there are letters everywhere! On the alphabet chart, on the rug, on our anchor charts, on the labels around the room. Once you identify a letter in your book, you can find that letter in the room. Then, try to "write" it in the air, on your desk, or on your knee with your finger to remember its shape.*

Teaching Tip This lesson helps children recognize letters no matter the font or placement: in isolation or within a word, written by hand or typed, or in a variety of fonts. "Writing" the letter also helps them to remember it.

Prompts

- What's that letter in your book? Can you find one in the classroom?
- Yes, that's a letter [__]. Try to "write" it in the air with your finger. Now "write" it with your finger on your knee.
- Yes, that's the same letter—this one is typed and that one is handwritten, but they are both a letter __.

Trace and Compare the Letters (Uppercase Versus Lowercase)

Strategy Name the letter. Trace the uppercase and lowercase letter with your finger. Notice what's the same and what's different between uppercase and lowercase.

Teaching Tip Make sure you have plenty of alphabet books with large uppercase and lowercase letters in a clear, clean font. Some alphabet books contain sentences on each page, which may be OK for some children but distracting for others. For example, *Creature ABC* (Zuckerman, 2009) would be a great choice for this strategy. Two two-page spreads are dedicated to each letter. The first of the spreads features a large uppercase and lowercase letter and a lively photograph of an animal on a white background. The next two pages feature a single word and photograph of another example of the same animal (e.g., *H* and *h* with a photo of a hippo; a photo of a different hippo and the word *hippopotamus*). *ABC: A Child's First Alphabet Book* (Jay, 2003) is another good choice. Each page features a large photograph with one simple sentence below (e.g., "[Letter] is for [thing]").

Prompts
- Trace the letters with your fingers.
- What do you notice is the same about the uppercase and lowercase letters?
- What's different between the uppercase and lowercase letters?

Skill
- **letter-sound knowledge**

Progression
Is paying attention to the print in books and is ready to develop letter-sound knowledge.

● ● ● ● ●

Research Link
In a large study of preschoolers exploring emergent literacy skills that contribute to emergent writing, both knowledge of the alphabet and awareness of print concepts contributed positively to letter writing (Puranik, Lonigan, & Kim, 2011).

Skill

- **letter-sound knowledge**

Progression

Is paying attention to the print in books and is ready to develop letter-sound knowledge.

Research Link

Although knowledge of letter names and knowledge of the sounds those letters represent are often thought to be the same ability, research by McBride-Chang (1999) indicated that is not the case. The two independently predicted later reading-related skills (phonological awareness, spelling, reading), meaning they represent different abilities.

Strategy Look closely at a letter on the page in your alphabet book. Trace it with your finger and say the letter name. Say the names of the thing(s) pictured on the page that are spelled with that letter. Then go back and say the first sound you hear at the start of each word.

Lesson Language *Let's look together at Lois Ehlert's* Eating the Alphabet: Fruits & Vegetables from A to Z *(1989). I'm going to open to the first page where I see the upper- and lowercase A. I'm going to trace the two letters with my finger and say A. Now I'll look around the page. I see an apple, an avocado, some asparagus. Let me go back to the first one and say it so I can hear the first sound by itself, aaaa-pple. Now I'll try avocado, aaaa-vocado. Great! Will you help me with the next page? That's right, that's the uppercase and lowercase B. What do you see on this page? Turn and tell your partner.* (Kids turn to a partner to name banana, bean, beet, broccoli.) *Now, say each word so you can hear the first sound.* (Kids turn to a partner to isolate the sound at the beginning of each word.) *Great! Off you go with a partner. Remember the steps—look, trace, say the letter name, say the word, say the letter sound at the start of the word.*

Teaching Tip For children ready for an extension, you can challenge them to come up with two other words they know that start with the same sound. You might suggest they look around the classroom to help.

Prompts

- Say the names of the things on this page that go with the letter __.
- Say the name of that animal. What's the first sound you hear?
- Ah, so one sound the letter __ can represent is the /__ / sound.
- Say the name of the letter. Now say the sound.

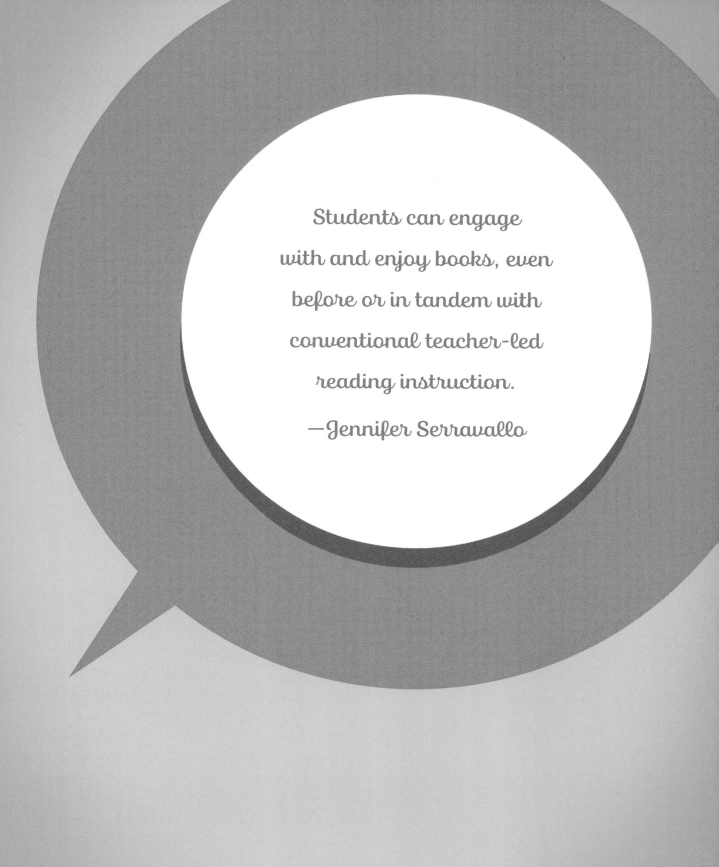

Students can engage
with and enjoy books, even
before or in tandem with
conventional teacher-led
reading instruction.

—Jennifer Serravallo

Engagement and Motivation

◎ Why is this goal important?

You could be the most eloquent teacher, the best strategy group facilitator, the most insightful conferrer. But if you send your kids back for independent reading and they don't read, then they won't make the progress you are hoping and working for. Research has shown that the amount of time that kids spend practicing reading, on task, with eyes on print, makes a huge difference to their success as readers overall, and across content areas (Allington, 2011; Anderson, Wilson, & Fielding, 1988; Cunningham & Stanovich, 1991; Krashen, 2004; Pressley et al., 2001; Stanovich & Cunningham, 1993; Taylor, Frye, & Maruyama, 1990).

An engaged reader is often one who is "motivated to read, strategic in their approaches to comprehending what they read, knowledgeable in their construction of meaning from text, and socially interactive while reading" (Guthrie, Wigfield, & You, 2012, p. 602). This definition of an engaged reader suggests that teachers need to work to help readers construct meaning (see Chapters 5 through 11), and that an engagement problem may actually be a symptom of something else—a child who is not understanding, for example (Ivey & Johnston, 2013). It also suggests that in classrooms where partnerships and clubs support kids' independent reading, readers are more likely to be engaged (see Chapter 12).

In addition to comprehension and social interaction, there are a few other ways to support motivation and engagement in reading. Helping children select books that are both readable and interesting is critical (Arzubiaga, Rueda, & Monzó, 2002; Ivey & Broaddus, 2007; Miller, 2009; Von Sprecken, Kim, & Krashen, 2000), as is readers' attentional focus and their ability to self-monitor and bring their focus back to reading. Stamina also comes into play; strategies can offer readers ways to increase the amount of time they can sustain their reading. When all these factors are in place, readers may attain what Atwell refers to as being "in the reading zone" (2007) or what Csikszentmihalyi calls a state of "flow" (1990).

Text choice
Selecting texts that are a good fit in terms of readability, background knowledge, and interest.

Stamina
Sustaining reading for extended stretches of time, persevering through challenges.

Attentional focus
Blocking out distractions (from the reading environment or from within the reader's own mind) to keep attention and focus on the text (includes *self-regulation* and *impulse control*).

Self-monitoring
Recognizing when one's mind is engaged with the text and when it's not, and utilizing fix-up strategies to reengage and understand.

Skills a reader might work on as part of this goal

Visualizing
Creating mental images as a way to engage with the text and follow the information or action.

Planning
Starting reading time with a clear intention, usually related to a reading goal.

Activating prior knowledge
Using relevant knowledge (about the topic, series, author, genre, etc.) before, during, and after reading to connect new to known and maintain engagement.

How do I know if this goal is right for my student?

One of my favorite tools for figuring out who needs support with engagement is the engagement inventory (Serravallo, 2010, 2015). Essentially a kidwatching tool, it can be used to record student behaviors and observable signs of engagement and disengagement. While we can glean some information about engagement from watching children, be aware that compliance and engagement are not the same; a student might *appear* focused on their reading, but in actuality they may have a wandering mind, may not be enjoying their book, or may be muscling through their reading only because they know that's what you expect. Be sure to combine this kidwatching with other ways of getting to know your students' engagement.

ENGAGEMENT INVENTORY
NOTE TO TEACHER: Kid-watch and record student behaviors during 5–10 minute increments.

Names	Time/Environment 10:05	Time/Environment 10:10	Time/Environment (interruption) 10:15	Time/Environment 10:20	Time/Environment 10:25	Notes
Tara	✓	✓	✓	✓	✓	
Marcus	T	T	Z	✓	✓	
Andrew	✓	✓	✓	T	T	
Ana	✓	✓	✓	✓	✓	
Maya	✓	✓	✓	✓	✓	
Jonas	✓	SB	Z	✓	✓	
Jaclyn	T	✓	✓	✓	✓	
Michael T.	✓	✓	W	T	✓	
Ella	✓	T	✓	✓	T	
Michael R.	✓	✓	✓	SB	Z	
Kim	T	✓	✓	T	T	
John	✓	✓	✓	✓	T	
Chelsie	✓	✓	✓	S	✓	
Merridy	✓	✓	✓	S	✓	
Jesus	T	✓	✓	✓	T	
Barb	✓	✓	✓	✓	T	
Katherine	✓	✓	✓	✓	T	

KEY: C = Chatting   ✓ = Engaged   S = Smiling   SB = Switching Books   T = Looking at Teacher   W = Looking Out Window   Z = Zoning Out

An engagement inventory is a tool you can use to observe signs of engagement and record student reading behaviors. From this observation, I can tell that both Kim and Marcus might benefit from strategies that would help them to stay focused and engaged the entire time, and to self-monitor (Strategies 2.14–2.26).

Interest inventories help you to learn about students' identities as readers and can help you facilitate reader-book matches. For students who need support with book choice, asking questions about activities outside of reading, like hobbies, favorite movies, or TV shows can often help.

In a conference or a written survey, ask readers to talk to you about their plan(s), goal(s), and purpose(s) for reading, and also about what they notice about their own engagement—do they tend to stay focused, monitor their comprehension, and/or have strategies to reengage if they find they become distracted?

Reading Interest Survey

Name: **Lola**

Do you like to read?
yes

How much time do you spend reading?
30 min /day

What are some of the books you have read lately?
nonfiction about animals, picture books

Do you have a library card? How often do you use it?
yes. I don't usually borrow books

Do you ever get books from the school library?
Yes. 2 every Friday

About how many books do you own?
too many to count!

What are some books you would like to own?
joke books, anything with a good story

Put a check mark next to the kinds of reading you like best and topics you might like to read about:

___ history	___ travel	___ plays	___ sports
✓ adventure	___ romance	___ poetry	✓ science fiction
___ biography	___ war stories	___ car stories	___ supernatural stories
___ humor	___ mysteries	✓ folktales	✓ how-to-do-it books
___ art	___ westerns	✓ novels	✓ astrology
___ detective stories			

Interest inventories help you learn about readers' identities and interests so you can better match them to books. I notice from this inventory that some of Lola's interests (TV, movies) dovetail with the books she says she's enjoying, but others (magazines like Ranger Rick and an interest in animals and space) may be an untapped source for finding new great reads (Strategies 2.1–2.6).

Reading Interest Survey

Do you like to read the newspaper?
no.

If yes, place a check mark next to the part of the newspaper listed you like to read:

___ headlines	___ editorials	___ sports
___ advertisements	___ columnists	___ entertainment
___ comic strips	___ political stories	___ current events
___ others (please list):		

What are your favorite television programs?
cartoons and some stuff on Disney

How much time do you spend watching television?
only a few shows a week

What is your favorite magazine?
Ranger Rick!

Do you have a hobby? If so, what is it?
I like ballet. I also like arts + crafts and science.

What are the two best movies you have ever seen?
Toy Story, Frozen.

Who are your favorite entertainers and/or movie stars? When you were little, did you enjoy having someone read aloud to you?
yes. I love being read to. I like anybody from Disney movies

List topics, subjects, et cetera that you might like to read about:
animals, space, folktales

What does the word 'reading' mean to you?
fun!

Say anything else that you would like to say about reading:
I like to read.

What Texts Might Students Use When Practicing Strategies from This Chapter?

The strategies in this chapter can be used when students are reading any type of text, in any genre or format. However, it's important to remember children's engagement is linked in part to their interest in the texts they are reading (e.g., Guthrie, Wigfield, & You, 2012; Hidi, 2001; see Strategies 2.1–2.8). Although some strategies in this chapter (Strategies 2.16–2.26, for example) can be shared with students reading texts they didn't choose—such as test practice material, textbooks, or other assigned reading—offering a wide range of choices is critical to supporting readers with this goal. Think short and long texts, stories and informational texts, and books about a wide range of topics written by authors from a diverse range of backgrounds. Consider, also, modality. Some children may be most engaged when reading on-screen, and others will find their best fit with paper books (Moyer, 2011).

How do I support students as they work on skills to help their reading engagement?

After evaluating a student's engagement, select strategies that you can model, that they can practice with you, and that they can use independently to increase their skills.

Although development is rarely perfectly linear, skill progressions can help us pinpoint where a student is now and what might come next. Use the if-then chart on page 63 to evaluate your students' reading and find strategies that will support their growth.

A Progression of Skills: *Engagement and Motivation*

If a student . . .

Needs support choosing texts that are of interest (and that they can read with comprehension, accuracy, and fluency).

Chooses appropriate texts and is ready to start identifying a purpose or making a plan for reading time.

Can sustain reading for a short period of time and is ready to improve attentional focus to increase stamina, and to monitor for meaning and fix-up and reengage as needed.

Then you might teach . . .

2.1 **Find Your Next Great Read**

2.2 **Consider Aspects of Your Identity to Help You Choose**

2.3 **Find Your Topic Territories**

2.4 **Seek Out Recommendations from Readers You Trust**

2.5 **Read a Review to Help You Choose**

2.6 **Sample the Book, Then Decide**

2.7 **Check the Book's Readability**

2.8 **If It's Not Working, Let It Go**

2.9 **Read with a Purpose in Mind**

2.10 **Make Reading Resolutions**

2.11 **Plan Goal-Focused Stopping Places**

2.12 **Prepare to Purposefully Pause**

2.13 **Plan Ahead for Unexpected Reading Moments**

2.14 **Choose Your Reading Environment**

2.15 **Vary the Length, Type, or Difficulty of Texts**

2.16 **Look Ahead, Take Breaks**

2.17 **Consider Mind over Matter**

2.18 **Retell and Jump Back In**

2.19 **Reread and Jump Back In**

2.20 **Restart Your Reading**

2.21 **Prime Yourself with Prior Knowledge**

2.22 **Fix the Fuzziness**

2.23 **Get Focused with Questions *Before* You Read**

2.24 **Ask Questions *as* You Read**

2.25 **Visualize to Focus**

2.26 **Monitor and Adjust Your Pace**

Strategy Name a book you remember loving, then type its title into a website such as Toppsta.com to see what recommendations pop up. As you read the reviews and summaries of the recommended books, think about what you loved about the original book and let that help you select your next great read.

Teaching Tip The online world is rich with algorithms designed to put products in front of us that we'll want to click on and buy. In the reading classroom, we can use this technology to help readers find books they really want to read. Browse websites such as Amazon, Toppsta, What Should I Read Next?, and Biblionasium—and go to your library with a list of sure-to-be-loved books in hand.

Prompts
- Which book do you most remember loving? Type that one into the website.
- Let's take a look together at some of the other books the website suggests.
- Can you see why this one is suggested to be similar to the one you loved?
- Read the summary before you decide.

Consider Aspects of Your Identity to Help You Choose

Skill

- text choice

Progression

Needs support choosing texts that are of interest (and that they can read with comprehension, accuracy, and fluency).

●○○

Hat Tip

Being the Change
(Ahmed, 2019)

Research Link

Students' book preferences have been shown to be correlated to gender identity more than sex (McGeown, 2012) and to race (Brown-Wood & Solari, 2021; Hardy et al., 2020), although other studies have found that it doesn't matter if the reader's race aligns with the main character, so long as the story is compelling (Jacoby & Edlefsen, 2020). These findings suggest children need access to reading materials that reflect a wide range of identities and experiences.

Strategy Reflect on your identity. How would you describe yourself? What groups do you belong to? What places matter to you? What do you most enjoy? Then, decide. Do you want to choose a book to see yourself, or do you want to read to discover something new?

Lesson Language *When you choose a new book, remember that you are also choosing to have a certain kind of experience. Sometimes you'll choose books that feel so familiar—where the character shares aspects of your identity, set in a place like the place you live, with themes that resonate with your life. Other times, you may choose to escape: to travel to a different time or location, to step into the shoes of a character so different from you and your experiences. To set yourself up to be engaged with your reading, think about what kind of experience you want to have. You can also reflect on whether the books you tend to choose fit into one category more than another and make plans to outgrow or balance your overall reading diet.*

Teaching Tip Be sure to check out resources for improving representation in your text offerings available through We Need Diverse Books (https://diversebooks.org/) and updated statistics through the Cooperative Children's Book Center at the University of Wisconsin-Madison School of Education (https://ccbc.education.wisc.edu/literature-resources/ccbc-diversity-statistics/) as well as the scholarship of Rudine Sims Bishop (see, for example, her paper from 1990).

Prompts

- Do you want to read about a character who is similar to you in some way or one who may have a very different experience?
- Now that you've reflected on your own identity, what do you think you might look for in a book?
- What do you notice about the books you tend to choose?

Reflect to Choose

- How would you describe yourself?
- What groups do you belong to?
- What do you most enjoy?
- What places/topics matter to you?

Read to See New Places | Read to See Yourself

Strategy Readers should be able to answer the question "Who am I as a reader?" One way to do this is to make a list of books (and movies and TV shows) you remember reading and loving and then another list of those you remember disliking. Look across the lists and ask, "What do my favorites have in common? What might help me to love a book?" You might think about types of characters, themes, topics, or the genre.

- -

Teaching Tip For children who need extra support with reflections or finding patterns, you could choose from the prompts that follow to guide their reflection in a conference or create a questionnaire with more guiding questions.

- -

Prompts

- Make a list of books (and movies and TV shows) you've loved the most.
- What patterns do you see?
- Is there anything similar about these books in terms of character? Theme? Topic? Genre?
- Write 3-5 titles of books you never finished or weren't excited about. Are there any patterns?

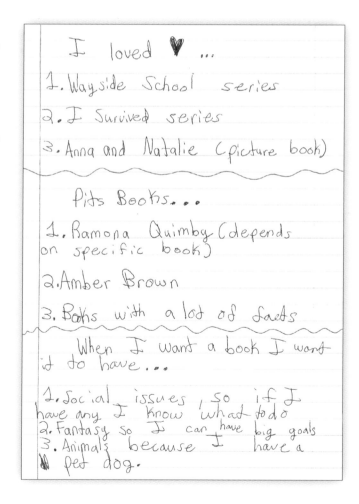

I loved ♥ ...
1. Wayside School series
2. I Survived series
3. Anna and Natalie (picture book)

Pits Books...
1. Ramona Quimby (depends on specific book)
2. Amber Brown
3. Books with a lot of facts

When I want a book I want it to have...
1. Social issues, so if I have any I know what to do
2. Fantasy so I can have big goals
3. Animals because I have a pet dog.

Progression

Needs support choosing texts that are of interest (and that they can read with comprehension, accuracy, and fluency).

Hat Tip

The Book Whisperer: Awakening the Inner Reader in Every Child (Miller, 2009)

Research Link

Over the decades, young people have reported spending more time engaging with other forms of media than with books (National Endowment for the Arts, 2007; Robinson & Weintraub, 1973). Studies of book choices have found that children tended to gravitate toward books with familiar characters or storylines from popular media, suggesting that familiarity and prior positive experiences may lead to greater engagement (Jacoby & Edlefsen, 2020; Williams, 2008).

Seek Out Recommendations from Readers You Trust

Strategy Think about someone who likes the same kinds of books you like. Remind them of your reading interests. Ask them for recommendations.

Teaching Tip Students may not know how to recommend books in ways that make others want to read them, so model good book talks during your literacy block. Point out, for example, how you use convincing language and how you mention specific parts—characters, themes, plot points—that you know will hook the reader (without giving it all away). Then, create a culture of book recommending in your classroom. Make time and space for it and encourage children to seek out recommendations from both peers and adults (librarians, parents, and caregivers, and you!). Consider encouraging children to create their own book trailers to share with friends: upload them to a Google Drive for all to access, create a bulletin board with QR codes to access them, or play select ones during class meetings. Students can also seek out recommendations on sites such as Toppsta (see Strategy 2.1).

Progression

Needs support choosing texts that are of interest (and that they can read with comprehension, accuracy, and fluency).

Prompts

- Who might you ask for a recommendation?
- Tell your friend what you're looking for in a new read.
- Based on what your friend has told you about that book . . . what do you think? Want to give it a try?
- Wow, that book sounds perfect for you, don't you think?

Research Link

In an international study of more than 1,000 adult avid readers, a significant number of respondents credited a "social influencer" who helped to provide access and facilitate choice for their lifelong reading habits and engagement with reading (Merga, 2017).

Strategy Locate reviews of a book you're considering by typing its title into Amazon, Goodreads*, or TikTok*. See what others have had to say about the book. Based on the reviews, consider if the book is a good fit for you and matches the reading mood you're in now.

Lesson Language *Have you heard that #BookTok has been helping titles to trend, launching careers of new authors, and giving new life to titles some have forgotten about? Not only that, but watching the video reviews of some "BookTokers" has inspired me to pick up quite a few books I wouldn't have otherwise considered. Maybe it'll do the same for you! TikTok also uses an algorithm to find patterns in the videos you've watched and can recommend others for you to explore based on those patterns. On Amazon and Goodreads you can also read from the tons of written reviews submitted by everyday readers. I like reading the five-star and one-star reviews the most to find out what people loved—or really disliked—about the book to help me decide if it's worth my time.*

Teaching Tip You could add lessons onto this strategy that help children with their critical reading of reviews. For example, looking across several reviews that mention common things (a pattern in the reviews) could mean that viewpoint is more likely to be something worth paying attention to. You may also teach them to be wary of extreme outliers. Also, remind them to consider who is giving the review. A review by someone who is a verified purchaser (on Amazon) or someone who has a copy of the book on camera (on TikTok) is likely more credible than a review from someone who might not even have the book.

*Note: The audience for TikTok reviews is young adult and teen, not any younger, so adjust your Lesson Language accordingly. Also be aware that Goodreads involves creating an account, and the site doesn't have a dedicated kids' section, so adult supervision is advised.

Skill
• **text choice**

Progression

Needs support choosing texts that are of interest (and that they can read with comprehension, accuracy, and fluency).

Research Link

There are, of course, many ways technology today can facilitate peer sharing around books. But even two decades ago, using extremely basic software, researchers were already reporting improvements in reading engagement after students were asked to create multimedia book reviews to share with their classmates (Reinking & Watkins, 2000).

Skill
• **text choice**

Strategy Read just enough to get the feel of the book—the first few pages or so—then think about how you feel. Does the author have your attention? Can you visualize what you're reading about? Are you eager to read the rest of the book? If so, the book may be a good fit for you. If not . . . move on!

Prompts

• How do you feel after the first bit?
• What grabs you here?
• Tell me if you'd like to keep reading. If yes, why?
• Do you feel like you were focused the whole time you were reading?

Progression

Needs support choosing texts that are of interest (and that they can read with comprehension, accuracy, and fluency).

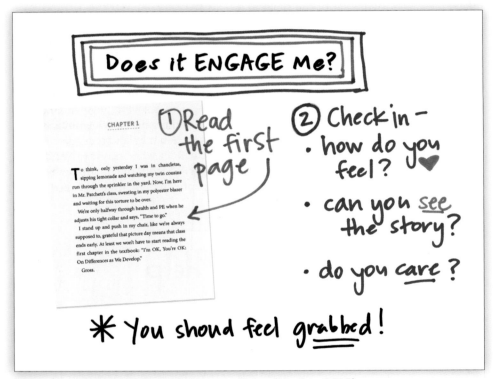

Text excerpt from *Merci Suárez Changes Gears* (Medina, 2018).

Research Link

Book choice is one critical key to increasing children's reading engagement. (Edmunds & Bauserman, 2006; Krashen, 2004). As students are apt to make book choices based on a book's cover image, title, number of pages, familiarity with the author, and so on (Merga & Roni, 2017; Williams, 2008), they may recognize after beginning the book that the content is not to their liking.

Strategy Read a bit (a page or two). Notice if you're able to read most of the words right away or easily figure out new ones. Notice if you read smoothly and with expression. Notice if you're understanding. If it feels challenging, decide if you want to use strategies to support your reading and keep the book or find something that feels more comfortable.

Lesson Language *Although interest in a book is a primary reason to choose it, you also need to make sure that the book is one you* can *read—a book that won't frustrate or confuse you or feel like so much work that you lose steam. In other words, the* readability *of the text needs to be a good match for you. There will be times that you feel up for a challenge and you're willing to work a bit harder without compromising engagement—maybe you'll plan to slow down, do some prereading on the topic in an easier text, or read with a friend. But sometimes you might decide the book is too much of a heavy lift for now, or won't keep your attention, and if so, you might want to save it for later.*

Teaching Tip Although it's important for children to have experience with and exposure to complex texts with the support of a teacher, books for independent reading need to be ones they can read with . . . well . . . independence! Many factors go into what is readable—from background knowledge on a topic to language complexity in the text to a student's motivation to read it and much more (Hoffman, 2017; Serravallo, 2018). It's important to offer children strategies to guide them to choose books they can read and want to read and not limit their choices based on text level.

Prompts

- After reading the first page, do you think you could read the words accurately and with fluency and understanding?
- You said it felt challenging. Are you up for the challenge (with a plan for some strategies to use to help you), or does it feel like one you want to save for another time?
- From the part you read aloud, it sounded smooth and accurate. Are you understanding?
- Check your accuracy, fluency, and understanding.

Skills

- **text choice**
- **self-monitoring**

Progression

Needs support choosing texts that are of interest (and that they can read with comprehension, accuracy, and fluency).

Research Link

Readers don't grow as much when they read too many easy books (Baker & Wigfield, 1999), and readers who spend too much time struggling with difficult texts may become frustrated and disengaged (Anderson, Higgins, & Wurster, 1985). Students need strategies to help them choose books that are both personally interesting *and* at a level of complexity that supports sustained engagement (Donovan, Smolkin, & Lomax, 2000; Fresch, 1995; Reutzel, Jones, & Newman, 2010).

Skills

- **text choice**
- **self-monitoring**

Progression

Needs support choosing texts that are of interest (and that they can read with comprehension, accuracy, and fluency).

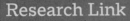

Research Link

In a large study of students in grades 4 and 6, researchers found that students with high and average scores on a reading achievement test completed significantly more of the books they started than their peers with lower scores (Anderson, Higgins, & Wurster, 1985), and in an earlier study, Mork (1973) found that low achievers often selected books that were too difficult.

Strategy Once you've selected a book, give it a chance and begin to read it using strategies meant to help you engage. But, if you get into the book, say about a quarter of the way through it, and you aren't loving it, ask yourself, "Do I want to finish this book, really? Or would I rather read something else?"

Lesson Language *Abandoning a book doesn't mean abandoning reading—in fact, letting go of a book may actually help you read more! Our classroom library, school library, town library, and local bookstores are absolutely filled with books written for children just like you. Even if you read every minute of every day, you still wouldn't be able to read them all! This means we can be choosy and make decisions about which books we pick up in the first place and whether or not to abandon a book if it's not working for us. I do this—I promise! Some books are a little slower to start, so I usually read several chapters (25 to 30%), but if by that point I'm not feeling it, I return it to the library, or pass it along to a friend who I think might like it better than I do. I've learned that if I try to stick with a book I don't love, I end up reading more slowly and it takes longer to get through it, which means I get to enjoy fewer books overall. So if you've given the book a good chance and it's not working for you, let it go and find another!*

Teaching Tip Although occasional book abandoning is a good idea to support engagement and overall high volume of reading, you'll want to keep an eye out for "serial abandoners" who seem not to finish anything. Those readers may need additional help with making choices to begin with, or they may need supports for their memory or their skills for synthesizing and adding up information over time (see Chapters 5–10).

Prompts

- Do you feel like you've given the book a chance? Have you read about a quarter of it?
- What are you going to choose to do: keep reading, or abandon the book?
- It's OK; abandoning this book makes more room in your reading life for a different book you might love!

Strategy Look at the text in front of you and think about your purpose for reading it: To learn information? To be entertained? To practice a goal such as reading with fluency? Jot a note to yourself, tell your purpose to a friend, or check your personal reminders such as your goal bookmark. Read with that purpose in mind.

Teaching Tip Do you frequently revisit and reread texts with your students? Some teachers, for example, engage children in shared reading lessons where they are guided to reread for different purposes each day. In that case, a brief menu of options based on what you do in whole-class or small-group shared reading lessons can encourage children to do this independently, with their self-selected books. For example, a first reading might be to practice decoding any unfamiliar words, then a second reading could be to work on fluency, then a third reading could be one where they practice retelling. Another best practice is for children to have individual goals based on assessment and goal-setting conversations; you may set children up with their own individualized menu of strategies they've learned that are aligned to their current goal.

Prompts
- Remind yourself of your goal. What will you practice as you read today?
- What will you try to do as a reader today?
- What are your plans for your reading time today?
- Jot a note to yourself so you remember what your focus will be during reading today.

Skills
- **planning**
- **attentional focus**

Progression

Chooses appropriate texts and is ready to start identifying a purpose or making a plan for reading time.

● ● ○

Research Link

Based on a review of both classic and more recent studies, Cartwright (2015) concludes that "skilled comprehenders approach texts with particular goals for reading, or a plan to understand the texts in a certain way for a particular purpose" (p. 40) and recommends teaching readers to make plans and keep strategies to accomplish goals in mind and apply them actively as they read.

Skills
- **text choice**
- **planning**

Progression

Chooses appropriate texts and is ready to start identifying a purpose or making a plan for reading time.

Research Link

Researchers studying the effects of goal setting on children's self-efficacy and reading comprehension found that students (low-achieving fourth and fifth graders) who were given specific goals reported greater self-efficacy than their peers who were merely told to work "productively" and that process goals (specific actions or strategies) were more effective for comprehension than product goals (specific knowledge about a topic) (Schunk & Rice, 1989, 1991).

Strategy Reflect on your reading history to make a plan for your reading future. You might look at the most recent books you've read and decide to expand your palate. You might think about your reading pace and want to make some changes. You might consider what purposes you had for reading in the past and make resolutions for reading going forward.

Lesson Language *As you get older, learn new things, and develop new interests, who you are as a reader and what you choose to read about will probably change as well. That's normal. But you can also be intentional about how you want to change as a reader. You can make plans to change. For example, I was on a walk with a friend recently who asked me for a recommendation for a novel to take on vacation. I thought back to all the books I've read in the last six months and realized every single one was for school, to learn new techniques to help me as a teacher. I had a really good reason for why I was doing that reading, but her question got me remembering how much I also enjoy stories and regretting that it wasn't a part of my current reading life. At that moment, I made a resolution to try to balance my reading a bit more, and since then I've kept a novel going while I'm also reading all these informational books to learn more about teaching.*

Prompts

- What are you thinking about your reading history?
- What resolution(s) do you want to make for the short-term future?
- Is there anything about your reading past you want to change going forward?
- You can think about reading rate or pace, the types of books you read, or what you read about.

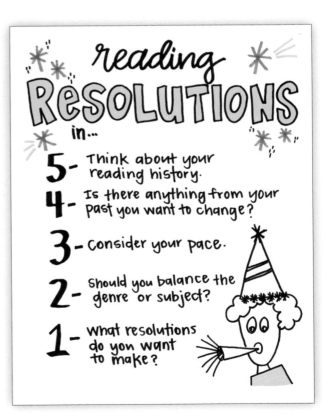

2.11 *Plan Goal-Focused Stopping Places*

Strategy Think about your goal. Set stopping places in your reading by marking them with a blank sticky note. When you get to a stopping place, pause and use the strategies aligned to your goal to do some thinking and practice with a strategy.

Lesson Language *You know what helps many people stay focused and engaged? When they are their own boss. And that's what I'd like you to be today—I'd like you to be the boss of your own reading. You all have goals for yourself as readers that we've discussed during conferences. Now, decide how often you'll stop to do some thinking or practicing and whether you'll take any notes on what you tried when you do.*

Teaching Tip To provide extra scaffolding, you might jot a quick goal-focused prompt or question on sticky notes for a student to preplant in their book. For example, you might write, "What new ideas do you have about the main character?" for someone with a goal of understanding character.

Prompts

- What's your goal? What strategies have you learned to help you with that goal?
- When you stop, what will you do? Jot? Stop and think? Stop and sketch?
- Think about how often you'll need to stop to stay focused.
- Let's look at how this book is organized. Now think about your goal. Where do you think it makes sense to stop?

Progression

Chooses appropriate texts and is ready to start identifying a purpose or making a plan for reading time.

● ● ○

Research Link

In a review of the literature on metacognition (i.e., evaluating and managing your own thinking), Jacobs and Paris (1987) found consistent evidence that what children know about making plans and setting goals, and keeping both in mind, can influence how well they are able to monitor their own reading. Skilled readers think strategically before, during, and after reading.

Skills

• planning
• attentional focus

Progression

Chooses appropriate texts and is ready to start identifying a purpose or making a plan for reading time.

● ● ○

Research Link

In a classic article, Paris, Lipson, and Wixson (1983) propose that children need three kinds of knowledge to read strategically. Declarative knowledge essentially defines—knowing what a story is, for instance. Procedural knowledge is understanding how to do something, such as how to skim for main ideas. However, truly strategic reading requires conditional knowledge—knowing when and why to use a strategy to achieve a particular goal (Paris & Cross, 1983).

Strategy Be clear about your purpose for reading. Read with that purpose in mind. When you come to a spot in the text that aligns to your purpose, stop and think, and possibly jot. You can jot to help you remember, to share with me (your teacher), or to share with a friend.

Lesson Language *Your purpose(s) for reading may change depending on the situation and the text you're reading. Perhaps you're reading a text in a genre you want to try out as a writer; in that case you may be reading to study the author's craft. Maybe you're in the middle of a chapter book that you're reading with your book club, and you're reading to generate ideas you want to talk about or debate. It could be that you're reading to gather information for a research report you're working on. Or something else! If you're clear on your purpose, you can read through that lens, expecting to find places in your book that will make you want to pause to think, and maybe even jot.*

Prompts

• What purpose do you have for reading? What will you keep in mind as you read?
• What kinds of things might you read that will cause you to pause and think/jot?
• I notice you've stopped to jot a few times. Do these jots align to your purpose?

Strategy Think about the moments you may have across your day to read, outside of school or scheduled reading time. Make a plan for what kinds of reading material, and how much, you want to bring with you.

Lesson Language *One of the habits many lifelong, truly independent readers share is that they carry books with them wherever they go in anticipation of moments when they might "find" a little reading time. Fifteen minutes on a car ride home, ten minutes waiting in a doctor's office, forty-five minutes sitting on the sidelines while your sister finishes her soccer game, five minutes at the end of the day as the buses are being called. These little bits of reading add up to a lot of minutes over time. You can think ahead and plan for these opportunities and make sure you have what you need to squeeze in more hidden reading moments across the day.*

Teaching Tip Frequent stopping and starting in longer novels may frustrate some readers or cause their comprehension to slip. In those cases, recommend (and provide access to) magazines, poetry anthologies, or other short form pieces they can finish in small amounts of time.

Prompts
- When do you think you might have time to read outside of school?
- Are you the kind of reader who can read a chapter book for a few minutes at a time, or would you rather pick shorter texts?
- Plan ahead for what you'll read.

Skill
- **planning**

Progression

Chooses appropriate texts and is ready to start identifying a purpose or making a plan for reading time.

Hat Tip

Reading in the Wild
(Miller, 2013)

Research Link

Since the 1980s, researchers have advocated for students to spend more time reading to support both fluency and reading achievement (Stanovich, 1986). However, one study found most reading programs only devote about 15 minutes per day to actual engagement with text (Allington, 2014). Strategies like this one are meant to help increase the volume of reading students do across the day—volume that adds up over time.

Skills

- **planning**
- **attentional focus**
- **stamina**

Progression

Can sustain reading for a short period of time and is ready to improve attentional focus to increase stamina, and to monitor for meaning and fix-up and reengage as needed.

● ● ●

Research Link

According to Powell, McIntyre, and Rightmyer (2006), "off-task" behavior during literacy lessons is often caused by students who resist "closed" learning environments with few opportunities for choice. In two studies exploring a more "open" approach, researchers found that more students (second, third, and fifth graders) preferred flexible seating options, which aided their engagement and ownership over learning (Cole et al., 2021; Stapp, 2019).

Strategy Choosing a reading environment is very important. Think about what you need—bright or dim light? Background noise or quiet? Hard or soft seating? Lying down or sitting upright? Plan out your reading space, give it a try, and reflect on how it went for you.

Teaching Tip Ideally, children are reading both at home and at school each day. Each location has its own limitations and parameters, and each offers different possible options and opportunities. Consider gearing this strategy toward the classroom environment for an in-school reflection, and then ask children to consider their home reading environment (with a reflection on how their reading went in their new reading space) for homework. Be mindful, however, that some children may have very little control over their home environment, and what is possible in terms of creating a reading space may vary dramatically among the students in your class.

Prompts

- What do you think you need from your environment to get the most reading done?
- Think about environments where you've been successful.
- Think about what tends to distract you. Choose a different type of spot.
- You considered where you'd do your best reading so thoughtfully. Give it a try and we'll talk in a couple days.

Strategy Consider what reading materials you'll need for a successful reading time. Consider if you'll want shorter or longer texts. Will you read stories, poetry, informational texts, or some mix of a variety of texts? Get your stack ready before you begin reading.

Lesson Language *Texts of different lengths, different genres, and different complexity each take a different kind of attention and focus, and demand different things from us as readers. Make a plan for your reading time that sets you up to stay focused for the entire time, or be prepared with other materials "on deck" for when you notice you need a change. For example, you might pause your reading of a longer book and move to some shorter texts when you notice your attention waning. You might vary the genre or type of text (articles, short stories, poems) to help you stretch your reading time.*

Teaching Tip This strategy is intended to help children stay focused on their reading for a longer stretch of time. For some children, varying what they read and giving them the option to switch between materials can help extend their reading. Keep an eye on the impact that switching between texts has on students' comprehension, and advise children to switch less frequently if doing so seems to have any adverse effects.

Prompts
- What else have you chosen to read during reading time?
- Let's make a plan for your reading time with these materials.
- Let's set a goal for how much you'll read before moving on to something else.
- Now that you've come to the end of reading time, reflect on how switching between texts helped, or didn't help, your engagement and comprehension.

Skills
- **planning**
- **attentional focus**
- **stamina**

Progression

Can sustain reading for a short period of time and is ready to improve attentional focus to increase stamina, and to monitor for meaning and fix-up and reengage as needed.

● ● ●

Research Link

Individual interest may help a reader stick with a relevant, but otherwise boring, text, whereas *situational* interest (i.e., quality or context, such as an especially well-crafted story or an informational text with stunning photographs) may maintain engagement even when the individual has no initial interest (Hidi, 2001). Varied reading can elicit situational interest so that readers may eventually develop individual interest in a topic, genre, or format (Schraw & Lehman, 2001).

Let's make a reading plan

1. STACK
What else have you chosen to read?

Length → Short or long?
Genre → Fiction or nonfiction?
Type → Poetry or anime? Magazine or digital?
Complexity → Challenge or quick read?

2. VOLUME
Set a goal for how much you'll read before moving on to something else.

3. TIME
Make a plan to stay focused the entire time. Switch between texts to keep motivated.

4. REFLECT
Consider how switching between texts helped or didn't help your comprehension.

Next time...

Skills

- **planning**
- **attentional focus**
- **stamina**

Progression

Can sustain reading for a short period of time and is ready to improve attentional focus to increase stamina, and to monitor for meaning and fix-up and reengage as needed.

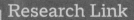

Hat Tip

I Am Reading: Nurturing Young Children's Meaning Making and Joyful Engagement with Any Book (Collins & Glover, 2015)

Research Link

Sanders and colleagues (2021) found that using timers to segment longer work periods into shorter ones, as well as looking ahead at larger tasks and breaking them up into smaller ones, supported self-regulation in students with emotional and behavioral disorders.

Strategy One way to increase the amount of time you read with focus is to set a time or page number goal. Set a personal quiet timer for a certain amount of time, or plant a sticky note on a spot where you'll take a pause. When you meet your goal, take the break you need (get up, stretch, let your mind wander for a moment). Then, repeat the process and get back into your reading.

Teaching Tip Teachers often ask me what type of break is appropriate. My suggestion is that the teacher decides on a "break" with the student, or the teacher decides for the student based on what they know about the child. Kids who are very physically active may need a break that involves getting up and moving to help get the wiggles out, such as stretching at their seat. On the opposite end of the continuum are children who may be very sleepy and need a break that will energize them, such as doing quasi-push-ups on their desk or placing their hands on the seat of their chair to do a quick lift-up. A Google search for "movement breaks for the classroom" will yield many specific ideas. Still other students may benefit from taking some time to stop and reflect on what they've read, perhaps even jotting a quick summary or idea. This last idea will help support comprehension, which is linked to level of engagement. No matter the type of break, over time, you'll want to coach the reader to extend the number of pages or amount of time they read before taking a break.

Prompts

- How many minutes/ pages do you think you can read before you need a break?
- So last time, you thought you'd take a break every __ minutes/ pages. How did that work for you?
- So last time you decided to take a break by __. How did that work for you?
- Plan out what you'll do for a break.

Strategy Sometimes the key to staying focused is *deciding* to stay focused. Tell yourself, "I'm going to stay focused on what I'm reading" and then hear yourself as you read. Read the words as if they are beautiful or as if what you're learning about is interesting. If you feel your mind wanting to do something else, or being pulled away, intentionally refocus on your book.

Lesson Language *Have you ever heard that when you smile—even if you're not in a good mood—it will actually change your mood from the inside out and it can make you happy? It's true! Sometimes doing something consciously can have an effect on something that we normally think is involuntary or out of our control. For example, when we read, the kind of attitude with which we approach our reading can change how much we understand and are able to focus on it. Approach reading by switching your brain on with a clear intention to stay focused right from the start.*

Teaching Tip Before you teach this strategy, make sure you've helped students choose texts that interest them and that aren't too challenging—a key first step to engagement. Also remember that students who normally focus easily may struggle when they read texts they haven't chosen (such as in testing situations) and can benefit from this strategy to apply to those sorts of situations.

Prompts
- Get your mind ready.
- Read it like it's the most interesting thing you've ever read.
- What will you tell yourself if you find your attention wandering?
- Do you see a difference in your attention?

Skills
- **planning**
- **attentional focus**
- **stamina**
- **self-monitoring**

Progression

Can sustain reading for a short period of time and is ready to improve attentional focus to increase stamina, and to monitor for meaning and fix-up and reengage as needed.

Research Link

Many students, especially those who struggle with reading, benefit from learning strategies that promote self-regulation, including being explicitly taught how to establish goals, self-monitor performance, and use self-instructions to direct the focus of their attention (Mason et al., 2013).

Skills

• **self-monitoring**
• **attentional focus**
• **stamina**

Progression

Can sustain reading for a short period of time and is ready to improve attentional focus to increase stamina, and to monitor for meaning and fix-up and reengage as needed.

Strategy Everyone's mind wanders sometimes; the important thing is that you are able to pull your attention back. Say to yourself, "No. I'm not going to think about that right now." Then, quickly retell what you remember about your book to jump back into it.

Teaching Tip Consider modifying the language of this strategy so it's appropriate for the type of text and complexity of text the student is reading. For example, children reading beginning reader books will mostly retell the whole book, and a student reading a chapter book may just retell the last chapter. A student reading an informational text won't *retell* but rather will *summarize* (give a main idea or topic and key details).

Prompts

• Say back what you remember.
• When/where did you find your mind wandering?
• Did your mind wander there? You know what to do. Show me.
• You're retelling before you jump back into the book—that's really going to help you stay focused.

Strategy As you read, be aware of your thinking. Sometimes your mind can leave the book to think about something else even when you're pronouncing the words on the page (out loud or in your head). When your mind isn't in the book, back up and reread. If you notice your attention shifting very often, consider whether the book is a good fit or if something in your environment is causing you to become distracted.

Lesson Language *I'm going to tell you about something that happens to everyone I know at one time or another—and I want you to think about whether it's ever happened to you. Sometimes, when a reader is reading, their eyes are working through the words, maybe even hearing the words in their head as they read, but the words are not connecting to meanings in their brain. They're thinking about something totally unrelated. Sometimes, I will go on like this for a few paragraphs before I realize, "I have no idea what I just read." How do I know I've lost my way? Maybe the setting in my book has changed and I realize I don't know how the character got there, or maybe the author is teaching about a new subtopic and I don't remember reading the rest of the last subtopic. In moments like this, you might even say, "Well then, you weren't even really reading, were you?" And you'd be right! When this happens, the most important thing to do is to stop and reread, not just plow ahead. Your comprehension and enjoyment of the text depend on it!*

Prompts

- Is your mind in the book, or just your eyes?
- What do you notice about your focus?
- I saw you caught yourself getting distracted, so you backed up to reread.
- Show me what to do when you get distracted.

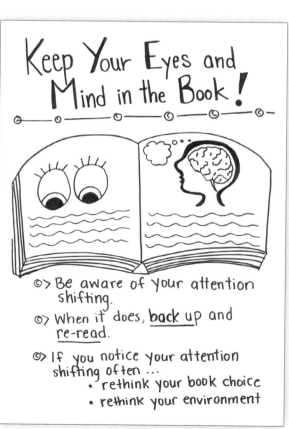

Skills

- **self-monitoring**
- **attentional focus**
- **stamina**

Progression

Can sustain reading for a short period of time and is ready to improve attentional focus to increase stamina, and to monitor for meaning and fix-up and reengage as needed.

Research Link

Although readers of all ability levels occasionally "zone out" while reading (Schooler, Reichle, & Halpern, 2004), maintaining focus is particularly challenging for those with attention-related disabilities.

Skill

- **self-monitoring**

Progression

Can sustain reading for a short period of time and is ready to improve attentional focus to increase stamina, and to monitor for meaning and fix-up and reengage as needed.

● ● ●

Research Link

Readers with and without identified learning disabilities benefit when they receive explicit instruction in Self-Regulated Strategy Development (SRSD), including how to self-monitor their comprehension and reread as needed (Hedin, Mason, & Gaffney, 2011).

Strategy When you get interrupted while you're reading or you come back from a break, take a moment to reorient yourself to what you're reading. Go back to the last thing you remember. Reread from there to get back into your book.

Prompts

- Go back to the last place you remember what you were reading about.
- You just took a break. How will you get back into it?
- Did rereading help?
- I notice you backed up to reread after your break.

Strategy Sometimes setting ourselves up for success helps us to stay focused and engaged. As you sit down to read, think about what you already know that can help you connect to your reading today. You can think about the text's structure or genre, what you know about the topic, what you know about other books by this author, or what you know about others in this series. Think about what might be new or different, and make a plan for how you'll work through the new parts.

Lesson Language *I want to show you how I would set myself up to read this book,* Inside Out and Back Again *(Lai, 2011). This is a novel in verse so I'm going to think about how I've read other novels in verse—I'm going to adjust my reading rate to go a little bit more slowly and maybe expect a lot of figurative language, for example. As I take a peek inside, I see it's set a while ago, in 1975, and begins in Vietnam. Since this is before I was born, and set in a country I've never been to, I'm going to need to be very careful to slow down and attend to details the author offers about the place and time. The blurb on the back says the book is about moving to a new country and experiencing grief. It also says there are themes of family strength. Although this character is so different from me in a lot of ways, I think I'll be able to connect with some of those themes in the story.*

Prompts

- What do you know about this series/author/genre?
- Tell me how you think the book will be structured.
- Talk about how you're getting ready to read this book.
- You used what you know about the series to explain the structure!

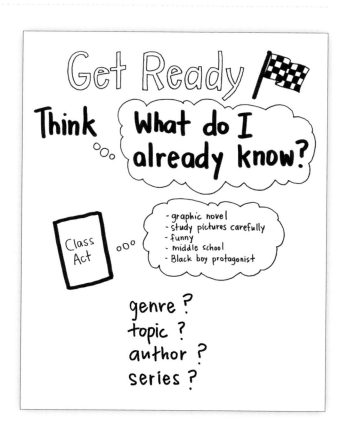

Skills
- **activating prior knowledge**
- **planning**
- **attentional focus**

Progression

Can sustain reading for a short period of time and is ready to improve attentional focus to increase stamina, and to monitor for meaning and fix-up and reengage as needed.

Research Link

In multiple recent and classic studies, researchers have found that skilled readers set themselves up before they read by exploring the text's content and structure (Duke et al., 2011; Pressley & Afflerbach, 1995), and they think about what they already know as they approach a new text (Pressley & Allington, 2014). Activating prior knowledge has significant positive impacts on comprehension (Kim et al., 2021).

Skills

- **self-monitoring**
- **visualizing**

Progression

Can sustain reading for a short period of time and is ready to improve attentional focus to increase stamina, and to monitor for meaning and fix-up and reengage as needed.

● ● ●

Strategy Sometimes when you're reading, you miss a little detail or some bit of information along the way that leaves you confused. When your understanding feels fuzzy—for example, you're confused about what's happening, how the information fits together; you can't picture what you're reading about; you've stopped reacting— you should back up and reread to fix the fuzziness.

Teaching Tip While working to develop this self-awareness in students, you may also choose to have children stop at predetermined spots in their books to check in using a series of questions to determine *if* anything is fuzzy. For example, when reading a story, they may ask themselves questions such as "Who is in this scene? What's happening? Where are they?" When reading informational texts, they may ask themselves, "How does this information fit together? What is the main thing I'm learning about?" You can direct them to reread and fix the fuzziness if they can't answer these comprehension-check-type questions.

Prompts

- Ask yourself, "Who is in this scene?" (*Pause for response.*) Now ask, "What is happening?" (*Pause for response.*) Now ask, "Where are they?" (*Pause for response.*) If you've got all three, read on.
- Ask yourself, "Can you list back some of the information you read in this section?"
- What felt fuzzy in that last part? What will you do to fix it?
- Check in. Is everything clear or is something fuzzy?

When Your Reading Leaves You CONFUSED or Feeling FUZZY, ASK YOURSELF...
1. What is happening?
2. Who is in the scene?
3. Where are they?
NOW...
Back up and re-read

Strategy Preview the text. Check your prior knowledge: What do you already know (about the genre, structure, author, series, topic, and so on) that will help you read this text? Ask some questions before you begin reading that align to your purpose for reading and your reading goal.

Teaching Tip The quality of students' questions, and the extent to which the questions are tied to students' goals and plans for reading, will factor into how helpful a questioning practice is at supporting comprehension and engagement. For example, making predictions can help to guide reading, by asking questions at the start of a book like, "I wonder if she'll regret lying to her mother or get in trouble?" or "In what ways will the community be affected if the city slashes the budget for public transportation?"

Prompts
- Try starting your question with who, what, where, when, or why.
- Think about your goal. What questions do you have connected to your goal and this text?
- Now that you've previewed this part of the book, what questions do you have?
- How much more do you think you'll need to read to answer that?

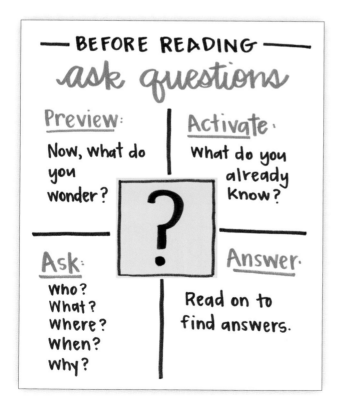

Skills
- **questioning**
- **activating prior knowledge**
- **planning**
- **attentional focus**

Progression

Can sustain reading for a short period of time and is ready to improve attentional focus to increase stamina, and to monitor for meaning and fix-up and reengage as needed.

Research Link

In one study of children referred to as "poor comprehenders," researchers Wong and Jones (1982) found that teaching students how to ask questions improved the types of questions children asked on their own to direct their reading and comprehension. Another study found that questions students asked that supported their interpretations and predictions were most beneficial (Cain, Oakhill, & Bryant, 2004).

Skills
- **questioning**
- **attentional focus**

Progression

Can sustain reading for a short period of time and is ready to improve attentional focus to increase stamina, and to monitor for meaning and fix-up and reengage as needed.

● ● ●

Strategy Be curious! Engage your mind by asking questions as you read. You can ask questions about your predictions, questions centered on the information you want to learn, or questions about ideas you have. Read on to try to answer the questions.

Lesson Language *Part of having your mind switched on and reading in a wide-awake way means coming to the text with curiosity. Similar to having a conversation with yourself as you read, you can ask and answer questions about what might come next, why a character did what they did, what you might learn, or why the author wrote something in the way they did. You can read to answer questions about the topic and seek out information. If it helps you, you can jot your wonderings and check back as you read on to see if you found some possible answers!*

Prompts
- Say, "I wonder . . ."
- Tell me about the conversation you're having with yourself.
- Try starting a question with who, what, where, when, or why . . .
- That's what you know so far. So what does that make you wonder?

Strategy Creating a picture in your mind that shifts and changes is essential to staying focused. Try to experience all the author is describing by using all your senses. Read a little, then pause. Think, "What do I see? Hear? Feel? Taste? Smell?"

Lesson Language *Much of being an engaged reader means understanding what you read—it's not enough to just say the words you're reading in your head. One of the best ways to make sure you are understanding is to keep a picture in your mind of what the author is describing. You may have heard before that readers "make a movie in their minds"—that means that the pictures you make aren't still; they move. As the character moves, the picture changes. If you're reading informational texts, you learn about the topic and you can actually see the animal doing the things the author describes in the book about reptiles or imagine the plates of the Earth shifting in the book on geology. Read a little. Stop and think about what you read. Use all your senses to add to your picture. Think, "What do I see? Hear? Feel? Taste? Smell?" You'll find that you'll be as engaged in your book as you would be if you're watching your favorite TV show!*

Prompts
- What do you see? Hear? Taste? Smell?
- How has your picture changed?
- Make the picture move.
- (*Nonverbal: gesture to nose, mouth, eyes to prompt for different senses.*)

Text excerpt from *An Enemy at Green Knowe* (Boston, 2002).

Skills
- **visualizing**
- **attentional focus**

Progression

Can sustain reading for a short period of time and is ready to improve attentional focus to increase stamina, and to monitor for meaning and fix-up and reengage as needed.

Research Link

Reading is not only transforming print into sounds, but using those sounds and words to construct a "situation model" (Kitsch, 1988), a visual and spatial mental representation that is animated by the reader's knowledge and changes as the reader moves through the text (De Koning & van der Schoot, 2013). Creating visual images while reading takes practice, often beginning with teacher modeling, and is essential for accurate reading comprehension (Hibbing & Rankin-Erickson, 2003).

Skill

• **self-monitoring**

Progression

Can sustain reading for a short period of time and is ready to improve attentional focus to increase stamina, and to monitor for meaning and fix-up and reengage as needed.

● ● ●

Research Link

A student's oral reading doesn't reveal what's going on in their mind. A reader with a quick pace may not be comprehending, whereas a reader who seems to be reading too slowly may, in fact, just be reading with extra care (Walcyzk & Griffith-Ross, 2007). Support and empower students to self-monitor their reading pace to make sure they are comprehending (Applegate, Applegate, & Modla, 2009).

Strategy The pace you read a certain text may depend on a lot of factors—how challenging the text is for you, what your purpose is for reading, how much background knowledge you already have about the topic, and so on. As you read, be aware of whether the pace at which you're reading is helping you to engage and understand; if not, adjust your pace.

Teaching Tip In a reading conference, you might ask a child to read a page to themselves, as you listen carefully for a smooth pace. Be mindful of the reasons why readers may choose to slow down (to monitor, to read more closely, to really hear their reading voice in their head) or speed up (to get to the exciting part, because the text is on the easy side for them), and there is of course variance in the average pace of each reader. The crux of this strategy is helping children to be aware if their pace is right for their purpose and their level of engagement and to adjust if they need to.

Prompts

• What do you notice about your pace?
• If you find your comprehension is breaking down, you may need to slow down a bit.
• I notice you're stopping a lot to jot. Is that helping you or is it slowing your pace down so much that it's getting in the way?
• If it feels comfortable and you're understanding, you're probably reading at a good pace.

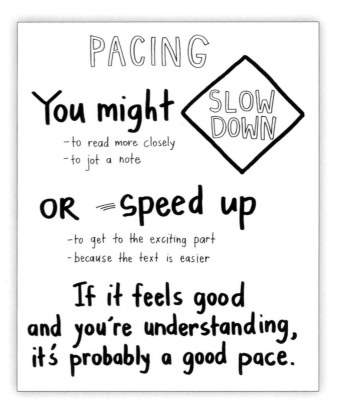

If you send your students off to read, and they don't engage with their reading, they won't make the progress you are hoping and working for.

—Jennifer Serravallo

Goal
3

Accuracy

◎ Why is this goal important?

To read with fluency and to construct meaning from a text, children need to read words accurately. Ehri and McCormick (1998) have found that accurate reading occurs in several ways:

- A reader may decode the word using grapheme-phoneme knowledge: identify the symbols (graphemes) that represent sounds (phonemes), segment the word, and blend the sounds together to pronounce the word.

- A reader may decode the word by analogy: recognizing how the word or parts of the word they are trying to read is/are similar to another word or word parts they already know.

- A reader may predict based on context, or a combination of context and some of the letters. (For more, see "The Role of Context in Reading with Accuracy" on page 94.)

- A reader may know the word on sight and read it automatically.

That last one—knowing the word on sight and reading it automatically— happens once a reader *orthographically maps* the word by decoding it and linking the pronunciation to its meaning (see diagram below; Ehri, 2014, 2017, 2020; Share, 1995, 2008). Many agree it takes a reader between one and four times decoding a word for it to become a sight word, though for those for whom reading is challenging, it can take more than ten (Blevins, 2016; Kilpatrick, 2015). Over time, we want *almost all* words to become sight words, not just high-frequency words, eliminating the need to decode except in really rare instances. The aim is for children to read with fluency (see Chapter 4) and for their minds to be freed up to think about the text and deeply comprehend (see Chapters 5–11), which is the whole point of reading (Castles, Rastle, & Nation, 2018; Ehri, 2005; Willingham, 2015; Wolf, 2007).

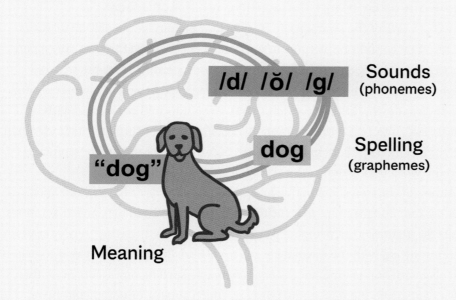

Different areas of the brain are responsible for recognizing a word's meaning, sounds (phonemes), and spelling (graphemes). For words to become sight words that can be read with automaticity, connections need to be made between these areas. This is known as *orthographic mapping*.

Strategies in This Chapter Complement, But Don't Replace, Phonics and Phonemic Awareness Instruction

Children deserve phonics and phonological awareness instruction that matches their needs, is assessment based, is well paced, is engaging, and provides the amount of repetition each child needs to learn (Kilpatrick, 2015; Mesmer, 2019; Snow, Burns, & Griffin, 1998).

As we know, an either-or approach—lots of isolated phonics without time for children to read, or lots of reading with only incidental or minimal phonics—will not help you reach *all* readers. In this chapter, you will find strategies meant to complement phonics instruction, which serve to remind students of what they know when they are reading connected text; the strategies are meant to support students' *application* and *transfer*.

Providing regular time for reading is critical—to help students move from slow and deliberate decoding to faster more automatic decoding, to encounter words again and again so they can become sight words, and to enable them opportunities to "self-teach" (Castles, Rastle, & Nation, 2018; Connor, Morrison, & Katch, 2004; Ehri & McCormick, 1998; Share, 1995).

The Role of Context in Reading with Accuracy

Note that none of the strategies in this chapter encourage prediction or guessing based on context or pictures or encourage children to attend to only a part of a word. Guessing doesn't often work very well, permits students to avoid attending to the orthographic sequence, and isn't something we should prompt kids to do (Gough, 1983; Kilpatrick, 2015). Even if a child guesses something that doesn't interfere with comprehension, and they get through that individual text, it doesn't help them in the long run because they can't orthographically map the word if they don't attend to its letters.

Although children shouldn't be *taught* to guess words or ignore their spellings, context and meaning are crucial as children read: both to form expectations about the identities of upcoming words and to confirm that what they've read is accurate, fitting with the meaning of the text (Ehri, 2020). Context also comes into play with homonyms such as *bat*, where one spelling represents more than one meaning and the reader must discern which applies, or with heteronyms (e.g., *desert*) where context helps with both meaning and pronunciation.

Tracking
Smoothly following words with one's eyes, maintaining a one-to-one match as each word is read aloud.

Decoding
Using a knowledge of letter-sound relationships to correctly pronounce words.

Skills a reader might work on as part of this goal

Blending
Combining separate sounds to correctly pronounce a whole word.

Self-monitoring
Being aware of one's own reading, and checking in to make sure the words a reader has decoded and pronounced make sense in context. Fixing mistakes at the point of error or after rereading.

◎ How do I know if this goal is right for my student?

You may use a variety of different types of assessments to better understand your students' word-level reading skills, to determine if this is the right goal for them, and, if so, which of the strategies within the chapter would be most helpful. For example, you might:

- Ask children to read from *word lists* of increasing complexity (i.e., beginning with single-syllable words, then moving on to multisyllabic words) to check their ability to read words in isolation. You may ask children to read real words and/or pseudowords. Understand that some of the real words may be in their sight word vocabulary, and in those cases you'd be assessing recall and automaticity rather than decoding and blending.

- Administer and evaluate *spelling assessments/inventories* that check on different word features and patterns that children are able to spell or find confusing, since there is often a relationship between spelling and decoding abilities (Blevins, 2016; Gentry & Graham, 2010; Willingham, 2015).

- Listen to students *read connected text and take notes on their reading*. See, for example, the Listening to Reading—Watching While Writing Protocol (Ward, Duke, & Klingelhofer, 2020). Be aware that in connected text, context supports the reader in a way that reading words in isolation does not. This type of assessment will be very helpful to see if a child catches errors and self-corrects—an important emphasis across the chapter. Be sure to watch for, prompt for, and support the ability to self-monitor and self-correct in *all* readers alongside *every* strategy.

What Texts Might Students Use When Practicing Strategies from This Chapter?

Making sure children have access to texts with the right supports and challenges is critical. First, consider what children have learned from phonics and offer texts that "reward attention to the words" by including words they *can* read when they use their phonics knowledge and apply their strategies (Duke, 2020). If the text has too many words that are beyond a child's decoding ability, they might be left to guess or become frustrated. Also be aware that texts that require a child to do too much decoding—even if they're successful at it—can make the reading slow and labored and, as a result, meaning-making becomes more challenging.

Depending on the reader, you may offer some combination of decodable texts, controlled vocabulary readers, multiple criterion texts, and/or authentic trade texts to help children practice decoding and at the same time monitor for sense, stay engaged, and develop their language capacities. Each text type has strengths and limitations (Gibson & Levin, 1975; Shanahan, 2019). I recommend looking at textproject.org for information to help you make decisions about what you might choose for both instruction and independent practice.

◎ How do I support students as they work on skills to help their accuracy?

After evaluating a student's accuracy, select strategies that you can model, that they can practice with you, and that they can use independently to increase their skills.

Although development is rarely perfectly linear, skill progressions can help us pinpoint where a student is now and what might come next. Use the if-then chart on page 97 to evaluate your students' reading and find strategies that will support their growth.

A Progression of Skills: Accuracy

If a student . . .	Then you might teach . . .

If a student . . .

Needs support tracking the print, attending to each word closely, looking at all the letters left to right, and using their knowledge of letter-sound correspondence to decode.

Then you might teach . . .

3.1   **Keep Your Eyes on the Words**

3.2   **Check the Beginning, Middle, and End**

3.3   **Choose a Way to Blend**

3.4   **Clip the Consonants**

3.5   **Say Each Sound Once**

3.6   **Say the Sound, Not the Name**

Has begun decoding and is ready to practice self-monitoring and correcting. These strategies need to be taught early and throughout all stages of word-level reading development.

3.7   **Fix It by Checking Each Letter**

3.8   **Fix It by Tracking Word by Word**

3.9   **Check In with Yourself, Reread, Fix Up**

3.10 **If You Slowed to Decode, Go Back over the Road**

3.11 **Whoa, Slow, Go**

Attempts to decode unfamiliar words, going left to right, blending letter by letter. Is ready to learn to be more flexible with sounds letters can represent, more alert to letter combinations that work together, and to decode by analogy.

Note: Strategies 3.13–3.19 offer a suite of options to explicitly remind children to remember what they know from phonics and apply it to their reading.

3.12 **Apply Phonics and Word Study to Book Reading**

3.13 **Remember: Try a Different Consonant Sound**

3.14 **Remember: Consonant Pairs That Make One Sound**

3.15 **Remember: Be Flexible with Vowels**

3.16 **Remember: Watch Out for Vowel Influencers**

3.17 **Remember: Try a Schwa**

3.18 **Remember: Look for Two or Three Vowels Together**

3.19 **Remember: Recognize Common Letter Sequences**

Is ready to decode longer, multisyllabic words by recognizing and correctly pronouncing words with more complex letter strings (*ough, ear*) and apply knowledge of syllable type and morphemes (meaning chunks such as *cycl, ing*), blending parts together. May also be working to refine pronunciations by figuring out what part of the word to stress.

3.20 **Cover and Slide**

3.21 **Write It, Read It**

3.22 **Take the Word Apart, Then Put It Back Together: Syllables**

3.23 **Take the Word Apart, Then Put It Back Together: Meaning Chunks**

3.24 **Ask: Where Do I Put the Stress?**

3.25 **Come Up with a Plan**

3.26 **Combine Word Syllables Across a Line Break**

Strategy When you come to an unfamiliar word, remind yourself of what you know to decode the word and blend the sounds. Try it. Keep your eyes focused on the word you're working on.

Teaching Tip Readers who find decoding difficult sometimes look away from the word (to pictures, to you, around the room, etc.) when they get stuck, and they may benefit from this strategy to stay focused on the text. In addition to the strategy, consider if the text is setting them up to be successful or if it's overly challenging and asking them to use phonics skills they do not yet have. For example, lower-level patterned books often include words that can only be figured out based on context or pictures, so shifting to decodable texts, at least until the student becomes more proficient with consistently decoding and attending to all letters and sounds in words, might help. When reading with a student, after an attempt or two using what they know, I will often say, "You worked hard and tried what you knew! Let me help. Watch me," and decode the word for them, pointing to letters as I say the sounds that match so we can stay in the flow of reading and not sacrifice energy, engagement, or comprehension.

Prompts

- Yes! You figured out the word by looking carefully at all the letters and blending the sounds.
- You're looking at me. Would you like help? Let's look back at the word.
- You stayed focused on the words on the page! Now reread the sentence to make sure what you read makes sense.
- (*If the child attempts the word and it's clear they are unable to read it because they don't know the word from their language or because they don't yet have the phonics knowledge required to decode it.*) Let me help you read it. Try the letter sounds you know, I'll help you with the others, and then we'll blend the sounds together.

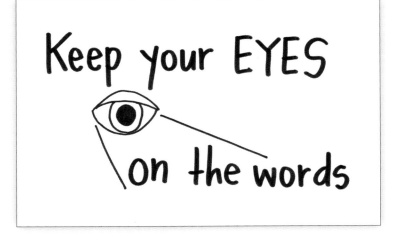

Skills

- **tracking**
- **decoding**
- **blending**

Progression

Needs support tracking the print, attending to each word closely, looking at all the letters left to right, and using their knowledge of letter-sound correspondence to decode.

Research Link

Using eye movement analysis in a series of studies, Justice and colleagues (2005) found that, prior to developing print awareness and decoding skills, beginning readers have their eyes on the text less than 7% of the time. Explicit scaffolding from adults may help guide young readers to visually attend to print.

Skills

- **decoding**
- **blending**
- **self-monitoring**

Progression

Needs support tracking the print, attending to each word closely, looking at all the letters left to right, and using their knowledge of letter-sound correspondence to decode.

Research Link

Research shows that even when we recognize and read words automatically, we are still looking through the whole word (Rayner, 1998). Beginning readers, however, frequently skip letters, guessing the word using only the beginning letters or the general shape (Gough, 1993; Gough & Juel, 1991; Rayner, 1988; Rayner et al., 2001). Unless they develop the skills to orthographically map all the sounds and letters in the word, children may approach a reading task as visual identification rather than truly understanding the written sound-letter system (Ehri, 2020).

Strategy Check the beginning of the word, sliding the sounds together. Check the middle of the word, sliding the sounds together. Check the end of the word, sliding the sounds together. Say the whole word, blending the beginning, middle, and end. Check to make sure the word you read makes sense and sounds right.

Lesson Language *It's important to look at every word, all the way through. If you change or drop off even one letter it could change the word completely! Imagine if I read the word* spitting *instead of* splitting! *Totally different words. Read at a speed that allows you to look through every word. Don't rush. And when you come to an unfamiliar word, be sure to read through the whole thing—the beginning, middle, and end—to figure it out.*

Prompts

- Check the beginning.
- You got the beginning and middle, but don't guess based on those parts. Look at the ending, too.
- I couldn't quite hear the middle part. Could you say each sound carefully?
- What you read matches the letters!

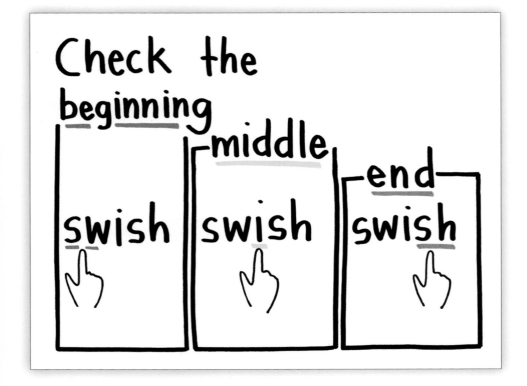

Strategy Option 1: Blend left to right, saying the sound(s) for each letter (group of letters) and sliding into the next sound(s) for the next letter(s). Option 2: Read the first part, then the second. Go back and blend the two parts together and continue to add on the third, and so on, until you read the end of the word.

Teaching Tip Depending on students' short-term memory and the length of the word they are decoding, they may be able to go left to right through the word (sequential blending) or they may benefit from learning how to gradually accumulate word parts (successive or cumulative blending) (Beck & Beck, 2013). For the word *incidental*, sequential would be *in-ci-den-tal . . . inncciideenntal*. Cumulative would be *in-inci-inciden-incidental*.

Prompts
- Try blending one part at a time.
- You blended the first two parts together. Go back and reread the two parts and add on the third.
- It seems like you're forgetting the first part of the word by the time you get to the end. Let's try to build the word by backing up and adding more each time.
- How will you blend the sounds together in this word?

2 Ways to Blend:
perplexing

① Read each part, slide into the next one

per-plex-ing

② Reread as you add more parts

P
per
perplex
perplexing

Skill
- blending

Progression

Needs support tracking the print, attending to each word closely, looking at all the letters left to right, and using their knowledge of letter-sound correspondence to decode.

●○○○

Hat Tip

Making Sense of Phonics: The Hows and Whys, second edition (Beck & Beck, 2013)

Research Link

In a study guided by the work of both Ehri (1995, 2002, 2005) and Beck (1989; Beck & Hamilton, 2000), researchers worked with students who struggled with reading beyond first grade because they failed to apply their knowledge of sound-letter correspondence across entire words. After an intervention designed to cue readers to attend to the graphemes in *all* positions of the word, children demonstrated gains not only in decoding but also comprehension and phonological awareness (McCandliss et al., 2003).

Skills

• **decoding**

• **blending**

Progression

Needs support tracking the print, attending to each word closely, looking at all the letters left to right, and using their knowledge of letter-sound correspondence to decode.

Hat Tip

"When Young Readers Get Stuck" (Duke, 2020)

Research Link

Research suggests that teaching connected phonation (stretching one sound to the next, like *fffaaannn*) at least with words with sonorous/stretchy sounds, is superior to segmented phonation for young readers (Gonzalez-Frey & Ehri, 2021).

Strategy Point under each letter (or letter combination) in the word, one at a time, left to right. Say each sound without adding any extra vowel sounds that aren't there. Blend the sounds together.

Teaching Tip The process of decoding words that have not been orthographically mapped (see pages 92-93) involves transforming graphemes (letters and/or letter combinations) into phonemes (the sounds the letters represent) and then blending the phonemes to form words with recognizable meanings. This strategy aims to support children with a key to blending: being careful not to add "uh" (or any other vowel sounds) after a consonant. For example, the letter *t* does not represent "tuh," and the letter *b* does not represent "buh." This additional vowel sound can interfere with blending and pronunciation. If students have a hard time cutting the extra sound off the consonants, you might direct them to *connected phonation* (stretching one sound to the next, like *crrraaash*), which is easiest to teach with words that have continuous sounds (/m/, /s/, /f/, /l/, /r/, /n/, /v/, /z/) and vowels.

Prompts

• Clip the sound—say just the consonant sound without adding a vowel sound.
• What sound do you say when you see that letter (those letters together)?
• Stretch that sound into the next sound.
• What word did you read?

Strategy Point under the word. Slide left to right, saying each sound only once for each letter or letter combination. Go back to the beginning of the word and blend the sounds together.

Lesson Language *I hear you saying the sound for each single letter (or letter combination) a few times in a row. That makes blending the sounds much harder. When I sound out* cat, *I will say three sounds. In this word, it's one sound for each letter. Listen: /k/ . . . /a/ . . . /t/ not /k/ /k/ /k/ /a/ /a/ /a/ /t/ /t/ /t/. Try your word again, but this time remember not to repeat any sounds.*

Teaching Tip When teaching students about letter-sound correspondence, and during practice applying this knowledge during reading and writing (such as during phonics, interactive writing, shared reading, or shared writing), be careful not to model repeating sounds. Teach students to say each sound once. This will help them blend the separate phonemes in the word without any extras. Blending can be very challenging for students with dyslexia. If you notice a student has difficulty blending individual sounds together, prompt them to "slide through" the sound (Duke, 2020) or ask them to "melt" the sounds together as they slide their finger under each letter or group of letters.

Prompts

- I think you said that letter sound twice. Just say each sound once.
- Say it only once, like you mean it!
- Blend the sounds together.
- Slide through the word, blending all the sounds together.

Skills
- **decoding**
- **blending**

Progression

Needs support tracking the print, attending to each word closely, looking at all the letters left to right, and using their knowledge of letter-sound correspondence to decode.

● ○ ○ ○

Hat Tip

"When Young Readers Get Stuck" (Duke, 2020)

Research Link

Researchers explored explicit instruction that included phoneme blending by pointing at the letters and stretching out the sounds without stopping, then quickly saying the word. Compared with their peers in the control group, students who received the supplemental instruction improved their reading accuracy, reading efficiency, oral reading fluency, and developmental spelling, and also grew in phonemic awareness and alphabetic knowledge (Vadasy & Sanders, 2008; Vadasy, Sanders, & Peyton, 2006).

Skill

- **decoding**

Progression

Needs support tracking the print, attending to each word closely, looking at all the letters left to right, and using their knowledge of letter-sound correspondence to decode.

● ○ ○ ○ ○

Research Link

Students may struggle to learn letter names because there is not always a clear connection between the name of the letter and its sound (Block & Duke, 2015; Ehri & McCormick, 1998).

Strategy Remember that letters are symbols for sounds. When you're decoding a word, say the *sounds* not the *letter names*.

Lesson Language *You know the letter "ess." We write it with a squiggly shape that looks like a small snake. That squiggly shape with the* letter name *"ess" represents the* sound /s/. *You also know the letter "tee." We write it with a cross shape. That cross shape with the* letter name *"tee" represents* sound /t/. *Remember when you're reading words, you want to say the* sound *and not the* letter name. *For example, look at this word:* (show the word *dog*). *If I read the letter names* d o g *and blend it together it would sound like "dee-oh-gee." It's great that you know the letter names, but when sounding out words we need to say the sounds those letters represent. So, if I say the sounds /d/ /aw/ /g/ and blend them together I get* dog!

Teaching Tip Knowing letter names helps when learning the alphabet, with alphabetization, and with labeling a letter no matter the font or whether it is uppercase or lowercase. However, knowing the sounds that letters represent is necessary for decoding and encoding words. Some letters are easier to learn because their sound comes at the beginning of the letter name. For example, the letter name *b* (i.e., "bee") starts with /b/ and the letter *k* (i.e., "kay") starts with /k/. However, letters that start with a vowel sound or that do not have the sound in the letter name are more difficult. For example, the letter *h* (i.e., "aych" in U.S. dialects) does not have the /h/ sound in it, and the letter *m* (i.e., "em") starts with the vowel sound /ĕ/.

Prompts

- What sound(s) does __ represent?
- That's the name of the letter. What sound does it represent?
- Point under each letter (or letter group) and say the sounds.
- Yes! You said all the sounds. Now blend them.

Strategy When you've tried reading a word but it doesn't sound like a word you know, or doesn't make sense in the sentence, try to find what needs fixing. Move your finger under each letter as you look across the whole word from left to right. Do not skip over any letters as one letter can be the difference in reading the word correctly.

Teaching Tip Playing matching games with visually similar words during phonics and word study instruction can help students attend carefully and closely to each letter. For example, you might have multiple versions of the same few words written in different fonts (e.g., *hot, hop, hat, hip*) and ask children to read through the word, and match the cards to other cards with the same word.

Prompts
- That was so close! Slide your finger under each letter to see if you can find the error.
- Make sure you are looking at and sounding out each letter correctly.
- Slowly slide your finger under the word as you focus on each letter.
- Now blend the word again with the right sound. Does the word make sense now?

Skills
- **decoding**
- **self-monitoring**

Progression

Has begun decoding and is ready to practice self-monitoring and correcting. These strategies need to be taught early and throughout all stages of word-level reading development.

● ● ○ ○

Research Link

A panel reviewing studies for the What Works Clearinghouse (U.S. Department of Education Institute of Education Sciences) identified about a dozen studies that provided strong evidence for teaching explicit decoding skills, including self-monitoring, or "fix-up" strategies. The WWC review panel recommended that students check to see if the word they have produced by blending sounds "makes sense" or is a "real word" (Foorman et al., 2016, p. 25).

Skills
- **tracking**
- **self-monitoring**

Progression

Has begun decoding and is ready to practice self-monitoring and correcting. These strategies need to be taught early and throughout all stages of word-level reading development.

Research Link

Young learners do not automatically understand the concept of a "word" because oral speech does not always contain the same pauses between words that we find in printed text. As a result, supporting students to match spoken words to written words while reading connected text is a crucial step in the development of phonological awareness (Flanigan, 2007; Morris, 1993).

Strategy If you find yourself skipping over words or losing your place on the page, slow down and use a tool (your finger, a note card, a bookmark) to help you track where you are and make sure you are reading every word on the page. Listen to yourself and make sure what you're reading is making sense. If not, you may have read a word incorrectly or skipped over a word(s).

Teaching Tip Skipping words or lines of text can impact comprehension. Sometimes even small words like *not, at, in, on,* if skipped or read incorrectly, change the meaning of the entire sentence (or passage). Be on the lookout for students who become overwhelmed with lots of text on a page and/or small print, and offer them tools such as a note card to move down the page, under each line or a bookmark with an opaque window cut out to track the print. Pointing at one word at a time is fine for brand-new readers, but an overreliance on pointing to single words as readers become more fluent causes them to read with less phrasing and prosody. (See more on fluency strategies in Chapter 4.)

Prompts
- Reread the sentence out loud.
- Do you hear a word that might be missing?
- Keep this card under each line as you read it, to help you keep your eyes on the words and not lose your place.

Strategy As you read, check in with yourself to make sure what you're reading makes sense. When it doesn't, reread. Find which word(s) you read incorrectly, then use your decoding strategies to fix it.

Teaching Tip Model reading a sentence accurately, pause and say, "Checking in with my reading. Yes, that all made sense," and then another with an error that doesn't make sense, pause and say, "Hm. Something is wrong there." (For example, you might misread the sentence "She hoped to make cookies with her mom tonight" as "She hopped to make cookies with her mom tonight.") Model rereading carefully to find which word(s) were read incorrectly, then model applying a decoding strategy students know that will help you figure it out.

Prompts
- Check yourself.
- Did that make sense?
- Yes, you caught yourself! Go back and reread to find the error.
- You're right, that word isn't __. What strategy can you try to help you figure it out?

Skills
- **self-monitoring**
- **decoding**

Progression

Has begun decoding and is ready to practice self-monitoring and correcting. These strategies need to be taught early and throughout all stages of word-level reading development.

Research Link

Denton and colleagues (2013) conducted a randomized controlled trial exploring a set of Tier 3 interventions for second graders, including teaching students to use context to self-monitor and self-correct errors. Students who received the intervention demonstrated significantly better growth in word identification, phonemic decoding, and fluency compared with their peers in the control group.

Skills

- **decoding**
- **self-monitoring**

Progression

Has begun decoding and is ready to practice self-monitoring and correcting. These strategies need to be taught early and throughout all stages of word-level reading development.

Research Link

Children need to slow down and actively decode, rather than mumble through or skip over unfamiliar words in an attempt to preserve their pace. Decoding each and every word on the page gives students the repeated exposure that leads to more accurate and fluent reading (Chard, Vaughn, & Tyler, 2002; Hudson et al., 2020; Padeliadu & Giazitzidou, 2018; Stevens, Walker, & Vaughn, 2017).

Strategy When you come to an unfamiliar word, it's important you slow down to decode it using a strategy(ies) you know that will work in that instance. Then go back and reread the sentence with the word you figured out to be sure it makes sense with the rest of the words.

Teaching Tip Fluent reading has three components: accuracy, pace, and prosody. When readers need to adjust their pace to attend more closely to a word to read it accurately, encourage rereading to smooth their reading out. Repeated readings of decoded words also help to develop automaticity with those words, as they become stored in memory as sight words, which also supports fluency. (To find more strategies to support readers' pace and prosody, see Chapter 4.) Be watchful, though: If a child needs to slow down to decode too many times, they may experience frustration and a breakdown in meaning-making, which will impact not only their enjoyment but also their ability to catch errors and self-correct. In this case, work to find texts that are more accessible, where most of the words are already part of the child's sight vocabulary, so there is less frequent word solving required.

Prompts

- I see you read that word by slowing down and breaking it up part by part. Now that you know the word, go back and reread.
- Zooming in on one word means you have to take a moment and zoom back out to the whole text. Reread this bit now that you know this word and see how it fits.
- Now that you figured it out, what will you do next?

3.11 *Whoa, Slow, Go*

Strategy When you decode a new word, stop and think if you have heard it before and know the meaning. It's a "whoa" if you aren't sure what it means and aren't sure if you are pronouncing it correctly—ask someone how to pronounce it and what it means (or use a resource). It's a "slow" word if you think you've heard it and might know what it means, but you aren't sure—say it a few times out loud, and reread the sentence to be sure of the word's meaning. It's a "go" if it's a word you can pronounce, and know what it means—keep reading!

Teaching Tip Phonological long-term memory, one of the three critical skills used to map the correct sequence of sounds in spoken language to the letters that represent them in speech, happens when a student reads a word and recognizes it as a word they have heard before, even if they don't know the meaning. This strategy encourages children to seek out the word's meaning and proper pronunciation to make that possible. For more support with helping children to understand word meanings, see Chapter 11.

Prompts
- Do you know what that word is?
- I can see you pronounced it correctly. Have you heard that word before?
- Say it a few times—whisper it to yourself—is it familiar?
- If you haven't heard that word before, seek help to pronounce it and know what it means.

Skill
- **self-monitoring**

Progression

Has begun decoding and is ready to practice self-monitoring and correcting. These strategies need to be taught early and throughout all stages of word-level reading development.

Research Link

Although it may be tempting to correct students' errors, this may lead readers to expect others to find their errors. Research shows that it is more effective to support students to self-monitor (Anderson & Kaye, 2017), though not all children use this metacognitive strategy automatically (Martin & Kragler, 2011) and will need support to develop their capacity for self-monitoring (Anderson & Kaye, 2017).

Skill

- **decoding**

Progression

Attempts to decode unfamiliar words, going left to right, blending letter by letter. Is ready to learn to be more flexible with sounds letters can represent, more alert to letter combinations that work together, and to decode by analogy.

 ●●●○

Research Link

Research has shown that only those children who already have some knowledge of phonological decoding (i.e., understanding that words are made up of parts, hearing the parts in the words, and being able to rhyme words they hear) are able to "decode by analogy" (Ehri & Robbins, 1992; Gaskins et al., 1988; Johnston, 1999; Peterson & Haines, 1992), and that it is easiest for beginners to make analogies between endings of words (Goswami, 1986, 1998; Goswami & Bryant, 2016).

Strategy When you're trying to decode a word, make sure you think, "Have I seen a word like this or letter pattern like this during word study or phonics?" If so, use what you know to help you read the word.

Teaching Tip Explicit instruction in phonics is crucial for students as they work to become strong decoders. Learning word families, root words, prefixes, and suffixes, for example, can be very supportive for developing readers. Tweak this strategy to match the features of words the student knows, and be specific about *what* phonics knowledge they should be keeping in mind and applying as they read. Note that Strategies 3.13–3.19 offer a suite of options to explicitly remind children to apply specific learnings from phonics to their reading.

Prompts

- You know __ and __ from phonics, so use that to help you read this word.
- We studied this spelling pattern! What sounds can you try?
- Use what you know to help you read that word.
- Yes! You remembered we practiced this during phonics. It's so important to connect what we do during that time to your book reading.

Strategy You know that some consonant letters can represent more than one sound. When you are having difficulty decoding a word, look to see if it has one of these letters. If it does, try another sound that letter can represent to fix it.

Teaching Tip Several consonants can represent more than one sound, depending on their location in the word and what letters come before or after. Some examples are the soft and hard *c* and *g*, *x* as in *xylophone* or *fox*, and the *y* that can act like a consonant (*yellow*) or vowel (*cry*). For some children, thinking of other words they know where the consonant is in the same position (e.g., *happy* can help them read *funny*) or remembering the pattern about the sound the consonant represents when it's next to certain letter(s) (e.g., *c* followed by *e* versus *o*) can help them use the correct sound. If remembering the patterns or decoding by analogy is challenging, or if they haven't yet learned the particular pattern, they can also just try the different sounds the letter can represent to see which one sounds right and makes sense (Block & Duke, 2015; Scanlon, Anderson, & Sweeney, 2010).

Prompts
- Try another sound for that letter.
- What's another sound that consonant represents?
- *C* can represent /s/ or /k/. Try both to see which one sounds right and makes sense.
- *X* can represent /z/ or /cks/. Which is it here?

Try a different consonant sound

C — Does it sound like cake or Ceiling?

g — Does it sound like giraffe or game?

y — Does it sound like yellow or sky?

Skill
- decoding

Progression

Attempts to decode unfamiliar words, going left to right, blending letter by letter. Is ready to learn to be more flexible with sounds letters can represent, more alert to letter combinations that work together, and to decode by analogy.

Research Link

Compared with vowels, consonants are more predictable in their letter-sound correspondence (Gates & Yale, 2011; Johnston, 2001). As a result, they present less of a challenge for beginning readers, but complete orthographic mapping requires an understanding of all the letters in a word.

Remember: Consonant Pairs That Make One Sound

Skill

- **decoding**

Progression

Attempts to decode unfamiliar words, going left to right, blending letter by letter. Is ready to learn to be more flexible with sounds letters can represent, more alert to letter combinations that work together, and to decode by analogy.

Research Link

Whether single or in a digraph or trigraph, consonants usually have only one or one of two sounds (Gates & Yale, 2011; Johnston, 2001). Furthermore, the different sounds are largely systematic and consistent: *ch* might sound different in *chin* and *chemist*, but the word *chin* will be pronounced the same every time—it is never pronounced /kin/ (Block & Duke, 2015).

Strategy You know that sometimes a pair of consonants represents only *one* sound. When decoding, read left to right, and when you come to any of these combinations, make sure to say one sound, not separate sounds for each letter. Remember: they can be at the beginning, middle, or ends of words!

Teaching Tip Consonant digraphs are when two consonant letters make one sound. Some examples include *ch, sh, ph, wh, th* voiced (as in *these*) and *th* unvoiced (as in *think*). There is even a less common consonant trigraph, with three letters making one sound: *tch* as in *hatch*. Students need to know the many letter-sound correspondences in English, not just one sound (phoneme) for each of the twenty-six letters (graphemes) of the alphabet. For children new to consonant digraphs, you might start with a list of words where the digraph is at the beginning (e.g., *phrase, shape, chip*), then move to end-of-word digraphs/trigraphs (e.g., *bath, click, graph, match*), and then eventually practice with middle-of-word occurrences (e.g., *toothless, wrecked, reaching, kitchen*). For children who are having difficulty, make sure they can first separate the sounds (phonemes) when they say a word, then show them with tiles or sound boxes how each sound corresponds to a single letter or letter pair/trio. This practice should happen during phonics/word study time, and then you can use this strategy to remind readers about what they know when they are reading connected text.

Prompts
- Are there two (three) letters in the word that should make one sound?
- Say the sound these two (three) letters make when they are together.
- Now read the word being sure you use the *one* sound these *two* (*three*) letters make when they are together.

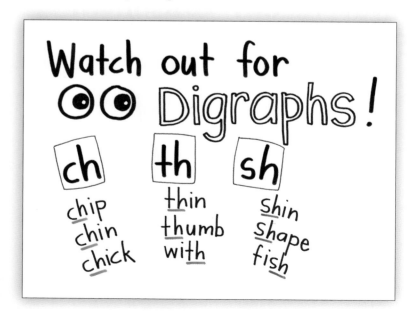

Strategy Be flexible about vowel sounds—try one sound, then another you know that the letter(s) can represent—until you read a word that sounds like a word you know and that makes sense in the sentence.

Lesson Language *We know that vowel letters can be tricky because they all can represent more than one sound. When you come to a word you don't recognize, one strategy is to try, try, and try the word again, using different sounds for the vowels in the word. For example, if I come to the word w-e-a-r I can try the long e sound for the ea like in the word ear ("/wēr/"). Let me be flexible. The ea might sound like a long a plus the r ("/wār/"). Wear, like wear clothes, or wear down. Now I need to check to see which pronunciation/word makes sense in the context of the text and sentence. The sentence says, "Her mom said, "Is that what you're going to wear today?" and the pronunciation /wār/ makes sense because she's talking about wearing clothes.*

Teaching Tip This is a very beginning strategy to introduce to readers before they know a lot of specific information about vowels and vowel combinations. (See also Strategies 3.16–3.18 for more specific strategies for vowels.) Also note that vowel pronunciations may differ based on regional variations, the speaker's first language, and other factors, so be aware that your own pronunciation may not be the same as that of your students. Be sensitive to the range of pronunciations in your classroom, and be supportive that those variations are equally correct (Motha, 2014).

Prompts

- Try another sound you know that vowel can represent.
- Try it again, with a different sound for that letter.
- That letter can also represent the sound /_/.
- Notice that vowel is next to another one. What do you know about what sound those two letters together represent?

Skill
- **decoding**

Progression

Attempts to decode unfamiliar words, going left to right, blending letter by letter. Is ready to learn to be more flexible with sounds letters can represent, more alert to letter combinations that work together, and to decode by analogy.

Hat Tip

Letter Lessons and First Words: Phonics Foundations That Work (Mesmer, 2019)

Research Link

Although written English has only five letters labeled as vowels (with *y* as a part-time member), spoken English is estimated to have fifteen distinct vowel phonemes (represented by single letters or multiple letters in combination), and vowels can sound different depending on dialect. Despite this complexity, Johnston (2001) revealed that the sounds of vowels follow specific rules, making it more practical to support students to recognize *patterns* rather than teaching them broad generalizations.

Remember: Watch Out for Vowel Influencers

Progression

Attempts to decode unfamiliar words, going left to right, blending letter by letter. Is ready to learn to be more flexible with sounds letters can represent, more alert to letter combinations that work together, and to decode by analogy.

Research Link

In a large study of word recognition, researchers looked at eight structural features connecting the orthography of words to their sounds. They found that vowel digraphs and silent markers made words more difficult for students to recognize. Interestingly, however, for the older students in the study, the presence of *r*-controlled vowels aided word recognition, indicating that understanding this feature of English orthography benefits decoding (Willson & Rupley, 1993).

Strategy Look past the vowel letter you're trying to decode. What letter(s) do you see? Ask yourself, "How do these letters impact the sound of this vowel?"

Lesson Language *When you are figuring out what sound a vowel letter represents, remember that the letters after the vowel letter can change the sound it represents. It can help to look through the word, beyond the vowel, then return to it to decode. For example, if I see the word* b-a-r, *I have to look past the* a *to know that the* r *will mean the word is pronounced /bar/. In the word* b-a-s-e, *the* e *will impact the pronunciation of the* a. *In this case, the word is pronounced /bās/. In the word* bat *I see only a consonant, so I know to use a "short* a*" sound for /băt/. Those are three words that all start with the letters* b *and* a *where the* a *represents a different sound because of the spelling in the rest of the word.*

Teaching Tip This repertoire strategy requires children to remember what they know about *r*-controlled vowels, vowel teams (digraphs and diphthongs), silent *e*, and schwa. If you haven't yet taught these features of English orthography during phonics, do that first, then return to this strategy. Also, it's important to be sensitive to the range of pronunciations in your classroom, and be supportive that those variations are equally correct (Motha, 2014). For example, note that /r/ in many regions of the United States is completely different from most of the rest of the world. In New England, for many speakers whose first language is not English, and even for people from England itself, /r/ is sometimes omitted, or less pronounced. Additionally, speakers of other languages, particularly Spanish and some of the southern African languages, may sometimes roll the *r*.

Prompts

- Do you see an *r*, silent *e*, other vowel?
- Could the [vowel] represent a schwa sound there?
- What other sound could that vowel letter represent?
- What's the influencer? Now say the sound that vowel letter represents.

Strategy If you try the short and long vowel sounds and neither seems right, try the schwa.

Teaching Tip A schwa is the sound any vowel may represent in the unaccented syllable(s) of a multisyllabic word (Block & Duke, 2015; Venezky, 1999). It can sound like a short *u* or a short *i*. As you've likely taught your kids during phonics, a schwa can be spelled with any of the vowel letters. The few generalizations on the chart will help children remember when a schwa sound is likely the right choice.

Prompts
- Could a schwa sound work here (*pointing to the vowel letter*)?
- You tried a long and short vowel sound and neither sounded right. What else can you try?
- That vowel comes right before an *l*. How should you read it?
- That vowel comes right before an *n*. How should you read it?

Skill
- **decoding**

Progression

Attempts to decode unfamiliar words, going left to right, blending letter by letter. Is ready to learn to be more flexible with sounds letters can represent, more alert to letter combinations that work together, and to decode by analogy.

Research Link

As the schwa sound is the most common vowel sound in the English language, found in nearly all words of three syllables or more, it is essential to know for accurate reading, especially of multisyllabic words, which are common in academic vocabulary. Because the schwa sound is determined by the rhythm of stressed and unstressed syllables, students need to "hear" this rhythmic pattern, even when reading silently (Weber, 2018).

Remember: Look for Two or Three Vowels Together

Skill

• **decoding**

Progression

Attempts to decode unfamiliar words, going left to right, blending letter by letter. Is ready to learn to be more flexible with sounds letters can represent, more alert to letter combinations that work together, and to decode by analogy.

Research Link

You may have heard (or been taught) that "when two vowels go walking, the first one does the talking," but in fact, that is true less than half the time (Carroll, Davies, & Richman, 1971; Johnston, 2001)!

Strategy As you read through the word, you may see two or three vowels in a row. Think about what you know: Do these vowels together represent just the sound of the first letter? Do they represent one unique sound? Do the sounds slide together? Should you break the word into syllables between the vowels? If you aren't sure, try more than one way to see which works.

Teaching Tip In some cases, two vowels together can sound like two sounds sliding together (e.g., *oi* as in *coin* or *ou* as in *mouse*). Other times, two vowels together represent a unique sound (e.g., *oo* in *book*), and the same combination of letters can at times represent different sounds (e.g., *oo* in *too* versus *look*). Still other times, there is a syllable break in between the vowels and each vowel sound is pronounced (e.g., the break between the *i* and *o* in *tedious*). Therefore, as students approach words with two or three vowels together, they'll need to be flexible in decoding (Duke, 2014a; Johnston, 2001). You can practice spotting vowel combinations by reading from categorized word lists, and then provide students with books or other authentic texts where they can practice what they've learned.

Two or Three Vowels Together

Use the Sound of the First Vowel	Doesn't Represent the Sound of the First Vowel	Two Sounds Together	Syllable Break Between Vowels
Coat /ō/	Friend /ĕ/	Boy /oi/	Lion (*li-on*)
Toe /ō/	Bear /âr/	Coin /oi/	Diary (*di-a-ry*)
Green /ē/	Beauty /ū/	Mouse /ou/	Piano (*pi-an-o*)
Peach /ē/	Great /ā/		Hilarious (*hil-ar-i-ous*)
Cue /ū/			Usual (*u-su-al*)
			Video (*vid-e-o*)

Prompts

• Do you see vowels that go together in this word?
• Try more than one way—break between the vowels, slide the sounds together, use the one sound for the vowel sequence—to see which one is correct.
• You put those two letters together to make one sound and you were able to read the word!

Strategy As you read through the word, you may see a sequence of letters that you've seen in other words you know. Remember what you know about the sound(s) that sequence represents, and say it rather than sounding it out letter by letter.

Teaching Tip As the words they decode become more complex, readers will need to recognize three (e.g., *ous*, *eau*) and four (e.g., *eigh*, *ough*, and *augh*) letter sequences that together represent a sound(s). If children approach words with these spelling patterns and try to sound out each individual letter, spend some time during phonics teaching them about these letter sequences: create word lists or webs with the same spelling pattern, read poems together that use words with the same spelling pattern again and again, and provide them with decodable readers where they'll have a chance to apply what they've learned.

Prompts
- Do you see a sequence of letters that go together in this word?
- Remember, *ous* together can represent one sound, /us/.
- Instead of saying one sound for each letter, remember these three (or four) letters go together to make the sound(s) __.

Look for
Letter Sequences

might	fair	weigh
sight	hair	sleigh
tight	stair	eight

Skill
- **decoding**

Progression

Attempts to decode unfamiliar words, going left to right, blending letter by letter. Is ready to learn to be more flexible with sounds letters can represent, more alert to letter combinations that work together, and to decode by analogy.

●●●○

Research Link

After analyzing 18,000 words to determine the utility of 23 commonly taught phonics rules, Caldwell and colleagues (1978) determined that many of them apply less than half of the time. However, they found greater consistency among units like *ine* and *ake*, which led them to recommend teaching specific patterns rather than broad generalizations, a finding later corroborated by Johnston (2001) after analyzing the 3,000 most frequent words in written English.

Skills

- **decoding**
- **blending**

Progression

Is ready to decode longer, multisyllabic words by recognizing and correctly pronouncing words with more complex letter strings and apply knowledge of syllable type and morphemes, blending parts together. May also be working to refine pronunciations by figuring out what part of the word to stress.

Research Link

Starting in the 1970s, scholars have advocated for successive blending, which requires fewer sound units to be held in memory at any one time. By reducing the burden on working memory, the reader may focus on other tasks necessary for successful decoding, such as scanning for digraphs, diphthongs, or other letter combinations where two or more letters contribute to a single sound (Resnick & Beck, 1976).

Strategy When you're trying to read a longer word, you can cover up the word with your finger, revealing the letters of the word slowly. Slide your finger across the word left to right to show more and more letters as you read them, blending the sounds together as you go.

Teaching Tip This strategy will support students with *successive blending*—continuously adding on more sounds as they look from letter to letter in the word. You can model this by slowly uncovering the letters of the word, one at a time, stretching the sounds (for example, plastic would be *pllllllaaasssstiiic*.) For readers with more experience with word parts, you may find that they can be taught (or that they automatically) uncover parts of words based on what they know about syllables or morphology (for example, in *plastic* they may uncover the *pl* and then the *as* and then the *tic* and read the word in three parts: *pl-as-tic . . . plastic*). (See Strategy 3.22 for help with teaching children about syllable division and Strategy 3.23 for help with meaning-based/morphological parts.) Whether they go one letter at a time or one part at a time, the point of this strategy is to help them not be overwhelmed by longer unfamiliar words and to instead slow down and look all the way through the word.

Prompts

- Cover the word. Slide your finger left to right.
- Before uncovering any more, blend the sounds those letters represent first.
- Blend as you go, let one sound slide into the next.
- I notice you read part by part. Did that help you?

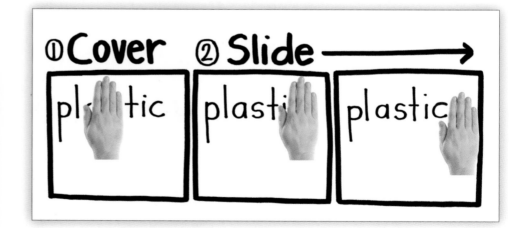

Strategy Write the word you're trying to read. As you write it, say the sounds each letter (or letter group) makes, then put the whole word together. Use decoding strategies you know to read it from the paper/whiteboard and then go back and read it in the context of the sentence.

Lesson Language *If you come to a word that is challenging to decode, you might try writing it down on a piece of scrap paper or dry-erase board. For example, as I came to this word* (point to a longer, more challenging word in a book, such as *encyclopedia*), *I knew I wanted to slow myself down. Watch me as I write the word, saying the sounds of each letter or group of letters as I go. The first part I see is en* (say /en/ not *e* and *n* as you write it on paper). *The next part is cy* (say /sy/ not "cee" and "y" as you write it), *and so on.* (After writing out the whole word part by part.) *I'm going to go back to the word and put the parts together.* "En-cy-clo-pe-di-a. Encyclopedia!"

Teaching Tip This strategy helps children pay attention to every letter in a word, as is required for full alphabetic decoding (Beck & Beck, 2013). The Lesson Language example shows how applying knowledge of familiar word parts can help with longer words, but the strategy can also be used with shorter, simpler words such as *play* where the reader would write each letter of the word, say a sound for each, then blend the sounds together.

Prompts

- What's the first letter or group of letters you'll write down?
- Say the sounds, not the letter names, as you write the word.
- Now that you've written it out, and said the sounds as you wrote it, go back to the beginning and blend the sounds together.

Skills
- **decoding**
- **blending**

Progression

Is ready to decode longer, multisyllabic words by recognizing and correctly pronouncing words with more complex letter strings and apply knowledge of syllable type and morphemes, blending parts together. May also be working to refine pronunciations by figuring out what part of the word to stress.

Research Link

Drake and Ehri (1984) showed a group of fourth graders correctly spelled words and then those same words broken into syllables. Then they guided the students to pronounce each syllable carefully before writing each word, to optimize the match between the letters and sounds. Compared with their peers in a control group, the students spelled more words correctly and remembered both silent letters and letters representing schwa vowels more accurately.

Skills

- **decoding**
- **blending**

Progression

Is ready to decode longer, multisyllabic words by recognizing and correctly pronouncing words with more complex letter strings and apply knowledge of syllable type and morphemes, blending parts together. May also be working to refine pronunciations by figuring out what part of the word to stress.

● ● ● ●

Hat Tip

A Fresh Look at Phonics: Common Causes of Failure and 7 Ingredients for Success (Blevins, 2016)

Research Link

There are three overarching skills relating to decoding multisyllabic words: analysis, pronunciation, and synthesis (Beck & Beck, 2013). Analysis is knowing *where* to divide words. Children know how to break a word apart into syllables based on what they know about morphology and/or what they've learned about syllable types (Bhattacharya, 2006; Bhattacharya & Ehri, 2004; Knight-McKenna, 2008).

Strategy Find the syllable breaks to read a longer word syllable by syllable. Remember there is at least one vowel in every syllable (see chart), so start by underlining (or finding) each vowel. Break the word apart keeping at least one vowel in each syllable. Pronounce each syllable. Blend them together.

Prompts

- You read that syllable by syllable—and it worked!
- Remember the syllable spelling patterns you know.
- Each syllable has at least one vowel. Where do you think the first break is?
- Make sure to keep blends and digraphs together within a syllable.

Syllables can help you figure out words

Here are some reminders:

V C C V — doctor — Divide between 2 middle consonants

V C V — visit — If the 1st vowel is short, divide after the consonant

V C V — paper — If the 1st vowel is long, divide before the consonant

C · LE — turtle — Divide before the consonant -le

V C C C V — extra — With 3 consonants usually split after 1st consonant

V C C C C V — instruct — With 4 consonants usually split after 1st consonant

(But keep digraphs and blends together!)

sunshine — For a compound word divide between the two words

V V — lion — Divide between two vowels if they aren't a pair

unhappily — Divide after a prefix and before a suffix

Strategy When you get to a longer word, take a moment to analyze its parts. One way to do this is to look for familiar meaning-based parts such as bases, roots, and affixes that you already know how to read. You might analyze the word out of order, but then go back and read it left to right, saying each part and blending the parts together.

Lesson Language *Longer words are often made up of parts that are familiar. Some parts are common prefixes:* re-, de-, un-. *Some parts are common suffixes:* -ing, -ed, -er. *And the middle parts are often parts we see in lots of other words, too, such as the word parts you've studied, bases, or root words. Sometimes you can take apart a longer word, find the smaller parts you recognize, then put them back together to make a whole. For example, if I come to the word spelled* i-n-d-e-p-e-n-d-e-n-t *, I can look for the parts I know. I know* in- *and* -ent, *and in the middle I see a word I know,* depend. *Now I can put it back together:* in-depend-ent. Independent!

Teaching Tip For more on helping children understand the meaning of words based on morphology, see Strategies 11.12 and 11.13.

Prompts
- Do you see any prefixes or suffixes?
- Try to take the word apart. What's the first part you see?
- Try covering the ending, now read the rest, and now put the ending back on.
- Blend the parts together.

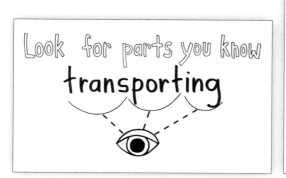

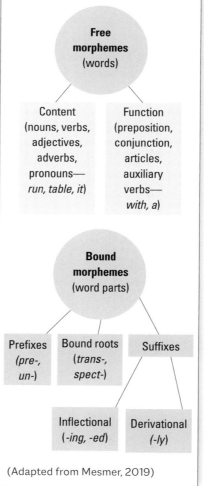

Free morphemes (words)

| Content (nouns, verbs, adjectives, adverbs, pronouns—*run, table, it*) | Function (preposition, conjunction, articles, auxiliary verbs—*with, a*) |

Bound morphemes (word parts)

Prefixes *(pre-, un-)* | Bound roots *(trans-, spect-)* | Suffixes

Inflectional *(-ing, -ed)* | Derivational *(-ly)*

(Adapted from Mesmer, 2019)

Skills
- **decoding**
- **blending**

Progression

Is ready to decode longer, multisyllabic words by recognizing and correctly pronouncing words with more complex letter strings and apply knowledge of syllable type and morphemes, blending parts together. May also be working to refine pronunciations by figuring out what part of the word to stress.

Hat Tip

A Fresh Look at Phonics: Common Causes of Failure and 7 Ingredients for Success (Blevins, 2016); ***Letter Lessons and First Words: Phonics Foundations That Work*** (Mesmer, 2019)

Research Link

Having a large phonological lexicon of familiar words and word parts (e.g., *-ing, ence, ip*) helps with both decoding and sight word learning. Systematic and explicit word study, including the etymology of roots, the meanings of various prefixes, and the connection between suffixes and tenses, supports this familiarity (Archer, Gleason, & Vachon, 2003; Ehri & McCormick, 1998; Nation & Cocksey, 2009).

Skills

- **decoding**
- **self-monitoring**

Progression

Is ready to decode longer, multisyllabic words by recognizing and correctly pronouncing words with more complex letter strings and apply knowledge of syllable type and morphemes, blending parts together. May also be working to refine pronunciations by figuring out what part of the word to stress.

Research Link

For children with phonological processing challenges, identifying or being aware of the stress in a word can be challenging, even if and when they speak with standard intonation patterns. In addition, there may be some stress patterns that vary according to region or dialect (for example, how do you pronounce *research*?) (Goswami et al., 2013).

Strategy If you sound out a word but the word you've pronounced isn't making sense—either it's not a word you've ever heard or it is a word but isn't making sense with the context—it could be that the stress is on the wrong syllable. Think about which generalization applies to this word (see chart). If you aren't sure, try it two ways to see which is correct.

Lesson Language *Consider the word* l-e-s-s-o-n. *It has two syllables:* les-son. *We could pronounce it* les-SON *or* LES-son. *Which one sounds like a word you know? And then there are words in English that are spelled the same but have different meanings depending on where you put the stress—you'll need to think about part of speech and use context to help you read the word correctly. Like this sentence, for example: "I need to desert my post." First, I'll break it into syllables:* des-ert. *Next, I'll think about the part of speech. Based on where it is in the sentence, I know it's a verb. It's something the speaker needs to do. So . . . the stress goes on the second syllable—*des-ERT. *When pronounced that way, it means to leave or give up on, not an arid region with sand and cacti.*

Teaching Tip For more on helping children think about the meaning of words that are spelled in the same way but pronounced differently, see Strategies 11.2 and 11.6.

Prompts

- Can you tell what the part of speech is?
- Since you know it's a verb, try to stress the second syllable.
- I heard you try putting the emphasis on two different syllables. Which one was correct?

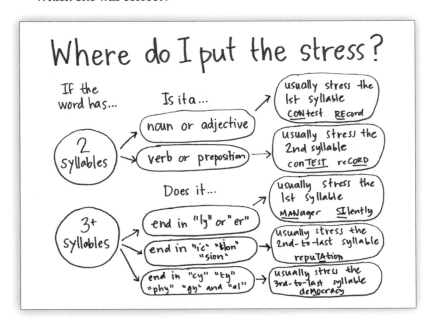

3.25 Come Up with a Plan

Strategy When you come to an unfamiliar word, you have options for how you can figure out the parts before you blend it back together. Think: Is this word best approached left to right, part by part, or by looking at parts out of order (and then returning to read the parts left to right)?

Teaching Tip Most times readers will move left to right through a word, read each part, and blend the parts together. Hierarchical decoding, or looking at the parts of a word out of order, requires a more complex understanding of how, for example, letter placement influences vowel sounds (in the word *tape* you have to notice the *e* at the end of the word, which influences the sound the *a* represents—for more see Strategy 3.16) and how double consonants influence the sound (for example, in the words *latter* and *later*) (Mesmer, 2019). For very long, complex words, or words with irregular spelling patterns, it may help to focus on the parts students can read (suffixes, roots, etc.), then be flexible with the parts they aren't sure about.

Prompts
- How will you approach this word?
- Look ahead to the end of the word. How does the *e* change the vowel?
- Look at the parts. Now go back to the beginning to read it.
- Now that you know what sound the vowel will make, slide through all the sounds to read the word.

Skills
- **decoding**
- **blending**

Progression

Is ready to decode longer, multisyllabic words by recognizing and correctly pronouncing words with more complex letter strings and apply knowledge of syllable types and morphemes, blending parts together. May also be working to refine pronunciations by figuring out what part of the word to stress.

Hat Tip

Letter Lessons and First Words: Phonics Foundations That Work (Mesmer, 2019)

Research Link

Beginning in the consolidated alphabetic phase, some readers may begin to decode hierarchically as they acquire a working implicit knowledge of how graphemes in one part of the word impact the pronunciation of graphemes in other parts of the word (Ehri & McCormick, 1998; Resnick & Beck, 1976).

Combine Word Syllables Across a Line Break

Skill

- **blending**

Progression

Is ready to decode longer, multisyllabic words by recognizing and correctly pronouncing words with more complex letter strings and apply knowledge of syllable type and morphemes, blending parts together. May also be working to refine pronunciations by figuring out what part of the word to stress.

Research Link

Research has demonstrated that text is easier to read when sentences are manipulated so that the ends of lines correspond to the ends of phrases (LeVasseur et al., 2006). Because beginning readers are inclined to stop at the end of a line, they need to be explicitly taught that the hyphen is a graphical clue that the word continues onto the next line.

Strategy When you see a word broken up across two lines, get ready to put the parts together. Read the first part at the end of the line, then the second part on the next line, then blend the two parts together.

Lesson Language *In the book we've been reading as a class, there have been lots of times when I came to a word at the end of the line that was not the whole word. It looks like this* (show an example under a document camera from a recent text the children are familiar with). *At first, it can seem tricky to figure words like this out because the whole word isn't together. But actually, in some ways it can be easier— the word is broken up into syllables, which will make decoding the longer word a bit easier. I can read the first part* doc- *and then the part on the next line* ument *and put them together to read the word:* "Docu-ment. Document."

Prompts

- Do you see a word broken up across the two lines?
- That's not a whole word, that's a part of the word—see the hyphen at the end of the line? The word continues on the next line.
- What strategy can you use to read it part by part?
- You read the first part, now put it together with the second part.

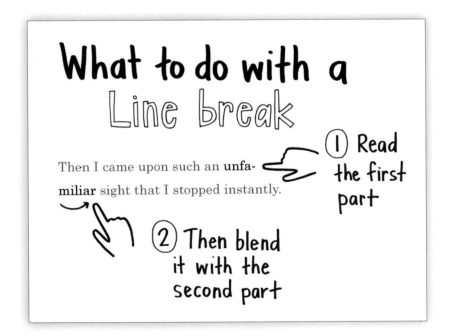

An either-or approach—
lots of isolated phonics without
time for children to read, or lots of
reading with only incidental
or minimal phonics—will not
help you reach all readers.

—Jennifer Serravallo

Fluency

◎ Why is this goal important?

When a child reads accurately and with automaticity, at an appropriate pace, and with prosody (i.e., proper phrasing, expression, and emphasis), they communicate that the text is making sense *and* they help themselves make sense of their reading (Klauda & Guthrie, 2008; Kuhn, 2008; Rasinski, 2010). Still, fluency isn't something that all readers automatically acquire; some readers need instruction and benefit from strategies to support their practice.

Fluency is a bridge between word recognition and comprehension, and "is a factor in both oral and silent reading that can limit or support comprehension" (Kuhn, Schwanenflugel, & Meisinger, 2010, p. 240). Try reading a text in a staccato, word-by-word, monotone fashion and you will likely discover you understand and remember very few, if any, of the words you said aloud. Many scholars agree that if you are able to improve your fluency, you will often improve your comprehension (e.g., Hudson et al., 2020; Lai et al., 2014).

That said, it is also possible for a child to be reading fluently but *not* comprehending. Have you ever met that child who reads a text sounding like they are reading lines for a Broadway audition, only to stop, be asked a simple question about what they just read, and have them tell you they don't remember a thing? In our attempts to teach children to read fluently, it's important that we don't send the message that reading is just about performing or reading fast (Applegate, Applegate, & Modla, 2009; Cartwright, 2010).

Skills a reader might work on as part of this goal

Expression
The aspect of prosody that includes reading to match the meaning and/or feeling of the piece, changing pitch to match end- and midsentence punctuation, and changing intonation for dialogue.

Inferring
Using background knowledge together with details in the text to understand meaning that influences prosody (e.g., when reading character dialogue based on feelings, emphasizing important words, and so on).

Phrasing (also known as *parsing*)
The aspect of prosody that includes pausing after meaningful phrases and attending to midsentence punctuation.

Self-monitoring
Attending to one's own fluency (during oral and silent reading) and rereading to improve fluency as necessary.

Emphasis
The aspect of prosody that includes stressing words in the sentence to match the author's meaning, and paying attention to text treatments (for example: bold, italics, or all caps).

Pacing
Reading at a speed that matches the reader's natural rate of speech.

What Texts Might Students Use When Practicing Strategies from This Chapter?

Students can (and should!) read with fluency in *any and all texts*. However, throughout this chapter, I'll also recommend specific text types that can help scaffold students' fluency learning as they work on certain strategies. These include:

Plays and scripts. Research has established that reader's theater encourages repeated readings and supports students with all aspects of fluency. Scripts—being all dialogue—also encourage expressive reading tied to character emotion.

Poems and songs. Keeping to a rhythm or beat can help children with their pacing, and the line breaks in these text types support phrasing. In addition, poems and songs are brief and you can encourage children to read them again and again.

Early chapter books. Page layouts in many popular series for young readers include longer sentences broken up across lines to support phrasing.

Texts with special typographical features. Look for books like Mo Willems' Elephant and Piggie series, *Yo! Yes?* by Chris Raschka, or *The Book with No Pictures* by B. J. Novak, which include bolded words, a variety of punctuation, different text treatments, and speech bubbles, which guide intonation and expression on every page.

How do I know if this goal is right for my student?

The best way I've found to understand students' fluency strengths and needs is to listen to them read aloud and take notes. First, choose a text they can read with a high level of accuracy. Then, as they read aloud, take notes on where and when they pause and how they change their voice to reflect the meaning on the page. Qualitative assessments like this will help you match students with appropriate strategies. I find quantitative assessments of fluency, such as timing readers with a stopwatch to get a word-per-minute (WPM) rate, less helpful for determining what strategies would help a student most. During WPM assessments, children may view their reading aloud as a race against the clock, rushing and skipping over opportunities to self-correct, or they may feel pressured and nervous, causing the results to be skewed.

Name: Julisa
Title: Moving Day Surprise

Voice up @ question mark

no expression for dialogue

A record of one student's reading fluency. Slashes (/) indicate pauses, and I've made notes about expression in the margins. Based on this record, I would say the student could work on reading more words in a phrase before pausing and attending more consistently to ending punctuation to inform intonation and expression (Strategies 4.8–4.13).

◎ How do I support students as they develop fluency?

After evaluating a student's oral reading, select strategies that you can model, that they can practice with you, and that they can use independently to increase their skills.

Although development is rarely perfectly linear, skill progressions can help us pinpoint where a student is now and what might come next. Use the if–then chart (adapted from the NAEP *Oral Reading Fluency Scale* [2018] and Zutell & Rasinski's *Multidimensional Fluency Scale* [1991]) on page 131 to evaluate your students' reading and find strategies that will support their growth.

A Progression of Skills: *Fluency*

If a student . . .

Needs general support with fluency at any developmental level.

Reads word by word and is ready to practice reading in longer phrases.

Reads in phrases and is ready to attend more closely to ending punctuation (and not insert ending punctuation that isn't there).

Attends to ending punctuation (periods, exclamation marks, question marks) and is ready to attend more closely to midsentence punctuation (commas, dashes, parentheses) and special text (italics, bold).

Reads in longer phrases, informed by midsentence and ending punctuation and is ready to consider meaningful context to influence expression and place emphasis on appropriate words.

Then you might teach . . .

4.1 **Reread for Fluency**

4.2 **Warm Up and Transfer**

4.3 **Coach Your Partner's Fluency**

4.4 **Act It Out to Smooth It Out**

4.5 **Listen to Yourself, Catch the Choppiness, Reread**

4.6 **Find a Good Pace: Fluent, Not Fast**

4.7 **Read in Your Head Like You Read Aloud**

4.8 **Scoop Up Words to Read in Phrases**

4.9 **Warm Up with Phrases**

4.10 **Read to the End of the Line**

4.11 **Drum the Poem to Find the Rhythm**

4.12 **Mind the Ending Punctuation**

4.13 **Snap to the Next Line**

4.14 **Let the Commas Be Your Guide**

4.15 **Attend to Extra Information: Parentheses and Em Dashes**

4.16 **Read with Emphasis: Bold, Italics, Underline, All Caps**

4.17 **Read with Emphasis: Infer from Context**

4.18 **Use a "This Is Interesting" Voice**

4.19 **Use a Character's Voice for the Words Inside Quotation Marks**

4.20 **Read It How the Author Tells You (Tags)**

4.21 **Make Your Voice Match the Feeling**

4.22 **Make Your Voice Match the Meaning and Genre**

4.23 **Be Your Own Director with Plays and Scripts**

4.24 **Find the Pauses in Poetry**

4.25 **Let the Rhyme Be Your Guide**

Strategy When you have to slow way down—to figure out a word, to check your understanding, because you found your phrasing was awkward—go back to the beginning of the sentence and reread. This time, read the words automatically, pause in places that make sense, and make your voice match the meaning.

Lesson Language *There are many reasons you may need to pause for a moment midsentence to figure out something—it could be you need to slow down to use decoding strategies to figure out a word, because you caught yourself reading something incorrectly, or because the sentence is long and complicated and you're slowing down to make sure you understand it. Whatever the reason, make sure you go back to reread. When you reread, make sure to read words you slowed to decode automatically. Make sure to match your voice to the punctuation. Make sure you are thinking as you read the sentence again. Rereading will both* help your fluency *and* help you better understand what you read.

Teaching Tip Research strongly supports rereading three to five times for optimal fluency benefit (Kuhn, Schwanenflugel, & Meisinger, 2010).

Prompts

• I notice you're stopping to figure out that word. Make sure you go back and reread the sentence once you figure it out.
• Now that you've figured it out, go back and read the whole sentence.
• Do you think you should reread that?
• It sounds like you slowed down a few times. Reread to make sure you're understanding.

Skills
• **self-monitoring**
• **pacing**
• **phrasing**
• **expression**

Progression
Needs general support with fluency at any developmental level.

● ○ ○ ○ ○

Hat Tip

The Fluent Reader: Oral and Silent Reading Strategies for Building Fluency, Word Recognition, and Comprehension, **second edition** (Rasinski, 2010)

Research Link

Repeated reading is one of the oldest and most studied fluency interventions, with hundreds of studies indicating moderate to high effect sizes across a range of ages and contexts (Padeliadu & Giazitzidou, 2018). Encouraging children to reread at a speaking pace can aid both their fluency and comprehension.

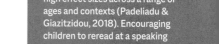

Skills

- **self-monitoring**
- **phrasing**
- **expression**
- **emphasis**
- **pacing**

Progression

Needs general support with fluency at any developmental level.

Strategy Warm up by rereading a familiar text, getting the feel for fluent reading. When you feel like the reading is easy and smooth, move to a new text. Try to make your voice sound just as smooth on the just-right text as it was on the text you've read many times, whether you're reading aloud or silently.

Lesson Language *Before an athlete goes onto the field or court for a game, they need to spend some time warming up. Warming up usually means doing easier exercises to get muscles ready to do the harder work of the sport. This can be true in reading, too. To do this, you take a text (for example, a book, poem, or song) that would be considered easier for you—something where you'll know all the words and you can read it smoothly without much effort because you're familiar with it. As you read it, be aware of your pacing, how you scoop up many words at a time in a phrase, and how you read it thinking about the meaning. After a minute or so of that, you should get the feel for it. Next, move to your new text. Try to make your voice sound just as smooth and expressive.*

Teaching Tip If you encourage students to warm up by reading texts you've used in shared repeated readings, they'll get the added benefits of your modeling.

Prompts

- (familiar text) That sounded smooth.
- (familiar text) I noticed you paused when you saw punctuation!
- (new text) Remember your pace with the familiar book? Do the same with this one.
- (new text) Scoop under these words.

Research Link

Multiple syntheses of existing studies have reported the benefits of repeated reading interventions, both with and without modeling and feedback (Chard, Vaughn, & Tyler, 2002; Hudson et al., 2020; Stevens, Walker, & Vaughn, 2017).

Strategy Choose who will be a reader and who will be a coach. Reader: read smoothly and with expression. Coach: give compliments and tips.

Lesson Language *Partners can help each other by listening and being a coach. As one of you reads aloud, the other can give compliments and tips to make the reading even smoother or more expressive. For example, if your partner sounds choppy or flat, you might say, "Go back and read that again" or "Make your voice match the feeling" or "Reread it so it's smoother." If the reading sounds smooth and expressive, point it out with a compliment like, "That sounded just like talk!"*

Teaching Tip As you observe a partnership working together you can coach the "coach," by whispering prompts (such as those below) and directing them to repeat the prompts to their partner. In almost no time, they'll use the prompts on their own, without reminders from you. As an added bonus, students doing the coaching or teaching will remember the kinds of things they say to their partner while coaching and may even apply it while they are reading their own texts.

Prompts
- Make your voice match the feeling.
- That was smooth reading!
- That sounded just like how you talk.
- I think that was a little choppy. Try it again.

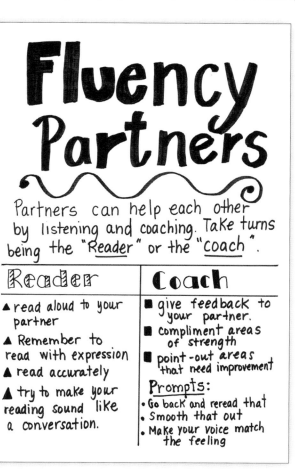

Skills
- **phrasing**
- **expression**
- **emphasis**
- **pacing**

Progression

Needs general support with fluency at any developmental level.

● ○ ○ ○ ○

Research Link

Studies have shown that peers of all ages can be effective fluency teachers for each other (Dufrene et al., 2010; Fuchs et al., 2001; Hofstadter-Duke & Daly, 2011; Josephs & Jolivette, 2016; Marr et al., 2011), and that the nature of performance feedback influences the aspects of fluency that improve as a result (Ardoin et al., 2013).

Skills

- **self-monitoring**
- **phrasing**
- **expression**
- **emphasis**

Progression

Needs general support with fluency at any developmental level.

Strategy Choose a book (or a play or script) to read with your partner that has two characters in conversation. Decide who will take on each role. Read your part using all you know about smooth and expressive reading, so you sound and act like the characters you're portraying. Reread to rehearse and improve your performance, just as actors do!

Teaching Tip Books in Mo Willems' Elephant and Piggie series are great choices for practicing this strategy. The books focus mostly on two characters, and most of the text is dialogue captured in speech bubbles. Because early chapter books like Saadia Faruqi's Yasmin series often have scenes of dialogue involving small numbers of characters, they are also good choices for practice. If you don't already have baskets of plays and scripts in your classroom library, consider creating one! There are many sites online with scripts to print for free, including those on Tim Rasinski's website (www.timrasinski.com). For a more advanced strategy leaning on the reader's theater research, see Strategy 4.23.

Prompts

- Read it again to practice.
- Use your voice to show how the character would say that.
- Now that you've acted it out once, think about what might change the next time you act it out together.
- You sounded just like the character!

Strategy Listen to yourself as you read. (You can either read with a quiet voice in a spot in the room that won't disturb anyone, or use a "phone.") As you listen, notice how you sound. If you catch yourself sounding flat or choppy, reread to make it sound more like how you'd talk.

Teaching Tip Tools like a "fluency phone" (sometimes referred to as a "whisper phone" or "read to self" phone) can be purchased or made with a piece of PVC piping. The curved tube allows for instant feedback as students read aloud, allowing them to better monitor and adjust their reading. If you don't have the tool, space children out around the room so they can hear themselves when reading at a whisper level.

Prompts

- Really listen to yourself as you read.
- As you listened to yourself read, do you think it sounded smooth or do you want to go back and reread?
- You really listened to yourself there—I noticed you went back to smooth out your reading.
- Read it in a whisper and listen.

Skills

- **self-monitoring**
- **expression**
- **phrasing**
- **pacing**
- **emphasis**

Progression

Needs general support with fluency at any developmental level.

● ○ ○ ○ ○

Research Link

The auditory feedback students get from hearing themselves read supports them to self-monitor, which has benefits for strengthening foundational decoding skills, like letter-sound relationships, as well as improving prosody and comprehension (Stouffer, 2011).

Skills
- **pacing**
- **self-monitoring**

Progression

Needs general support with fluency at any developmental level.

● ○ ○ ○ ○

Research Link

Researchers caution against "fast reading" being confused with "fluent reading" (Rasinski, Homan, & Biggs, 2009). An appropriate pace is usually one that is not too slow *or* too fast, as fast reading may not result in good comprehension (Applegate, Applegate, & Modla, 2009). Providing a model of fluent oral reading helps students internalize its sound.

Strategy Listen to yourself as you're reading, whether you're reading aloud or silently. If you're losing track of the text's meaning, slow down. Read smoothly, pausing at the punctuation, but don't rush.

Lesson Language *Sometimes in an effort to smooth out your reading and become more fluent, you may find yourself speeding up or rushing. Be careful! Don't read so fast that you lose track of what the words are saying and meaning. The best pace for you is one that can help you keep track of what you're reading, and it usually is about the same pace as the speed you talk when you're telling about, teaching, or explaining something.*

Teaching Tip This is a great strategy for students who are still developing their fluency, but as they develop and become more experienced, readers will learn to match their reading pace to their reading purpose—sometimes speeding up when they're reading just for pleasure, other times slowing down when they need to attend closely to information.

Prompts
- Does reading at the speed you're reading now allow you to think and understand?
- It feels like you're rushing a bit. Slow down so you can read smoothly and with understanding.
- That pace feels natural, about the same speed you speak.
- How did that pace feel—too fast, too slow, or just right?

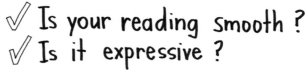

Strategy When you read aloud, your pacing, phrasing, and expression all impact how you understand. When you read silently, be sure you are hearing your own (well-paced, smooth, expressive) voice in your head. If you notice you can't hear it, switch to reading aloud a bit before returning to silent reading.

Teaching Tip Students will most likely practice most of the strategies in this chapter orally at first—whether with you in conferences, in small groups, during a shared reading lesson, or when paired with another reader in class. Oral reading gives children a chance to hear themselves read, adjust, and revise their prosody. You can also make it explicit that any of the strategies students practice aloud at first can, and should, also apply when they are reading silently. As Rasinski and colleagues (2011) stated, "[A]lthough fluency is normally considered within the domain of oral reading, silent reading fluency is a salient concept in reading" (p. 95).

Prompts

- Try to read the next part silently, but listen to your own voice in your head.
- It's silent to me, sitting next to you, but you should still be hearing yourself.
- If you come to a moment of beautiful language, pause and read aloud.
- If you stop hearing yourself, read aloud a bit.

Skill

- **self-monitoring**

Progression

Needs general support with fluency at any developmental level.

Research Link

Eye movement studies that track where a reader fixates have indicated that skilled readers read with prosody and stress/emphasis even when reading silently, which helps to preserve comprehension (Ashby, 2006).

Progression

Reads word by word and is ready to practice reading in longer phrases.

●●○○○

Hat Tip

Comprehension from the Ground Up: Simplified, Sensible Instruction for the K–3 Reading Workshop (Taberski, 2011)

Research Link

One study showed robust gains in *phrasal reading*—an important component of fluency—when students engaged in repeated readings of texts with visual cues that separate the phrases (also known as *phrase-cued text*) (LeVasseur, Macaruso, & Shankweiler, 2008).

Strategy Instead of reading word by word, try to scoop up a few words at a time. Read all the words in one scoop together, before pausing. Then scoop up the next few words.

Lesson Language *Instead of reading word by word (which may sound like a robot), it's important to try to read a few words together, without pauses between each word. You can slide your finger in a scoop under the few words you're going to read as a group. Pause, and then scoop up the next few words. So, instead of sounding like this: "This. Is. A. Dog. He. Likes. To. Play. Ball." It'll sound like this: "This is"... "a dog"... "he likes"... "to play ball."* (Give children a contrastive example by first demonstrating—pointing word by word for the first reading, and then later sliding your finger under the words to scoop a phrase as you read them.)

Teaching Tip Some students may benefit from the support of having phrase breaks indicated for them (this is known in research as "phrase-cued text"). You can take a photocopied text, add slash marks where a reader should pause or curved lines under a group of words, and coach students as they read to the slash/end of the curved line. (See Research Link.)

Prompts
- What words will you scoop up together?
- That sounded word by word; try it again by scooping.
- Let me show you where to pause (add scoops or slashes), and you read the words.
- Repeat after me. (*Read in phrases and have the student read the same words you just read.*)

Strategy Warm up by reading a list of common phrases. Notice the feel of reading a group of words smoothly, without a pause. Read these and other phrases you come upon in your reading smoothly, without a pause.

Teaching Tip This is a good strategy for readers who need to develop automaticity at the phrase level and/or readers who need help knowing how to group words within a sentence into syntactically appropriate groups. Search for Fry's or Dolch's phrases using Google to find lists (or go to www.timrasinski.com /presentations/fry_600_instant_phrases.pdf for a complete list of Fry's phrases), and select those at about the same level of complexity as what students will encounter in their books; choose short and simple phrases for those reading lower-level texts (i.e., those in the first 100 most common list), and more sophisticated phrases for those reading higher-level texts (i.e., those in the 300s or 400s groups).

Prompts
- Warm up with these phrases. Now let's try it in your book.
- (*Nonverbal: slide a finger under the phrase to indicate it should be read in one breath.*)
- That word is __ (e.g., *in, at, with*) so see if the next few words will go together. Yes? Read it as a phrase.

WARM UP phrases

A long time

All day long

She said to go

There was an old man

A number of people

Over the river

It turned out well.

Most of the animals

Try your best.

Tell the truth

Where in the world?

The tall mountains

A few children

A long life

Progression

Reads word by word and is ready to practice reading in longer phrases.

Hat Tip

The Fluent Reader: Oral and Silent Reading Strategies for Building Fluency, Word Recognition, and Comprehension, **second edition** (Rasinski, 2010)

Research Link

In one study of fourth graders, researchers found that an understanding of *simple* sentences (either in speech or written) correlates to comprehension of complex sentences encountered in text (Sorenson Duncan et al., 2021). In a separate study of adolescent readers, the ability to read in phrases was associated with syntactic understanding, which impacts comprehension (Nomvete & Easterbrooks, 2020).

Skill

• phrasing

Progression

Reads word by word and is ready to practice reading in longer phrases.

Research Link

Studies stretching back to the 1940s indicate that assisting students to identify meaningful phrases in text, starting with small chunks and progressing to entire sentences, promotes fluency and comprehension (Rasinski, 1990).

Strategy Read all the words on one line in one breath. Pause only if there's punctuation telling you to, then move to the next line.

Lesson Language *In the books you used to read, one short sentence went across the bottom of a page. Now that you're reading books with longer sentences, you'll find that the sentence is sometimes broken up for you. When you're reading these books, let the line breaks help you with your phrasing. The words on a line are meant to go together, so try to read them without pausing, and keep going until the end punctuation.*

Teaching Tip Several early chapter book series (see Poppleton [Rylant], Henry and Mudge [Rylant], and Frog and Toad [Lobel]) break longer sentences up into shorter lines. The additional white space and fewer words on each line give extra support to students practicing their phrasing. After some practice with this strategy, you'll notice students are reading in more than 3–5 word phrases, and you'll want to move them on to a strategy like "Snap to the Next Line" (Strategy 4.13) so they don't pause at the end of a line. The line breaks serve as a temporary scaffold.

Prompts

• After a quick pause at the line break, keep going on the next line. You haven't reached the end of the sentence yet.
• Show me where you're going to pause.
• I heard two pauses on that line. Try it once more, but don't stop until the end of the line.
• Read it like this. (*Read a line; have the child repeat.*)

Strategy Read the words. Drum the beat of the poem with your fingers on the desk, clap it, or come up with a beatbox rhythm to say to the beat. Read it again, this time to the beat.

Teaching Tip Making children aware of rhythm in poetry may support their phrasal reading and help them to internalize syntax in a way that's helpful for both fluency and comprehension. Try this with poems that have a predictable meter, nursery rhymes, or rap or songs where the "drum beat" will be easy to find. For example, Eloise Greenfield's poem "Rope Rhyme" is a great choice. Show students how to find the beat by clapping it or drumming it (bum bum bum-de-dum bum bum bum . . .), practice it a few times, then have students try it with new poems on their own.

Prompts
- Can you hear the beat? Drum it on the table.
- I'll drum it for you; you read the words.
- I'll read the words; you drum the beat you hear. Now you try to read it and drum it on your own.

Skills
- **phrasing**
- **pacing**

Progression

Reads word by word and is ready to practice reading in longer phrases.

Research Link

In a study of 150 preschoolers, those who performed well on a beat synchronization task outperformed their peers on all preliteracy measures (Bonacina et al., 2021). In another study, rhythm was positively related to both phonological awareness and naming speed among first graders and was a predictor for their reading ability in grade 5 (David et al., 2007).

Skill

• **expression**

Progression

Reads in phrases and is ready to attend more closely to ending punctuation (and not insert ending punctuation that isn't there).

Research Link

Spectrographic analyses of first-grade readers over time have indicated that students who had fewer inappropriate pauses in their reading during grade 1 tended to have more "adult-like" prosody (such as rising or dropping pitch at the end of sentences) by the end of grade 2, which was associated with better comprehension in grade 3 (Miller & Schwanenflugel, 2008).

Strategy To be sure you're attending to the ending punctuation, look ahead to the end of the sentence. Notice if there is an exclamation point, question mark, or period. Make your voice match the punctuation.

Lesson Language *As we've talked about before, readers do more than just read the words—they also read the marks on the page. Ending punctuation gives us a really big clue about how the sentence should be read. Most sentences will end with a period that just marks a stop and slight voice drop. But if a sentence ends with a question mark, you should read it like you're asking a question. If you see an exclamation mark, that means the sentence is expressing a strong emotion—like happiness, anger, or surprise—and your voice should communicate that. If you read a sentence with the wrong expression, it may change the meaning of the sentence and confuse you.*

Teaching Tip For a more advanced version of this strategy, engage children in an exploration of the different pitches they might use for any individual mark based on the meaning of the sentence and which words within the sentence are emphasized. For example, you might think about the different ways you could read the simple question, "Is that yours?" Notice how it's a slightly different question depending on which of the three words you emphasize.

Prompts

• Peek at the end of the sentence—what punctuation do you see?
• Yes! Your voice matched the punctuation.
• That's a (question mark/exclamation mark/period). Make your voice (rise/drop).

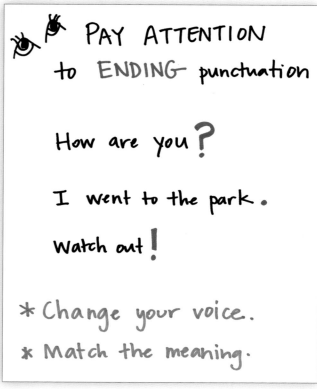

Strategy Sentences only sometimes end at the end of the line. If you don't see ending punctuation (., !, ?, . . .) at the end of the line, you need to snap your eyes to the next line quickly. Try reading with only the briefest pause or break between the end of one line and the beginning of the next.

Lesson Language *In the books you're reading now, you'll notice many more words fit onto the page without much white space. In these denser texts, a sentence might start anywhere on a line, wrap around to the next line, and finish somewhere in the middle of the next one. As you read, you need to snap your eyes quickly from one line to the next if there's no ending punctuation to stop you. Read the whole sentence together, even when it's broken up across a line. For example, it should sound like this.* (Model reading seamlessly one sentence that's broken up across a line.)

Teaching Tip This strategy is best for readers who are proficiently reading in longer phrases, and are reading at least until the end of a line with appropriate phrasing (see Strategy 4.10: "Read to the End of the Line" for more).

Prompts
- Keep going through the line break.
- Did you see ending punctuation there?
- I could tell you snapped your eyes to the next line.
- You paused only when you saw punctuation!

Skill
- **phrasing**

Progression

Reads in phrases and is ready to attend more closely to ending punctuation (and not insert ending punctuation that isn't there).

 ○ ○

Research Link

Because many sentences do not have prosodic information other than the final punctuation, chunking information can be a challenge (Schreiber, 1991). Research has demonstrated improved fluency, and fewer false starts, when text is altered so that the ends of lines correspond to the ends of phrases (LeVasseur et al., 2006). Though all text isn't laid out this way, teach students that meaningful phrases often span line breaks.

Skills

- **phrasing**
- **expression**

Progression

Attends to ending punctuation (periods, exclamation marks, question marks) and is ready to attend more closely to midsentence punctuation (commas, dashes, parentheses) and special text (italics, bold).

Research Link

Researchers have noted that skilled readers do not rely solely on end punctuation to guide their prosody; context and usage of the comma also matters. For example, commas after introductory phrases, quotations, and single words in a list were all marked differently (Miller & Schwanenflugel, 2006).

Strategy The punctuation inside a sentence gives you direction about how to read the sentence. The marks show you how the words are related and which ones go together. When you come to a punctuation mark in the middle of a sentence such as a comma, your voice should reflect the break between two groups of related words, usually with a very short pause and a slight change in pitch.

Lesson Language *Lynne Truss's picture book* Eats, Shoots & Leaves (2006) *is a book of paired sentences—the words stay the same but the punctuation changes. For example, the first two pages feature the sentences "Slow, children crossing" and "Slow children crossing" with accompanying illustrations. On the page with punctuation, we see a crossing guard alerting a motorist to take caution and go slowly as kids are trying to get to school safely. Without the comma, it's the children who are slowly crossing a bridge. In the books you're reading now, be on the lookout for commas that chunk information in ways that will help you understand the sentence and know where to pitch your voice a bit. Groups of words before, after, or in between punctuation marks are meant to be read together. Your voice should indicate that you are moving from one group of words to the next anytime you see punctuation inside a sentence.*

Teaching Tip For readers just beginning to pay attention to commas, directing them to notice commas and take a slight pause may be enough. Proficient readers, though, recognize a range of comma uses in a sentence (lists, after introductory clauses, to indicate a parenthetical, etc.), and the commas influence not only *phrasing* but also *expression*. So, tweak this strategy for more experienced readers to explore the impact commas have on pitch as well (see Research Link for more).

Prompts

- Read all the words up to this comma in one breath.
- Which words will you read together?
- I could hear your voice showing the move from one group of words to another. I noticed you paused at the comma (or colon or dash).
- Did you hear your change in pitch at the comma?

> 'Commas' mean P·A·U·S·E,
>
> I ate roast chicken, mashed potatoes, and green beans for dinner.

Attend to Extra Information: Parentheses and Em Dashes

Strategy Notice the type of extra information set off by em dashes or parentheses. Think about the context and the purpose. Read the extra information with expression that matches the meaning.

Lesson Language *Just like commas and end marks, parentheses and em dashes indicate pauses, but they also cue expression in a really big way. Writers typically use these marks to add a little extra information to the running text, something we do all the time when we talk to each other. We interrupt what we're saying to add a little detail and make something clearer. Well, parentheses and em dashes are the tools writers use to bring this same conversational "sound" to their writing. When you see these marks, think about what you understand from the text up to that point and how the marks are being used to direct your expression, and reread if your first go doesn't match the meaning.*

Consider the following examples. How do you imagine someone would say this if they were talking?

- *"You're really bugging me today—you came in my room, you took my stuff, you broke my toy—I need you to get out!" I'd read this list of three things inside the dashes with extra emphasis, maybe even building up to the third item, as if she's getting angrier with each action she mentions.*
- *"Mr. Cantor—a newbie—was always making mistakes." "A newbie" feels like a little extra info to me, so I'd read it as an aside, with a drop in my voice.*
- *"She couldn't get enough of the National Parks (views, mountains, fresh air) so she traveled to one every chance she got." In this case, what's in the parentheses is a list of things she loves, so I'd slow down, lingering on each one as if appreciating it.*

Prompts

- Do you think what's in the parentheses is an aside, or do you think it needs extra emphasis?
- Reread that part, but this time read what's in the parentheses like a whisper.
- How will you read what's offset by dashes?
- Think about the purpose of the extra information.

Watch for extras in your reading !

( ) and — might mean to read softer or with emphasis

ex. Next Tuesday (my birthday) is going to be fabulous.

This morning was awful— I tripped, missed the bus, and forgot my lunch.

Progression

Attends to ending punctuation (periods, exclamation marks, question marks) and is ready to attend more closely to midsentence punctuation (commas, dashes, parentheses) and special text (italics, bold).

● ● ● ● ○

Research Link

In one study of third-grade readers, researchers found that students didn't attend to parenthetical information with appropriate prosody, positing they lacked experience with this type of information and didn't understand the function of the parenthetical (Schwanenflugel, Westmoreland, & Benjamin, 2015).

Skills

- expression
- emphasis
- self-monitoring

Progression

Attends to ending punctuation (periods, exclamation marks, question marks) and is ready to attend more closely to midsentence punctuation (commas, dashes, parentheses) and special text (italics, bold).

Research Link

In a case study of first graders and their use of multimodal features in picture books, researchers found that students did not automatically rely on typography as much as punctuation or illustrations, but they still identified instances where students altered their reading of the text based on a changed typographical feature (Kachorsky et al., 2017).

Strategy When you see bolded words, italics, words underlined, or words in all caps, that's a signal to read the word(s) with emphasis. Base *how* you emphasize the word on what you understand about what's happening in that text at that point.

Teaching Tip Check out B. J. Novak's *The Book with No Pictures* or Mo Willems' Elephant and Piggie books for lots of fun opportunities to practice responding to text treatments with a change in emphasis—stress, tone, or even volume!

Prompts

- With emphasis on that word, how does it change the meaning?
- Let me hear you read it, emphasizing that word.
- I see (bold/caps/italics, etc.). Do you? Show me where.
- Yes! I could hear you emphasize the word that's italicized.

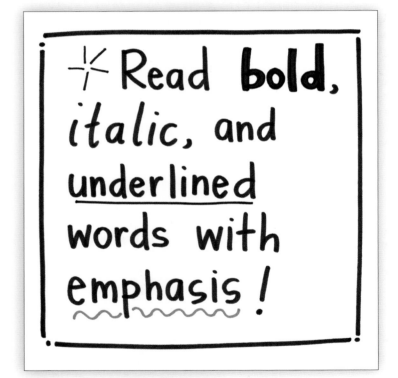

Strategy If there is no special text treatment to tell you which word(s) in a sentence to emphasize, think about the context. Does it suggest emphasis? If it does, think about how where you place emphasis impacts the meaning. If your inferred emphasis doesn't match the meaning, reread emphasizing a different word (or words).

Lesson Language *The word or words you do or don't emphasize can impact the meaning of a sentence. For example, consider a short sentence like "This is my house." Depending on how you read it, it can mean different things.*

"This is my house." (A simple declarative statement with no emphasis)
*"**This** is my house." (It's this one, not that one)*
*"This is **my** house." (It's mine, not yours or someone else's)*
*"This is my **house**." (I'm not talking about any other place)*

Sometimes, based on context, it makes sense to emphasize a word even if there is no special text treatment to guide you. How do you know when you need to add emphasis? You look for the meaning to suggest it. For example, if you found this sentence in this context:

As we walked down the street, I told my new best friend that I couldn't wait until I could show her my room. "This is it! This is my house."

How would you read it? Would you add emphasis? If so, on which word? If the way you read it the first time doesn't match what you're understanding in the text so far, try emphasizing a different word.

Prompts

• Do you think any words in this sentence need emphasis?
• When you emphasize that word in the sentence, how does it impact the meaning?
• Based on the context, which word should you emphasize in this sentence?
• When you stress that word, it means __. Do you think that fits with the context?

Skills

• **expression**
• **emphasis**
• **self-monitoring**
• **inferring**

Progression

Reads in longer phrases, informed by midsentence and ending punctuation and is ready to consider meaningful context to influence expression and place emphasis on appropriate words.

Research Link

As a number of scholars have highlighted, written text does not contain many prosodic cues, so readers need to rely on context and comprehension to decide on appropriate pitch, stress, emphasis, and pauses (Miller & Schwanenflugel, 2008; Schreiber, 1991).

Skills

- **expression**
- **emphasis**
- **pacing**
- **self-monitoring**

Progression

Reads in longer phrases, informed by midsentence and ending punctuation and is ready to consider meaningful context to influence expression and place emphasis on appropriate words.

Strategy Read an informational text with a "wow" tone of voice. Slow your pace. Be careful to emphasize the part of the sentence that's most interesting or surprising. Raise your voice at questions.

Lesson Language *If you read information, fact after fact, in a monotone, flat voice, it'll be harder to stay engaged and harder to understand. Instead, try to read information that excites or surprises you in a voice that shows it's interesting. When you read in a "Wow! I never knew that!" tone of voice, you'll perk up, and click into what the sentence is teaching you. Listen for the difference.* (Model reading a sentence in a flat, monotone voice and another with great expression, like the information is the best thing you've ever heard.) *Turn to your partner: How would you describe the difference? Which sentence did you understand better?*

Prompts

- Your tone was flat there; try to make it sound like the information is amazing!
- You just made that sound interesting!
- What's the "wow" part of that sentence? Can you reread it, trying to emphasize that part with your voice?

Research Link

Some researchers argue that the term *intonation* (rise and fall of pitch) is more appropriate than *expression* (a particular way of phrasing) when orally reading informational texts (Kuhn, Schwanenflugel, & Meisinger, 2010), and that informational texts have a unique way of being read aloud (e.g., Carlson et al., 2009; Shattuck-Hufnagel, Ostendorf, & Ross, 1994).

Strategy In a story, everything inside of quotation marks is dialogue. Read it so it sounds like the character is talking. Switch out of the character's voice when you come to the dialogue tag (which tells you who is talking and how they speak).

Lesson Language *Be careful to pay close attention not only to the words, but also the marks on the page. For example, it's very important to know when, in a story, a character is speaking. The author helps us by using quotation marks. (Show example from a big book and/or hand-drawn large quotation marks.) When you see the first or* opening *mark, you can think of it like the character opening his or her mouth—it's the start of the talking. The voice you use has to change to a character voice. Then, when we see the quotes again, like right here* (point to example), *that's the* closing *of the quotation marks, and the closing of the character's mouth. Open quotes, open mouth. Closed quotes, closed mouth. Open quotes, start sounding like the character. Closed quotes, stop sounding like the character. Let's try it together.*

Prompts
- There's the quotation mark! Switch to your character's voice.
- I can tell you paid attention to the quotation marks because I could hear the character's voice.
- That's a tag. Switch out of the character's voice.
- The dialogue and narration sounded the same. Go back and try it again.

Skill
- **expression**

Progression

Reads in longer phrases, informed by midsentence and ending punctuation and is ready to consider meaningful context to influence expression and place emphasis on appropriate words.

Research Link

In a study of third-grade readers, researchers found that fluent readers mark linguistic focus features—such as dialogue tags indicating direct quotes—as well as sentence information in their oral reading prosody (Schwanenflugel, Westmoreland, & Benjamin, 2015).

Pay Attention to Quotation Marks

> Look! A talking hint.
>
> this is called a speaker tag
>
> My mom looked at me as I nervously clutched my backpack.
> "Are you okay, J.D.?" she asked.   Mom talks
> "Well, Mom, I'm a little scared," I said.
> "Do you still want to do this?" she asked.   J.D. talks (switch your voice)
> "I have to, Mom, the whole CITY is coming!"
> "Well, YOU were built for this moment. You're my child, J.D. We Joneses don't let nerves stop us!"   Mom again (change your voice)

talking starts

talking stops

Open quotes, open mouth

Closed quotes, closed mouth

Excerpt from *J.D. and the Great Barber Battle* (Dillard, 2019).

Read It How the Author Tells You (Tags)

Skill

- expression

Progression

Reads in longer phrases, informed by midsentence and ending punctuation and is ready to consider meaningful context to influence expression and place emphasis on appropriate words.

● ● ● ● ●

Research Link

A small study of third-grade students found that, although reading dialogue resulted in slower and less accurate oral reading, students recalled more from the dialogue than from the narrative portions of the same text. The greater attention students devoted to prosody while attempting to mimic the characters' speech may have made the dialogue sections more memorable, but they also required a greater cognitive load (Cohen, Krustedt, & May, 2009).

Strategy When you see dialogue in a story, pay attention not only to what the character says but also *how* the character says it. Sometimes, the author will just write "said." But if the author tells you *how* the character says it (e.g., *whispered, shouted, pleaded*), read it with a tone that matches the tag.

Lesson Language *The other day I was reading out loud to my daughter. It was a new book we'd never read before, so I didn't know it. I was reading along and I got to some dialogue. I was thinking, based on what had happened so far, that the character was shouting for help, so I read it like this.* (Read in a shouting voice.) *"But won't you please help?" But then I noticed, right after the dialogue marks ended, the author told me how she meant for me to read it. The dialogue tag said, "whispered Jonas." I apologized to my daughter—"I'm so sorry! I read that wrong!" And I went back and reread like this.* (Reread in a whisper.) *"But won't you please help?" That little change in my tone made me think very differently about the character, what he was feeling, and what was happening right there in the story. It started as a shout for help—with a tone of impatience, maybe even annoyance. But a whisper for help is different. It's more pleading, more desperate. Those dialogue tags sure are important in helping us figure out* how *the character is talking so we can better understand the story.*

Prompts

- Check the tag. Now read it how the author intended.
- Yes—you paid attention to the tag. So what are you thinking about the character now?
- The tag says __, but you read it like __. Give that one more try.
- Show me how you'll read it.

THE READING STRATEGIES BOOK 2.0

Strategy Think about how the character feels. Think about how you sound when you feel like that. Read the dialogue or narration to match the character's feelings.

Teaching Tip This strategy can be modified for readers at different levels. For children in books that have heavy picture support, you can cue them to check the picture to see the facial expression of the character, then to make their voice match how the character is feeling. For children reading books without picture support, you might prompt them to think about how the character might be feeling based on dialogue or actions. This is an extra step, as children will have to first be able to infer, and then they are able to adjust their expression. For more support with teaching children how to infer character feelings, see Chapter 6.

Prompts
- How is the character feeling?
- How would it sound when that character talks?
- Yes! Your voice sounded (sad or happy or mad).
- Check the dialogue tag. Does that help you think about the feeling? Now make your voice match it.

Make your voice match the mood.

When Luca got sick his whole neighborhood ached.

As they talked, Ellie realized she really wasn't afraid anymore.

Skills
- **expression**
- **inferring**
- **self-monitoring**

Progression

Reads in longer phrases, informed by midsentence and ending punctuation and is ready to consider meaningful context to influence expression and place emphasis on appropriate words.

Hat Tip

Comprehension from the Ground Up: Simplified, Sensible Instruction for the K-3 Reading Workshop (Taberski, 2011)

Research Link

After receiving explicit instruction in the "grammatics" of quoted speech, a small group of second graders expanded their repertoire of strategies for reading dialogue with good expression, including paying attention to the illustrations, plot, "teasing words," text treatments and punctuation, and the grammar of individual sentences (French, 2012).

Skills

- **self-monitoring**
- **expression**
- **pacing**

Progression

Reads in longer phrases, informed by midsentence and ending punctuation and is ready to consider meaningful context to influence expression and place emphasis on appropriate words.

Research Link

In a study of second-grade readers, researchers established a link between good reading prosody and reading comprehension. Readers across skill levels used their prosody to help them understand more difficult texts (Benjamin & Schwanenflugel, 2010). Different genres require different styles of intonation and expression (Kuhn, Schwanenflugel, & Meisinger, 2010).

Strategy Stay focused on what's happening, what you're learning about, or the meaning the author is trying to get across. Be aware of the genre of the text, and what you know about how it sounds to read that sort of text aloud. Make sure your pacing and expression match the type of text and what the text is about.

Lesson Language *As you read, it's important to think about the kind of text you are reading and what the author has written, and make your voice match that meaning. Let's practice with a few types of texts. The first is a story,* Islandborn *by Junot Díaz (2018). In this sentence "Lola, you see, loved to draw, but she had left the Island when she was just a baby so she didn't remember any of it," I am thinking about how she feels left out. Since this is narration, I am going to use a voice like the voice-overs you hear in movies, narrating what's happening, but with a tone of sadness to match how Lola might be feeling. Here's a different text:* Can We Save the Tiger? *by Martin Jenkins (2011) is an informational text with a call to action. Check out the last two sentences of the first page: "In fact, some have coped so badly that they're not here anymore. They're extinct." My tone? I want to communicate that the author and I(!) are concerned about the endangered animals. I also feel like I want to read that last sentence slowly, with emphasis on* extinct, *to match the emphasis the author places on the idea by making it such a short, direct sentence.*

Prompts

- What kind of text is this? Show me how you'd read that.
- Did how you read that make sense with the story?
- I could tell you were thinking about the kind of text this was.
- The way you read it matched the mood at this point in the story!

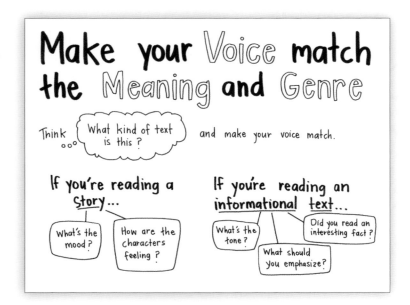

Strategy Where you pause and how you read dialogue can slightly alter the meaning or communicate different things about a character. Reread the play or script, paying close attention to the character and the context (plot, setting). Read the stage directions carefully. Consider where to pause and what expression to use.

Lesson Language *When you're reading a part in a play or script, it's important to think like a director and decide how you will perform your part. Be sure to reread the script several times, carefully attending to the plot, the tone, the punctuation, the stage directions—all the information that's there to help you interpret your part—so you really understand what's happening and can decide how you'll portray the character through the dialogue. For example, based on context, you might pick up on whether the character is saying something in a sarcastic or literal tone, or interpret that a character is nervous and decide to deliver dialogue in a rushed voice; if they are distracted or sleepy, the dialogue may have a lot of extra pauses. You might even decide where to place pauses for a comical effect.*

Teaching Tip Emergent bilingual students, students with certain reading disabilities, and students in need of additional support, including older students (Keehn, Harmon, & Shoho, 2008), may benefit from having a teacher or other adult model reading the text aloud in preparation for students to read the text themselves (Clark, Morrison, & Wilcox, 2009; Lekwilai, 2014).

Prompts
- What are you trying to show about the character?
- What's the tone of this scene? Think how will you change your reading of the dialogue to match it.
- Try the pause in another place. Which one matches what you think this scene is about?

Skills
- **phrasing**
- **expression**

Progression

Reads in longer phrases, informed by midsentence and ending punctuation and is ready to consider meaningful context to influence expression and place emphasis on appropriate words.

Research Link

An action research study involving students who were learning English (Liu, 2000) and another study focused on students the researchers termed "struggling readers" (Tyler & Chard, 2000) found that reader's theater is a motivating activity that promotes both comprehension *and* fluency because students must work to understand meaning, interpret the text, and perform based on those interpretations.

Skills

- **self-monitoring**
- **phrasing**
- **pacing**

Progression

Reads in longer phrases, informed by midsentence and ending punctuation and is ready to consider meaningful context to influence expression and place emphasis on appropriate words.

Research Link

Classroom-based and clinical studies have found benefits to using poems and songs to support fluency, as well as other goals related to reading including decoding, accuracy, engagement, and comprehension (Iwasaki et al., 2013; Nichols et al., 2018).

Strategy Read the poem a few times to understand its meaning. Think about where it makes sense to pause based on line and stanza breaks, punctuation, text treatments, and most of all, meaning. Read it aloud a few ways until it sounds right—how you read it should match the meaning.

Lesson Language *Everything a poet does is intentional—layout, line breaks, punctuation (or not)—but the conventions you typically use to guide your reading of prose are often very different in poetry. Because of this, knowing when to pause in a poem requires more interpretation. Sometimes, you will pause when you come to white space—a line break, a stanza break, or spaces the author left in the middle of a line. Other times, you might see uppercase letters or italics that mark a change and suggest a pause. Still other times, poets may use punctuation just like you see in other texts and it can guide you. No matter what, let the meaning of the poem help you decide how it should be read.*

Teaching Tip This strategy is most helpful for *free verse* poetry. You might compare a more interpretive poem like "There Was No Wind" (Nye, 2008) to a poem like Langston Hughes' "April Rain Song" where each line feels like a sentence (though there is no ending punctuation) and pausing at the end of each line break may feel like a more obvious decision. Keep in mind that some poets make decisions about line and stanza breaks more for visual reasons than to direct how a reader might read it aloud, so keep meaning in the forefront as you find the pauses that make sense.

Prompts

- Look for line or stanza breaks or punctuation to direct your pauses.
- What is this poem about? Keep that in mind as you read.
- Where does it make sense to pause?
- Do your pauses match the meaning?

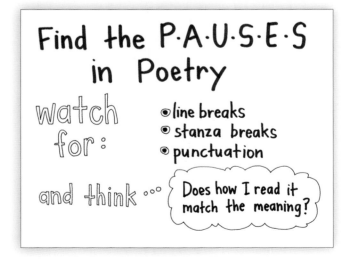

Strategy Notice rhyming words in the poem. Use the rhyme to help you find the beat. Then decide how you'll read. Will you linger on the rhyming words? Pause right after a rhyming word? Put emphasis on the rhyming word? Read it several times until it sounds right.

Lesson Language *In 2017 at age 12, Solli Raphael was the first youth to win the Australian Poetry Slam (https://www.australianpoetryslam.com/champions). When you listen to him perform his poetry, you'll notice a rhythm and a beat that propels his performance. This rhythm is tied in part to the rhyme—he tends to slow down or emphasize the rhyming words, sometimes even taking a pause after the rhyming word and the first word after it.* (Play the video of the performance and clue kids in to listen for the rhyming words.)

> *Evolution/confusion/contribution/solution/evolution*
> *Survive/alive*
> *Buyer/admire/desire/high wire*

Check out Jesse Oliver's poem. He does something similar with rhyme and also with alliteration. What do you notice about how the rhyming words help with the rhythm and therefore with pausing, expression, and emphasis? (Play the performance [same site as above], and invite students to listen in for these words.)

> *Guys/high/why*
> *Diplomacy/potency*
> *Silenced/seldom/seen/scene*

Teaching Tip These slam poetry examples would be great for upper elementary or middle school readers. For younger readers, consider familiar nursery rhymes and songs.

Prompts
- Find the rhyme.
- Read it with a beat, paying attention to the rhyming words.
- Each time you come to a rhyming word, will you emphasize the word? Linger for a bit?

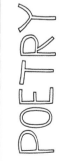

Watch for RHYMES

POETRY

Will you linger?
Will you p·a·u·s·e ?
Will you emphasize ?

☆ Try it several times until it sounds right.

Skills
- **self-monitoring**
- **phrasing**
- **expression**
- **emphasis**
- **pacing**

Progression

Reads in longer phrases, informed by midsentence and ending punctuation and is ready to consider meaningful context to influence expression and place emphasis on appropriate words.

● ● ● ● ●

Research Link

A group of researchers explored the connection between speech rhythm sensitivity and children's reading development with a group of lower elementary students over time. They found that speech rhythm sensitivity was able to predict differences in word reading and phrasing skills in a reading fluency measure one year later (Holliman, Wood, & Sheehy, 2010).

Goal 5

Comprehending Plot and Setting

◎ Why is this goal important?

To help students achieve that lost-in-a-book, engaged experience that makes reading enjoyable, they have to understand what's happening and how the events connect to form a cohesive plot, know where the action is taking place, and create mental images of what they are reading.

In fictional stories, writers craft stories with plots that include some conflict and resolution or a journey and where change happens over time (Burroway, 2003). Even in true stories, the author has made intentional decisions about what events to include and which to leave out to shape a narrative that follows a logical order and is engaging to read. Regardless of whether the story is completely imagined or rooted in reality, when readers explicitly learn about story structure and the predictable elements of plot, they are better able to predict, remember, and recall the events and comprehend the narratives they read (Dickson, Simmons, & Kameenui, 1998; Fitzgerald & Teasley, 1986; Pearson & Fielding, 1991; Renz et al., 2003; Short & Ryan, 1984). This type of explicit instruction is especially critical for those who struggle with comprehension (National Reading Panel, 2000).

A story's setting(s), the place(s) and time(s) where the action unfolds, is not "merely scenery against which the significant takes place"; they anchor the plot (Burroway, 2003, p. 129). Readers must be able to visualize the setting to feel oriented. In fact, research has found that readers who successfully comprehend tend to be "imaginative readers" who actively select which information in a text is most important to focus on, link information from the text with their background knowledge, and organize information in their minds (National Reading Panel, 2000; Pressley, 2002a; Sadoski & Quast, 1990; Woolley, 2010). As the texts they read become more complex, readers should also consider why the setting matters and the ways it impacts characters and events.

Determining importance
Identifying the most important events in a plot, usually anchored to the problem or what a character wants.

Retelling/ summarizing
Recounting the events in a plot (whether the plot is linear, or includes multiple plots, flashback, and so on) in sequence. Retellings tend to be more detailed; summaries tend to be shorter and include only the most important events.

Inferring
Developing ideas about plot and setting that aren't explicitly stated in the text, including making predictions.

Visualizing
Picturing beyond the author's description, invoking multiple senses beyond seeing (hearing, feeling, smelling) as appropriate.

Skills a reader might work on as part of this goal

Self-monitoring
Asking and answering questions, being aware of when the plot is making sense and the setting is clear, and using strategies to address confusion.

Synthesizing
Understanding how events in the story connect, such as causes and effects, or problems and resolutions.

Building knowledge
Searching out information (about setting(s), for example) to add to the details the author provides.

Activating prior knowledge
Using knowledge of places and times, plot structures, series, genre, and so on to comprehend.

◎ How do I know if this goal is right for my student?

To assess student comprehension of plot and setting, ask students to respond to prompts and questions about a text or excerpt, and then evaluate the quality of their responses. The text can be short (short story, picture book, something from a children's magazine) or long (chapter book); can be one you choose or they choose; and you can decide to read it aloud or have them read it independently. Plant questions at key points in the story, or ask them to read the whole story and respond by jotting or talking about the story when they're done.

Here are some prompts and questions you can use that align to this goal:

- Retell the most important things from this book/chapter in the order they happened.
- What problem(s)/obstacle(s) is your character dealing with?
- Describe the setting. What do you picture?
- How does the setting impact the character(s)?

> toad will not leave frog alone when he wants to be alone.

This student's jot about the problem in a story reveals that she is able to identify a main problem for the main character. She is ready to connect plot events that relate to that main problem (Strategies 5.16, 5.18), and eventually to notice multiple aspects of a story's main problem(s) (Strategies 5.20, 5.21).

> In Japan it is really hot and humid. But when the sun goes down it look really beautiful to see the sunset. Also there was lots of lanterns over the Ohta River. The candles shown very brightly.

After reading this student's thinking about the setting, I notice he is able to identify the place (Ōhata River, Japan) and time (at sunset) and offer some details ("hot and humid") that indicate he's visualizing. He is ready to infer based on setting(s), such as how setting(s) contributes to mood or impacts characters or plot (Strategies 5.27–5.32).

What Texts Might Students Use When Practicing Strategies from This Chapter?

Strategies in this chapter will help readers who are reading narratives of any type, format, or genre that have plots and settings, whether fictional (e.g., historical fiction, mystery, realistic fiction chapter books, graphic novels, and so on) or informational (e.g., biographies, historical accounts). When students first begin working on this goal, they may find it helpful to start with shorter narrative texts (e.g., fictional picture books, picture book biographies, early reader chapter books, and so on) that have fewer plot events and books with some picture support (e.g., picture books, graphic novels, and so on) to support visualization. To practice the more sophisticated strategies (beginning with Strategy 5.23), students will need to be reading narratives with more complex plots and settings.

◎ How do I support students as they develop their understanding of plot and setting?

After evaluating a student's verbal or written responses about the plot and setting in their text(s), select strategies that you can model, that they can practice with you, and that they can use independently to increase their skills.

Although development is rarely perfectly linear, skill progressions can help us pinpoint where a student is now and what might come next. Use the if–then chart on page 163 to evaluate your students' reading and find strategies that will support their growth.

A Progression of Skills: *Comprehending Plot and Setting*

If a student...

Needs support naming and visualizing the setting and/or understanding what's happening on an individual page or a moment in the story, and how events in the plot connect. Could practice retelling or summarizing stories with a simple plot sequence.

Retells in sequence but may include too few or too many details. Is ready to identify a character's main problem or motivation in the story and determine the most important plot events connected to it.

Is able to identify one problem and is ready to consider multiple aspects (internal, external) of a story's problems/conflicts and track how they are solved or resolved by the story's end.

Retells sequential narratives and is ready to learn to retell or summarize stories with more complex plots (jumps in time, foreshadowing, flashbacks, etc.), or infer to create theme or idea-based retellings.

Is able to visualize and describe a setting and is ready to infer based on setting(s), such as how setting(s) contributes to mood or impacts characters or plot.

Is ready to analyze stories using prior knowledge of plot archetypes, how a plot follows a literary tradition, or how a writer's plot choices may allude to traditional stories.

Then you might teach...

5.1	Touch, Look, Retell
5.2	Say What's Most Essential
5.3	Think: Who's Speaking?
5.4	Think: Where Am I?
5.5	Map It
5.6	Use Your Senses
5.7	Learn More About the Setting

5.8	Know the Book's Structure: One Story or Multiple Episodes?
5.9	Tap into Title Power
5.10	Let the Blurb Help You
5.11	Preview, Then Predict
5.12	Predict the Plot in a Series Book
5.13	Form Genre-Based Expectations of the Plot
5.14	Use Story Elements to Identify Problem(s)
5.15	Find the Problem by Focusing on Reactions
5.16	Summarize with "Uh-oh ... UH-OH ... Phew!"
5.17	Summarize Based on What a Character Wants
5.18	Summarize with "Somebody ... Wanted ... But ... So ..."
5.19	Record Each Chapter's Main Event

5.20	Identify Internal and External Problems
5.21	Track the Problems as They Snowball
5.22	Notice If Problems Are *Solved* or *Resolved*

5.23	Summarize Based on Theme
5.24	Flag Flashback(s) and/or Backstory
5.25	Use Two (or More!) Plot Mountains
5.26	Follow the Story's Ups and Downs

5.27	Consider the Importance of Setting to the Plot
5.28	Consider How the Setting Impacts the Character
5.29	Mind the (Setting) Gaps
5.30	Use Notes and Features to Prime and Deepen Knowledge
5.31	Analyze Historical Contexts
5.32	Consider Levels of Setting: Micro-, Meso-, Macroenvironment Systems

| 5.33 | Use Basic Story Archetypes to Think About Plot |
| 5.34 | Consider Literary Traditions to Compare and Contrast Plots |

Strategy When you finish reading a book and want to go back to retell, you can touch the first page where something important happened, look at any pictures on the page, and tell what happened. Then turn until you find a page with another important event: touch, look, retell. Keep going through the entire book.

Teaching Tip As written, this strategy will work best for children who are reading and retelling picture books or short beginning reader books. For children reading early chapter books or longer chapter books where there are many more pages, you can modify the lesson by teaching them to "flag" pages with sticky notes where main events occurred (either as they are reading or after reading), then touch the pages with the sticky notes to retell the big events in sequence. Also be sure to check out the strategies to support children with more challenging plot structures later in the chapter (Strategies 5.24, 5.25, and 5.26).

Prompts
- Touch the page. What happened first?
- Look at the picture to remind you of what happened in this part.
- Find the page where you read about the next important event.
- Instead of touching every page, remember, just touch the ones with the big events.

Skills
- **determining importance**
- **retelling**

Progression

Needs support naming and visualizing the setting and/or understanding what's happening on an individual page or a moment in the story, and how events in the plot connect. Could practice retelling or summarizing stories with a simple plot sequence.

Research Link

Using the book as a tactile scaffold may improve the quality of young readers' retelling, as they are free to focus on remembering key events, with the book supporting their retelling of those events in order (Reed & Vaughn, 2012).

Say What's Most Essential

Skills

- **determining importance**
- **summarizing**

Progression

Needs support naming and visualizing the setting and/or understanding what's happening on an individual page or a moment in the story, and how events in the plot connect. Could practice retelling or summarizing stories with a simple plot sequence.

Research Link

First graders who received explicit instruction in identifying key story elements (e.g., characters, setting, and plot) in authentic texts outperformed peers in a control group in identifying important parts of the story and providing longer and more sequentially organized retellings. They were also more likely to report the importance of looking for key elements when reading narratives (Baumann & Bergeron, 1993).

Strategy Name the main character(s). Say where the story takes place. Say one sentence for the beginning of the story. Say one sentence for the middle of the story. Say one sentence for the end of the story.

Lesson Language *Let's retell* My Papi Has a Motorcycle *(Quintero, 2019). Let's start with the characters: "This is a story about a little girl and her father, whom she calls Papi." Now the setting. Well it changes a bit throughout the story, so I'll say it like this: "They start off at their home and go for a ride around their city on his motorcycle." Now the beginning: "In the beginning of the story, her papi comes home from work and they get on his motorcycle to go for a ride." Now the middle. Hm, there are a lot of pages in the middle. What's the most important part? Maybe instead of just picking one page, I can summarize the things they do across the entire middle: "In the middle, they pass lots of familiar places as they ride on the bike, like the market, the murals, the shaved ice shop, her abuelito/a's house, and more." Now the end. How does the whole story end up? "They finish their ride by returning home and enjoying a shaved ice together."*

Teaching Tip This strategy can be used to support children who are reading shorter texts (e.g., picture books, early readers) to retell the whole book and can be used for children reading longer texts (e.g., chapter books or biographies) to retell a chapter.

Prompts

- Start with the characters and the setting.
- Just tell me using one sentence—what is the most important thing that happened in the beginning?
- Can you say that in a shorter way?
- What's the most important thing that happened in the middle?

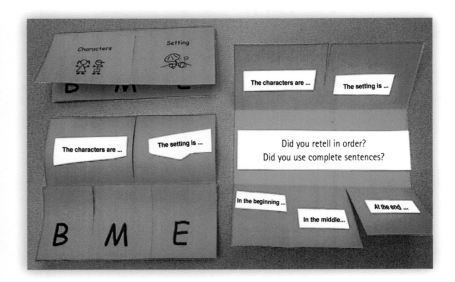

Strategy Create a mental picture of the characters in the scene. As you read a line of dialogue, imagine who said it. Notice when the next sentence of dialogue is on a new line with new opening quotes—visualize the other character in the scene speaking.

Teaching Tip Tracking who is speaking in a scene is critical to understanding what's happening (i.e., the plot events). In some stories, the author won't always indicate who said the dialogue, making it more challenging to follow the action. Visualizing who is speaking and being able to follow back-and-forth dialogue without tags (e.g., *she said, he whispered*) will help readers keep track of what's happening.

Prompts
- How do you know who is speaking?
- Describe what you picture. Can you see the two characters talking? Who is talking in this sentence?
- Let's backtrack to where we last saw a dialogue tag. Take it from there—who do you think is speaking now?
- It will alternate between the two speakers. So who is this?

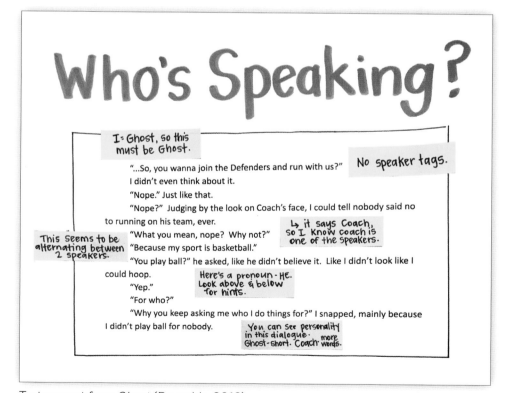

Text excerpt from *Ghost* (Reynolds, 2016).

Skill
- **visualizing**

Progression

Needs support naming and visualizing the setting and/ or understanding what's happening on an individual page or a moment in the story, and how events in the plot connect. Could practice retelling or summarizing stories with a simple plot sequence.

● ○ ○ ○ ○ ○

Research Link

Research suggests that comprehension difficulties often stem from a reader's failure to form clear mental images from text, particularly readers with identified learning disabilities (Bishop & Adams, 1992). However, not all readers automatically create mental images and can therefore benefit from modeling and guiding questions that help them to "see" characters (and other story elements) in their mind's eye (Algozzine & Douville, 2004; McTigue, 2010).

Think: Where Am I?

Skills

- **visualizing**
- **inferring**

Progression

Needs support naming and visualizing the setting and/or understanding what's happening on an individual page or a moment in the story, and how events in the plot connect. Could practice retelling or summarizing stories with a simple plot sequence.

Research Link

Researchers found that instructing less skilled comprehenders to look for clues in a text to establish specific locations and events (that are otherwise implicit) helped them to make a greater number of inferences (Yuill & Joscelyne, 1988).

Strategy Pay close attention to the first sentence(s) of the chapter and any picture there may be to clue you into the setting. Make sure you're clear on where the chapter is taking place. When you start a new chapter, think about how the character got from the setting in one chapter to the setting in the next.

Lesson Language *You may need to slow down your reading at the start of the chapter, at a break within the chapter, or with page turns (in graphic novels) to check the pictures (if there are any) and the words for clues about where the character is, when it is, and to think about how they got there. Since many of you are choosing graphic novels now, let's take a look at how the author of* American Born Chinese *(Yang, 2006) alerts us in pictures and words to setting (place and time) changes. I notice on page 36 they're inside a classroom, and on page 37 they are outside. There is no narration or dialogue telling me about the setting change, so I have to notice it and imagine how they got from one place to another. In this case, I'd guess the bell rang, they had lunch, and now they're out at recess. Other times, I get notes in these boxes in the upper right-hand corner. Look at the top of page 36, it says, "Two months later . . ." so that helps me understand how much time passes between page 35 and page 36.*

Teaching Tip Be sure to introduce children to midchapter scene markers such as a series of asterisks centered on the page or a decorative scroll that indicates the passage of time and the need to employ this strategy in the middle of a chapter. For students reading graphic novels, point out the differences between boxes that include time marker information and speech bubbles that show dialogue.

Prompts

- Reread the first page. Are there any details there about where or when this chapter happens?
- How do you think the characters got from there to here?
- Can you find a sentence that tells you about the setting?
- I noticed you read the clues at the start of the chapter carefully to figure out the new setting!

5.5 Map It

Strategy Sketch a map of the setting(s) based on the details the author provides and what you visualize. When a character travels from place to place, refer to the map to track the character's journey. Add on to your map any time your character goes to new places.

Teaching Tip Pausing to take time to draw a map will be most helpful for students reading books with complex or unfamiliar settings like those in fantasy or historical fiction. In some books, especially fantasy fiction, authors may include a map of the world of the story. For children reading books like this, draw their attention to the map, encourage them to study it before reading, and reference it while reading to stay oriented to the setting and setting changes.

Prompts
- Recall the place(s) you've read about. Draw a map showing all those places.
- Where is this place compared to that one?
- Show me on your map where the character is in this scene.
- From this chapter to this chapter, show me on your map where the character travels.

Progression

Needs support naming and visualizing the setting and/or understanding what's happening on an individual page or a moment in the story, and how events in the plot connect. Could practice retelling or summarizing stories with a simple plot sequence.

Research Link

Narrative cartography, the "graphic representation of the spatial configuration of the world represented by the text" (Ryan, 2020), may support readers to improve connections between the words on the page and their "mental representations" (Kintsch, 1988) by helping them connect the "verbal code" of the text with the "nonverbal code" of mental images (Sadoski & Paivio, 2012).

Use Your Senses

Skill

- **visualizing**

Progression

Needs support naming and visualizing the setting and/or understanding what's happening on an individual page or a moment in the story, and how events in the plot connect. Could practice retelling or summarizing stories with a simple plot sequence.

Research Link

Fifth graders instructed in a Sensory Activation Model strategy (Algozzine & Douville, 2004), which guided them to think about a story using all five senses, were able to construct more images in written responses than their peers who were guided to use visual-only imagery.

Strategy Add to your reading experience by going beyond a basic image of what you *see* as you read. Use your imagination to make the picture (what's illustrated, or what you see in your mind) *move*. Then, ask yourself, "What would I *hear*, *smell*, and *feel* in this place?"

Lesson Language *At the beginning of* New Kid *(Craft, 2019) we can see Jordan at home. He lives in a city in a brownstone house. Those details are literally there in the illustrations. But we can use our imagination to make what we see move, like a movie. And we can go beyond the picture or our mental movie to add other senses. I can imagine* hearing *the sounds of traffic, their neighbor sweeping the front stoop, the dog barking. I can imagine* smelling *the exhaust from the cars. When Jordan pulls up to his new school, Riverdale, my image needs to change. This new place feels more open and spacious than the city. I can imagine* hearing *birds chirping and kids laughing and chatting. Lockers slamming shut. I can imagine* smelling *freshly cut grass. I imagine* feeling *the warm sun and breeze of a September morning.*

Prompts

- What do you see? Can you make your mental picture move?
- Use your imagination. What do you hear? Feel?
- Imagine yourself to be in the place. Use all your senses to describe what it's like there.
- Add in other sensory details.

Strategy Identify the setting (time, place) of your book. Search for more information from other texts, videos, or images, or interview people you know familiar with the time and place. Build your knowledge so as you read, you can add more to your mental picture beyond what the author describes.

Teaching Tip The amount of knowledge a reader has about a topic has a strong correlation to how well they'll be able to comprehend. In well-written stories, the author will do some building of the world (through description in the narrative itself, in an author's note or prologue, and so on), but depending on the reader's prior knowledge, it may or may not be enough for them to visualize and/or understand the significance of the setting and the impact the setting has on characters. When readers choose texts outside of the content you're studying in class, they can search the internet for images and videos, look for picture books, or interview people who've experienced a setting to help them better understand and visualize it.

Prompts
- What are some of the key words about this setting you might use in your search?
- Who do you know in your life who might be able to describe what it was like then/there?
- Think about what you learned about this setting from your research. How can you use that as you read to add to your mental picture?

"My dad was the strongest man I knew, but the Depression brought him to his knees."
(memory of boy at age 12)
from www.allabouthistory.org

Skills
- **building knowledge**
- **visualizing**

Progression

Needs support naming and visualizing the setting and/or understanding what's happening on an individual page or a moment in the story, and how events in the plot connect. Could practice retelling or summarizing stories with a simple plot sequence.

Research Link

In a study of age-related differences in inferencing, researchers found that knowledge that could be easily accessed was twice as likely to be used to make inferences during text comprehension (Barnes, Dennis, & Haefele-Kalvaitis, 1996). Receiving information about the setting has been shown to improve recall and perceived ease in understanding a story (Harris et al., 1980).

Know the Book's Structure: One Story or Multiple Episodes?

Skill

- **synthesizing**

Progression

Retells in sequence but may include too few or too many details. Is ready to identify a character's main problem or motivation in the story and determine the most important plot events connected to it.

Research Link

In a typical narrative plot, a character(s) has to resolve multiple issues—written across episodes—to solve a problem or get what they want. Research has shown that young children often have difficulty seeing the causal connections between these episodes (van den Broek, 1989), indicating that they may benefit from instruction that helps them be more clear.

Strategy After you read the first chapter, think, "Was the main problem solved?" If so, then the next chapter will likely be a new story with the same characters, but a new problem and solution. If the answer is no, then the story will probably continue into the next chapter, and the problem won't be solved until the end.

Lesson Language *You are ready to read chapter books! Look at these great choices I have for you—Mr. Putter and Tabby (Rylant), Frog and Toad (Lobel), Jo Jo Makoons (Quigley), Minnie and Moo (Cazet), Meet Yasmin (Faruqi)—so many series to read! As you get ready to read these books, I want to make you aware of something that can sometimes be tricky. The structure of the books isn't always the same: Sometimes these chapter books will be a collection of different stories. Other times they will be one long story broken up into a few parts. And sometimes, certain titles in the same series are set up in different ways.*

Prompts

- What's the problem in this story?
- You got to the end of this chapter. Was the problem solved?
- You're at the start of a new chapter. Is it a new story or the same one?
- Yes! New problem means new story.

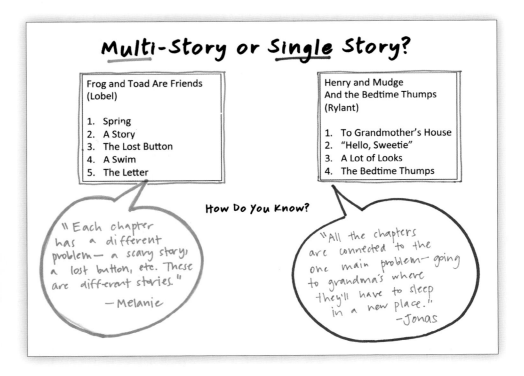

Strategy Read the title (of the book or chapter). Keep the title in mind as you read. Pay close attention to those events that connect back to the title.

Lesson Language _The title is a carefully chosen part of any book. In some chapter books, the title might either announce a main problem very clearly, or connect closely to the main problem. For example,_ Yasmin the Builder _(Faruqi, 2018) is about when Yasmin needs to come up with an idea for a building project at school but she's having a lot of trouble, and the most important events connect to how she solves that problem. This book,_ Rich, _from the Dyamonde Daniel series (Grimes, 2017) is about when Dyamonde wants to get rich by winning a $100 award from her library's poetry contest, but when she learns that her classmate is living in a homeless shelter, her ideas around money change. You can also get help from chapter titles! Take a look at_ Definitely Dominguita: Knight of the Cape _(Jennings, 2021). The first chapter is titled "A Dare," so you should know that by the end of the chapter you'll know what the dare is. Chapter 2 is called "A Problem," so you can check with yourself at the end of that chapter to make sure you know what the problem is!_

Teaching Tip Note that with beginning chapter books, titles will often function as names or labels, as the examples in the Lesson Language suggest. As texts get more complex, titles may leave a reader wondering why the book was titled what it was until the end. These types of titles may invite readers to infer or interpret deeper meaning such as theme or symbolism (see Strategy 7.14 for one way to help readers with this). In more complex chapter books, chapters are less likely to be titled than just simply numbered, and when there are chapter titles, they may be more symbolic or connected to theme (see _Esperanza Rising_ [Ryan, 2000], for example).

Prompts

- Reread the title. Does it say what the problem is?
- How does the character's problem connect to the title?
- Where in the book did you find the problem? Let's check to see if it matches the title.
- Keep the title in mind. What's the most important part of this chapter?

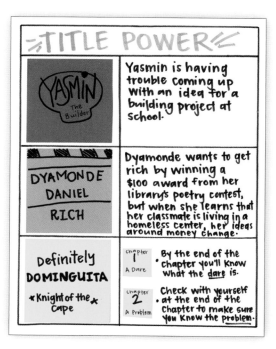

Progression

Retells in sequence but may include too few or too many details. Is ready to identify a character's main problem or motivation in the story and determine the most important plot events connected to it.

Research Link

Searching the title for clues about the plot is the first step (_T_) of a prereading protocol known as TELLS Fact or Fiction (Idol-Maestas, 1985). Then, (_E_) examine and skim pages for clues, (_L_) look for important words, (_L_) look for hard words, (_S_) think about the story settings. In a small study of strong decoders, readers' comprehension improved using the protocol with teacher-guided assistance.

Let the Blurb Help You

Skills

- **determining importance**
- **activating prior knowledge**

Progression

Retells in sequence but may include too few or too many details. Is ready to identify a character's main problem or motivation in the story and determine the most important plot events connected to it.

Research Link

Reading the blurb is one method of previewing a text and providing students with key concepts, vocabulary, and/ or conceptual frameworks that can help them understand new material. In a study comparing various prereading strategies with fifth graders, researchers found that when teachers provide students with information that helps them understand a text, comprehension improves (Dole et al., 1991).

Strategy Read the blurb on the back cover or inside flap. Ask yourself, "Are there clues about the genre or structure of the text? Are there hints about what the most important issues are in this story? Do I have a sense of what problems the main character might face?"

Teaching Tip A single blurb won't have all these types of information. Study a variety of them with your students to help them notice and name the types of information often found in book blurbs.

Text Structure or Format	Figure out how the book might be organized. For example, if it says "five wonderful stories . . . ," then you know you're going to read a collection of different stories in one book. You might also get information about other ways the structure is unique, such as whether the story has alternating narrators or if it's a graphic novel, for example.
Genre	Look for genre or text type words such as "In this suspenseful page-turner . . ." or "Historical fiction at its finest . . ." and remember what you know about books in that genre.
Main Problem	Look for key phrases like "Find out what happens when (character) has to deal with . . ." or "(Character) has a lot to be unhappy about . . ." that will highlight the problem(s).
Theme	Sometimes the book's blurb (or the review quotes) will come right out and tell you what some of the important ideas in the book might be (e.g., "A heartwarming story about the importance of being kind to others").

Prompts

- How will the information in the blurb help?
- What will the structure of the book be, based on what you read?
- Do you have any ideas about the main problem the character will face?
- Let's talk about what a theme in this book might be, based on the blurb.

Strategy Preview the book (title, cover, blurb, first couple of pages). Think about what you already know (about the topic, genre, series) that can help you understand this story. Make predictions about how the plot might unfold.

Lesson Language *Even if a book is new to you, you might already know more about it than you expect! Take a look at the title and the picture on the cover. Read the blurb on the back and/or the first couple of pages. Think: Does the book include places you have visited, or places similar to places you know? Does the story seem to include one of your hobbies, or something else that you like to do? Does this book remind you of books you have read before? What do you know about books in this genre? Have you read another book in the series? Using what you already know about how a book "like this" might go, make predictions about the plot.*

Teaching Tip Readers do not approach a book as a blank slate—they bring a wealth of experience to their reading: personal, cultural, and their accumulated experience with stories. Helping them activate what they already know will help them to better understand the text they are about to read.

Prompts

- Preview the book. What do you know from prior knowledge that may come in handy when reading this book?
- You've read others in the series, right? What do you know about how those plots go that might help you predict this one?
- Think about what you know about the genre to help you predict.

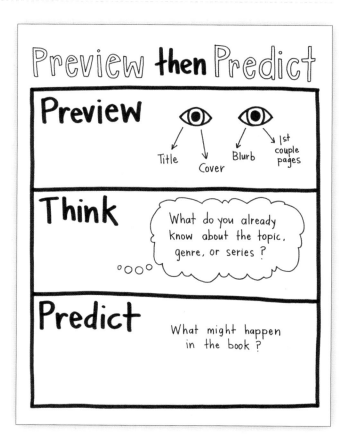

Skills

- **activating prior knowledge**
- **inferring**

Progression

Retells in sequence but may include too few or too many details. Is ready to identify a character's main problem or motivation in the story and determine the most important plot events connected to it.

Research Link

In a small but classic study, Hansen (1981) supported second graders to make inferences by making them aware—via a visual metaphor—that using their prior knowledge was an effective tool to understand new text. Children were asked about possible prior experiences, and then prompted to hypothesize about something similar happening in a story. Students in the experimental group outperformed their peers on an assessment of comprehension.

Predict the Plot in a Series Book

Skills

- **activating prior knowledge**
- **inferring**

Progression

Retells in sequence but may include too few or too many details. Is ready to identify a character's main problem or motivation in the story and determine the most important plot events connected to it.

● ● ○ ○ ○ ○

Research Link

Transitional chapter book series offer many benefits to newly independent readers, including grade-appropriate vocabulary, supportive illustrations, a single plot, and short chapters (Liang & Lowe, 2018; McGill-Franzen & Ward, 2018). Their formulaic plots make them easy to understand and remember, while still allowing students to make inferences and practice other important comprehension skills (Greenlee, Monson, & Taylor, 1996; McGill-Franzen & Ward, 2018).

Strategy When you start reading a new book in a series, think, "What do I already know about what might happen in this story from reading other books in this same series?" Think about the types of problems and/or how a character solves the problem. Predict how this new book in the series will go.

Lesson Language *One of the great things about reading in a series is that a lot is the same from book to book, so a new book can feel as familiar as an old friend. Many of the characters are the same, and the plots often follow a similar pattern. When you read a new book in a series, you should use what you already know about series books to help you. For example, if you're reading a book from the My Furry Foster Family series (Michiko Florence), you should expect that in every book Kaita will be fostering a different animal, and she needs to work through problems unique to the animal to help them find forever homes. Knowing how the plots of other books in the series go will help you understand where in the story arc you are in your current read. This can help you to figure out what's most important, to retell what you've read so far, and to predict what might come next.*

Prompts

- How might the plot of this one go based on what you know about the other books in this series?
- Tell me the gist of the plot from the other books you've read in this series.
- What's similar about all the books in this series?
- So you know the other books in the series tend to __. How does that help you think about the plot in this one from the same series?

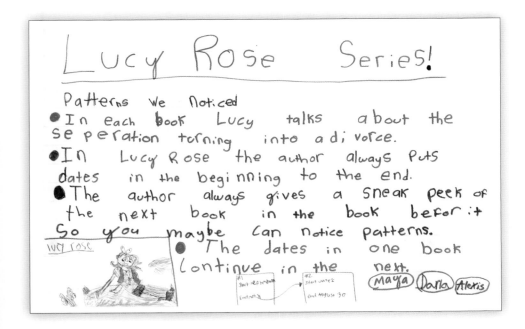

Strategy Identify the genre of the book (from the title, the blurb, a review, and so on). Think, "What do I know about how the plots of stories in this genre tend to go?" As you read, connect events in this specific story to your general expectations based on genre.

Teaching Tip The general genre knowledge readers use with this strategy can help them get ready to read, track plot events as they read, and summarize the most important events after they've finished the book.

Prompts

- The blurb says this is a ___. What do you know about the plot of that kind of story?
- Say, "This is a [genre] so I expect . . ."
- Use what you know to help you predict.

Skills

- **activating prior knowledge**
- **inferring**

Progression

Retells in sequence but may include too few or too many details. Is ready to identify a character's main problem or motivation in the story and determine the most important plot events connected to it.

Research Link

In a study with students in grades K through 2, researchers found that even very young children had a working knowledge of genre, with a particularly well-developed knowledge of the features of narrative texts. Looking across the age groups, they found that students develop more knowledge of genre forms and functions over time (Kamberelis, 1999; Kamberelis & Bovino, 1999).

Use Story Elements to Identify Problem(s)

Skill

- **determining importance**

Progression

Retells in sequence but may include too few or too many details. Is ready to identify a character's main problem or motivation in the story and determine the most important plot events connected to it.

Research Link

An awareness of story elements gives readers a common "story grammar" they can use to have more precise discussions and to develop deeper understandings about how these elements interact and influence each other in a story (Dymock, 2007).

Strategy Think through story elements to find the problem(s). Ask yourself: Is there a problem one character has with another? Is there a problem brought on by the setting? Is there a problem based on something the character wants but can't have? Is there a problem connected to a theme or social issue within the story?

Teaching Tip This lesson could be modified for those reading beginning chapter books where problems are usually one-dimensional and simple, and for those students reading higher-level chapter books, where problems are often complex and multidimensional. The example in the chart below was created by students who were reading Pam Munoz Ryan's (2000) *Esperanza Rising*, which is a text typically read at the end of fifth/beginning of sixth grade. Note the number of problems!

Prompts

- Where or when does the story take place? Does that seem to be adding to the problem?
- What is a theme in the story? Is the character's problem connected to that?
- Name a character. Does that person contribute to the problem?
- Is there more than one problem? Think about setting, character, theme.

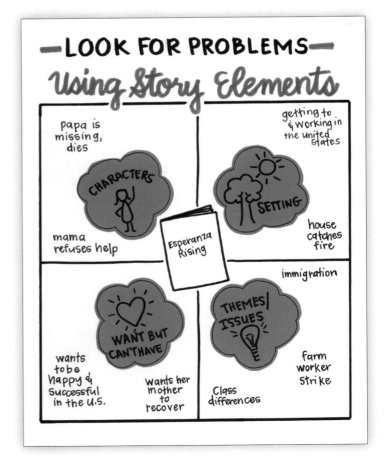

Strategy To find a problem, notice moments when the character acts, feels, or reacts as if there is a problem. Reread the scene to better understand what caused the problem.

Lesson Language *Problems help to focus the plot of the story and help you retell based on what's most important. If you pay close attention, you can see (in the pictures) and read when the character has a problem. They may look upset (or sad or worried). The narrator might describe a character's feeling ("She was so upset" or "He couldn't believe his bad luck"). Or there may be things the character says that let you know he or she is having a problem. For example, in* Ty's Travels: Lab Magic *(Lyons, 2022), we see the main character, Ty, disappointed that he can't go inside the lab at the science museum. The illustrator draws him with a frown on his face and his eyes closed, his mom comforting him. The text reads, "Oh no! Momma sees a sign. Ty is too little. Momma hugs him" (p. 12). Both the pictures and words (especially, "Oh no!") help us figure out that Ty is having a problem in this moment of the story.*

Prompts
- How's the character reacting?
- Check the character's face in the picture.
- Does the character say anything to show his or her feeling?
- Yes, that's something the character says. What does that reaction tell you about what he or she is feeling?

Skill
- **determining importance**

Progression
Retells in sequence but may include too few or too many details. Is ready to identify a character's main problem or motivation in the story and determine the most important plot events connected to it.

Research Link
Younger readers tend to focus on *what* is happening in a story rather than *why* (Stein & Levine, 1990). Research has shown that focusing on the perspectives of characters helps readers to better identify the story's central problem (Emery, 1996).

Find the Problem by Focusing on ——Reactions——

Ty has a frown on his face and his eyes are closed.

"Oh no! Momma sees a sign. Ty is too little. Momma hugs him."

TY'S TRAVELS
Lab Magic

Yasmin, already feeling scared, tries to hide the problem by shoving it into her desk. Then realizes a new problem.

The next morning at school, the students showed their homework.

Yasmin shoved her blank paper into her desk.

At lunch she realized she'd forgotten her lunch box. "Oh no!" she wailed. Her day was getting worse and worse.

YASMIN
The Writer

Skills

- **determining importance**
- **summarizing**
- **synthesizing**

Progression

Retells in sequence but may include too few or too many details. Is ready to identify a character's main problem or motivation in the story and determine the most important plot events connected to it.

Research Link

In a classic study on story structure, Mandler and Johnson (1977) found that readers can make sense of complex twists and turns in a story as they are reading it, but when it comes time to recall that story, they tend to simplify it using familiar story schema. This suggests a graphic organizer (such as a story mountain showing rising and falling action) could help readers remember a story's structure.

Strategy When you summarize, think about the problem (uh-oh), how the problem gets worse (UH-OH), and how the problem gets solved (phew!). Use a story mountain with these parts to summarize, touching the parts of the mountain as you go.

Lesson Language *If I were going to summarize the true story* The Floating Field: How a Group of Thai Boys Built Their Own Soccer Field *(Riley, 2021), I could start off with the uh-oh—the problem. In this story, the problem is that a group of soccer-loving boys in a Thai fishing village only had a sandbar to practice on, and when the tide came in their "field" was underwater. They decided to build their own field, but then things got more challenging—UH-OH! Gathering materials was hard, they were building without a plan, the boards and nails they used bent and split, and the villagers called them crazy. But then they successfully finished their floating field, the villagers started to cheer them on, and they got to play in a tournament (phew!).*

Teaching Tip A straightforward *problem → problem worsens → solution* plot structure is most common in beginning chapter books. As texts get more sophisticated, characters often have multiple problems, different problems emerge over the course of the story, and problems may be multidimensional. Following the plot may be further complicated by going backward and forward through time via flashbacks and/or foreshadowing (or even flashforwards), as well as multiple plot lines. See Strategies 5.24–5.26 for ideas that align to features of these more complex texts.

Prompts

- Start with the uh-oh. What's the problem?
- Talk about how the problem gets worse.
- Where are you on the story mountain now? Point to it.
- And how does the story end up? What's the phew?

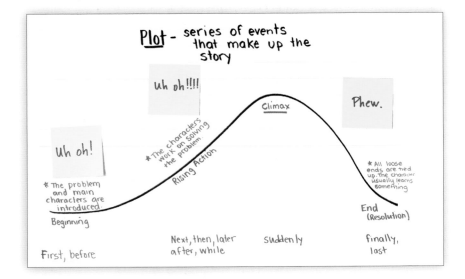

Summarize Based on What a Character Wants

Strategy Think about what the character really wants. Then, think about the most important events (in each scene or each chapter) that connect back to what the character wants. Summarize by saying the events in the order they happened.

Lesson Language *Sometimes it's hard to focus your summary when there are so many events! If you think about what the character wants as the driver of the plot, it can help you summarize with more focus. For example, early on in* Fauja Singh Keeps Going: The True Story of the Oldest Person to Ever Run a Marathon *(Singh, 2020), we learn that Fauja "longed to join [his friends] when they ran and jumped" and played, but he was too weak. Knowing that the main thing he wants is to be strong and active, we can sift through the events to tell only those that connect to it—that he took his first steps at age 5, that he practiced working and walking on his farm until age 15 when he could finally walk a mile. We learn that at age 81, he moved to England and was lonely and bored and noticed people running on TV and decided to give it a try. He loved running outside, exploring his new town, and making friends, and then at age 89 he became one of the oldest people to ever complete the London Marathon. Then, he ran the New York City marathon at 93, and the Toronto marathon at age 100! There are other events that help tell the story like when he ate daal for dinner, or when he met his coach, but when you're briefly summarizing and need to pick just the most important events, stick to those that connect to what the character wants most.*

Prompts
- What does this character want?
- You are telling me everything; what is most important, based on what the character wants?
- Now that you've identified what the character wants, list events in order that connect to that goal.
- Does that event connect back to what the character wants?

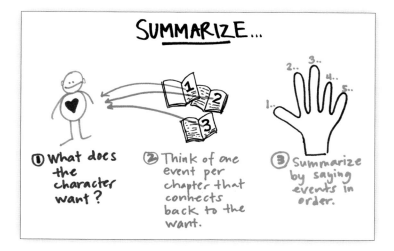

Skills
- **determining importance**
- **summarizing**
- **synthesizing**

Progression

Retells in sequence but may include too few or too many details. Is ready to identify a character's main problem or motivation in the story and determine the most important plot events connected to it.

Research Link

A number of scholars define a narrative as a story with characters, settings, and events, with each event motivated by a character's goal (Bower & Rinck, 1999; Mandler & Johnson, 1977; Richards & Singer, 2001; van den Broek et al., 2003). Readers who clearly see the connections between the events and the characters' goals can more easily visualize, understand, and remember the story (Bower & Rinck, 1999).

- **determining importance**
- **summarizing**
- **synthesizing**

Progression

Retells in sequence but may include too few or too many details. Is ready to identify a character's main problem or motivation in the story and determine the most important plot events connected to it.

Research Link

In a narrative, the protagonist usually has a main goal, but this typically involves one or more subgoals (van den Broek & Trabasso, 1986). In a study with third and fifth graders, students tended to remember the main goal, which often resulted in retelling other story events in relation to that goal and were more successful remembering external actions compared with internal motivations (Goldman & Varnhagen, 1986).

Strategy Think first, "Who is the main character?" Then, "What does the main character want?" Then, "What gets in his or her way?" And finally, "How does it end up?" Be sure the ending connects back in some way to the problem.

Lesson Language *Remember* Islandborn *by Junot Díaz (2018)? Watch me as I summarize this story by thinking, "Somebody wanted ... but ... so ..." Somebody ... the main character is Lola. What did she want? She wants to be able to share about her country with her class. But? What was the problem? Everyone else in the class seems excited and ready to share about their countries, but Lola can't remember anything because she left her island when she was very young. So? What does she do about it? How does it end up? Well, I need to make sure I connect back to what she wanted (to share) and the obstacle (she can't remember). So, what she did was she interviewed members of her community and family. From the stories they told, she remembered and imagined and was able to share the island that is a part of her with her class.*

Teaching Tip You have likely noticed that this strategy is a combination of sorts of Strategies 5.16 and 5.17. I've purposely included three variations of strategies related to summarizing plot because different students will respond to different scaffolds and because different stories might lend themselves to slightly different approaches to summarizing. I've also intentionally included a variety of story types/genres in the three Lesson Language examples—fiction, biography, historical account. Any of these three strategies could work with any of these genres.

Prompts

- What does the character want?
- What is one obstacle to the character getting what they want?
- Connect the ending to what the character wants.
- That ending clearly connects to what the character wants.

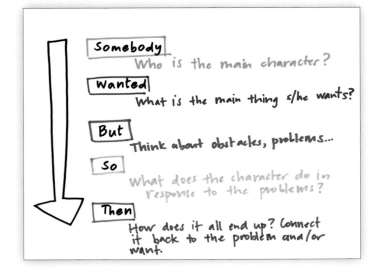

Record Each Chapter's Main Event

Strategy Each chapter will have at least one important event connected to a problem. To remember the event, stop and jot about it or sketch it on a sticky note at the end of each chapter (sometimes you can use the chapter title to help). When you pick the book back up to keep reading, you can scan all your jots or sketches to remind yourself of what you read.

Teaching Tip For this strategy, you can offer students sticky notes, a notebook, or a paper with spots to jot after each chapter, like the student work sample on this page. Some teachers prefer sticky notes because the notes stay next to where the thinking occurred, and you or the student can quickly reread them within the context of the page. Other teachers prefer paper notes because you can easily collect and review them before tomorrow's lessons. Still others like students to use a notebook so they can refer back to their work and it stays neatly in one place. Adapt this lesson to your style!

Prompts

- Check the chapter title.
- What's the most important thing that happened?
- If you had to say the most important thing in one sentence, what would it be?
- Reread your sticky notes to remember the most important event from each chapter.

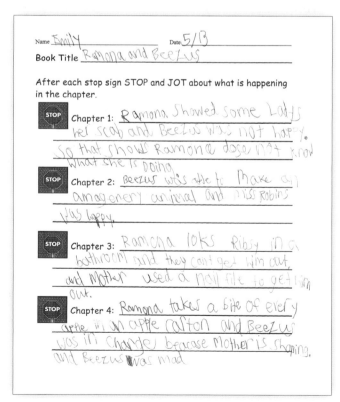

Skill

- **determining importance**

Progression

Retells in sequence but may include too few or too many details. Is ready to identify a character's main problem or motivation in the story and determine the most important plot events connected to it.

Research Link

In a review of research on main ideas and events, Williams (1988) points out that students are not often provided with specific "relevance signals" (van Dijk, 1979) that cue a reader to focus on certain aspects of the text. Younger readers may be more attracted to details that have personal meaning or are interesting and therefore need additional support to focus on key events (Williams, 1988).

Skills

- **determining importance**
- **synthesizing**

Progression

Is able to identify one problem and is ready to consider multiple aspects (internal, external) of a story's problems/conflicts and track how they are solved or resolved by the story's end.

Research Link

In a review of research, Feathers (2002) cited multiple findings reporting that young children tend to retell stories as a sequence of actions, often omitting motives and other internal states. However, although young children do not automatically include the thinking of characters in their spontaneous retellings, they can answer questions about internal responses, if asked directly (Stein & Glenn, 1979).

Strategy Watch out for problems that happen inside a character's heart and mind (internal) and problems a character experiences when things happen to them (external). Jot them down when you see them. Think about how they are connected.

Lesson Language *In* Merci Suárez Changes Gears *(Medina, 2018), Merci deals with lots of external problems and obstacles (other characters, her circumstances, events beyond her control, challenges with the setting), and the author helps us understand how they connect to Merci's internal problems (her feelings, concerns, worries, or conflicting thoughts). For example, at school, she feels like an outsider because she's a scholarship student while her classmates are rich and privileged. The circumstances outside of her control—being less wealthy than peers—are an external obstacle, and how it makes her feel othered is something she feels internally. Merci also feels a lot of pressure—an internal problem—as she struggles to maintain the B+ she needs to keep her scholarship when she has so many other things to do (sports, a job, help with her ailing grandfather)—an external problem. Each of these problems connects to multiple other events in the story. When you're on the lookout for both the internal and external sides of the problems, it can help you track all the important events in the plot.*

Prompts

- To find the main character's external problems, consider how other characters are impacting them or what circumstances are outside of their control.
- To find internal problems, consider how the character is acting, reacting, thinking, or feeling.
- How do those problems connect?
- The internal problems are __. The external problems are __.

Xiomara:

Internal *Whats bothering her on the inside?*	External *Whats bothering her on the outside?*
- she feels like she takes up too much space	- she feels like she takes up too much space because everyone is constantly telling her to be smaller, especially her mami
- she feels angry and upset at her mami	- she feels this way because her mami won't let her have any freedom
- she feels guilty	- she feels guilty because she isn't the daughter her mami wants her to be
- she feels upset and frustrated	- she feels upset and frustrated because her mami burns her book of all the poems shes ever written, and she grounds Xiomara for disobeying her.

Strategy Notice one main, central problem the character is dealing with. Track how other problems add onto or connect back to the main problem.

Lesson Language *When one action or event causes many other similar actions or events, we call it "snowballing" because it's like a snowball that just keeps gathering more snow, getting bigger as it rolls on. In books, characters' problems often seem to snowball as more and more details and events keep adding to their problems. For example, in Merci Suárez Changes Gears (Medina, 2018), we learn early on that Merci is being bullied by Edna Santos at school. As we continue reading, we can track the details and events that add to this problem, making it even bigger: the differences in social class between Edna and Merci, Edna's jealousy when a boy she likes starts paying attention to Merci, and even the distraction of the bullying that Merci doesn't have time to deal with.*

Prompts

- What is a main, central problem the character is dealing with? (With another character? With the setting?)
- Is there another problem that happens with that character, in that setting?
- How does that smaller problem relate to the main problem?
- In each new scene, check to see if any new problems emerge that connect to the main one you identified.

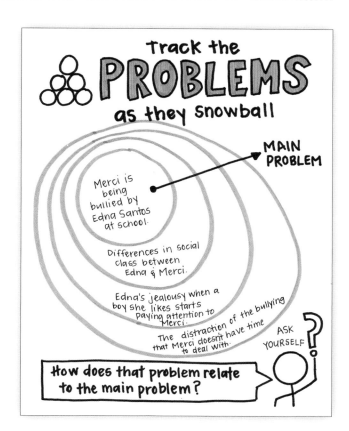

Skills

- **determining importance**
- **synthesizing**

Progression

Is able to identify one problem and is ready to consider multiple aspects (internal, external) of a story's problems/conflicts and track how they are solved or resolved by the story's end.

Research Link

To understand a story as a coherent whole, readers must see the "causal network" that connects its sequence of key events (van den Broek & Trabasso, 1986). Students with certain identified learning disabilities may need additional support in seeing these connections. Compared with their peers, their retellings often include fewer goal-related events (Renz et al., 2003).

Notice If Problems Are Solved *or* Resolved

Skills

- **determining importance**
- **synthesizing**

Progression

Is able to identify one problem and is ready to consider multiple aspects (internal, external) of a story's problems/conflicts and track how they are solved or resolved by the story's end.

Research Link

Postdiction (i.e., thinking back over what you've read to see if predictions matched outcomes) has a powerful effect on both comprehension and perceived enjoyment. In one study, researchers found that college students judged high-surprise endings to be interesting if the predicted problem was solved, but not if the ending was predictable or if the outcome was merely resolved (Iran-Nejad, 1987).

Strategy At the end of the story, remind yourself about the main problem the character has been dealing with. Think about how events at the end of the story connect to the main problem. Consider if the problem was *solved* (all fixed!) or *resolved* (wrapped up in some way) at the end.

Teaching Tip In beginning chapter books, problems are generally completely solved at the end. But as novels get more complex, and the problems the characters deal with become more complex, too, it's likely that some of the issues are *resolved* rather than *solved*. Take a look at the chart to see examples from *Yasmin the Builder* (Faruqi, 2019), *Ty's Travels: Lab Magic* (Lyons, 2022), and *Merci Suárez Changes Gears* (Medina, 2018).

Prompts

- What main problem(s) from throughout the story are resolved or solved at the end?
- Would you call this ending a *solution* (all problems are solved!) or *resolution* (things get wrapped up)? Why?
- List all the problems the main character dealt with. How does the author wrap up those problems at the end of the story?
- Remember, a resolution might be *internal:* the character grew, accepted, or changed because of it.

✓ Solved or Resolved?

	PROBLEM	SOLUTION/RESOLUTION
Yasmin The Builder	Yasmin can't figure out what to build.	She gets an idea and is celebrated. **S**
Ty's Travels	Ty is upset because he is too young to participate in the lab at the science museum.	His family makes him one at home where he can do all the experiments he missed out on. **S**
Merci Suárez Changes Gears	Merci's grandfather, Lolo, has Alzheimer's and the family is keeping the secret from her.	**R** She accepts the diagnosis. He's not miraculously better - that unfortunately isn't possible - but she comes to terms with it and grows and changes and matures through the process.

Summarize Based on Theme

Strategy Stop and ask yourself, "What was this story *really* about?" Make your answer to that question the first sentence in your summary. Next, tell just the events that best support that idea. Finish with a closing statement about how the events connect back to what's most important.

Teaching Tip Consider providing an annotated summary during your lesson like the example from *After the Fall* (Santat, 2017) below. To be successful with this strategy, students will need to be able to state a message, lesson, or theme. You can see Chapter 7 for ideas on how to help students with this at various levels of text difficulty.

Prompts

- What is this story *really* about?
- What parts of the story best support that idea? Tell them in order.
- That happened, but does that support your idea?
- Only tell the parts that go with your idea.

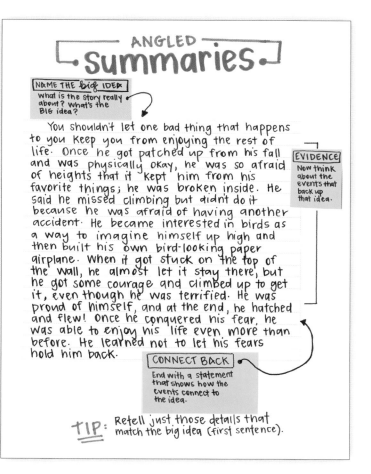

Skills

- **summarizing**
- **determining importance**
- **synthesizing**
- **inferring**

Progression

Retells sequential narratives and is ready to learn to retell or summarize stories with more complex plots (jumps in time, foreshadowing, flashbacks, etc.) or infer to create theme or idea-based retellings.

Research Link

The identification of themes can be challenging for students, partly because the definition is often fuzzy. This fuzziness can be clarified by offering a structure tied to story grammar (Williams, 1988). In a research program spanning many decades, Williams and colleagues have helped students of various ages and abilities focus on what is important in a text by means of a "theme scheme" (Williams, 2005).

Skills

- **inferring**
- **determining importance**

Progression

Retells sequential narratives and is ready to learn to retell or summarize stories with more complex plots (jumps in time, foreshadowing, flashbacks, etc.) or infer to create theme or idea-based retellings.

Research Link

Research indicates that readers do not remember stories in the order they are written, but rather reorder the events into a linear fashion (Prouty, 1986). However, one study found that this ability improves over time (Stein, 1978), possibly indicating that older students are more aware of nonlinear storytelling techniques and are therefore better prepared to recognize and process them (Stein & Glenn, 1979).

Strategy Notice when events in the story flash back to the past to give background or where a narrator offers backstory. Flag the flashbacks and/or backstory with sticky notes in your book. Think (and maybe jot) about what is revealed or what you're learning about the character(s) from the moment, and/or consider why the author may have included it.

Teaching Tip Flashbacks alter the movement through time in a story, and some students may need additional support noticing when the scene within a scene jumps back in time. Point out that some authors will alert you to a change in year. In other cases, flashbacks might be in a different tense than the main narrative, in a different font, or be marked with a chapter or section break. In still other cases, a flashback could begin with the narrator saying something like, "I remember when . . ." Still other times, a reader will need to pay attention to the age of the character in each scene, and notice when the character's age is less than their age in the main narrative to infer it's a memory or flashback. Backstory, on the other hand, is often a moment of exposition where the narrator explains something to the reader that gives additional information.

Prompts

- Show me where the flashback begins.
- Look for dates, a change in age, memories, or dream sequences.
- Is that part of the story moving forward, or is the narrator giving you backstory?
- Think about what you now know about the character from the flashback or backstory. How does that make you think about the story in a new way?

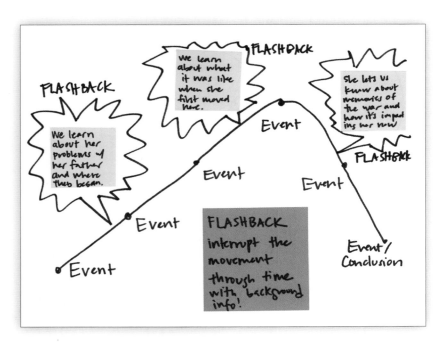

Strategy Keep two (or more!) "plot mountain" graphic organizers in front of you as you read. As you come to a new, significant event, think about which plot that event aligns to. Add it to that plot mountain. Use the plot mountains to help you retell.

Teaching Tip Alert children to various ways that authors unfold two (or more) plots across a book. Sometimes, they may notice that the character has a journey or trajectory in a couple of different *places* (see the *Joey Pigza* [Gantos, 1998] example in the figure below). Other times, there may be two (or more) *time periods* (*A Long Walk to Water* [Park, 2010] has narratives from both 2003 and 1983 in each chapter, with a clear heading, font color, and style difference to help the reader keep track). Still other stories alternate storytellers from chapter to chapter, where the plot usually moves forward through time, but from different characters' perspectives.

Prompts
- Notice the dates at the start of each chapter. How does that help you track the plots?
- Think about what event that new event connects to.
- Add the event to your plot mountain.
- Retell the events in the order they happen in [setting]. Now retell the events that happen in [setting].

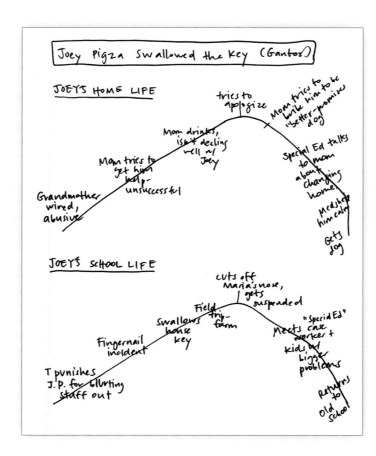

Skills
- **determining importance**
- **retelling**

Progression

Retells sequential narratives and is ready to learn to retell or summarize stories with more complex plots (jumps in time, foreshadowing, flashbacks, etc.) or infer to create theme or idea-based retellings.

Research Link

Fifth-grade students who used a graphic organizer to visually represent the key elements of a narrative were able to recall more elements of a text than their peers in a control group (Reutzel, 1985).

Skills

- **determining importance**
- retelling

Progression

Retells sequential narratives and is ready to learn to retell or summarize stories with more complex plots (jumps in time, foreshadowing, flashbacks, etc.) or infer to create theme or idea-based retellings.

Research Link

In an overview of story maps, Davis and McPherson (1989) provide evidence from multiple studies that the use of a graphic representation for story elements and their relationships has a positive effect on reading comprehension.

Strategy Take note of (and draw) the "ups" (striving toward a goal, attempting to solve a problem) and the "downs" (new problems or obstacles, or an unfolding event or resolution). Use your line drawing to help you remember the story's ups and downs to retell the story.

Lesson Language *Some stories follow a simple plot structure, sometimes called an arc or mountain. We start drawing the arc when we learn about a problem the character has or something they want. The arc then moves up as events and obstacles follow that complicate things, until the plot reaches a turning point or climax (the top of the arc or mountain), and then the line moves back down as the plot is resolved. However, some stories have a plot that unfolds with many ups and downs along the way, sometimes in each chapter. One way to track this is to draw a downward line each time the character faces a problem, an upward line as they are working to solve the problem or get what they want, and another downward line as the problem is resolved. You can take quick notes on the plot events that correspond to each up and down to help you review, remember, and retell the story.*

Prompts

- You noticed a new problem. How will you show that on your plot diagram?
- Will that be an up line or down line?
- Now that you've got a line drawing of the plot, use that diagram to help you remember and retell the story.

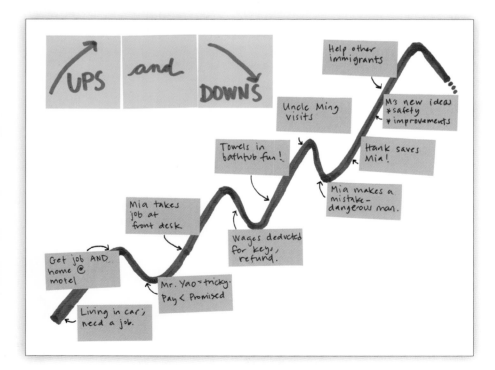

Consider the Importance of Setting to the Plot

Strategy Think about the setting of the story. Ask yourself, "Does the setting play an important role in the events of the story? If the story were set someplace else, or at a different time, how would it be different?"

Lesson Language *In Kelly Yang's* Front Desk *(2018), Mia and her family are recent immigrants from China who have settled in California. The fact that they are here, in this particular place and time in the United States, in the 1980s, impacts their lives in so many ways—the tension of holding on to Chinese culture and language while also fitting into life in the United States, the economic challenges of being an immigrant, the racism. The motel where they live and work also represents so much—opportunity, home, community—and impacts them in so many ways. The setting is such an important part of everything that happens in the story. Now, contrast that to one of the many set-in-a-school stories we have in our classroom library such as* Yasmin the Builder. *Yes, it matters that it's in school, but it really could be just about any school, anywhere—it's just background and doesn't really matter to the plot.*

Prompts
- How important is the setting?
- Describe the setting. How does it impact the story?
- Let's imagine some other places the story might be set. Would that change the story?
- Can you name a specific example of how the setting is important to the story?

Skills
- **visualizing**
- **inferring**
- **determining importance**

Progression

Is able to visualize and describe a setting and is ready to infer based on setting(s), such as how setting(s) contributes to mood or impacts characters or plot.

Research Link

In a large study with sixth graders, participants read stories with variable settings to explore if they influenced reading comprehension. Comprehension scores on locally set stories were higher than either foreign-set stories or those with a nonspecific location (Craddock, 1981).

Consider How the Setting Impacts the Character

Skills

- **visualizing**
- **inferring**

Progression

Is able to visualize and describe a setting and is ready to infer based on setting(s), such as how setting(s) contributes to mood or impacts characters or plot.

● ● ● ● ● ○

Strategy When the author describes the setting, slow down. Picture the details the author is giving you about the time and place. Notice what's happening in the time or place alongside what a character thinks or feels. Think, "How does the setting impact the character?"

Lesson Language *In* A Long Walk to Water *(2010), Linda Sue Park offers lots of descriptive details about the setting and what life is like for villagers in Sudan—a place many readers in the United States may know little about. For example, details such as "there was only heat, the sun already baking the air" and "dust" (p. 1) "spiky plants" and "thorns" (p. 8) deepen our understanding of the character's struggle on her journey, the pain and exhaustion, as she walks for hours during the dry season to get the water she and her family need. This description is in stark contrast to the moment when she arrives at the pond. With descriptions like, "the horizon gained color . . . from hazy gray to olive green" and "so much life" and "many kinds of birds, all flap and twitter and caw" (p. 14), we can sense the momentary relief this setting brings her.*

Prompts

- Show me where the author describes the setting in detail.
- Say back the details you learned about the setting. Now describe how it's impacting the character.
- Why might the setting be important?

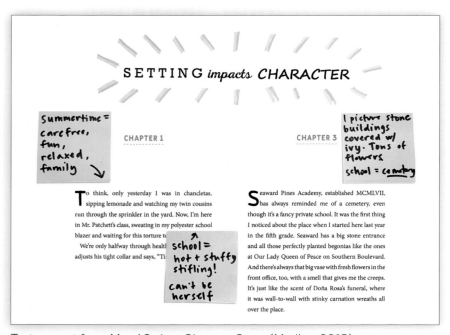

Text excerpt from *Merci Suárez Changes Gears* (Medina, 2018).

Research Link

According to Dual Coding Theory (Sadoski & Paivio, 2012), a mental representation of a text includes both verbal information and nonverbal information from all five senses. Rather than a static image, the mental representation constantly changes as new information is added, such as when a character moves from place to place.

Mind the (Setting) Gaps

Strategy Sometimes you'll find yourself slightly confused or just curious about the setting. When you are, think, "What do I know about this time and place? What questions do I have?" Jot notes. Then, read on to try to answer your questions.

Lesson Language *When you read more challenging texts, often ones that are set in made-up places or in historical times, you'll find that there are gaps in your understanding. Sometimes, the author will assume you know something or will slowly give you more information as the story goes on. This means you don't have all the information up front, and instead, you need to construct it yourself. Keeping track of what you know, and what questions you have, will help you sort between what's confusing and what's clear in your mind. As you read on in the story, you should be able to respond to or answer your questions based on what you're learning in the text.*

Teaching Tip This is, essentially, a KWL strategy, angled to support a student's understanding of setting. They can use the same procedure to help self-monitor, question, and clarify confusion with *any* story element.

Prompts

- What do you know about the time and place?
- What details did the author give you? What are you curious about? What's confusing?
- Think about what's important to know, that you haven't learned yet.
- I noticed you followed up on a question. That's going to help you understand!

Stacy

All the Way to the Top
By Annette Bay Pimentel

Fact	Question	Response
:Jennifer Keelan-Chaffins was born with Cerebral Palsy.	Why were People so cruel isth to People with disabilities?	I think everyone is equal, no matter if they have disabilities.
:Jennifer Keelan-Chaffins Participated in her first Protest, Arizona, in 1987	Why didn't her neighborhood School let her, and her friends eat at the Cafeteria?	
+Her School says that "Jennifer doesn't belong there, because she uses a wheel chair.		
		When she went to her New School her classmates were so confused, because she has a wheel chair.
		She got bullied, and felt left out.
		This makes me think she doesn't give up on anything.

Skills
- **activating prior knowledge**
- **determining importance**
- **inferring**
- **self-monitoring**

Progression

Is able to visualize and describe a setting and is ready to infer based on setting(s), such as how setting(s) contributes to mood or impacts characters or plot.

Research Link

In an article summarizing early cognitive work on story structure, Bower (1976) shared findings that the more straightforward a plot is, the easier it is to remember. Because a complicated story is more challenging to recall, an external memory aid, such as note taking, can be helpful.

Use Notes and Features to Prime and Deepen Knowledge

Skill

• building knowledge

Progression

Is able to visualize and describe a setting and is ready to infer based on setting(s), such as how setting(s) contributes to mood or impacts characters or plot.

Strategy Look for extra features such as historical notes, author notes, or maps in your book—sometimes they're in the beginning, sometimes they're at the end. Don't skip them! Spend time with these features before or after the story, depending on their placement.

Lesson Language *When you have little or no background knowledge about the time period, look for historical notes and features to give you background. For example, in* A Long Walk to Water *(Park, 2010), the author includes a map at the beginning of the book as a helpful reference to orient you as you read—and since it comes before the story, you should study it before you begin reading. At the end of the book, she includes an author's note that explains more about the Sudanese Civil War in the 1980s and the peace accord that ended it, provides information about other military conflicts in Africa, and shares about the Water for Sudan nonprofit started by Salva, one of the book's main characters. The additional information comes after you've already read about these events and the character in the book itself and are almost certainly wanting to know more.*

Teaching Tip Though the example in the Lesson Language is for historical fiction, you'll often find similar features in realistic fiction, biography, fantasy, and more.

Prompts

• What did you learn from the historical notes to help you understand the setting?
• After reading the story, what do you wonder about? Check the historical notes to see if your questions might be answered.
• Think back to events. How do details from the notes help you picture it better?

Research Link

In an extensive review of 183 books, articles, and research reports, Dochy and colleagues (1999) established a firm case for the importance of background knowledge to learning outcomes, including reading comprehension. If students do not already have this knowledge, the additional features of a book are one convenient source of information directly related to the content of the story.

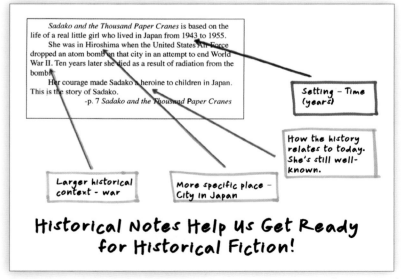

Text excerpt from *Sadako and the Thousand Paper Cranes* (Coerr, 1977).

Strategy Think about the setting of the story as including both the time and place in history. Consider the details about the social, economic, and political environment of that time and place. Consider what effects the environment has on the character(s).

Lesson Language *When you read historical fiction, it's so important to really understand the historical environment. It's more than just saying "Northeastern United States, 1942." It helps to go a little deeper, thinking about different aspects of what life was like then, to best understand the characters, why they do what they do, and how their environment impacts them. You should consider the social environment—think for example about the kinds of social issues that existed in that time and place or what expectations there were for different groups of people. Think about the economic environment—what sorts of jobs were available? What did being in different social classes mean at that time? Think also about the politics of the time—who was in power and what were their beliefs about how to lead the place? What laws existed and how might those impact the characters? When an author writes historical fiction, he or she carefully considers all the aspects of the environment, and it's important that you, as a reader, do as well!*

Prompts

- What do you know about this time and place?
- Can you get information from the text, historical notes, or prologue?
- Think about social issues. What's at play here?
- Talk about what you know so far about the economics/politics of this time.

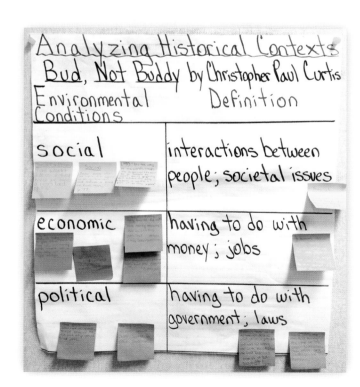

Skills

- **activating prior knowledge**
- **inferring**

Progression

Is able to visualize and describe a setting and is ready to infer based on setting(s), such as how setting(s) contributes to mood or impacts characters or plot.

Hat Tip

Teaching Interpretation: Using Text-Based Evidence to Construct Meaning (Cherry-Paul & Johansen, 2014)

Research Link

After participants in one study read a story about baseball, researchers found essentially no difference in the retellings of good comprehenders with little background knowledge and weak comprehenders with substantial background knowledge: knowledge closed the gap between the two groups (Recht & Leslie, 1988). The use of videos, articles from the popular press, and informational texts helps to build critical background knowledge (Lupo et al., 2018).

Consider Levels of Setting: Micro-, Meso-, Macroenvironment Systems

Skills

- **determining importance**
- **inferring**

Progression

Is able to visualize and describe a setting and is ready to infer based on setting(s), such as how setting(s) contributes to mood or impacts characters or plot.

Hat Tip

Fresh Takes on Teaching Literary Elements: How to Teach What Really Matters About Character, Setting, Point of View, and Theme (Smith & Wilhelm, 2010)

Research Link

Supporting students to develop a multilayered perspective on setting requires *historical literacy* (Downey & Long, 2015): activating prior knowledge, previewing the new text, and then building historical knowledge by collecting evidence, analyzing and evaluating, making connections between the various sources and the target text, and synthesizing to try and understand why events unfold in a particular way.

Strategy Notice and name the aspects of a character's environment. This may be based on information the author has given you or on what you can infer based on text details. Then, think about which of these is important based on the conflicts the character is experiencing.

Lesson Language *If I were to think about* Front Desk *(Yang, 2018), I might consider a few levels of setting for Mia, and how each is important to understanding her and the struggles she's facing. The immediate setting, the microsystem, is the motel and the community of people there who become like family, and the motel owner who's making things more challenging. A mesosystem is California in the 1980s, in a country new to them, and factors that make it challenging for immigrants to get ahead. The macrosystem includes Communist China, the place Mia and her family left behind in hopes of a better life, and the place where her extended family (who chose not to immigrate) still resides.*

Prompts

- Describe the character's local setting—home, school, community.
- What are you thinking about the setting?
- Let's think more broadly. Describe the larger setting.
- What information do you have about the global or political environment?

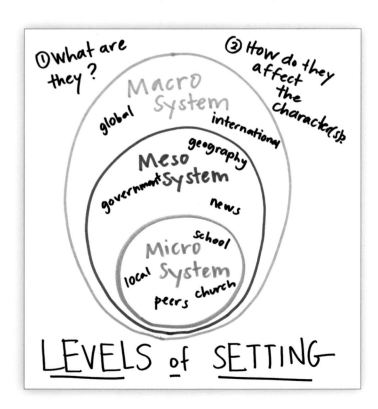

Strategy Review the story archetypes you know. Consider which type(s) best fit the story you're reading. Use the basic plot trajectory of the story archetype to help retell the most important events from the story you read.

Lesson Language *Depending on who you ask, there are a handful (3? 7? 12?) of different basic plots, sometimes called "story archetypes." Recognizing a story's "type" can be a tool to help us make connections between and across stories, to compare and contrast, and to consider why the author may have made the plot choices they did. Knowing the story type may also help you to summarize the key events of the story based on the type. For example, identifying the movie* Jingle, Jangle's *plot as "a story of rebirth" could help you focus on how the character is developed in the beginning (once joyful toymaker, Jeronicus's business is ruined when a thief takes an important design, his daughter moves away, and he loses his creative spark), how the character's circumstances change in the middle (when his granddaughter, Journey, visits and brings inspiration), and how the ending connects (Jeronicus successfully resumes inventing toys and repairs his relationship with his daughter).*

Prompts
- What are the story types you know?
- Name which of the story types best matches the story you're reading.
- Say, "I know __ about the story type. In the story I'm reading . . ."
- Retell the story using what you know about that story archetype.

Skills
- **activating prior knowledge**
- **retelling**
- **determining importance**

Progression

Is ready to analyze stories using prior knowledge of plot archetypes, how a plot follows a literary tradition, or how a writer's plot choices may allude to traditional stories.

● ● ● ● ● ● ●

Research Link

Although repeated exposure provides readers with "story schemata" that correspond to common, archetypical stories in a cultural context, they are often unaware of these schemata. Once someone makes the shared elements of these stories explicit, they are easier to understand and remember (Morrow, 1985; Stein & Glenn, 1979).

Consider Literary Traditions to Compare and Contrast Plots

- activating prior knowledge
- synthesizing

Progression

Is ready to analyze stories using prior knowledge of plot archetypes, how a plot follows a literary tradition, or how a writer's plot choices may allude to traditional stories.

● ● ● ● ● ● ●

Research Link

In their classic work explaining their theory of story schemata, Mandler and Johnson (1977) suggest that readers learn the essential components of stories from folktales, fables, and myths. To be remembered, stories from these oral traditions were reduced to their most essential elements.

Strategy Think about the traditional stories you know. Does the book you're reading remind you of any of those stories? Compare and contrast the plots of each.

Lesson Language *Children's literature today sometimes stands on the shoulders of classic stories such as those found in mythology, fairy tales, fables, and religious texts from across cultures. When you can make a connection between the plots of a current book and a traditional story, you can then consider what's the same and different, and that comparison can help you consider what events are most important and help you develop ideas. For example, Grace Lin has said her book* Where the Mountain Meets the Moon *is a Chinese story in the tradition of* The Wonderful Wizard of Oz *(Baum, 1900). There are similarities between the two: you might note that in both stories, a female main character goes on a quest, meets magical creatures along the way, and realizes the importance of home. But noting the differences also helps you pay attention to important events, details, and ideas in the more modern story. For instance, you may pay close attention to the impact of setting on the characters, consider the way Lin uses Chinese folklore throughout and how that impacts the narrative, and pay attention to thematic differences between the two stories.*

Prompts

- Does this story remind you of any traditional stories you know?
- Name some similarities between the traditional story and this one.
- Say, "In the traditional story . . . but in this one . . ."

When readers explicitly learn about story structure and the predictable elements of plot, they are better able to predict, remember, and recall the events and comprehend the narratives they read.

—Jennifer Serravallo

Goal 6

Comprehending Characters

◎ Why is this goal important?

Character development is often intertwined with plot development; characters are the actors connecting the events of the story. Characters help readers stay engaged while reading: they can become our friends, can reflect our experiences and help us feel seen and understood, can help us learn about lives outside of our own, and can help us think differently about or better understand people in our own lives (Bishop, 1990; Emery, 1996; Roser et al., 2007). Research has also found that readers who are able to empathize with characters have better overall comprehension of the story (Bourg et al., 1993; Phillips, 1988).

Literary characters are inventions of a writer's imagination. Though "characters" in historical accounts, biographies, or true accounts are real people, authors decide which events from their lives to include and how to portray them. No matter the narrative genre, readers need to pay attention to details that the author includes, connect what they read to their background knowledge about people (Culpeper, 1996, 2014), and work to learn, think about, and understand characters.

200

They may, for example, learn to track and consider

- what characters look like, how they dress, what possessions they keep
- what characters say and how they say it
- what is left unsaid by and about the characters
- thoughts characters have that are revealed through the narrator
- the moods and emotions of characters
- characters' actions
- how characters respond to events and other characters
- backstory and beliefs of characters
- the opinions characters have about each other.

Of course, the age and maturity of the reader, as well as their ability to understand human emotions and traits in life, will impact how well they can infer and interpret emotions and traits of characters in their books (Emery & Milhalevich, 1992; Shannon, Kame'enui, & Baumann, 1988). With explicit strategy instruction and scaffolds, however, a reader's ability to understand characters will improve (McTigue et al., 2015).

Skills a reader might work on as part of this goal

Activating prior knowledge
Using knowledge of people in real life, or knowledge of texts (series, genre, and so on), to comprehend.

Self-monitoring
Being aware of who the characters are, how they relate to each other, and what you know about them, and rereading as necessary to fix confusion.

Determining importance
Knowing who is in the story and what details help a reader understand something about each character, and paying attention to those details.

Synthesizing
Putting together ideas and information about characters from across a text to come up with theories or interpretations, to articulate change, to understand cause and effect, and to understand motivations.

Inferring
Using information from the text and the reader's own background knowledge to think about feelings, traits, motivations, and relationships of main, secondary, and tertiary characters. Making predictions.

Analyzing
Examining specific character traits, or other aspects of characterization, to compare or contrast, or consider author's craft.

Visualizing
Using details from the story to imagine characters' actions and expressions.

◎ How do I know if this goal is right for my student?

To assess a student's comprehension of character feelings, traits, relationships, change, and so on, ask them to respond to prompts and questions about a text or excerpt, and then evaluate the quality of their responses. The text can be short (e.g., short story, picture book, something from a children's magazine) or long (e.g., chapter book); it can be one you choose or they choose; and you can decide to read it aloud or have them read it independently. Plant questions at key points in the story, or ask them to read the whole story and respond by jotting or talking about the story when they're done.

Here are some prompts and questions you can use that align to this goal:

- Who are the main characters?
- Who is telling this story?
- Describe the kind of person your character is.
- How is the character feeling?
- How has the character changed?
- Describe the relationship between [character] and [character].
- Putting together all you know, what theories do you have about your character?

> Lincoln is a very kind and thoughtful person.
> I know this because in the text it states
> that Lincoln felt bad for his former
> school because Lincoln new school always
> beats his old school.

This student's jot shows she's able to name two similar traits about the main character and provide text evidence for why she used those adjectives. However, in the book she's reading, I know the characters are more complex than her response indicates. Therefore, she's ready to think about motivations, compare characters, or notice changes in characters (Strategies 6.10–6.13) and eventually to think about how the characters in her books are complex (Strategies 6.14–6.17).

> Koya is a person who wants to be happy because
> she wants to make others happy, and
> hides her anger and pretends to be
> happy instead of showing her anger when
> she has some anger.

This student sample shows how a reader can notice complexity and nuance within a character—that her motivations (wants to be happy and make others happy) cause her to pretend and hide how she really feels. This reader might benefit from additional strategies that help her to think about character complexity as more than just feelings (Strategies 6.14–6.17) and eventually to synthesize traits to come up with interpretations and theories about the character (Strategies 6.18–6.21).

What Texts Might Students Use When Practicing Strategies from This Chapter?

The strategies from this chapter will help when students are reading any narrative text types or genres that have characters—either people or animals, whether fictional (e.g., historical fiction, mystery, realistic fiction chapter books, graphic novels) or informational (e.g., biographies, historical accounts).

How do I support students as they develop their understanding of characters?

After evaluating a student's verbal or written responses about the characters in their book(s), select strategies that you can model, that they can practice with you, and that they can use independently to increase their skills.

Although development is rarely perfectly linear, skill progressions can help us pinpoint where a student is now and what might come next. Use the if-then chart on page 205 to evaluate your students' reading and find strategies that will support their growth.

A Progression of Skills: *Comprehending Characters*

If a student . . .

Needs support identifying the narrator and characters and determining important information about characters from text and/or pictures.

Identifies characters, can name important details explicitly from the text, and is ready to infer what characters think and feel and support their thinking with text evidence.

Can infer a character's thoughts and feelings at specific points in the text and is ready to start synthesizing inferences to identify patterns, infer motivations, compare characters, and recognize changes in the character.

Is able to infer about characters and synthesize information across the text. Is ready to think in more nuanced ways to analyze how characters can be complex (i.e., multiple or conflicting motivations or traits).

Is ready to synthesize multiple traits to develop a theory or interpretation of a character, describe character relationships, and name the impact that one character has on another.

Is able to form theories and is beginning to understand character relationships. Is ready to analyze those relationships and consider point of view and characters' perspectives and how they impact the story. May also analyze characters based on a knowledge of archetypes and allegories.

Then you might teach . . .

6.1   **Identify Characters Using Pictures and Names**

6.2   **Identify Who's Telling the Story**

6.3   **Role-Play to Understand Characters**

6.4   **Say What's in the Bubble**

6.5   **Think About How the Character Is Feeling**

6.6   **Put On the Character's Face**

6.7   **Add Text Clues and Background Knowledge to Get Ideas**

6.8   **Study Talk and Actions as Windows into Traits and Feelings**

6.9   **Back Up Ideas About Characters with Evidence**

6.10   **Look for a Pattern**

6.11   **Track Feelings as They Change**

6.12   **Empathize to Understand Motivations**

6.13   **Compare Characters**

6.14   **See More Than One Side**

6.15   **Notice When a Character Acts Out of Character**

6.16   **Find Complexity During Conflict(s)**

6.17   **Consider Conflicting Motivations**

6.18   **Notice Interactions to Infer**

6.19   **Look Across Notes to Develop Theories**

6.20   **Consider When Internal and External Are at Odds**

6.21   **Be Aware When a Character Is Unaware**

6.22   **Analyze Character Relationships**

6.23   **Analyze Author Choices: Point of View and Perspective**

6.24   **Identify Archetypes**

6.25   **Consider Characters as Allegorical Figures**

Strategy As you read a book, remind yourself who the characters are. Look at the illustrations to see who is pictured. Look for names in the story. List (aloud or on a sticky note) the facts you know about them from the book.

Lesson Language *Let's revisit Chapter 1 of* Yasmin the Builder *(Faruqi, 2019). On the first page we can look at the illustration first. There's Yasmin! She's one character, and the facts we know about her from this chapter are that she's one of the students in the class, and she doodles and sketches and can't figure out what to draw. Who else? Look at the text. Whose names did we read? Ms. Alex! We know she is the teacher. Then we notice the narrator mentions "the class" and we see a group of students on the next page in the illustration. Do we know any of their names specifically? I see the name "Ali," and there is an illustration of him on the opposite page. He says he wants to get started on the project and that it's boring that the teacher is making them sketch. Keeping track of who's who, and what we know about them, is essential to following the story.*

Prompts
- Check the illustrations—who do you see pictured?
- Check the words. What names do you see?
- Yes, __ is one of the characters. Now list what you know about them.
- Say, "The character is __ and from the story I know __ . . ."

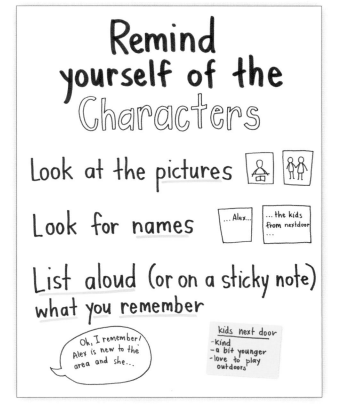

Skills
- **determining importance**
- **self-monitoring**

Progression

Needs support identifying the narrator and characters and determining important information about characters from text and/or pictures.

● ○ ○ ○ ○ ○

Research Link

In a small qualitative study, first graders who were prompted to think specifically about characters before each day's read-aloud of a chapter book became more adept (over the course of the book) at identifying traits rather than actions and focused more on the characters' thinking and feeling rather than physical descriptions (Roser et al., 2007).

Skills

- **self-monitoring**
- **determining importance**

Progression

Needs support identifying the narrator and characters and determining important information about characters from text and/or pictures.

Research Link

According to Bruce's *A Social Interaction Model of Reading* (1981), the interaction between an author and a reader can be complicated by the inclusion of a narrator, who is a creation of the author, but who does not necessarily speak with the author's voice. To make sense of this complexity, beginning readers need support in identifying "who" is telling the story.

Strategy Ask yourself, "Who is telling this story? Is it one of the characters from the story or a narrator who isn't part of the story?" Pay close attention to the narration, and the dialogue tags. If a character is telling the story, you'll see *I, me, we, my*.

Lesson Language *The narrator is important! The narrator can give us information about the characters by describing them. Or, if the narrator is one of the characters, you may also learn about what that character is thinking and feeling. Let's look at a few books to see if we can tell if the narrator is a character (and if so, who it is) or isn't a character.*

J.D. and the Great Barber Battle (Dillard, 2021) begins, "'Sit still and look straight into the mirror,' my mom said as she turned on a set of clippers" (p. 7). I see the word my *so the narrator is the main character (who is probably J.D., from the title and the cover of the book). Let's look at another one:* Sona Sharma, Very Best Big Sister? *(Soundar, 2020). Here are a few sentences from early in the story, "Sona and Elephant often play in the garden . . . They read books, make up stories, and watch noisy squirrels race around." Well, we know Sona is the main character from the title—is she telling the story? No. A person wouldn't call themselves by their own name, and I also see the word* they *to talk about Sona and Elephant. That means this story is told by a narrator who is not one of the characters in the story.*

Prompts

- Can you tell who the narrator is?
- Look carefully at the pronouns. Do you see *I, my,* or *me*?
- Take a look at dialogue tags to clarify who is speaking and if the speaker is also the narrator.
- Yes, that's right—*he, she, they* in the narration means it's not the main character telling the story.

Strategy With a partner, choose a scene. Act out the scene as if you are the characters (or use puppets). Try to talk in the voice of the character and move like the character would move. When you finish acting out the scene, stop and talk about what you think about the characters.

Teaching Tip Sometimes the best way to get to know characters is to pretend to be them—to do what they do, say what they say, and act how they act. Many author websites have printable resources of the characters in some of the books you are reading to your children or that they are reading independently (see, for example, Dav Pilkey's website www.pilkey.com or Mo Willems' website www.pigeonpresents .com). These resources offer quick and easy ways to make puppets, but you can also set children up to create their own puppets and props during a choice time or center time. See *A Quick Guide to Boosting English Language Acquisition in Choice Time, K–2* (Porcelli & Tyler, 2008) for more ideas on how to use choice time to support comprehension and enjoyment of stories.

Prompts
- How would your character act?
- Make the puppet talk in the voice of your character.
- Now that the puppet acted like the character, how do you think he or she felt?
- Based on what the character did or said, what are you thinking now?

Skills
- **visualizing**
- **inferring**

Progression

Identifies characters, can name important details explicitly from the text, and is ready to infer what characters think and feel and support their thinking with text evidence.

Research Link

Reader's theater has benefits for fluency (see Strategy 4.4 and Strategy 4.23, for example) including for very young readers (Moran, 2006), but also requires a thorough understanding of character. Researchers have described how comprehension is supported when students role-play with puppets (Peck & Virkler, 2006; Zuljevic, 2005).

- **inferring**
- **visualizing**

Progression

Identifies characters, can name important details explicitly from the text, and is ready to infer what characters think and feel and support their thinking with text evidence.

Research Link

In a study to investigate how discussing character perspectives would impact children's ability to infer character motives (Emery & Milhalevich, 1992), researchers reported a statistically significant improvement in perspective-taking with sixth graders, but no change with fourth and fifth graders. With age, students may improve in their ability to understand the perspectives of others (Shannon, Kame'enui, & Baumann, 1988); younger students may need more instruction.

Strategy Pause and think, "What might this character be thinking or saying here?" Even when the text doesn't tell you, you can imagine and infer. Pause on the page and put a thought or speech bubble above the character in the picture, point and say, or jot, what the character might be thinking or saying.

Teaching Tip For beginning readers, I try to keep stopping and jotting to a minimum and instead direct them to simply flag pages with blank sticky notes and/ or to use quick symbols to hold on to thinking. You can also create speech bubbles and thought clouds and affix them to tongue depressors. Children can use these as tools independently and with partnerships. For children who are ready to stop and jot a phrase or sentence, you can give them sticky notes with bubbles (or have them draw their own) and they can affix them to the page and jot what the character might be thinking or saying. When students read books without pictures, they can still use this strategy—the speech or thinking bubble image can serve as a quick prompt to remind them to pause their reading and think. In the figures, you can see variations of this strategy.

Prompts

- What just happened? So, what might your character be thinking?
- What words might your character say in their head or out loud?
- Before you turn the page, pause and think about what they would be thinking.
- Put your thought bubble on the page. Now say what the character might be thinking.

Think About How the Character Is Feeling

Strategy Imagine yourself to be in the same situation as the character, or remember a time when you were. Think about how you felt or would feel. Then, use a word to describe that feeling.

Lesson Language *Characters in our stories have feelings, just like people in our lives have feelings. We can use specific words like* happy, excited, amazed, nervous, sad, *or* worried *to talk about those feelings. Let's think about the scene in* Sona Sharma, Very Best Big Sister? *(Soundar, 2021) where she's talking to her elephant about the news that she's going to be a big sister. Maybe some of you have experienced that, maybe others would need to imagine what it would be like to learn that a new baby is about to join your family. Let's notice what she says and does and think about how she might be feeling. When Elephant responds to her news with, "That's a good thing, no?" she responds, "I don't know." Then, she says she "doesn't want to share" her family. What words describe how she's feeling right now? Maybe nervous? Or uncertain? Or possibly a bit worried? The author doesn't use those words, but we can think about how she's feeling based on what she says and does and use our own words to describe it.*

Prompts
- Notice how the character talks. How do you think they feel?
- Use a word to describe the feeling.
- Reread this scene. What is the character doing and saying?
- Say, "If I were [character] in this situation, I'd be feeling . . ."

> # Think about how the character is feeling
>
> | **Imagine** | being in the same situation as the character (or remember a time when you were) |
> | **Think** | about how you would feel (or how you felt) |
> | **Describe** | that feeling with a word
> ※ You can use a chart to help you! |

Skills
- **visualizing**
- **inferring**
- **activating prior knowledge**

Progression

Identifies characters, can name important details explicitly from the text, and is ready to infer what characters think and feel and support their thinking with text evidence.

● ● ○ ○ ○ ○

Research Link

Looking beyond the field of literacy (Emery & Milhalevich, 1992), researchers have found that with instruction, both elementary-age students (Elardo & Caldwell, 1979; Emery, 1996; Hodges et al., 2018) and adolescents (Chandler, 1973; Thein, Beach, & Parks, 2007) improved their ability to identify and understand the perspectives of others. This instruction is especially vital when supporting students to understand cultural perspectives different from their own (Thein, Beach, & Parks, 2007).

Skills

- **determining importance**
- **inferring**

Progression

Identifies characters, can name important details explicitly from the text, and is ready to infer what characters think and feel and support their thinking with text evidence.

Research Link

In a small study examining second graders' ability to use illustrations to make inferences about characters, researchers found that students used facial expressions and body posture to interpret what characters were feeling and thinking, both at particular points in time and when characters experienced changes in their internal state (Willson, Falcon, & Martinez, 2014).

Strategy Pay close attention to the picture. Look at the expression on the character's face. Make the face yourself. Think, "How is the character feeling?"

Lesson Language *Sometimes you may hear people say to "put yourself in the character's shoes" when they want you to try to understand and feel what the character is feeling. But feelings aren't in shoes! Feelings show up on your face and body. When you are happy, you smile—smile with me. When you are sad, you frown—let me see you look sad. Well, characters in your books have feelings, too. When you can't figure out how they are feeling right away, you can make your face match the face of the character. You can think about how you feel when you make that face to better understand how the character must be feeling. You can check the "How Are You Feeling?" chart to see which face most closely matches the one you're making to know what word to use to describe the feeling.*

Prompts

- Check the face of the character in the picture.
- How do you feel when you make that face?
- I see your face changed. What feeling matches that?
- Check the feelings chart to find a word that matches that feeling.

Add Text Clues and Background Knowledge to Get Ideas

Strategy Pay attention to text clues about the character. Then think, "What do I already know about people from my life who remind me of this character?" This is your background knowledge. Finally, put the text clues and your background knowledge together to come up with your own ideas about the character.

Lesson Language *When I read* Thank you, Omu! *(Mora, 2018), I was immediately reminded of my grandmother. Just like Omu in the book, my grandmother loved to cook and most of all loved to share her cooking with others. My grandmother took pride in her cooking and was famous (within our family) for a particular recipe she called "pizza fries" that meant as much to our family as Omu's red stew likely meant to her whole community. In the book, each time someone knocked on Omu's door and complimented the smell of her stew, she gave them some! Just like my grandma would make sure anyone who visited left with full bellies. Do you see how I'm connecting specific details from my background knowledge about a person to specific details in the story about the character? Now I'm going to think beyond what the text says and say some ideas about Omu, based on those connections. I think Omu is the kind of person who brings all kinds of people together. She's generous and proud. She gave until she had no more for herself! But at the end, everyone she shared with came to give back to her, and it makes me think that she is also a model who helps others be better, more generous.*

Prompts

- What details does the author give you about the character?
- Who does this make you think of in your own life?
- What ideas are you having about the character?
- That's something the author told you. What do you think about the character?

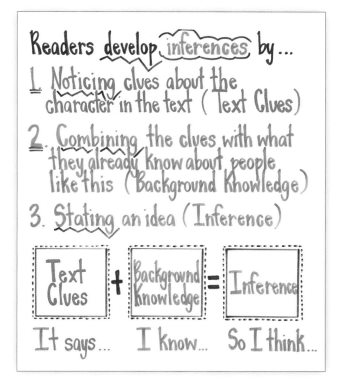

Skills

- **inferring**
- **activating prior knowledge**
- **determining importance**

Progression

Identifies characters, can name important details explicitly from the text, and is ready to infer what characters think and feel and support their thinking with text evidence.

Research Link

The process of reading involves making connections between the real world and the world of the story. Children bring their history of relationships to a text (Matthews & Cobb, 2005), which supports the bidirectional development of social imagination: what students know about how people interact in the real world influences their understanding of characters in stories, and vice versa (Lysaker et al., 2011).

Study Talk and Actions as Windows into Traits and Feelings

Skills

- **determining importance**
- **inferring**

Progression

Identifies characters, can name important details explicitly from the text, and is ready to infer what characters think and feel and support their thinking with text evidence.

●●○○○○

Research Link

Culpeper (1996, 2014) offers *attribution theory* as a framework for how a reader uses behavior clues to understand a literary character's thoughts and feelings. In the same way that we gather and make inferences about others in the real world, we gather similar clues in a narrative to construct understandings of characters.

Strategy Notice what the character says. Notice how they say it. (Pay attention to dialogue tags, descriptions of character actions, and any illustrations.) Ask yourself: "What words would I use to describe a character who talks and acts like this?"

Lesson Language *Let's revisit the first scene in* New Kid *(Craft, 2019). The dialogue tags and accompanying actions tell us so much about the characters. Let's see what we can infer about their traits and feelings. Look at the dialogue on pages 2 and 3 as Jordan's mom is going on and on about the private school she's enrolled him in. She says things like "Why can't you see how AMAZING this place is?" or "This is one of the best schools in the entire state! It looks like Harvard or something." Let's look at her actions here—she's got a huge smile on her face, and she's turned to the computer with her back to Jordan who seems to be groaning, rolling his eyes, and crumpling in his chair. He seems frustrated and nervous! How might we describe his mom's feelings and traits? I would say she's excited and enthusiastic about the school. She really loves her son and wants what she thinks is best for him. But I notice she's not even looking at him. She's kind of ignoring what he wants and how he feels, so we could say she's determined to put him in this school no matter his opinion.*

Prompts

- Can you point to a dialogue tag? Read it carefully. What does it make you think?
- What is the character saying?
- That word definitely matches the dialogue and action.
- That's an important tag to pay attention to—it shows *how* the character said something.

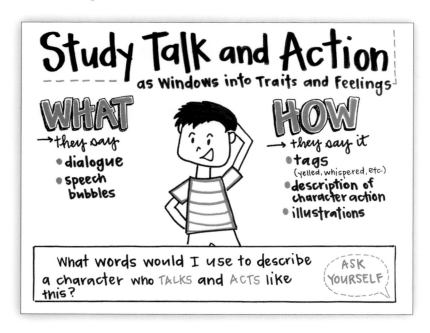

Back Up Ideas About Characters with Evidence

Strategy Focus on an idea you've had about the character: think about it or jot it on a sticky note. Reread to find a line where the character says or does something that connects to the idea. Explain *how* that line supports your idea.

Lesson Language *One idea I have from* My Papi Has a Motorcycle *(Quintero, 2019) is that Daisy's papi is loving and keeps her safe. I'm going to jot that idea down on a sticky and hold it in my hand so as I look from page to page for evidence, I can reread to remember the idea I'm trying to support. The first thing that happens is that he gets home from work. Let me see if there are any supports on these pages for my idea. (Read idea aloud.) Well, when he gets home, she immediately stops what she's doing and runs to him. She's so excited—you only act like that for someone you love and are happy to see. But wait—I'm trying to prove* (look at sticky note) *that he is loving, so let me keep looking. On the next page, I see him giving her a big whole-body hug, which shows their love. And then he puts a helmet on her to keep her safe. It also says he's careful with her ponytail and that his hands feel "like all the love he has trouble saying." There's more—those are just the first few pages—but do you see how I'm looking at all the details from the text and pictures with my idea in my mind and in my hand on a sticky note to find text evidence?*

Prompts
- What's the idea?
- Reread to find the part that gave you that idea.
- Explain how that moment in the story connects with your idea.
- That piece of evidence really works—I can see how that part gave you the idea.

Theory:

Min Li is a very kind and selfless person.

Proof:

When she went to see the man of the moon she asked her friend, dragons question instead of hers.

Proof:

She bought a gold fish that she really liked, but then she gave it away so her parents did not have to feed it.

Skill
- **determining importance**

Progression

Identifies characters, can name important details explicitly from the text, and is ready to infer what characters think and feel and support their thinking with text evidence.

⚫⚫○○○○

Research Link

Using the Chart for Multiple Perspectives (CHAMP) graphic organizer, researchers supported students to infer the thoughts and emotions of characters using both text evidence and picture evidence. When students went beyond just identifying emotional states to justifying them based on evidence, they developed a more thorough understanding of the story (McTigue et al., 2015).

Skills

- **inferring**
- **synthesizing**
- **determining importance**

Progression

Can infer a character's thoughts and feelings at specific points in the text and is ready to start synthesizing inferences to identify patterns, infer motivations, compare characters, and recognize changes in the character.

●●●○○○○

Research Link

Building upon previous studies on inferring while reading, Peracchi and O'Brien (2004) found that college-age readers construct a mental "profile" based on what they learn about a character across a text. Readers then use this collection of traits to predict what a character will do next in a story. However, if information is presented that conflicts with their mental character profile, readers are able to modify their prediction.

Strategy Often, traits are revealed through behaviors a character repeats again and again. Try looking at the character in multiple parts of the story. Think to yourself, "What actions, or thoughts, or dialogue repeats? Where is there a pattern?" Use pattern(s) to name a trait(s).

Teaching Tip In texts beginning readers read, you can often help children to distinguish between traits and feelings of a character—which are often confused—by telling them that feelings change while traits stay the same. For example, Frog is always patient and a good friend (traits), though sometimes he's happy and sometimes he's not (feelings). However, as texts get more complex, so do the characters. New traits emerge across the story, and some of their traits may change. For example, in *Front Desk* (Yang, 2018), Mia's mom shows a pattern of behavior that indicates she cares deeply for her family. Later, when she discourages Mia from focusing on writing, her passion, you can see the negative effect this has on Mia. Yes, she still cares, but you start to see some of her flaws as well. Therefore, this strategy will work best when children are reading texts where characters are less complex and nuanced. Look for strategies later in this chapter to support readers' inferences of traits and feelings in more complex texts.

Prompts

- Check your trait list. What word(s) describe the character?
- Do you see a pattern?
- How is the character behaving again and again?
- What's the same from page to page or part to part?

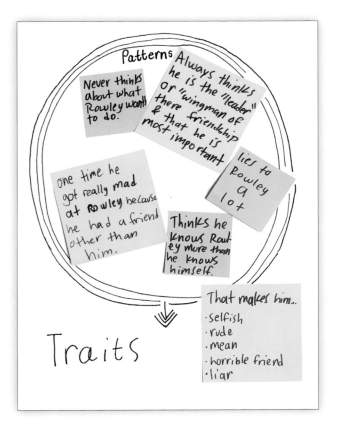

Track Feelings as They Change

Strategy Think about how the character is feeling at one point in the story and what caused them to feel that way. Jot a word or sketch a picture to capture your thinking. Now, look at how the character feels in a later scene. Jot or sketch the new feeling and event. Look across the sticky notes to explain how the feelings changed and what caused those changes.

Lesson Language *When something fun happens—you are having a birthday party, your mom buys you an ice-cream cone, or you learn to ride your bike by yourself—chances are you are smiling, saying "Yay!" and feeling happy. But, when something goes wrong—you did your homework but you forgot it at home, you get sick, or someone teases you—chances are you feel upset. The characters in the stories you read will have ups and downs, too. Events will happen and characters will react. You can track both how they feel and what made them feel that way.*

Teaching Tip In the previous chapter, Strategy 5.26 invites readers to track events of a complicated plot using a modified story mountain with ups and downs. You can modify that and add emotions to the underside and plot events to the top of the line so readers track both events and feelings across the story.

Prompts
- How might he or she be feeling here?
- Is this feeling the same or different?
- You understand the feeling at the beginning. What is the character feeling at the end?
- You looked closely at the words and pictures to figure out the feeling.

Skills
- **inferring**
- **determining importance**
- **synthesizing**

Progression
Can infer a character's thoughts and feelings at specific points in the text and is ready to start synthesizing inferences to identify patterns, infer motivations, compare characters, and recognize changes in the character.

●●●○○○○

Research Link
In a series of experiments with college undergraduates, Rapp and Kendeou (2007, 2009) found that initial ideas about a character remain remarkably stable and often do not keep pace with how a character may grow and change. In fact, readers read more quickly when they encounter actions that are consistent with the established behavior of a character than if the actions are unexpected.

Skills

- **inferring**
- **visualizing**
- **synthesizing**

Progression

Can infer a character's thoughts and feelings at specific points in the text and is ready to start synthesizing inferences to identify patterns, infer motivations, compare characters, and recognize changes in the character.

Research Link

Readers who empathize have both a better understanding of the emotional states of characters and a better overall comprehension of the story (Bourg et al., 1993; Bourg, 1996). Phillips (1988) found that the ability to empathize with characters was one of the strategies that explained differences between good and poor comprehenders in sixth grade.

Strategy Notice what's happening to the character (how other characters are treating them, what is going right or wrong for them). Think about *why* the character might be doing or saying something. Then, imagine yourself to be in the character's position. What would you say or do? Does thinking about this help you understand the character's motivations?

Lesson Language *If you go up to your mom and give her a big hug, there would be a reason for it, right? If you stop playing a game with a friend—you wouldn't do it randomly. If you work really hard on a project for school, and I ask you, "Why?" you could give me an answer, right? Well, characters are just like people in real life—they have reasons for doing the things they do. One of our jobs as readers who are trying to understand characters is to go a step beyond just saying what they do and try to say why they do it. Now, the tricky thing is, the character will rarely say, "The reason I'm doing this is . . ." just like we don't always explain our reasoning in real life without some prompting. So that means as readers we have to piece together the information in the story. Sometimes imagining ourselves to be in the character's position helps us to make an inference.*

Prompts

- Name what the character does or says. Now think, "Why did they do or say that?"
- Remember what the character wants. Why might they be acting/talking like this?
- Say, "In this situation, I'd feel or act __, so I think my character might be doing this because __."
- Use words like *maybe* or *because . . .* to explain a possible motivation.

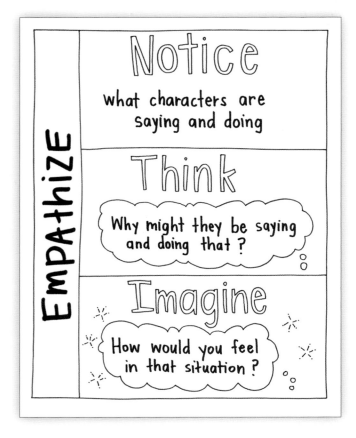

Strategy Think of two characters from within one book or from two different books that are similar. Use categories to compare them (some ideas are: traits, how they handle challenges, likes and dislikes, interests, change, lesson learned). Explain what's similar within each category and/or what's different.

Lesson Language *To compare two somewhat similar characters, it can be helpful to think in categories. We could, for example, see some similarities between Jordan in* New Kid *(Craft, 2019) and Merci in* Merci Suárez Changes Gears *(Medina, 2018): both are middle school students (age) on financial aid/scholarship (class) to attend a school (setting) where part of their struggles (problems) include trying to fit in to an unfamiliar environment. They both feel like outsiders, deal with bullies and teachers who misunderstand and mistreat them, and confront their own racial and class identities in juxtaposition to their peers. But there are important differences as well: their special interests and talents (Jordan—art; Merci—sports) and why they matter, how the setting (Washington Heights, New York City; Florida) impacts them, their home lives and the people who support them, how they handle obstacles (withdrawing or speaking up or going with the flow), and how they change (or don't) across the book. Thinking about similarities and differences in categories helps us pay attention to characters more fully and know them more deeply.*

Prompts

- Think about the categories you can use to compare.
- What's similar and different about your characters' identities? Interests? Traits?
- Compare each character when they deal with a problem or obstacle. What's similar and what's different?
- Look back across your comparisons. Describe the similarities and differences.

Bree from Swim team | Mary Anne from baby-sitters club

Traits
• Shy
• nervous
• awkward
• gets hopes up

Traits
• Shy
• nervous/awkward
• cries a lot

Changes
• get less shy

Changes
• get less shy
• be more brave

Lessons learned
• the more shy you are, the less you will make friends

Lessons learned
• just be brave and take a chance, and then you will have more fun.

Skills

- **synthesizing**
- **analyzing**
- **inferring**

Progression

Is able to infer about characters and synthesize information across the text. Is ready to think in more nuanced ways to analyze how characters can be complex (i.e., multiple or conflicting motivations or traits).

Research Link

Young children tend to have a narrow vocabulary (e.g., *happy, mad, sad*) for emotions (McTigue et al., 2015). Intentionally teaching vocabulary used to describe emotions, which may be supported by associating words with illustrations in picture books (Nikolajeva, 2013) or other drawings, supplies readers with the language necessary to express their thoughts about characters with more precision (Kucan, 2012).

Strategy Push yourself to name many traits your character has shown across the story, especially different traits in different situations. (Use a character trait list to help.) Sort traits into two categories—helpful traits and traits that create obstacles. Describe your character in sentences, showing their different sides.

Teaching Tip Consider creating a wall in your classroom where you hang photocopied covers of past read-alouds, with character webs or a list of traits below each. Encourage discussion during the read-aloud to help children think about characters in multiple ways, and generate a list of different sides of their character and why and how they act like that. These can serve not only as a reminder that characters are complex, but also as a "vocabulary wall" of sorts to help students reference words to describe the characters in books they are reading independently.

Prompts

- The trait you just said is __. Does acting that way cause more problems?
- Do you feel like you're seeing your character from more than one side?
- Say, "Sometimes my character __, but when __, they act __."
- Say, "Often my character seems to __, but sometimes __."

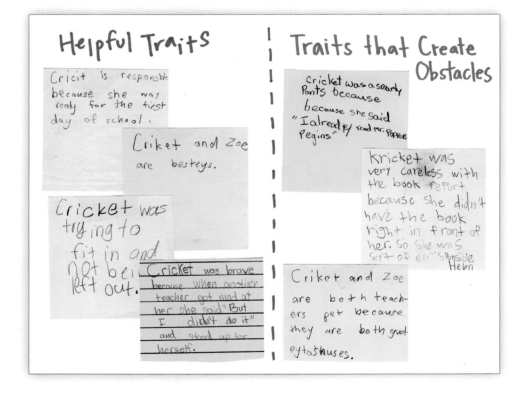

Strategy Notice when a character behaves in an unusual way. Jot a note about how what they say or do seems different or surprising. As you continue reading, figure out if the behavior simply shows you a different side of the character (they go back to behaving the same way) or if it indicates a clear change (they act in the new way from here on out). Form an idea or theory.

Lesson Language *In* Front Desk *(Yang, 2018), we get to know Mia in the beginning as someone with a positive outlook who really respects and looks up to her parents. She's quiet, she helps out around the motel, and when she gets upset or frustrated, she keeps her feelings inside. But by the middle of the book, she starts to speak up more. She debates Jason in class with vigor, she writes a letter to the mean girls who are teasing her, she enters an essay contest even though she got a C– in English and her mom is telling her she should focus on math, and she demands justice for Hank who is falsely accused of stealing a car. She's not keeping things inside anymore! The first time I saw her speaking up I was surprised, but once I saw the behavior repeat, I knew I was witnessing a change. On the other hand, I was shocked when Mia's mom discouraged her and told Mia that she is "a bicycle and the other kids are cars" (p. 145) when it comes to writing in English, because she's usually so supportive of Mia and just wants her to be successful. But after that, she continued to support and care for Mia, so I realized that she probably said that because she didn't want to see her fail or be disappointed. She didn't change, we just saw a different side.*

Prompts
- What's unusual about the character's behavior in this part?
- Do you think the character has changed or are you seeing another side of them?
- Talk about why you think they've changed.
- Based on all you know so far, make a theory.

Skills
- **inferring**
- **determining importance**
- **synthesizing**

Progression

Is able to infer about characters and synthesize information across the text. Is ready to think in more nuanced ways to analyze how characters can be complex (i.e., multiple or conflicting motivations or traits).

Research Link

A reader's initial thoughts about a character are resistant to change, even after being presented with contradicting information (Guéraud, Harmon, & Peracchi, 2005; O'Brien et al., 1998). As a result, students need extensive support to revise their mental representation of characters to comprehend changing or conflicting behaviors (Rapp & Kendeou, 2007, 2009).

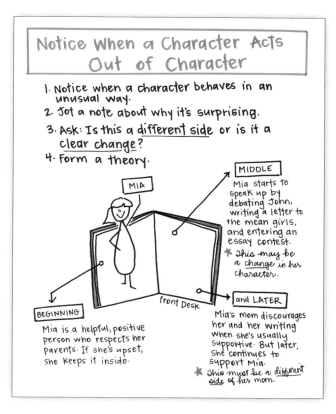

Notice When a Character Acts Out of Character

1. Notice when a character behaves in an unusual way.
2. Jot a note about why it's surprising.
3. Ask: Is this a <u>different side</u> or is it a <u>clear change</u>?
4. Form a theory.

MIA

MIDDLE
Mia starts to speak up by debating John, writing a letter to the mean girls, and entering an essay contest.
★ This may be a change in her character.

BEGINNING
Mia is a helpful, positive person who respects her parents. If she's upset, she keeps it inside.

front Desk

and LATER
Mia's mom discourages her and her writing when she's usually supportive. But later, she continues to support Mia.
★ This must be a different side of her mom.

Skills

- **determining importance**
- **inferring**
- **analyzing**
- **synthesizing**

Progression

Is able to infer about characters and synthesize information across the text. Is ready to think in more nuanced ways to analyze how characters can be complex (i.e., multiple or conflicting motivations or traits).

Research Link

Hancock (1993a, 1993b) found that readers (in grade 6) who chose places to pause and write in literature response journals often wrote entries focused on characters, providing advice in "real time" as the characters navigated the hurdles and conflicts of the plot.

Strategy Pause at a point of conflict in the story. Notice how the character acts before, during, and after the conflict. Describe the character in a way that shows the character's complexity, or different sides of them.

Lesson Language *Conflicts and obstacles test us as people, just as they do the characters in the stories we read. Sometimes people reveal a new side to themselves—sometimes positive, sometimes not so positive—in these moments. In* Sona Sharma, Very Best Big Sister? *(Soundar, 2020). Sona experiences conflict when her mom (Amma) wants her to play a guessing game about her soon-to-be-born sibling. Really, she doesn't want to be a big sister at all—she likes being the baby of the family. Before that moment, Sona is feeling nervous but she's quiet and only shares her feelings with her toy elephant. But then she cries, has a big outburst, and collapses into her mother's arms for comfort. After that moment she's with her grandfather (Thatha) and she's playful and silly and lighthearted. The moment of conflict brought out big feelings and dramatic actions, but we see different sides to her before and after that moment.*

Prompts

- Reread a point in the story where there's conflict.
- What was the character like before this? Now?
- What's the character like after?
- Describe the character to show both sides.

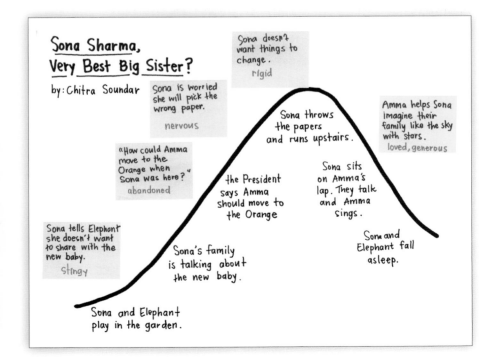

Strategy Identify the different things a character wants, or a goal(s) they are trying to accomplish. Consider if these motivations are in sync or at odds. Use your thinking about their motivations to uncover complexity in the character.

Lesson Language *In* Where the Mountain Meets the Moon *(Lin, 2008), Minli begins her journey wanting to save her village and family by helping her home, Fruitless Mountain, to once again grow green so they can all prosper. As she's away from home, she grows homesick and wants to return, at odds with her original goal of completing the journey, but she continues on because of the love she has for her family. She also meets and befriends a dragon whom she grows to love and wants to help—he wants to join her on her journey to ask the Old Man of the Moon why he can't fly. When Minli gets her chance to meet the Old Man of the Moon, whom she believes has the power to help change her family's circumstances and answer the dragon's question, she only is allowed to ask one question. Her two motivations—helping her family or helping the dragon—are at odds. Noticing her behaviors and choices in moments when her different motivations collide helps us understand her better—we can conclude she is wise, brave, and deeply good.*

Prompts
* Name one of the character's motivations. What is another?
* Are those motivations in sync with what the character wants, or are they at odds?
* Based on how the character acts as they work toward their goal(s), use words to describe them.

Consider a Character's Motivations

What do they want?   **What are their goals?**

Motivations

Minli wants to help her family and village prosper.

Minli wants to help Dragon.

Are they in sync or conflicting?

conflicting

What does that tell you about the character?

Minli is wise, brave, and good.

Skills

- **determining importance**
- **inferring**
- **synthesizing**

Progression

Is ready to synthesize multiple traits to develop a theory or interpretation of a character, describe character relationships, and name the impact that one character has on another.

Strategy Notice a place where a secondary character is interacting with a main character. Think about how a secondary character's actions are impacting the main character by how the main character feels, thinks, acts. Shift your perspective. Think about how the main character's actions and words are causing the secondary character to feel, think, and act. What ideas do you have about each of them and about their relationship?

Lesson Language *Let's look at the scene from* New Kid *(Craft, 2019) when Jordan meets the quarterback at his new school, Andy. Jordan is overwhelmed, a bit nervous, and just trying to take it all in. Here comes Andy who pats him on the head, calls him short, and proceeds to have negative things to say about just about every other student in school such as a "show-off," "awkward," and so on, and tells him to keep away from them all (p. 28). Let's look at this moment through Jordan's eyes. I'm thinking that what Andy's doing is but making him feel anything but welcome. He's probably making him feel like fitting in at this new school will be impossible. That it was a mistake to even enroll here. OK, now let's see it from Andy's eyes. I think he's a little fascinated or interested in the "new kid." He could be trying to sabotage his time at the new school by making it seem like nobody is worth getting to know or maybe he's jealous of him because he's likely to get attention. Or perhaps he wants to be his friend so he's making everyone else seem undesirable. No matter what he wants, I don't feel like they are going to be friends based on how Jordan is responding to him.*

Prompts

- Find a place where the characters are interacting.
- How is (character name) treating (character name)?
- That's a thought about one character. What do you think about their relationship?
- Explain how (character name) is causing (character name) to feel.

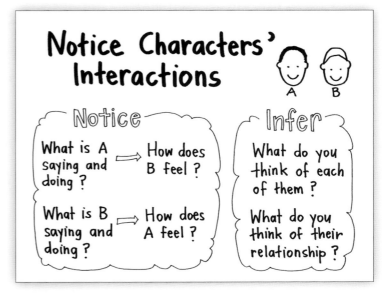

Strategy Collect your notes about one character's traits, feelings, wants, motivations. Lay them all out and look across them to see connections. Consider *when* or *why* a character acts in these similar and different ways. State a theory (a big idea) about who the character *really* is or what they *really* want.

Lesson Language *Let's look across the ideas we jotted at individual spots in the story* After the Fall *(Santat, 2017), combine them, and craft a theory. In one spot we jotted, "He's avoiding the things he loves because he's afraid." In another spot we jotted, "He wants to fly and be free." In another spot we wrote, "He's proud of himself for taking a risk." To put them together into one theory statement, we could ask ourselves, "When does he act one way? When does he act another?" Maybe we could say something like, "Humpty's accident and his feelings after it kept him from living his life fully, but having something that really mattered to him kept him focused and helped him to persevere."*

Prompts
- Start with all the jots you have about the same character—their traits, feelings, wants, and so on.
- Make sure your thoughts about the character are from different spots in the book.
- Yes—I think those traits show different sides to the character. So as you look across them, what theory do you have?
- Say, "My character is sometimes __ when __, but other times seems more __ because __."

Skills
- **inferring**
- **synthesizing**

Progression

Is ready to synthesize multiple traits to develop a theory or interpretation of a character, describe character relationships, and name the impact that one character has on another.

Research Link

As readers organize the information in a story into a coherent mental model, researchers suggest that younger students may create a *causal inference schema* that emphasizes actions and external events, and older readers may generate a *social inference schema* that emphasizes the internal thoughts and feelings that propel the motivations and goals, and subsequently the observable actions, of the story (McConaughy, Fitzhenry-Coor, & Howell, 1983).

Character
Eddie Ventura

Trait energetic
He has a fun time with his friends and he's always happy.

Trait Determined
while he plays sports, he can focus on something he needs to do.

Trait generous
when he sees someone needs help, he will go out of his way to help them.

Theory

My theory about Eddie is that he he is a little bit firm outside, but he is soft inside. When he is hanging out and eating pizza with his friends, he plays around and he's energetic. But he focus and he's determined when he plays baseball. I think that's changed him, in the beginning he could barely be determined to do things. But sports made him be more determined.

Consider When Internal and External Are at Odds

Skills

- **determining importance**
- **inferring**
- **analyzing**
- **synthesizing**

Progression

Is ready to synthesize multiple traits to develop a theory or interpretation of a character, describe character relationships, and name the impact that one character has on another.

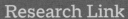

Research Link

Readers of all ages are prone to forming initial impressions of characters that remain stable even in the face of conflicting information (Rapp & Kendeou, 2007, 2009). Furthermore, readers are apt to make predictions that are trait-consistent with a character rather than trait-inconsistent (Rapp, Gerrig, & Prentice, 2001). Therefore, reconciling inconsistent external actions with internal motivations is challenging on a basic psychological level, particularly for younger readers.

Strategy Notice when a character's external actions are out of sync with the character's internal thinking and feelings. Ask yourself, "How do others see this character? Who does this character want to be?" Infer their traits and motivations.

Lesson Language *Meg Medina is a master of developing characters—let's revisit the first chapter of* Merci Suárez Changes Gears *(2018) to pay attention to how she helps us get to know Merci and to see what we can infer based on the clash of external (actions, dialogue) and internal (feeling, thinking). From her actions and dialogue, we see someone who wants to lead, to be in charge. For example, she convinces her friends to take a shortcut, asking them to follow her, using her "take-charge voice" that she's been practicing. But when we pay attention to her thinking and feelings in this same section, we know that she's a bit self-conscious about her hair, about the fact that her parents purchased the cheapest package on picture day, about her left eye that wanders, about feeling babyish around the older kids who call her and her friends "cute" in a voice you'd use to talk to kittens. So who she wants to be to others is someone who's got it together, self-assured, a leader. But on the inside, she's struggling with her own self-esteem. This is only Chapter 1, so as we keep reading, we'll pay attention to times when who Merci is on the outside clashes with how she's really thinking and feeling on the inside and also when the two are the same.*

Prompts

- Can you find a moment when what the character says conflicts with what the character thinks?
- Look at the internal thinking alongside the action.
- I can tell you picked up on the differences between thoughts and actions.
- Say, "My character is saying/doing __, but is thinking/feeling __. So I think . . ."

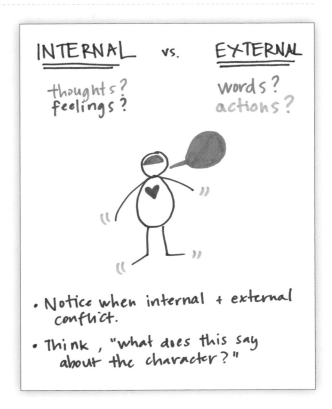

Strategy Notice when you as the reader know more about what's going on in the story than the character does. Articulate what it is the character doesn't know. Think about why it matters and what it might show about them. Consider how their not knowing could present a problem for them.

Lesson Language *Sometimes in stories, readers know things that characters don't know. In stories narrated in third person, the narrator sometimes comes right out to explain something the character doesn't know. For example, in* A Long Walk to Water *(Park, 2010), after Salva makes it safely across the rushing river filled with crocodiles, the narrator explains that "at least a thousand people had died trying to cross the river that day" (p. 79). Imagine how it would have been for Salva if he had known how lucky he was at that moment in the story? Would it have changed anything for him? Could he have continued on, or would he have been overcome with grief for all those that didn't make it? On the other hand, when a character is the narrator (first person), we usually have to infer that we know something the character doesn't know. For example, Merci is the narrator in* Merci Suárez Changes Gears *(Medina, 2018), and by Chapters 3 and 4, it's clear to us as readers that Lolo has advancing Alzheimer's and it's going to be a real challenge for Merci and her family, but Merci herself doesn't realize this. We might describe her at this point with words like* innocent, naive, *or* childlike, *and we can trace how her not knowing impacts her character development across the book.*

Prompts

- What does the character seem to be aware and unaware of?
- What does the character seem to be missing?
- Yes—you identified something we know as readers that the character doesn't know. Now talk about what ideas you have about the character.
- How does that lack of awareness impact the character?

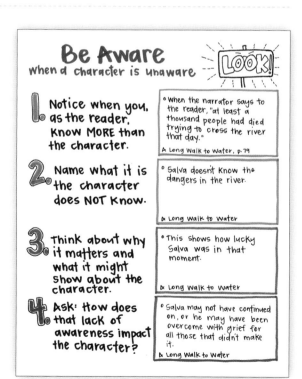

Skills

- **inferring**
- **synthesizing**

Progression

Is ready to synthesize multiple traits to develop a theory or interpretation of a character, describe character relationships, and name the impact that one character has on another.

●●●●●○

Research Link

Authors plan for readers to experience emotions like surprise and suspense by thoughtfully structuring the knowledge states—who knows what when—of various agents (i.e., characters, the narrator, the reader). In a series of experiments, Graesser and colleagues found that readers must construct and keep track of the knowledge states of multiple agents to both understand the story and experience the emotions intended by the author (e.g., Graesser et al., 2001; Graesser & Klettke, 2001).

Skills

- **inferring**
- **synthesizing**
- **analyzing**
- **determining importance**

Progression

Is able to form theories and is beginning to understand character relationships. Is ready to analyze those relationships and consider point of view and characters' perspectives and how they impact the story. May also analyze characters based on a knowledge of archetypes and allegories.

Research Link

In a pair of small studies, researchers used *character story event maps*, graphic organizers that help track characters, actions, and the implications of those actions, to support adolescents with comprehending novel-length stories (Drill & Bellini, 2022; Williamson et al., 2015).

Strategy Pay attention to how specific characters interact within a scene. Describe the qualities of their relationship. Notice when these same characters are in a scene together again. Describe qualities of their relationship at this moment. Put these ideas together to form a theory.

Lesson Language *Most relationships—in real life and in books—exist on a continuum. We need to expect that like a plot mountain, relationships between characters will have their ups and downs and sometimes shift at points of conflict or change. For example, think about Jordan's relationship with his mom (a minor character) in* New Kid *(Craft, 2019). In an early scene we see her so excited to send him to Riverdale School, but she ignores his quiet protests and the feelings that go with them. Later, when she showers him with hugs and calls him her "sweet potato" and "baby," Jordan just smiles and doesn't seem bothered (although his dad points out that she's babying him). And again later when she and Jordan's dad argue about him doing well in school versus pursuing his passion for art, Jordan is seated between them, both literally and figuratively in the middle of the argument. The illustration shows him shrinking down to the size of a baby. From these three scenes, I might say that Jordan's mom babies him and tries to control his life because she wants what's best for him, and that he mostly goes along with her, perhaps out of respect or because it's just normal for her to be the family decision-maker.*

Prompts

- You said ___ about their relationship in an earlier scene. As you reread this scene, what new thinking do you have?
- Put together the ideas you had about these characters' relationship in these few scenes. What's a theory you have now?
- What does their relationship tell you about each of them?

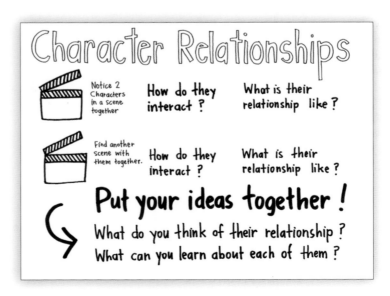

Analyze Author Choices: Point of View and Perspective

Strategy Identify the point of view (first, second, third) that the author chose. Consider why the author chose that narrator—how does it help you understand or relate to the characters? How does it impact how you experience the story? Now consider the *perspective* the narrator has. How does the narrator's identity impact how we experience the story? Understand the character(s)?

Teaching Tip This strategy is a more sophisticated version of Strategy 6.2 because it invites students to go beyond *identifying* the narrator to *analyzing* both the author's choice of narrator and that narrator's perspective (a unique viewpoint). Perspective is influenced by a first-person narrator's identity—their personality, socioeconomic status, cultural background, language, and so on. Both point of view and perspective impact how readers experience all elements of the story. Authors use narrators to help us feel closer to a character (first person) or more distant (third person). You might explore a variety of points of view and perspectives by reading a bit from a range of books including alternating first-person narrators (e.g., *Saving Mr. Terupt* [Buyea, 2015]), alternating third-person narrators (e.g., *Ground Zero* [Gratz, 2021]), alternating narrators with text style changes in a graphic novel (e.g., *Invisible Emmie* [Libenson, 2017]), and consistent first person (e.g., *New Kid* [Craft, 2019]) and third person (*A Long Walk to Water* [Park, 2010]).

Prompts

- How might this scene have been different if a different character had narrated it?
- How does the author's choice of point of view change how we experience the story?
- What do you know about the identity of the first-person narrator? How does who they are shape what we as readers experience?
- How does the narrator's perspective impact our empathy (who we are siding with, caring about, and so on)?

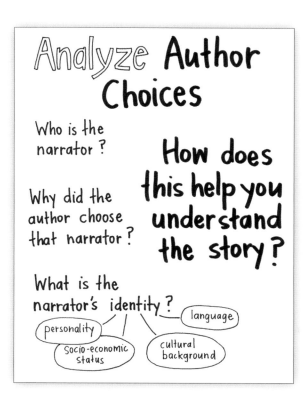

Skills
- **inferring**
- **synthesizing**
- **analyzing**

Progression

Is able to form theories and is beginning to understand character relationships. Is ready to analyze those relationships and consider point of view and characters' perspectives and how they impact the story. May also analyze characters based on a knowledge of archetypes and allegories.

Research Link

Graesser and colleagues explain that with first-person narration, the perspective of the narrator, the protagonist, and the reader are fused, while third-person narration creates emotional distance between the narrator and the characters (Graesser & Klettke, 2001). In a study of college students, participants were better able to recall stories written in first-person, indicating the strong emotional connection that readers make with that perspective (Graesser et al., 1999).

Skills

- **inferring**
- **analyzing**
- **activating prior knowledge**

Progression

Is able to form theories and is beginning to understand character relationships. Is ready to analyze those relationships and consider point of view and characters' perspectives and how they impact the story. May also analyze characters based on a knowledge of archetypes and allegories.

● ● ● ● ● ●

Research Link

Authors use archetypes, which vary based on cultural traditions, as a shorthand for communicating a character's essence. However, if the reader is unable to generate a complete or accurate mental model of that archetype, their understanding will quickly break down. This potential for misunderstanding is particularly acute if the author and the reader do not share the same cultural knowledge (Adams & Bruce, 1982).

Strategy Identify a character's archetype. Think about the strengths and weaknesses typically associated with that archetype. Use what you know about the type to predict how they'll act and to compare and contrast them as a character with other characters you know who fit the same archetype.

Teaching Tip Archetypes are character types that may be based on patterns of human behavior and/or common types in literature. They can help readers get to know characters quickly and provide important foils in a story. For example, Minli in *Where the Mountain Meets the Moon* (Lin, 2009) could be considered a classic hero. She is different from everyone she knows in both her physical appearance (glossy black hair and pink cheeks, shining eyes, and a smile, compared with the plain townspeople) and her traits (always ready for adventure, quick thinking, resourceful). Though at times she feels guilty for leaving home and is homesick, she is determined to complete her quest to save her village and family. A reader could predict early on that she would complete her quest if they know about this character type from other stories and could do some analysis comparing her to other explorer/ hero types such as Lyra Belacqua or Katniss Everdeen. There are examples of other archetypes in this story—the Magistrate Tiger (villain), the Buffalo Boy (orphan), Dragon (sidekick), Ba (storyteller)—that you could explore.

Prompts

- Does your character seem to fit with any of the archetypes you know?
- If your character fits with that archetype, what are some of the traits (strengths and weaknesses) you'd expect them to have?
- Based on that archetype, what can you predict about the character's actions/ journey?
- Use the archetype to help you compare/ contrast this character to others from different stories.

Identify Archetypes

Archetype	Example
Hero	T'Challa from *Black Panther*
Jester	Dory from Finding Nemo, Fool from King Lear
Magician	Gandalf from The Lord of the Rings
Outlaw	Batman
Explorer	Huckleberry Finn, Odysseus
Sage/ Mentor	Moana's Grandmother, Tala
Innocent	Tiny Tim from A Christmas Carol
Caregiver	Mrs. Luella Bates Washington Jones from "Thank You, Ma'am"
Bully	Draco Malfoy from Harry Potter
Orphan	Snow White

Does your character fit with archetypes you know?

What are some traits you would expect them to have?

What can you predict about their actions and journey?

Strategy Identify the larger point the story is trying to make (about society, religion, politics, human nature). Focus on a specific character within the story. Consider what that character might represent in the context of the story's larger meaning.

Teaching Tip Allegorical figures are characters that are important to the story *and* could be considered symbolic. Often, but not always, the character stands for something related to religion, politics, or morality. Some examples from classic stories include the tree in *The Giving Tree* (Silverstein, 1964), which could be considered a symbol for a mother who gives and gives until there is nothing left. The pigs in *Animal Farm*, most would agree, stand for specific members of the Bolshevik Leadership (Orwell, 1945). In *Where the Mountain Meets the Moon* (Lin, 2008), the Old Man of the Moon is an all-knowing character who lives atop a mountain reading "The Book of Fortune," containing the wisdom of all the world since the beginning of time. In a story that's in part about the importance of faith, who does that remind you of? (Multiple faith traditions, of course, have an all-knowing presence at their center.)

Prompts

- What are some of the themes/big ideas in this story?
- Are there any characters in this story that might stand for something or someone connected to that theme?
- What are some examples from the text that support that interpretation?
- Think about society, religion, politics, and human nature to help you consider what this character might represent.

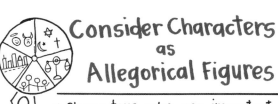

Skills
- **inferring**
- **analyzing**
- **activating prior knowledge**

Progression

Is able to form theories and is beginning to understand character relationships. Is ready to analyze those relationships and consider point of view and characters' perspectives and how they impact the story. May also analyze characters based on a knowledge of archetypes and allegories.

Research Link

Reporting from his own fourth-grade classroom, a teacher-researcher shared how the use of an allegorical picture book allowed him to have discussions about an otherwise challenging topic, in this case, the fraught history of immigration to America, both historic and current. He used the book as a bridge between the past and the present, between the story and reality, and between different texts (Cipparone, 2014).

Comprehending Theme

◎ Why is this goal important?

Stories are often rich with layers of deeper meaning, but these meanings don't just jump off the page at a reader. To read between the lines, think beyond what's literally in the text, and think "off" the page, readers need imagination, the ability to think abstractly, and an awareness of what to look for (Seifert, Dyer, & Black, 1986). This kind of thinking—picking up on themes, considering social issues, and interpreting symbolism—changes the reading experience: stories can now help us make sense of our world, feel something, question our own beliefs. Without these understandings, one could argue that readers misunderstand or, at the very least, *miss* a lot of what the story is about (Dimino et al., 1990; Gurney et al., 1990).

Children at any age or grade level can (and should!) have their own interpretations about the meanings of texts. These interpretations should be rooted in the details of the text, but two readers reading the same story may interpret themes differently, because the prior knowledge, experiences, and identities they bring to the text are unique (Rosenblatt, 1978). As children begin to infer themes, they may talk about them using individual words and short phrases, and over time they will learn to elaborate on their thinking and find symbolism related to those themes.

Although in books for beginning readers, themes are often easily accessible (e.g., "fitting in" or "friends are important"), as students progress through more challenging texts, themes often get to be more and more like life itself—multi-dimensional, contradictory, messy (Applebee, Langer, & Mullis, 1987; Sweet & Snow, 2003). When symbolism starts to appear, students can understand more of the text when they consider how people, places, or objects might represent something beyond their physical description.

What is a Theme?

The word *theme* is used in a variety of ways across research literature, practitioner-authored materials, and curriculum. In this chapter, I'm using the term *theme* to refer to either a single *word*, a *phrase*, or a *statement* that captures a reader's idea of what the story is *really* about because the idea is threaded across the story. Themes go beyond a retelling of plot events, are generalizable, and can often be applied to the reader's life (e.g., "I should be more courageous").

When a theme is stated as a single word or phrase, it's generally a *concept* (e.g., "courage," "good versus evil") and may or may not relate to social issues (e.g., "poverty," "ableism").

When a theme is expressed as a statement, it's generally a full sentence that elaborates (or provides commentary) on the single-word theme. These statements may contain a value judgement ("courage is important") or not ("some people have courage") (see Williams, 2005; Williams, Brown, et al., 1994; Williams, Lauer, et al., 2002).

Skills a reader might work on as part of this goal

Analyzing
Considering how an author develops a theme or symbol within a story, or thinking across texts to compare and contrast themes or symbols.

Determining importance
Identifying moments in a story that reveal important meanings related to a message, lesson, or theme.

Inferring
Using information from the text and the reader's own background knowledge to construct personal understandings, including predictions, about themes (e.g., messages, lessons, morals) and symbols.

Activating prior knowledge
Using knowledge of themes and ideas in other stories or in life to comprehend.

Synthesizing
Putting together information and ideas from across a text to interpret a story's theme(s), or an author's uses of symbolism.

◎ How do I know if this goal is right for my student?

To assess student comprehension of themes, ask students to respond to prompts and questions about a text or excerpt, and then evaluate the quality of their responses. The text can be short (e.g., short story, picture book, something from a children's magazine) or long (e.g., chapter book); it can be one you choose or students choose; and you can decide to read it aloud or have them read it independently. Plant questions at key points in the story, or ask them to read the whole story and respond by jotting or talking about the story when they're done.

Here are some prompts and questions you can use that align to this goal:

- What lesson(s) can we learn from reading this story?
- What does this story teach you about people/life/our world?
- What themes are showing up in this text?
- What have you learned about [social issue or topic] from reading this book?
- What might [symbol] represent?
- Are there any examples of symbolism in this text?
- Explain how this theme shows up in this book.

> A lesson I learned from reading this book was that fighting with your best friend isn't fun and it's okay to be sad.

This young reader shows he's able to articulate *two* lessons using universal (not book-specific) language. This is the limit of theme work he can do since the books he's reading don't yet have symbolism. I might choose to help him do similar work on different books (Strategies 7.16–7.21), or choose a different goal for him.

> The monster might represent her anger trieing to get out when she's tring to keep her good self in her because she doesn't like anger.

This response from a student reading a chapter book shows an understanding that something concrete (the monster in her dreams) can represent something abstract (her anger trying to get out). This student could work more on thinking about the importance of symbols as they connect to theme(s) in the story (Strategies 7.22–7.24).

> The theme of this book is that you should make new friends and keep your old friends. This theme relates to the title of the book (Taking Sides) because in the story Linc has two different groups of friends, his old school and his new school. In the end Linc must choose which group of friends.

This reader has connected the story's title to one possible theme or interpretation and has provided some explanation of her thinking. She's ready to learn strategies for inferring multiple themes (Strategies 7.19–7.20).

What Texts Might Students Use When Practicing Strategies from This Chapter?

Strategies in this chapter will help readers who are reading narratives of any type, format, or genre that are fictional (e.g., historical fiction, mystery, realistic fiction chapter books, graphic novels) and many that are not (e.g., biographies, memoir).

◎ How do I support students as they develop their understanding of themes?

After evaluating a student's verbal or written responses about the themes in their book(s), select strategies that you can model, that they can practice with you, and that they can use independently to increase their skills.

Although development is rarely perfectly linear, skill progressions can help us pinpoint where a student is now and what might come next. Use the if-then chart on page 237 to evaluate your students' reading and find strategies that will support their growth.

A Progression of Skills: *Comprehending Theme*

If a student . . .

Can understand a story on a literal level using book-specific language and is ready to infer a lesson, often from a moment in the book, or understand morals (as in fables) that are explicitly stated.

Is ready to understand theme as a concept inferred from synthesizing details across a section or the whole text and then articulated as a single word or phrase (e.g., friendships, love, fitting in).

Is able to infer theme(s) as a single word or phrase and is ready to elaborate or provide commentary to articulate theme(s) as statements, and infer multiple themes based on different plotlines, perspectives, and so on.

Is ready to identify symbols and motifs that connect to theme(s) and use prior knowledge to interpret their meaning(s).

Can identify theme(s), and is ready to analyze thematic elements within one text and/or across texts.

Then you might teach . . .

7.1	Think About the Moral of the Story
7.2	Give Advice to the Character
7.3	Look Up to Characters
7.4	Learn from Character Changes
7.5	Notice How Characters Respond
7.6	Pay Attention to "Aha Moments"
7.7	Notice When Wise Characters Teach
7.8	Connect Texts to Texts to Find Lessons
7.9	Find Different Lessons Within a Series
7.10	Find Theme Hints in Blurbs

7.11	Label a Theme (as a Concept/Idea)
7.12	Distinguish Between Plot Events and Theme(s)
7.13	Find a Story's Theme(s) by Focusing on Character
7.14	Find Theme Hints in Titles
7.15	Identify Social Issues

7.16	Say More About a Theme
7.17	Say More About Social Issues, and Take Action
7.18	Consider Last Words
7.19	Find Different Themes in Different Plotlines
7.20	Consider Characters' Identities for Different Perspectives on Themes
7.21	React to What's Unfair

7.22	Recognize Objects as Symbols
7.23	Draw from Your Symbol Bank
7.24	Look for Symbolism in Setting

7.25	Analyze the Development of Theme
7.26	Connect Texts to Analyze Theme
7.27	Analyze Satire

Strategy Read the fable. Read the moral of the story. Put it into your own words. Think about whether the main action in the story is positive or negative, whether the outcome is positive or negative. Think, "How does this story connect to and teach me this moral?"

Teaching Tip In fables (such as those by Aesop), a very short story is followed by a "moral" or lesson, which the author clearly states for the reader—usually a virtue the reader is meant to live by (e.g., being brave, friendly, helpful, truthful) or a cautionary tale of something not to do. Since fables are examples of classic literature, lessons from these stories often show up in contemporary children's literature. Therefore, when beginning to teach about themes, using fables provides two clear benefits. First, students can read a lesson right on the page (without having to infer it) and consider the connection between the events of the story and the lesson. Second, fables introduce readers to a variety of lessons and how they are phrased in universal language so they can look for similar ideas in the literature they read.

Prompts

- Read the moral of the story. Put it into your own words.
- How do the events of the story teach this moral?
- How does the character in the story learn this lesson? How do you as a reader learn it?
- Reread the fable and talk about the parts that go with this moral.

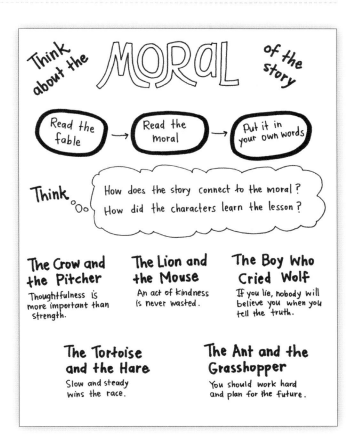

Progression

Can understand a story on a literal level using book-specific language and is ready to infer a lesson, often from a moment in the book, or understand morals (as in fables) that are explicitly stated.

Research Link

Dorfman has proposed a model for understanding theme that includes (1) a positive or negative central action, (2) a positive or negative outcome, and (3) a coherent and morally understandable connection between them. If any of those three components is unclear or misunderstood, the reader has a difficult time identifying the point of the story (Dorfman, 1988; Dorfman & Brewer, 1994).

Skills

- **activating prior knowledge**
- **determining importance**
- **inferring**

Progression

Can understand a story on a literal level using book-specific language and is ready to infer a lesson, often from a moment in the book, or understand morals (as in fables) that are explicitly stated.

● ○ ○ ○ ○

Research Link

In *bibliotherapy*, readers learn to problem solve and acquire coping skills (Lindeman & Kling, 1968; Pardeck & Markward, 1995) as they identify with issues characters face in books (Forgan, 2002). The process, however, can be reversed. By linking their lived personal experiences and knowledge to what a character is experiencing, students can consider how they might address the problems characters face (Cook, Earles-Vollrath, & Ganz, 2006).

Strategy Notice when a character acts in a way that surprises or worries you. Think, "Should they be doing that? What have I learned in my life that they could learn?" Give advice to the character by saying, "You should/shouldn't __ because __."

Teaching Tip For a variety of spins on this strategy, you can get more specific by asking children to pay attention to different aspects of character actions: something a character does again and again (a pattern), something a character does that you think is a mistake, something a character does to try to solve a problem, or something a character does to another character.

Prompts

- What is the character doing in this scene that you're paying attention to?
- Notice a mistake the character makes again and again.
- Say "Try to (or not to) __ when you __."
- Start with, "You should/shouldn't __."

Strategy List a character's positive traits. Think about when and why you see those traits based on how the character acts. Then think, "What lesson can this character teach me?"

Lesson Language *There are some people in your life you look up to. Perhaps the person shows courage, even when something is scary. Perhaps the person is kind, even when other people are being difficult. Perhaps they are patient, even during times when you'd be easily frustrated. People like this inspire us; they're role models. Characters in our books can be role models, too, and we can learn from the traits we see in them. For example, it would be difficult not to notice all the times Omu shares her stew in* Thank You, Omu! *(Mora, 2019), even though it means there is nothing left for her, and not think, "It's good to share when you can. I think I should share more, too."*

Prompts
- How would you describe how the character is acting here?
- What are you learning from this character?
- Say, "__ taught me that if __, you should __."
- Say, "__ is acting like __, so I'm learning __."

Skills
- **inferring**
- **synthesizing**
- **determining importance**

Progression

Can understand a story on a literal level using book-specific language and is ready to infer a lesson, often from a moment in the book, or understand morals (as in fables) that are explicitly stated.

Research Link

Based on the hypothesis that well-written books offer a depth of emotional experience, an analysis of 76 Newbery Medal books revealed characters who demonstrated eight widely agreed upon positive traits: compassion, respect, discipline, loyalty, courage, responsibility, forgiveness, and justice (Leal et al., 2000).

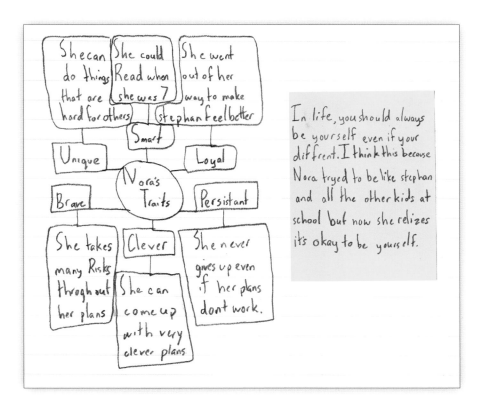

Skills

- **inferring**
- **synthesizing**
- **determining importance**

Progression

Can understand a story on a literal level using book-specific language and is ready to infer a lesson, often from a moment in the book, or understand morals (as in fables) that are explicitly stated.

Research Link

Going beyond the physical actions and deriving meaning from the psychological motivations of characters is particularly challenging for young students, although research indicates that inferencing abilities develop with age and practice (e.g., Beach & Wendler, 1987).

Strategy Pause in a place where the character's feelings or traits change. Notice what causes the character to change. Think, "What did they learn in that moment of change?"

Lesson Language *In* After the Fall *(Santat, 2017), Humpty was sad, afraid, and he missed being on the wall and doing what he loved—birdwatching. When he conquered his fears and climbed the wall, his feelings changed dramatically. He went from feeling sorry for himself to mustering up courage. In that moment, I could think about why his feelings changed—he set aside his fears and did what he truly wanted and needed to do. He learned it's important to follow your heart and dreams and be true to yourself. He also learned that by having courage, he could do great things.*

Prompts

- What were you thinking about the character at the beginning? When and where does it change?
- Find a place where the character's feelings/traits change.
- Based on this moment when they changed, what do you think the character learned?
- What does the change in feelings teach you?

Strategy Consider the actions of one character and how they impact another character. Notice how the character responds. Think, "What can I learn from their response?"

Lesson Language *When I read* Fauja Singh Keeps Going *(Singh, 2020), I noticed how Fauja responded to the way other characters treated him. For example, when he was a child, most of his family members would say "He's too weak," but his mother would tell him every morning, "You know yourself, Fauja, and you know what you're capable of. Today is a chance to do your best" (unpaginated). What did Fauja do? How did he respond? He practiced walking, getting stronger each day, and eventually at age five—he began to walk! What can we learn from this response? Perhaps that we can accomplish more when we listen to those who encourage us. Or that hard work pays off. Or that we should focus on what matters most.*

Prompts
- Name two characters who interact. How does one affect the other?
- Name the effect [character's] actions have on [character].
- What are you learning and thinking about based on how one treats the other?
- Say, "[Character] acts [behavior] toward [character], and that's teaching me . . ."

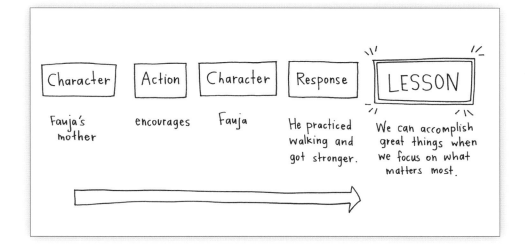

Skills
- **inferring**
- **synthesizing**
- **determining importance**

Progression

Can understand a story on a literal level using book-specific language and is ready to infer a lesson, often from a moment in the book, or understand morals (as in fables) that are explicitly stated.

Research Link

Although all stories provide opportunities for learning social-emotional skills, research has shown that students who experience difficulties with social interactions particularly benefit from reading instruction that focuses on inferring the thoughts and feelings of others (Lysaker et al., 2011).

Skills

• **inferring**

• **determining importance**

Progression

Can understand a story on a literal level using book-specific language and is ready to infer a lesson, often from a moment in the book, or understand morals (as in fables) that are explicitly stated.

Hat Tip

Notice and Note: Strategies for Close Reading (Beers & Probst, 2012)

Research Link

Moments of reflection near the end of a text are closely tied to the author's purpose (Deane, 2020). However, the author does not always state directly their intended message, and it may even be intentionally ambiguous; therefore, a reader must read the text closely to infer what the author is signaling (Goldman, McCarthy, & Burkett, 2015).

Strategy Look for a moment, often toward the end of the book, where the character reflects on what's happened in the story. Reread it. Ask yourself, "What can I learn from this passage?"

Lesson Language *When a person realizes or comes to understand something they haven't realized or understood before, we call this an "Aha moment." Sometimes a character's "aha" will be in their dialogue (especially when the story is told in third person). For example, in* Islandborn *(Díaz, 2018), after Lola interviews her family and community about her island, longing to spark her own firsthand memories, she says to her teacher, "I realized that I don't have to feel bad because even if I'd never set foot on the Island it doesn't matter: The Island is me" (unpaginated). Yes, she even says "I realized!" Her aha moment is right there, clear as day for us to notice and think about. When the book has a first-person narrator, then the aha moment may be in the character's narration, such as in* Merci Suárez Changes Gears *(Medina, 2018). The last page or so of the book is filled with Merci's reflections, making sense of the story she's just told, making her ahas public for all her readers to learn from, too. Here's just one of the sentences, where on the one hand she's wishing that everything could stay the same and then realizing, "Then again . . . it means that I wouldn't grow up at all. Staying the same could be just as sad as Lolo [Merci's grandfather] changing" (p. 355).*

Prompts

• Can you find a spot where the character reflects?
• Based on the reflection, what are you thinking about?
• What does the character's reflection help you to learn?

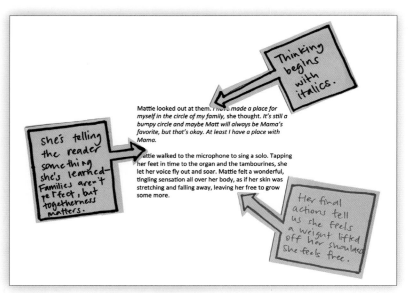

Text excerpt from *Circle of Gold* (Boyd, 1996).

Strategy Look for a place where a secondary character (often one who is older or wiser) gives advice to a main character, either directly or indirectly. Think to yourself, "What is the older character teaching the younger one?" Then, try to put the lesson in your own words, stating what it is that you, the reader, might also learn.

Lesson Language *You may have a person in your life who is older and offers you advice—maybe it's a parent, a grandparent, or a teacher. They may do it directly, "Have you ever considered . . . maybe you should try . . . ," or indirectly (by telling you a story from their childhood, for example). Many characters in the books you're reading also have people who offer them advice, and when you notice this, you can learn from that advice, too. For example, in* Where the Mountain Meets the Moon *(Lin, 2008), the author intersperses the narrative with stories that Minli's elders (her Ma and Ba) tell to teach and explain. Each of those short stories teaches Minli lessons that we as readers can learn too.*

Prompts

- Who in this story is an older and wiser character?
- Does anyone in this story give advice to another character?
- Put that character's advice in your own words.
- What's the lesson that you think you might learn from that?

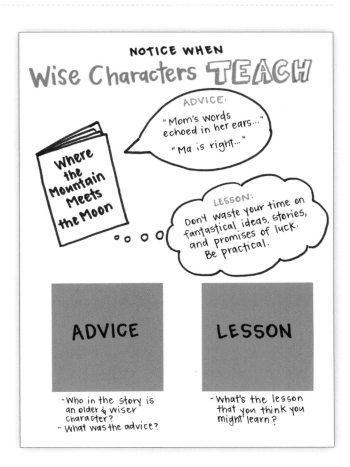

Skills

- **inferring**
- **determining importance**

Progression

Can understand a story on a literal level using book-specific language and is ready to infer a lesson, often from a moment in the book, or understand morals (as in fables) that are explicitly stated.

●○○○○

Hat Tip

Notice and Note: Strategies for Close Reading (Beers & Probst, 2012)

Research Link

Carl Jung (1959) suggested that the Wise Old Woman/Man is an archetype, a motif deeply embedded in the *collective unconscious*, who appears in stories across time and cultures to impart the wisdom of experience. Identifying this character allows the lead character, and by extension, the reader, to gain knowledge (Renga & Lewis, 2018).

Connect Texts to Texts to Find Lessons

Skills

- **activating prior knowledge**
- **analyzing**
- **inferring**

Progression

Can understand a story on a literal level using book-specific language and is ready to infer a lesson, often from a moment in the book, or understand morals (as in fables) that are explicitly stated.

● ○ ○ ○ ○

Research Link

Scholars from diverse disciplines refer to *intertextuality*, the idea that texts do not exist in isolation but are written and interpreted in relation to other stories (Deane, 2020; Wilkie-Stibbs, 2006). Readers notice aspects of stories that resemble, echo, or transform stories they have previously encountered (Bloome & Egan-Robertson, 1993; Deane, 2020).

Strategy Remember the stories you've read and what lessons you learned from reading them. Think about the story you're reading now. Do any of the lessons from the other books apply to this one?

Teaching Tip When they first talk about lessons, some children often stick too closely to literal details in the plot. For example, they'll say, "If you have a pair of extra shoes, you should give them to someone who needs them," instead of phrasing the lesson in a universal way, such as "Be grateful for what you have and share when you can." Discussing books with common lessons is one way to help children understand these ideas in a more conceptual way and talk about them using more universal language. To facilitate this talk, you might create a "wall" with common lessons and place book titles below them that teach similar things. Or start with book titles (ones you've read aloud together) and list the lessons they explore underneath. When children can identify multiple texts that have a common theme, they're able to look beyond the specific details of each story to see the ideas that they have in common.

Prompts

- What other books does this one remind you of? Why?
- Look at lessons we've identified in other stories. Are any of them true in this book, too?
- What lessons from that book apply to this one as well? What is different?
- Can you make a connection with lessons?

to find LESSONS

Be grateful for what you have and share when you can.	With hard-work, belief in yourself & determination, you can accomplish anything.	The bond between siblings is powerful.	It is unfair to judge someone at first glance. Everyone has a story.
- Those Shoes by Maribeth Boelts	- Firebird by Misty Copeland	- Unbound by Joyce Scott	- Milo Imagines the World by Matt de la Peña
- December by Eve Bunting	- The Floating Field by Scott Riley	- Fighting Words by Kimberly Brubaker Bradley	- The Junkyard Wonders by Patricia Polacco
- Christmas in the Trenches by John McCutcheon	- The Year We Learned to Fly by Jacqueline Woodson		

Strategy Identify the different problems in the books you've read from within the same series. Think about a lesson the character learned based on each problem. State different lessons for each book.

Teaching Tip *In series books, many things stay the same—characters, settings, sometimes even the general plot structure. However, the key obstacles and plot events do change from book to book, and so can our takeaways as readers. Consider the Dyamonde Daniel series. In* Almost Zero *(Grimes, 2010), Dyamonde learns to be grateful for what she has and to share with those who are in greater need. In* Make Way for Dyamonde Daniel *(Grimes, 2009), she learns how important it is to get to know someone and not make assumptions about their actions.*

Prompts
• What problem does the character deal with in each book?
• Name a lesson you can learn connected to each problem.
• What does the character learn? Now say it as a lesson you as the reader can learn.
• Since the problems and plots are different, the lessons should be, too.

Skills
• **activating prior knowledge**
• **inferring**

Progression

Can understand a story on a literal level using book-specific language and is ready to infer a lesson, often from a moment in the book, or understand morals (as in fables) that are explicitly stated.

Research Link

While reading a single story, readers must constantly update what they know about the characters and the plot (Donovan & Rapp, 2018). But in a series book, the process of *updating* is less critical because readers are familiar with the recurring characters, settings, and plot patterns, freeing them up to focus on the differences between installments, including the problem, resolution, and lessons learned (McGill-Franzen & Ward, 2018).

Skills

- inferring
- determining importance

Progression

Can understand a story on a literal level using book-specific language and is ready to infer a lesson, often from a moment in the book, or understand morals (as in fables) that are explicitly stated.

● ○ ○ ○ ○

Research Link

Exploring how middle school students select books, researchers found that half of the students referred to the blurb (Gerlach & Rinehart, 1992). In another study, middle schoolers reported that book blurbs generally did a good job communicating plot events, providing them with information necessary to predict what the book would be about (Rinehart et al., 1998).

Strategy Before reading the book, read the blurb to see if you can identify the character's struggles or a central problem in the plot. Then, predict, "Based on the struggles/problems they'll deal with, what lessons would I expect the character to learn in this story?"

Lesson Language *On the back cover blurb for* J.D. and the Great Barber Battle *(Dillard, 2021), we learn about many of the obstacles J.D. will face in the story. First, he gets a bad haircut from his mom before the first day of school. After that, he decides to "take matters into his own hands" and finds out "that unlike his mom, he's a genius with the clippers." He opens his own barbershop in his bedroom. Everyone starts talking about him and his success. But then, the owner of the only official local barbershop realizes he's losing customers and tries to shut down J.D.'s business. So his problems are he's embarrassed, which leads him to start his own business (successfully!), but then he has to "battle" for his ability to continue doing business. Maybe this book will be about how you should work hard and not give up when you really want something.*

Prompts

- Read the blurb to identify some problems/obstacles the character will face in the story.
- You can think about what someone would learn from solving those problems.
- What do you think the character might learn from dealing with these problems?
- You predicted the lesson would be ___. Now that you've read the story, what are you thinking now?

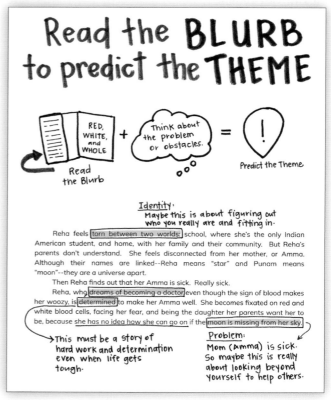

Text excerpt from *Red, White, and Whole* (LaRocca, 2021).

Strategy Think back to the events of the story you've read so far, quickly summarizing or stating the gist of the events. Then, think, "What's a word or short phrase that captures a theme (as a concept/idea) this story explores?" Use the list of common themes to help.

Lesson Language *One way to think of theme is as a concept, or idea, about life or people that the story explores. Themes can help us label and organize our thinking, like sorting similar objects into buckets. They help us think about the* so what *of any one book and also make connections between books (for example, both of these books are about friendship). A few common themes show up again and again in books, and as a starting place, you could consider if any of those themes are explored in the text you're reading.*

Teaching Tip A quick Google search for "common themes in literature" will yield lots of possibilities like the ones you see on this chart. Include ones you think your students are most likely to understand and find in the books they are reading. If you introduce them individually and with examples, students will be more likely to see them in other texts.

Prompts
- Say the gist of the story. Now say, "So what about it?"
- Check the list of common themes. Think about whether any of those relate to the story.
- Yes, a story can have more than one theme.
- Think, "What's a word or phrase that names something this story is *really about?*"

Skills
- **inferring**
- **determining importance**
- **synthesizing**

Progression

Is ready to understand theme as a concept inferred from synthesizing details across a section or the whole text and then articulated as a single word or phrase (e.g., friendships, love, fitting in).

● ● ○ ○ ○ ○

Research Link

Work by Lehr (1988, 1991) indicates that students as young as five and six are able to identify and match stories by theme (e.g., friendship, courage), before they are able to name the theme itself. The ability to verbalize the similarities between stories improves with age, particularly with wide exposure to literature.

Skills

- **inferring**
- **determining importance**
- **synthesizing**

Progression

Is ready to understand theme as a concept inferred from synthesizing details across a section or the whole text and then articulated as a single word or phrase (e.g., friendships, love, fitting in).

Research Link

Research indicates that identifying theme is especially challenging for students with certain learning disabilities, often because they use background knowledge inappropriately when they infer or they impose their personal point of view (Williams, 1993). Building from this research, Williams and colleagues (1994) designed a successful program to support students with learning disabilities to understand the concept of theme, identify themes, link theme to story events to improve literal comprehension, and apply themes to their lives.

Strategy To figure out what a story is *really* about, keep track of important plot events, especially those connected to the main problem(s) and (re)solution(s). Then, jot words or phrases that name the themes that relate to an important event or a pattern of events.

Lesson Language *The author of a story crafts a plot with carefully chosen details. We can follow the details to understand the sequence of events, but then as readers, we don't just read for what's literally there, we have to think about it, too! For example, in* Thank You, Omu! *(Mora, 2018), one of the first plot events is Omu cooking a delicious stew. I think about this event and I ask myself, "What does it relate to? Maybe . . .* pride, hard work." *Next, Omu shares her stew with the boy and this makes me think about* generosity, sharing, helping, *so I jot these words next to this event. As I continue reading, I notice that each time she shares with someone, they say, "Thank you," so I jot the word* gratitude. *Do you see that the author doesn't explicitly say any of these words and phrases I jotted—words like* pride, generosity, gratitude? *I moved from the specifics of what happened in the book to these more abstract words that are themes I know from life and that we often see in books.*

Prompts

- Name a main plot event in one quick sentence from these pages.
- What's a theme that relates to that event?
- That's the pattern of events . . . so now think about the theme that connects to it.
- Yes, as you list new plot events, you can also come up with new themes that relate to those events.

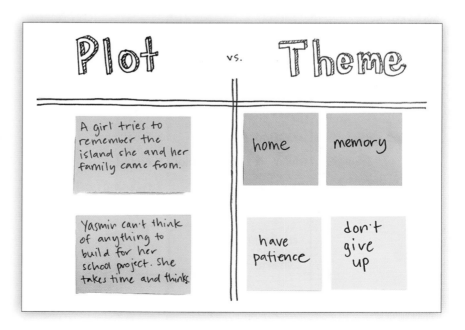

Find a Story's Theme(s) by Focusing on Character

Strategy Describe something about a character—a trait, a feeling, a motivation, and so on—based on how they handle what happens in the story. Then, use a word or phrase to name a theme that the character description makes you think about.

Lesson Language *When reading* The Floating Field: How a Group of Thai Boys Built Their Own Soccer Field *(Riley, 2021), I know that the boys wanted to get better at soccer, even without a proper field to practice on, and I remember that the townspeople called the boys crazy for building their own field. But the boys just blocked them out, stayed focused, believed in themselves, and got it done. If I used a word to describe the boys, I'd say they are* determined. *Now let me think, "What themes does being* determined *suggest? The importance of hard work. Teamwork. Staying focused on goals." Notice that I moved from a word I'd use to describe the characters to naming themes related to that trait.*

Prompts

- Name a theme that is showing up in this story based on what you are thinking about the characters.
- You might say, "I think it could be __ (theme) because __."
- Think about the character's traits or feelings. What theme relates based on the thinking you're doing about characters?

Skills

- **inferring**
- **determining importance**

Progression

Is ready to understand theme as a concept inferred from synthesizing details across a section or the whole text and then articulated as a single word or phrase (e.g., friendships, love, fitting in).

Research Link

When teachers guided second- and third-grade students to focus on the main character and the story's central problem, and to evaluate the outcome of the story, identify what the main character learned, and how that lesson could be applied to their own lives, the students were better able to identify themes that were the focus of instruction (Williams et al., 2002).

Progression

Is ready to understand theme as a concept inferred from synthesizing details across a section or the whole text and then articulated as a single word or phrase (e.g., friendships, love, fitting in).

Research Link

In a study with seventh and eighth graders (Gerlach & Reinhart, 1992), researchers presented the students with ten books and asked them to think aloud as they explored them. Students reported using the title as one of the primary ways to choose and gain information about the book.

Strategy Reread the title of the book. Think about how the title connects to what you read in the book. State a theme that seems to be a thread throughout the book and that is also reflected in the title.

Lesson Language *Titles often hint at the most important events, or ideas, in a book. Here are some examples. In* Merci Suárez Changes Gears *(Medina, 2018), change plays a major role—in part it's a coming-of-age story, but Merci also learns to adapt and deal with changes outside of her control, such as her grandfather's Alzheimer's. In* Fauja Singh Keeps Going *(Singh, 2020), we learn how important it is to keep going—to pursue dreams, to shut out the voices of naysayers, and the value of determination. In* After the Fall *(Santat, 2017), we see that you only truly learn what you are capable of after you fall . . . and get back up again.*

Prompts

• What's a concept or idea that you found throughout the book that connects back to the title?
• Consider why the book may be titled that.
• Are there any key words in the title that might be key words in a theme?
• That theme fits with the story! Is there another theme you think might also fit?

Strategy List all the issues your character deals with in the story. Then, decide which are *personal* issues and which are *social* issues. Consider the social issues. Think, "Which of the social issues are also *themes* in the story because they show up again and again?"

Lesson Language *When the author includes problems, obstacles, and conflicts in a story, it adds tension and suspense. It also can help readers think, and learn. One type of problem characters may deal with is called a* social issue, *which is a problem that exists within a society that many people deal with and try to solve and is often outside of any one character's control. For example, in* Front Desk *(Yang, 2018), Mia deals with many* personal *issues or problems: her mom doesn't understand her passion for writing, the motel owner docks the family's pay for something outside of their control, and so on. But* social *issues also are a really big part of the book— racism and prejudice, mistreatment of immigrants, and the effects of poverty, to name a few. They show up again and again in the story and are themes.*

Prompts
- Check the chart. Are any of the social issues on the chart part of the story you read?
- That sounds like a *personal* issue. It's something affecting the character.
- What makes that a *social* issue rather than a *personal* issue?
- Is the character part of a group of people who face common challenges?

Skills
- **analyzing**
- **synthesizing**
- **determining importance**

Progression

Is ready to understand theme as a concept inferred from synthesizing details across a section or the whole text and then articulated as a single word or phrase (e.g., friendships, love, fitting in).

● ● ○ ○ ○

Research Link

Readers need *critical literacies* to think deeply about the issues discussed within a story, as well as how and why the author has approached those topics in that particular way (Luke, 2012). Describing the impact of an interdisciplinary unit on (im)migration in a third-grade classroom, Brownell and Rashid (2020) present compelling evidence that children are capable of grappling with weighty social issues within and across multiple texts.

Skills

- **inferring**
- **synthesizing**

Progression

Is able to infer theme(s) as a single word or phrase and is ready to elaborate or provide commentary to articulate theme(s) as statements, and infer multiple themes based on different plotlines, perspectives, and so on.

Strategy Think about a theme you've identified as a single word or short phrase. Then ask yourself, "So what about it?" Think back to moments that connect to one theme. Then, say more. The sentence you say may be a general observation or a value judgement.

Lesson Language *Any one book can be about many things. For example, some themes I thought about when reading* My Papi Has a Motorcycle *(Quintero, 2019) are family, community, fatherhood, change, and love. Those single words are a start, but I can think more deeply about them. For example, I can think about moments in the story that got me thinking about* community—*the main characters are always happy to see others in the community, they have special relationships with various community members, they have memories with the people in their community. Now, I can ask myself, "So what about* community?" *and say more. For example, "Community can be like an extended family" or "Community is what makes people feel at home." Notice that I don't use any specific character names or settings anymore. I'm talking about the theme in a universal way, that can apply to other books or my life.*

Prompts

- List some themes that are showing up in your book.
- Ask yourself, "So what about __?" Say more.
- Think about moments in the story that connect to that theme.
- Use the theme in a sentence. Say it in a way that isn't just about this book.

Research Link

In an extensive program of research using a "theme-scheme" series of questions, Williams and colleagues have demonstrated that students in both elementary and middle school, including those with learning disabilities, can benefit from specific instruction that supports them to understand and identify themes (Wilder & Williams, 2001; Williams, 1993, 2005; Williams, Brown, et al., 1994; Williams, Lauer, et al., 2002).

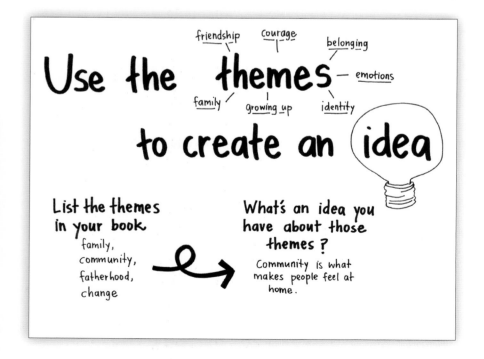

Strategy Notice if the character is dealing with any social issues that you recognize. Then think, "What is the character learning that connects to the issue? What might I (or others) learn? How might I take action?"

Lesson Language *Characters in stories are often dealing with social issues like people in real life—issues such as homelessness, gender inequality, racial prejudice, poverty, and more. When we find these sorts of issues in our books, we can think about what we might learn from the character's experience with that issue, and our reading experiences can inspire us to take action in real life. In* Front Desk *(Yang, 2018), Mia and her family face many challenges related to being immigrants: job choices are limited and other workers can mistreat, deceive, and take advantage of them. But she also learns that when the immigrant community sticks together, supports each other, and stands up to mistreatment, they are able to make changes. As a reader, I am thinking about what I learned from the book and also what I might do in my life. For example, I'm thinking about how it's important to speak up against injustice and also to be careful not to support businesses that mistreat or exploit workers.*

Teaching Tip Be sure students know what a social issue is (see Strategy 7.15) before teaching this strategy.

Prompts

- What social issues are you finding in your book?
- Based on what happens in the story, what does the character learn?
- Based on what you learned related to the social issue in the book, name how you may take action.
- That's the issue. How could reading this book change someone's opinions or actions related to this issue?

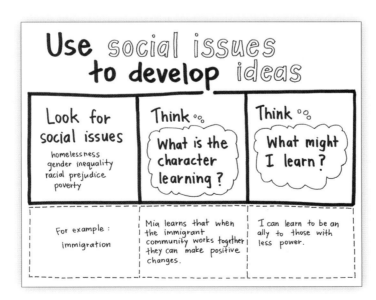

Progression

Is able to infer theme(s) as a single word or phrase and is ready to elaborate or provide commentary to articulate theme(s) as statements, and infer multiple themes based on different plotlines, perspectives, and so on.

Research Link

In a classic article, Cunningham and Foster (1978) describe sixth graders using a story diagram (Guthrie, 1977) to first identify the theme and resolution of a short story and then piecing together the plot, reversing the expected order of understanding. Knowing where to find the resolution can serve as an anchor for the analysis of a story.

Strategy Think about themes in the story. Reread the ending. Study the narrator's or character's last words. Think about what these last words mean, and how they connect to a theme. Say more about that theme after rereading the ending.

Lesson Language *In some ways, the ending of a book can be the key to understanding the story as a whole. After everything has wrapped up and you've learned what happens to the characters, most authors craft an ending designed to leave you thinking about what it all means. For example, in* Sona Sharma, Very Best Big Sister? *(Soundar, 2020), Sona struggles the entire book with accepting that her mom is having a baby and her world is about to change. So the themes I'm thinking about are* acceptance *and* change. *The story ends with the two sisters (and Sona's trusted "friend," her stuffed Elephant) alone in the nursery:*

> "She loves me," said Sona.
>
> "She loves me too," said Elephant.
>
> Minmini gave a little gurgle.
>
> "And we both love her," said Sona.

I can be the kind of reader who doesn't just breeze past the ending, but one who instead stops to think about it and have my own ideas about the story. Here, for example, I can see that Sona is more than accepting—she's truly loving—her new sister, Minmini. I can say more: I realize that although change can be hard, it can be rewarding too.

Prompts

- Look again at the ending. What are you left thinking about?
- How does that ending connect to theme(s) in the book you were thinking about?
- What ideas do you have after reading the ending of the book?
- What did you learn?

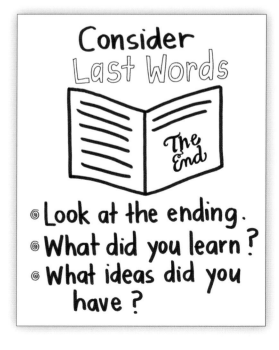

Strategy Track the journey of the character across a plot—how they change, the obstacles they face, the way they (re)solve their problems. Know that in each plot, there is likely to be at least one theme. Identify different themes in different plotlines in the same book.

Lesson Language *Within a book, there may be several themes: a character may learn different lessons as they face different obstacles and find different resolutions. For example, in* Merci Suárez Changes Gears *(Medina, 2018), when Merci is at school, we can learn about what it's like to have less money than most of your peers (based on how Merci is treated as a scholarship student), and when she's at home, we learn about the challenges of supporting a family member with Alzheimer's.*

Prompts
- Identify the different plotlines. Think about characters and settings.
- What did the character seem to learn in this plotline? How about this one?
- Talk about what each plot is mostly about. Now what does the character learn in each?
- Summarize the plots in this story. What lessons can you learn from each?

Skills
- **inferring**
- **determining importance**
- **analyzing**
- **synthesizing**

Progression

Is able to infer theme(s) as a single word or phrase and is ready to elaborate or provide commentary to articulate theme(s) as statements, and infer multiple themes based on different plotlines, perspectives, and so on.

●●●○○

Research Link

In literature circles, a group of fourth-grade students discussed the novel *Hoot* (Hiassen, 2002). At first, they focused mostly on concrete components, such as character descriptions and plot events. Over time, they began making more inferences and thinking more abstractly, supported by the unusual structure of the selected novel where two distinct plots eventually intertwine and dovetail around common themes (Barone & Barone, 2019).

Consider Characters' Identities for Different Perspectives on Themes

Progression

Is able to infer theme(s) as a single word or phrase and is ready to elaborate or provide commentary to articulate theme(s) as statements, and infer multiple themes based on different plotlines, perspectives, and so on.

Research Link

Literature can reinforce, or disrupt, how readers think about different identities and infer themes related to them (Bean & Moni, 2003). For example, studying depictions of (dis)ability in contemporary YA novels, Curwood (2013) found complex and realistic portrayals of characters with physical, mental, and emotional disabilities, an improvement from the negative and often condescending portrayals in classic literature.

Strategy Consider a character's identities. Each identity matters in the story: what problems they have, how they deal with those problems, and what they learn. Then think, "What themes are connected to the character's multiple identities?"

Lesson Language *Any one character—or person in your life—belongs to many groups and identifies in a number of different ways. Let's consider a character from* Sona Sharma, Very Best Big Sister? *(Soundar, 2020). What do we know about Sona that makes her a unique, multidimensional character? Which of these identities matter to what she learns in the story? Let's check the chart. How about Sona's age? Does age matter at all in this story? How does it factor into the problem and what she learns? How about family makeup? How does that factor into problems and what she learns?*

Prompts

- Let's think about the character's various identities.
- How does that specific identity matter to the story, the character's problems, and/or what they learn?
- Can you think of a theme that emerges because of the character's identity as a (specify an identity category)?
- That's one theme based on the character's identity as a (specify one identity category). Can you think of another?

Strategy Let yourself react in moments where what's happening to a character seems unfair. Ask yourself, "Why am I feeling this way? Who am I upset with in this story? What's the root of the issue?" Let your answers to these questions help you say more about themes.

Lesson Language *When something strikes you as being unfair, there are usually lots of reasons why you feel that way, so it's a good idea to pay attention in those moments. For example, I had a strong reaction to unfairness in* Front Desk *(Yang, 2018) when Hank is falsely accused of stealing a car from the motel parking lot. To make matters worse, his employer learns about the baseless accusation and fires him. Then Hank doesn't have the money he needs to pay for his room. It's just one unfair thing after another. It made me think about how false accusations can have really terrible consequences, and how people are supposed to be innocent until proven guilty, but how in reality, that's not what always happens. What makes matters even worse is that Hank doesn't have a lot of money to hire a lawyer to protect him against the injustice, and he needs his job and can't easily get a new one. That makes me think about economics and how those who have money have power (to get out of situations like this), but those with less money can get stuck.*

Prompts
- Is there anything in this story that you feel is unfair? What's your reaction?
- Now that you've described what's unfair, talk about what is at issue here.
- Say, "An issue I see is . . . and my idea about it is . . ."
- What are your thoughts or ideas about this issue?

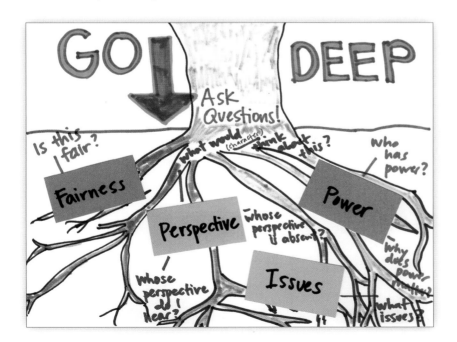

Skills
- **inferring**
- **determining importance**
- **synthesizing**

Progression

Is able to infer theme(s) as a single word or phrase and is ready to elaborate or provide commentary to articulate theme(s) as statements, and infer multiple themes based on different plotlines, perspectives, and so on.

●●●○○

Research Link

A reader's *aesthetic* responses (Rosenblatt, 1978) connect them with a text personally and emotionally. Even very young children respond with passion when confronted with injustice and suffering in books and will share their thoughts and emotional responses when provided with a supportive environment to do so (Chafel & Neitzel, 2005, 2012; Sychterz, 2002).

Skills

- **inferring**
- **synthesizing**
- **determining importance**

Progression

Is ready to identify symbols and motifs that connect to theme(s) and use prior knowledge to interpret their meaning(s).

Strategy Notice when an object keeps reappearing in a story or is described in detail. Consider what is important about that object, or why it matters. Ask yourself, "Is this connected to a theme in the story? What might the object symbolize or represent?"

Lesson Language *Have you noticed in our read-aloud* Front Desk *(Yang, 2018) that the tip jar keeps showing up in the story? It's even on the cover! We might think about why it matters to Mia—she's trying to save up to be able to pay the entry fee for the essay contest. We might think about how it's described—she places it front and center on the desk, but she keeps it a secret from Yao and her parents. Why does that matter? What might it represent? Well, maybe the jar represents her hopes and dreams—the money would literally help her out of her situation if she won the essay contest. And she sort of keeps her dreams of being a writer secret from her mom who's been critical of her writing, just like she keeps the tip jar secret. When she has to use the money she's worked so hard to collect to pay for her mother's hospital visit, she feels momentarily hopeless.*

Teaching Tip Remember that a symbol could be something an author intentionally crafted, but it could also be that the reader interprets something as symbolic.

Prompts

- What objects show up across the story, again and again?
- What objects do you notice being described in a lot of detail by the narrator or characters?
- List some concepts or ideas that the object could represent.
- Think about how that object is important, or why it matters, to help you figure out what it might symbolize.

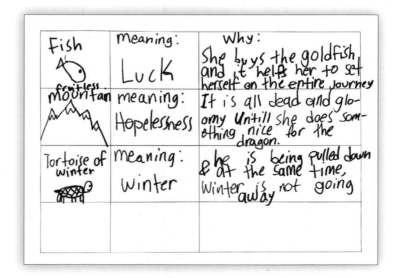

Strategy Check your symbol bank to see what an object, color, animal, and so on often symbolizes in literature. Think about which (if any) of those representations fits in the context of the story you're reading. Explain how that interpretation applies.

Lesson Language *A symbol bank is a useful tool for collecting symbols you have discovered and your interpretation(s) of their meaning(s). As you add to your symbol bank, and include different ideas about what each symbol might represent, remember that the same symbol can mean dramatically different things in different stories or even have different meanings depending on context within the same story. For example, the color red could represent either love and courage, or anger and war, depending on where, when, and how it's used in the text. Water might symbolize cleansing or life or clarity, but if the water is a turbulent sea, it might symbolize death or emotional volatility.*

Teaching Tip For readers in middle school and beyond, incorporate symbolism from classic texts such as mythology, religious texts, fables, and so on. Refer to the chart for examples.

Prompts
- What might this [object/animal/color] represent in this story?
- Check your symbol bank to see if any common symbols are showing up in your book.
- Yes, that's one interpretation of that symbol. Name some others.
- Name the different ways we know that symbol is used. How is it used in this text?

Use Your Symbol Bank

Colors		Animals	
Red	passion, love, anger	Bear	strength
Orange	energy, happiness	Dove	peace, love, purity
Yellow	happiness, hope	Fox	intelligence, mischief
Green	growth, peace, jealousy	Rabbit	good fortune, self-improvement
Blue	calmness, depression	Owl	wisdom, intuition
Purple	royalty, creativity	Snake	evil

Objects		Seasons/Weather	
Heart	love	Spring	beginning, rebirth
Key	answer, solution	Summer	maturity, knowledge
Fire	knowledge, passion	Autumn	aging, decline
Crown	wealth, royalty	Winter	death, sleep, stagnation
Crossbones	death, danger	Storms	anger, trouble
Water	birth, rebirth	Winds	change
		Full moon	danger, weirdness

What might ____ represent in this story?

What representation fits best with this story?

Skills
- **inferring**
- **activating prior knowledge**
- **analyzing**
- **synthesizing**

Progression

Is ready to identify symbols and motifs that connect to theme(s) and use prior knowledge to interpret their meaning(s).

Research Link

Based on a large body of research showing that students struggle to identify and interpret symbols in literature, Peskin and Wells-Jopling (2012) examined whether this ability improves with age-related cognitive development. When provided with concrete scaffolds, students in grades 6, 9, and 12 showed improvements in symbolic interpretation, indicating that difficulties with symbolism are more likely related to a lack of experience with and knowledge about symbols than to maturity.

Look for Symbolism in Setting

Skills

- **inferring**
- **synthesizing**
- **determining importance**
- **activating prior knowledge**

Progression

Is ready to identify symbols and motifs that connect to theme(s) and use prior knowledge to interpret their meaning(s).

●●●●○

Research Link

According to an analysis by Thomas (1986), the four most common settings in fairy tales are the woods, castles, towers, and huts. Because of the foundational influence of these traditional stories on Western literature, the symbolic power of these four settings reverberates in modern stories and imbues them with meaning.

Strategy Consider how a setting is important to the events of the plot and how that setting impacts the character. Now, consider whether that setting might be symbolic in some way based on what you know about that kind of place (from life and other literature) and/or how it aligns to a theme of the story.

Lesson Language *An author's choice of setting can have both literal and symbolic importance. In* Islandborn *(Díaz, 2018), though the story takes place in a classroom and around Lola's neighborhood, the Island is an important setting to the main character and to the story. Lola interviews family and community to understand specific details about the Island for a project she's doing in school, and most of the book is the various characters talking about it and describing it. But you could also interpret the Island as being symbolic—for example, of Lola searching for and yearning to be in touch with her own identity and roots, and who she is deep down.*

Teaching Tip Interpreting settings on a symbolic level is common in allegorical stories such as *Animal Farm* and other classic literature such as *Alice in Wonderland, Moby Dick*, or *The Great Gatsby*. Readers can find examples in current children's and young adult literature as well, including picture books (such as *Islandborn*). Also, setting isn't the only story element that can have both literal and symbolic meanings. Be sure to look at Strategy 6.25 for a way to teach that *characters* can be symbolic in allegorical stories.

Prompts

- Say, "The setting is important to the story because . . . Also, it might symbolize . . . "
- Think about the impact(s) the setting has on the character.
- That's what the setting literally is. Now consider what deeper ideas it might connect with.
- What might that place symbolize?

Look for Symbolism in Setting—

📖 Text	🏠 Setting	🔍 Symbolism	💡 Theme
Alice in Wonderland	- Wonderland	- the wonders of this strange land: a child navigating an adult world	- growing up
The Great Gatsby	- Roaring 20s	- the promise of prosperity and romance	- money can't buy: love, happiness, etc.
The Lottery	- picturesque New England town	- maintaining peace and order	- people will go to any lengths (even violent) to maintain order
Moby Dick	- Captain Ahab's ship while sailing the ocean	- isolation (oceans are vast and seemingly alienated from man)	- being isolated or alienated from community

Strategy Choose a theme that is developed across a story. Analyze its development by breaking the theme into parts either sequentially (beginning/middle/end; problem/resolution) or by literary element (character, plot, setting).

Lesson Language *Throughout* A Long Walk to Water *(Park, 2010), we could infer one theme around the importance of family or how family can serve as an emotional anchor. To analyze the development of the theme, I can think about it sequentially (for example, Salva thinks about being with his brothers at the beginning of the story, looks for his family along his journey, is relieved to meet up with his Uncle Jewir, and searches for his mother at the refugee camp) or based on different characters (for example, not only does Salva's narrative concern family but so does Nya's story) or based on different settings (for example, the importance of family for Salva in Sudan and the importance of family in America). At the end when Nya's and Salva's stories get tied together, their family problems are also resolved.*

Prompts

- Break the story up into parts. Explain how the theme shows up in the beginning, middle, and end.
- Determine *what* develops the theme, and then explain *how* it develops.
- How do different characters' traits, actions, and motives develop the theme?
- How does the theme play out in different settings in the book?

Analyze the Development of the Theme

Sequentially $1 \to 2 \to 3$	How does the theme show up in the beginning, middle, and end of the story?
Notice Characters ☺ 🙂 ☺	How does each character develop the theme?
Notice Settings 🏙	How does the theme play out in different settings in the book?

Skill

- **analyzing**

Progression

Can identify theme(s), and is ready to analyze thematic elements within one text and/or across texts.

●●●●●

Research Link

Ironically, one of the themes in the research on theme instruction is how difficult it is for readers to analyze themes (Sosa et al., 2016)! In a successful intervention with adolescent English learners, researchers and their teaching partners developed a set of eight cognitive strategies for before, during, and after reading, including sentence starters and explicit instruction on the difference between topics and themes (Olson et al., 2010).

Skills

- **synthesizing**
- **analyzing**

Progression

Can identify theme(s), and is ready to analyze thematic elements within one text and/or across texts.

Research Link

In a review of research on "multiple source use" when analyzing literature, Bloome and colleagues (2018) highlight that readers must construct accurate mental models of both stories to make comparisons between them. They found that using multiple texts may improve a student's understanding of each text.

Strategy Identify two books that have a similar theme. Ask yourself, "How does the theme develop in similar ways in each book? How does it develop differently?"

Teaching Tip See Strategy 7.8 in this chapter for a way for children to connect stories with similar lessons and Strategy 7.25 to help students to analyze theme in a single story. This strategy is more sophisticated as it asks readers to do both: compare *and* analyze. For example, you might compare themes in *New Kid* (Craft, 2019) and *Merci Suárez Changes Gears* (Medina, 2018). In both books, the main characters (Jordan and Merci) struggle in a school environment that feels culturally different from their home and community, they must navigate between two worlds, and they work to stay true to themselves. However, Jordan's challenges have more to do with race, whereas Merci's are more about class. You might also consider how each character's home environment and families help or hinder them as they navigate two worlds. This comparative analysis allows readers to articulate unique ideas more precisely from each text and consider author's craft in the development of the themes.

Prompts

- What other books does this one remind you of? Why?
- What are a few themes in this book? What book(s) also explore one of those themes?
- Compare how the authors of each book explore this theme in ways that are unique.
- Remember, when you analyze a theme's development you're breaking it into parts— chronologically, or by story element, for example.

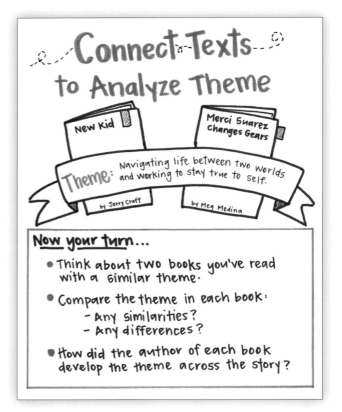

Strategy Identify what the satirical piece is about on a literal level. Summarize it in a sentence or two. Then, consider what the author/creator may be trying to say on a symbolic level by considering who or what is the target of the joke or commentary. Identify what details are real and factual and what details are exaggerated or invented to be humorous and make a point.

Teaching Tip Satire is prevalent in popular media as a way to provide humor and social criticism. Look for age-appropriate pieces from the online publications *The Onion* or *McSweeney's*, cartoons such as those in *The New Yorker* or *The Far Side*, sketch comedy like *All That*, Banksy's artwork, or films such as *The Lego Movie*. This is a strategy for more advanced readers because typically an entire piece is satirical and the reader must consider many parts to analyze satire effectively. But sometimes you will find satire embedded in a story that's not satirical, and when you do, this may be a good place to introduce it to more beginning readers. For example, in *New Kid* (Craft, 2019), Jordan is a cartoon artist and some of his cartoons appear throughout the story. Encourage children to think about what Jordan is going through and what he's trying to say or target in each of his pieces.

Prompts
- Who or what is the target of this piece?
- Identify the main topic. What is it literally saying? What about it is satirical?
- What details are exaggerated or fake to make that point?
- What bigger idea do you have after considering the satire?

Skills
- **inferring**
- **analyzing**
- **determining importance**
- **synthesizing**

Progression
Can identify theme(s), and is ready to analyze thematic elements within one text and/or across texts.

Research Link
Researchers found that when college students read a satirical short story, they were inclined to understand the stories literally (McCarthy & Goldman, 2015). However, when the instructional tasks guided them to produce interpretations, they were able to change their perspective and see beyond the text when cued to grasp meaning beyond the literal story.

Comprehending Topics
and Main Ideas

◎ **Why is this goal important?**

Various types of well-crafted, engaging informational texts for children often
include zinger, wow-worthy, incredible things to learn. The thing is, as cool
as it is to know some stand-out information, children are more likely to learn
and remember what they read when they can create mental files, storing and
organizing the details inside categories (Armbruster & Armstrong, 1993). These
categories may be the topics, subtopics, and/or main ideas of the text. Learning
how to understand what a whole text, or portions of texts, are *mostly about*
is therefore critical to comprehension (Williams, 1988). Of course, a reader's
ability to comprehend a text's main idea(s) depends in part on the amount of
background knowledge they have about a topic (Dole et al., 1991; Langer, 1984;
Snow, 2002). However, research has also shown that strategies that explain
how to determine a main idea are helpful (Seidenberg, 1989; Stevens, 1988). For
example, one study found expert readers often need to think through a process
and apply strategies to construct a main idea (Afflerbach, 1990).

The task of understanding the most important content varies depending on the complexity of the text. Most of the expository texts in your classroom library are likely to be informational texts. When children begin reading informational texts, the books they encounter are likely to be a collection of information about a broad *topic*, clearly stated. As they become a bit more complex, books tend to have *simple main idea(s)* often stated somewhere in the text—for example, in an introduction highlighting the main idea and/or in headings and topic sentences that spell it out clearly (see Strategies 8.3 and 8.5). Moving up in complexity, informational texts will usually have multiple main ideas, which readers often must infer. These multiple main ideas may provide more than one perspective or point of view on a topic, or they may explore different aspects of the topic. As texts become even more dense and are filled with significant amounts of information and various text features, readers will need skills to read, comprehend, and use those features well (see Chapter 10 for more support). They will then need to synthesize the text content and the text features together to determine *complex main idea(s)*.

Topic	Simple Main Idea(s)	Complex Main Idea(s)
African animals	Elephants are interesting creatures.	People both cause the elephant poaching problem in Africa *and* they can offer solutions.
Weather	Climate change is a big problem.	Climate change is having a terrible effect on people, wild animals, and other living things, but people can and should work together to fix it.
Atoms	Carbon is an important common element because it is found in living things.	Scientists have found ways to manipulate atoms to benefit people, though this nanoscience is still a work in progress.

As texts get more complex, so do their main idea(s).

Synthesizing

Putting related information together and identifying what that information has in common. Tracing relationships between different ideas in the text to see how they connect as a single topic or main idea.

Inferring

Determining main idea(s) when they are not explicitly stated in the text.

Determining importance

Identifying topic(s) and/or main idea(s) that are explicitly stated in the text. When these are not stated outright, finding the most important information in a text and articulating what that information has in common, either as a broad topic or as a main idea that makes some type of statement about that topic.

Skills a reader might work on as part of this goal

Questioning

Reading with a focus based on curiosity, and seeking out answers from within the section.

Analyzing

Identifying text structures to consider how parts are related and support a main idea. Considering an author's choices (of words, details, and so on), which may communicate authority or bias. Comparing and contrasting the development of main ideas across texts.

◎ How do I know if this goal is right for my student?

To assess student comprehension and their ability to determine topic(s) and main idea(s), ask students to respond to prompts and questions about a text or excerpt, and then evaluate the quality of their responses. The text can be short (e.g., an article, a portion of a textbook, or chapter from a longer work) or long (e.g., an informational picture book); it can be one you choose or they choose; and you can decide to read it aloud or have them read it independently. Plant questions at key points in the text, or ask them to read the whole text and respond by jotting or talking about the story when they're done.

Here are some prompts and questions you can use that align to this goal:

- What is the topic of this text?
- What is this [article, book, chapter, and so on] mostly about?
- What is the main idea?
- What two or three main ideas are explored in this text?

> To teach/inform you about how the everyday things that happen to your body (cough, sneeze, burp, hiccup, blink, yawn, sweat, shiver) ~~and~~ & why/how they happen

This response shows a reader who understands the complexity of this book's main idea—that it informs, and explains why and how—*and* that it deals with a broad topic (the body) and subtopics (cough, sneeze, burp, and so on). I would introduce some additional strategies that help the reader to see complexity in texts with a variety of structures (Strategies 8.13–8.17), and then to move on to analysis (Strategies 8.18–8.19).

> One main idea is, artists use special things. Another, is that no matter how old, you can be an artist.

When asked to determine the main idea(s) from an entire book, this reader was able to think about a main idea of two separate chapters focused on what artists use and famous artists. A good next step for this reader is to help her synthesize information from across the longer text to state a main idea in original language (Strategies 8.6–8.12).

What Texts Might Students Use When Practicing Strategies from This Chapter?

The strategies in this chapter are most helpful for students who are reading expository texts that are informational, persuasive, or procedural and that focus on topic(s) or idea(s). Here are a few examples:

Informational picture books. Short texts that use both pictures and words to tell about a topic such as the Bill of Rights, the solar system, gorillas, and so on.

Textbooks. Subject-area (science, history) course books.

Feature articles and op-eds. Short articles, such as those found in popular children's magazines, which center around a topic, often with some slant, perspective, or angle.

Procedural/how-to texts. Texts written to teach the reader how to do or make something (e.g., recipes, craft books, owner's manuals, and so on), which often include lists of materials and explanatory steps.

How do I support students as they work to determine topic(s) and main idea(s)?

After evaluating a student's verbal or written responses about the topic(s) and main idea(s) in their reading, select strategies that you can model, that they can practice with you, and that they can use independently to increase their skills.

Although development is rarely perfectly linear, skill progressions can help us pinpoint where a student is now and what might come next. Use the if-then chart on page 271 to evaluate your students' reading and find strategies that will support their growth.

A Progression of Skills: Comprehending Topics and Main Ideas

If a student . . .	Then you might teach . . .
Names topics and is ready to start identifying a text's subtopics.	**8.1 Identify Subtopics** **8.2 Notice What Repeats**
Is able to identify topic(s) and subtopic(s) and is ready to articulate a simple main idea that's stated explicitly in the text.	**8.3 Look for Main Ideas in the Introduction** **8.4 Look for Main Ideas in the Conclusion** **8.5 Clue In to Key Sentences**
Is able to recognize a main idea when stated explicitly in the text and is ready to begin synthesizing information to state a main idea in original language or to infer a main idea.	**8.6 Name the *What* and *So What*** **8.7 Ask Questions, Form Main Ideas** **8.8 Survey the Text** **8.9 Paraphrase Each Chunk, Then Put the Pieces Together** **8.10 Sketch Each Chunk, Then Put the Pieces Together** **8.11 Add Up Details to Determine Main Idea** **8.12 Shrink-a-Text**
Is able to synthesize information to state or infer a main idea and is ready to consider structure to determine multiple main ideas or a main idea with complexity.	**8.13 Consider Structure to Find Main Idea(s)** **8.14 Consider Structure: Problem/Solution** **8.15 Consider Structure: Cause and Effect** **8.16 Consider Structure: Compare and Contrast** **8.17 Consider Shifting Structures**
Is able to identify complex main ideas and is ready to read critically to analyze an author's craft, authority, or bias, or compare and contrast main ideas from different books on the same topic(s).	**8.18 Notice the *What* and the *How* of Information** **8.19 Research and Recognize the Author's Authority and Bias** **8.20 Compare and Combine Main Ideas Across Texts**

Strategy Identify the topic of the whole book. After you read the first page, spread, section, chunk, or chapter, state what that *part* is mostly about. As you continue to read, notice whether the next part offers more information about the same subtopic, or if the author has moved on to a new subtopic.

Lesson Language *In the book* Nano: The Spectacular Science of the Very (Very) Small *(Wade, 2021), we can figure out from the title that the whole book will be about very small things. As I flip through the book, I notice there are no headings or chapter breaks, so I need to be thinking about subtopics as I organize the information.* (Read aloud the first two pages.) *OK, so these first two pages are really about* materials *and how everything is made of some kind of material.* (Read aloud next two pages.) *Hm. Are these two pages still about materials? Sort of. But the author is sort of zooming in more, and talking about what the materials are made of.* (Read the next two pages.) *Still about materials or a new subtopic? It's like she's zooming in even more. Now she's talking about* atoms*. Atoms are what materials are made out of. These six pages I just read all go together of course, because the whole book is about one topic. But these* two *pages give us information about a more specific subtopic—atoms. Do you see how I paused to think about subtopics to help me group the information together before reading on?*

Teaching Tip For students reading more complex texts where the whole book is about one *main idea* rather than just a topic, tweak the language of this strategy slightly. Ask them to look for a main idea(s) of each part and an overarching main idea(s) of the whole text.

Prompts
- What is this *part* of the book mostly about?
- That's the topic of the whole book. Name the subtopic of just this two-page spread.
- Is this next part about the same subtopic as the last part, or did the author move on to a new subtopic?
- Now that you've finished the book, name all the subtopics the author writes about in this book.

Skills
- **synthesizing**
- **determining importance**

Progression
Names topics and is ready to start identifying a text's subtopics.

Research Link
Multiple studies have found that when a reader encounters a sentence that introduces a new topic, they spend more time with that sentence (Hyönä, 1994; Hyönä, Lorch, & Kaakinen, 2002), and the greater the shift in topic, the longer the duration of the pause (Lorch, Lorch, & Matthews, 1985; Lorch, Lorch, & Morgan, 1987). These findings suggest readers are actively monitoring a mental list of topics (Kieras, 1981).

Skills

- **determining importance**
- **synthesizing**

Progression

Names topics and is ready to start identifying a text's subtopics.

Research Link

Because the repetition of specific words is such a predictable and consistent marker of a conceptually linked portion of text, computers have been "taught" to use the strategy of identifying the frequency and distribution of words to subdivide a text into subtopics (Beeferman, Berger, & Lafferty, 1999; Hearst, 1997).

Strategy To figure out what a part or section is mostly about, it's helpful to pay attention to the word(s) you see again and again. Then think, "If the whole book is about __, based on the word(s) that repeat, this *part* is about __."

Lesson Language In Every Breath We Take: A Book About Air *(Ajmera & Browning, 2016), let's look to see if we notice words repeating.* (Read aloud the text and look at the photos on the first four pages.) *Notice any words repeating? That's right—air. We'd expect that of course because the whole book is about air. Maybe this is just the introduction to the big topic of the book. Let's keep reading to see if we notice a subtopic, based on repeating words.* (Read aloud the next two pages.) *Any repetition of words here? Yes, we noticed "pushes air out" and "in and out" and "into your lungs." I think these pages are really about the subtopic of how air moves.* (Read aloud the next two pages.) *Did you catch it? I read "needs clean air . . . needs clean air . . ." so that must mean these pages are about the subtopic of how all creatures need the air to be clean.*

Prompts

- What words repeat on each page?
- State the subtopic of just this part.
- The subtopic is a *part* of the overall topic.
- You found a repeating word! Now, what's the subtopic?

Strategy If the book or article you're reading has an introduction, read it carefully, maybe even twice. Consider if each sentence is giving you information about how the text will go, background information on the topic, or is presenting an idea about the topic.

Lesson Language *In* Climate Change and How We'll Fix It *(Harman, 2020), the author begins the book with a long two-page introduction. Let's read it closely to see what exactly she's introducing.* (Read first page aloud.) *Hm. The first page of the introduction seems to be mostly setting up the topic—she defines some terms like* climate, climate change, *and* climate crisis. *Oh—but in this one spot she shares an idea about the topic. She says, "Basically, the Earth is getting hotter—and this is throwing things off balance and affecting other natural systems. Not good" (p. 4). Hm, she says "not good," and we have to wonder if a main idea of the book might relate to this. Let's see.* (Read next page aloud.) *Ah, so this next page tells us some things about how the book is organized, but then look at the very last paragraph that starts with this sentence, "One last, very important thing before you read on—try to remember that although climate change is worrying, it's also fixable" (p. 5). We can keep that idea in mind as we read and consider what information might support it or if we need to add on to the idea to capture the main idea(s) of the whole book.*

Prompts

- Read the introduction carefully.
- What job does each part of the introduction have (set up, share an idea, and so on)?
- What's the main idea so far, after reading this introduction?
- Point to the sentence that seems to be sharing an *idea* about the topic.

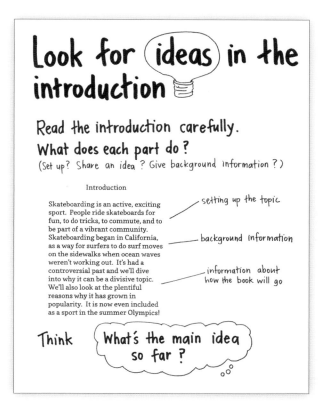

Progression

Is able to identify topic(s) and subtopic(s) and is ready to articulate a simple main idea that's stated explicitly in the text.

Research Link

In a review of research on various "text signals," Lorch (1989) reported that readers were better able to remember information included in an introductory preview and had an easier time grouping associated information when the relationships were included in the preview (Glover et al., 1988). Overviews can provide a coherent structure when the organization of the text is not obvious (Lorch, Lorch, & Matthews, 1985).

Look for Main Ideas in the Conclusion

Skills

- **determining importance**
- **synthesizing**

Progression

Is able to identify topic(s) and subtopic(s) and is ready to articulate a simple main idea that's stated explicitly in the text.

● ● ○ ○ ○

Research Link

In a series of experiments exploring overviews and summaries, Hartley and Trueman (1982) found that, when they included main ideas, these types of consolidating paragraphs helped readers to remember them. Lorch (1989) suggested that main ideas may be clearer and more direct in a summary (such as a concluding section) than in the body of the text.

Strategy If the book or article you're reading has a conclusion, read it carefully, maybe even twice. Notice the idea(s) the author presents to sum up the text. Think back to what you read and ask yourself, "What information from the text fits with those idea(s)?"

Lesson Language *Sometimes the author of an informational text will sum up the main idea(s) at the end—to reiterate what they hope is a main takeaway, so you don't miss it! Let's take a look at* Art of Protest: Creating, Discovering, and Activating Art for Your Revolution *(Nichols, 2021). The last part is called "Over to You," and it acts like a conclusion, wrapping up the book, with parting words such as "I hope this book has helped you understand and believe in the power of art as protest" (p. 74) and "Start MAKING. Start CREATING THE CHANGE that's needed for a BETTER WORLD" (p. 78). Considering what was included across the whole book, the ideas in this last part bring it home: Any of us can create art to use in protest, and when we speak up for change, it can make the world a better place.*

Prompts

- Read the conclusion carefully.
- Does any part of the conclusion state an idea (or ideas) that seem to sum up the most important information in the book?
- Yes, I agree that's an idea the author is leaving you with. How does it fit with the whole book?
- Point to the sentence that seems to be sharing an *idea* about the topic.

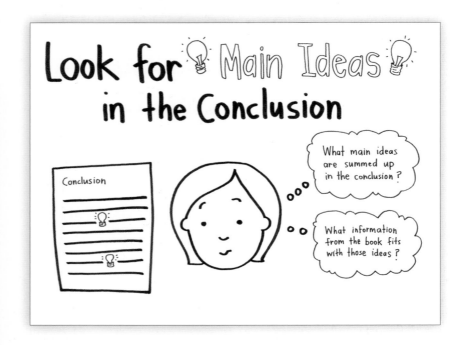

8.5　*Clue In to Key Sentences*

Strategy See if you can identify a single sentence—somewhere in the beginning, middle, or end—that seems to sum up the main idea: what the whole part or section is mostly about. When you think you've found it, check the other information to make sure it supports the main idea. It doesn't *all* have to, but *most* should. If you find that most of the information doesn't support that sentence, try a different sentence.

Teaching Tip As you explore informational texts in your classroom, you'll notice that some are well organized: they contain very clear sections and subsections labeled with headings and sentences that state a main idea. Reading researchers say that texts like these are *considerate* because they support comprehension (Anderson & Armbruster, 1984; Armbruster, 1984). Other books in your collection may have little to no support for readers to figure out main idea(s), sometimes because of an author's stylistic decisions and sometimes because they are just extremely complex. In these cases, readers likely won't find a main idea clearly stated and will need to employ different strategies to infer it. In *Climate Change and How We'll Fix It* (Harman, 2020), readers will find a key sentence on the upper left-hand side of each two-page spread announcing the main idea in bold. Each subsection on the spread has a clear heading and the key sentences are easy to spot somewhere within the section. On the other hand, *Nano: The Spectacular Science of the Very (Very) Small* (Wade, 2021), while less dense and simpler, is written in a beautiful, almost poetic way, but contains no headings to alert the reader to a shift in subtopics. *The Secret of the Scuba Diving Spider . . . and More!* (Rodríguez, 2018) incorporates narrative to tell stories about various animals, or the scientists studying them, alongside the information about the animals themselves. As you make a choice about whether this strategy will work, be sure to assess not only the reader but also the text the reader is reading.

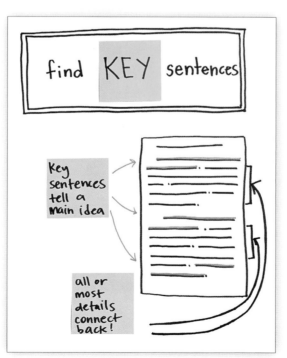

Prompts
- Do you see a sentence that tells you what this section is mostly about?
- I agree—all the details connect back to this one sentence.
- Which sentence seems like a main idea?
- Now read on, and check each sentence to make sure it connects with the main idea.

Skills
- **determining importance**
- **synthesizing**

Progression

Is able to identify topic(s) and subtopic(s) and is ready to articulate a simple main idea that's stated explicitly in the text.

●●○○○

Research Link

Readers have an easier time remembering, understanding, and identifying main ideas when they are clearly stated in the first rather than the last sentence of a paragraph (Flood, 1978; Kieras, 1981). A main idea located in the middle of a paragraph is the least supportive. However, strategies can help readers successfully identify a main idea, regardless of its placement in the text (Stevens, 1988).

Skills

- **determining importance**
- **inferring**
- **synthesizing**

Progression

Is able to recognize a main idea when stated explicitly in the text and is ready to begin synthesizing information to state a main idea in original language or to infer a main idea.

Research Link

Young children can be taught to recognize an author's voice, point of view, and perspective, and that they have the agency to respond to that voice with their own perspectives (O'Hallaron, Palincsar, & Schleppegrell, 2015). Known as *reflection literacy* (Hasan, 1996, p. 408), readers use inquiry and analysis to construct their own understanding from what the author has presented, rather than simply receiving knowledge from someone else.

Strategy First, identify the main topic (of the whole text or a section). Then ask yourself, "So what about it?" To answer that question, collect information related to the topic and identify the angle, idea, or perspective that the author brings to the topic.

Lesson Language *You can easily see from the title that* Every Breath We Take: A Book About Air *(Ajmera & Browning, 2016) is a book about . . . air! And this one called* The Science of an Oil Spill *(Wang, 2015) is about oil spills. And* The Secret of the Scuba Diving Spider . . . and More! *(Rodríguez, 2018) is about the special kind of spider pictured on the front. You can tell the topics without even reading the books! After you collect information, notice what the author writes about and how they write about it, then step back from the text to ask yourself, "So what about it? Out of all the books in the world on this topic, what is the big idea the author wants me to take away from this book?" For example, when I read the one about air, the author kept talking about how air is so important for every living thing and that we need clean air to survive.*

Prompts

- What's the topic of the book? Check the title.
- That's the topic. What's the main idea?
- Say, "The *what* is . . . The *so what* is . . ."
- What do you think the author is trying to say about that topic?

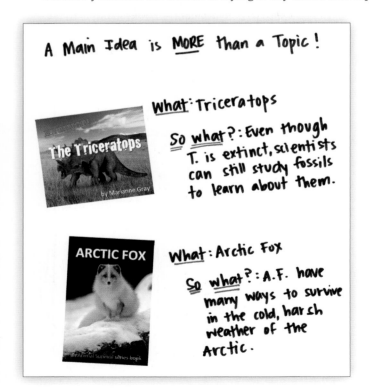

8.7 *Ask Questions, Form Main Ideas*

Strategy Preview the text (or section) to figure out the topic(s). Wonder and ask questions about the topic(s). As you read, try to answer your questions. At the end of a part or the whole text, think back to your questions and answers and form a main idea by asking yourself, "What does it seem like the text is mostly about?"

Lesson Language *As I look across these few pages in this section of* Bei Bei Goes Home: A Panda Story *(Bardoe, 2021), I see a number of photos of very young pandas. I'm thinking the topic of this section will be about baby pandas. I am wondering what baby pandas are like and also how fast they grow. (Read the section aloud.) Let me think back to my questions. I learned that a baby panda is called a cub, about their tiny size when they are born, how the mother nurses the cub, how pandas usually give birth to twins but only care for one of them, how a cub is totally dependent on its mother, and how it triples in size within three weeks. If I put together my question and all the answers I got from reading the section, I could think that the main idea is about how panda cubs need a lot of care to survive.*

Prompts

- Preview the text. What does it seem like the main topic(s) of this section will be?
- What are you wondering? You could jot it down or just keep it in your mind as you read.
- Reread (or think back to) your questions and answers.
- Based on all your questions and answers, what's the main idea?

Skills

- **determining importance**
- **questioning**
- **inferring**
- **synthesizing**

Progression

Is able to recognize a main idea when stated explicitly in the text and is ready to begin synthesizing information to state a main idea in original language or to infer a main idea.

●●●○○

Research Link

In one study, middle school students who scored below grade level on comprehension received strategy instruction to use self-questioning to identify main ideas. Another group was taught to pair self-questioning with prediction. Both groups outperformed the control group in comprehension measures, with the students who paired self-questioning with prediction receiving higher scores and the students who initially had the lowest comprehension scores showing the greatest gains (Nolan, 1991).

Progression

Is able to recognize a main idea when stated explicitly in the text and is ready to begin synthesizing information to state a main idea in original language or to infer a main idea.

Research Link

Although "picture walks" are common in classrooms when previewing narrative picture books, employing an equivalent "text feature walk" is less common in classrooms when engaging with expository texts (Kelley & Clausen-Grace, 2008). Teacher modeling accompanied by think-alouds can support students in identifying the purpose and usefulness of the various features, and how those features in combination can assist in making predictions (Kelley & Clausen-Grace, 2010).

Strategy Look around a page spread (or the pages of an article) and notice what jumps out at you—the heading(s), title(s), and visual(s). Ask yourself, "What does it seem like it is mostly about?" State a possible main idea. Then, read with that main idea in mind. Check the information you learn to see if it fits with your statement or if you need to revise it based on new information.

Prompts

- Look around the page. Tell me what you see.
- If you put all the visuals and headings together, what do you think it's mostly about?
- Check the information to make sure you have the correct main idea.
- Do you have any changes to make to your main idea statement, after reading the information?

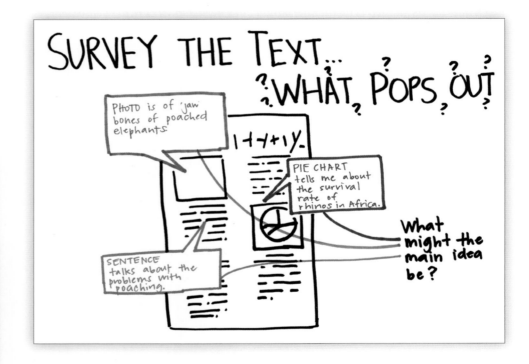

Paraphrase Each Chunk, Then Put the Pieces Together

Strategy Stop after every paragraph or short section. Think, "How can I say what I learned in my own words?" Jot a note in the margin. At the end of the article, read back over your margin notes and think, "So, what's this whole article mostly about?"

Teaching Tip Some readers who have had little exposure to informational texts need to learn to slow the pace of their reading, especially compared with how they read narrative texts. Strategies like this one ask readers to stop and chunk the information as they go as a method of monitoring their comprehension. The marginal notes help them to offload information they would otherwise have to hold in their memory, making it easier for them to synthesize the information at the end to generate main ideas.

Prompts

- Stop there. Jot a note.
- Don't write the same thing the author wrote; think and try to say it on your own.
- Look back across your notes. What is the *whole* article about?
- It seems like slowing down your reading pace is helping you to think about main ideas as you go.

Skills

- **determining importance**
- **inferring**
- **synthesizing**

Progression

Is able to recognize a main idea when stated explicitly in the text and is ready to begin synthesizing information to state a main idea in original language or to infer a main idea.

● ● ● ○ ○

Research Link

Schumaker, Denton, and Deshler (1984) developed a strategy called RAP: *R*ead a paragraph, *A*sk yourself "What are the main ideas and details of this paragraph?" and *P*ut the main idea and details into your own words. In numerous studies, students who use the RAP strategy were able to identify and recall more main ideas and had better overall comprehension (Ellis & Graves, 1990; Hagaman, Luschen, & Reid, 2010; Hagaman & Reid, 2008; Katims & Harris, 1997; Lauterbach & Bender, 1995).

Sketch Each Chunk, Then Put the Pieces Together

Skills

- **determining importance**
- **inferring**
- **synthesizing**

Progression

Is able to recognize a main idea when stated explicitly in the text and is ready to begin synthesizing information to state a main idea in original language or to infer a main idea.

Research Link

High school students who used drawings to summarize main ideas in a chemistry textbook scored better on a comprehension test than students who used only words or a combination of pictures and words (Leopold & Leutner, 2012). Drawing to capture main ideas is particularly useful for topics like chemistry or biology where the physical drawing is clearly connected to the mental model the reader constructs to understand the phenomenon (Schwamborn et al., 2010).

Strategy Stop after every paragraph or short section. Think, "What is this part mostly about?" Draw a quick sketch to hold on to that thought. At the end of the text, look back over your sketches and ask yourself, "Putting together all the sketches, what's this whole article mostly about?"

Lesson Language *I have the perfect book to practice this strategy—Art of Protest: Creating, Discovering, and Activating Art for Your Revolution (Nichols, 2021). I think it's perfect because it's about art and we'll be sketching, but also because the visuals don't really match the information in the text exactly, so adding your own sketches will help you monitor and hold on to information. Let's try reading one heading and section here on page 20, and then try drawing a quick sketch that will help you remember the most important idea from that part. Starting with "Craftivism." (Read section aloud.) It seems like this is about how even do-it-yourself art with yarn, paper, or quilting can be used in activism. And most of the section talks about origami. I think I'll draw a sketch of a ball of yarn and a paper crane to remember what this was mostly about.*

Teaching Tip This is similar to Strategy 8.9, but sketching might appeal to some students more than capturing their thoughts in words, and some may even want to do a combination of the two. For students reading articles, sketches could happen right in the margins on the page. For students reading a book, they could either sketch on sticky notes, or set up a 2 × 3 grid in their reader's notebook where they sketch, storyboard style, as they go.

Prompts

- What's that section mostly about? Stop and sketch what you see in your mind.
- Decide how much you'll read next before sketching again.
- Look back at your sketches— what's the article mostly about?
- I can see why you drew that sketch—it matches the information from that section.

Strategy Focus on one section. Read several paragraphs. List several pieces of information that seem to connect because they are about the same subtopic. In your own words, name what the section is mostly about. As you read on to collect more information, you may need to revise your main idea.

Lesson Language *Let's focus on the chapter "Oil Spill Impacts" in* The Science of an Oil Spill *(Wang, 2015). I'm going to read the first two pages aloud. (Read.) Now, let's list out information that seems to go together. We learned that oil can spread quickly in water, be absorbed into soil, poison water supplies, and take a long time to clean up. On this page, we learned it can smother plants and small creatures and ruin protective layers of feathers and fur on aquatic birds and marine mammals. And let's not overlook the map and caption that show us where dead birds were collected after the* Deepwater Horizon *spill. Adding up all this information, I would have to say that oil spills cause harm to living things and the environment in many ways.*

Prompts
- List pieces of information that fit together.
- What does all that information have in common?
- That's the subtopic; what's a main idea about the subtopic?
- Yes, that's a main idea statement—you told me the *what* and the *so what*.

Skills
- **determining importance**
- **inferring**
- **synthesizing**

Progression

Is able to recognize a main idea when stated explicitly in the text and is ready to begin synthesizing information to state a main idea in original language or to infer a main idea.

●●●○○

Research Link

The term *seductive details* refers to interesting, but inessential, information in a text that can potentially distract a reader. In a classic study involving both adults and children, researchers prepared informational texts that either contained, or did not contain, seductive details. Participants of all ages who read the texts with seductive details were less able to identify main ideas (Garner, Gillingham, & White, 1989).

Skills

- **determining importance**
- **inferring**
- **synthesizing**

Progression

Is able to recognize a main idea when stated explicitly in the text and is ready to begin synthesizing information to state a main idea in original language or to infer a main idea.

Research Link

Observing readers from fifth grade through college, Brown and Day (1983) crafted rules for summarizing: (1) delete unnecessary or redundant information, (2) decide on a category for items in lists, and (3) select or compose a topic sentence to capture the main idea. Composing a topic sentence was the most challenging task. Guiding questions and partner feedback can support students in this process (Nelson, Smith, & Dodd, 1992).

Strategy Read a chunk of text. Decide what it's mostly about. Try to shrink everything you just read into one sentence. Discuss your statement with a partner. Revise your statement if you agree revision is needed.

Teaching Tip As texts get more complex, the main idea(s) of sections may be less obvious. Readers need to synthesize, put main idea statement(s) into their own words, and decide what information is less critical to consider when stating a main idea. Encouraging children to lean on partners to discuss what main idea statement they came up with, and why, and giving them an opportunity to revise with feedback, can be a great support.

Prompts

- Read a chunk together. Now one of you: say what that chunk was mostly about.
- Explain why you think that's what it's mostly about.
- Do you agree with your partner that that's what the chunk was mostly about?
- You worked together to come up with a one-sentence summary of that part that's clear and concise.

Strategy At the end of a chunk of text, pause and think, "How does the information in these sentences *fit together*?" Look for conjunctions *within* and *across* sentences to help you. Use the chart for support. State a main idea that captures how the information is related.

Teaching Tip This "umbrella" strategy is meant to get readers thinking about the connection between structure and meaning. When a reader can categorize the overall structure of a paragraph, section, or entire book into a broad "bucket" of logical or rhetorical relations, it helps them to see which information is most important. Meyer (1985) has defined five broad categories of text structures; you can find more detailed strategies to help readers with three of the five on the following pages (Strategies 8.14, 8.15, and 8.16).

Text Structure	Description	What to Look For
Collection	Related ideas, events, items are grouped and possibly numbered.	first, second, third . . . in addition, also another, furthermore
Cause and Effect	Relationship between ideas where one thing causes another.	cause, because of effect, affects as a result, so
Problem-Solution or Question-Answer	Portions of text respond to each other, with a consistent topic in both parts.	trouble, difficulty to solve, in response recommend, suggest why?, because. . .
Compare-and-Contrast	Points out similarities and differences between topics.	whereas, on the other hand all but have in common, share, same as
Description	Elaborates on a topic through attributes, specifics, data, and so on.	for example, instance specifically, such as namely, properties of . . .

Based on Meyer (1985) and Meyer and Ray (2011).

Skills

- **inferring**
- **synthesizing**
- **analyzing**

Progression

Is able to synthesize information to state or infer a main idea and is ready to consider structure to determine multiple main ideas or a main idea with complexity.

Research Link

Meyer (1985) collapsed the broad categories of Grimes (1975) and her own previous work (Meyer, 1975, 1981) to create five categories that describe how information within a text can be related: collection, causation, response, comparison, description. Just and Carpenter's (1980) theory of comprehension includes readers taking time to process relationships between information within and across sentences to understand.

Consider Structure: Problem/Solution

Progression

Is able to synthesize information to state or infer a main idea and is ready to consider structure to determine multiple main ideas or a main idea with complexity.

Research Link

In a study with high school students reading a problem-solution text (Meyer, Brandt, & Bluth, 1980), researchers wondered what percentage of skilled readers would use the text's structure to make sense of the information and if they could be taught to use specific words that signal the problem-solution structure. They found that good readers remembered more ideas and made use of the signal words more frequently.

Strategy Look for key words that signal a problem-solution structure in a text or part of a text. Identify the problem(s). Then, notice what solution(s) the author offers. After that, state a main idea of the text that captures both the problem(s) and the solution(s).

Lesson Language *In* The Science of an Oil Spill *(Wang, 2015), four chapters are dedicated to explaining how oil spills happen and the problems they cause. The fifth and final chapter, titled "Oil Spill Response and Intervention," gives some ideas about solutions. The author first shares how cleanups utilize booms, skimmers, and chemicals called dispersants and how experts nurse the affected wildlife back to health. At the end, though, she says, "It is important to prevent oil spills before they happen" and suggests proper equipment maintenance, stricter rules, and governance. Since the whole text is organized in a problem-solution structure, I'm going to state a main idea in a way that captures both: "Oil spills cause tremendous harm and are challenging to clean up; therefore, people need to do more to prevent them from happening in the first place."*

Teaching Tip This is the first in a suite of strategies that clue readers into specific text structures they can use to help them identify key information and relationships between those pieces of information and to state a main idea. Keep in mind that an author may use different structures in different sections of a text (see Strategy 8.17), or there may be an overarching structure for the entire text.

Prompts

- Identify a problem. Identify a solution.
- Where will you look to read about the solution the author proposes?
- Make sure your main idea statement includes both the problem *and* the solution.
- You can state your main idea as "If . . . then . . ." or "When . . . we should . . ."

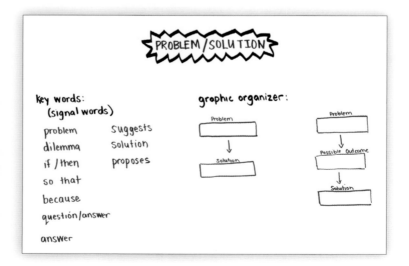

Strategy Look for key words that signal a cause-and-effect structure in a text or part of a text. Identify the cause(s). List out what happened (or could happen) as a result—the effect(s). When you think, "What's this all *mostly about*?" make a statement that includes both the cause(s) and effect(s).

Lesson Language *In the introduction to* Art of Protest *(Nichols, 2021), the author uses a cause-and-effect structure to explain how she witnessed social injustices as a child growing up in Mississippi and Tennessee and how that led her to use art to bring people together and raise their collective voices. By the end of the introduction, she invites the reader to notice social movements, campaigns for justice, climate issues, and the like and to "use art as a language and instrument that can help you champion your chosen cause" (p. 9). After reading the book, I'm considering if I can use an "If . . . then . . ." language frame to capture a main idea. Maybe something like, "If you notice a social issue and feel called to act, then you can use art as a way to protest and be part of the change needed to make the world a better place."*

Prompts
- You identified the structure as cause and effect—make sure your main idea statement tells *what happened* (the cause[s]) and *what were the results* (the effect[s]).
- You can say, "If . . . then . . ."
- How can you tell this is written using a cause-and-effect structure?
- Does the entire text describe causes and effects or just this part?

Skills
- **inferring**
- **synthesizing**
- **analyzing**

Progression

Is able to synthesize information to state or infer a main idea and is ready to consider structure to determine multiple main ideas or a main idea with complexity.

● ● ● ● ○

Research Link

In a study with adults (Meyer & Poon, 2001), readers who received specific strategy training on how to identify a text's structure remembered more information than those who received no training and had better recall of the most important information. Researchers hypothesized that the structure training helped readers to use signal words to identify key information and then to organize it more effectively in their memory.

Skills

- **inferring**
- **synthesizing**
- **analyzing**

Progression

Is able to synthesize information to state or infer a main idea and is ready to consider structure to determine multiple main ideas or a main idea with complexity.

Research Link

Research suggests that even very young children may benefit from instruction about expository text structure. In a pilot study with preschool children, researchers found that the participants made gains in mapping two targeted text structures, including compare/ contrast (Culatta, Hall-Kenyon, & Black, 2010).

Strategy Look for key words that signal a compare-and-contrast structure in a text or part of a text. Think about what the author is comparing. Identify the similarities and think about what they have in common. Identify the differences and think about what they have in common. Then, craft a main idea statement that uses those commonalities to talk about *both* things.

Lesson Language *If the text is organized to compare and contrast two (or more) things, then the main idea should include both things. For example, in* Can We Save the Tiger? *Jenkins (2011) compares the endangered tiger to the partula snail across eight pages in the book. Both animals are endangered, and the author says that he considers them both to be special. But there are differences. Tigers need a lot of space while the snail needs very little, a tiger is also valuable (for their skin or to make medicines), and tigers are killed by people directly while the snails are dying because of a new species that people introduced to their ecosystem. Now, if I only mentioned tigers in my main idea statement, then I'd only be giving part of the idea, not the main idea. I have to put it all together into one statement like this: "Both the tiger and partula snail are endangered although they are very different animals and are under threat of extinction for different reasons."*

Prompts

- You can say, "Both . . . however . . ." to describe similarities and differences.
- List back all the information you learned about their similarities. What's one statement that summarizes that information?
- List back all the information you learned about their differences. What's one statement that summarizes them?
- Make sure you have both the similarities and differences in your main idea statement.

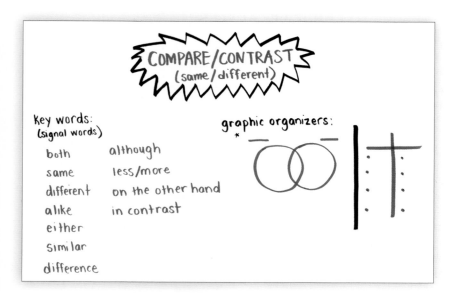

8.17 Consider Shifting Structures

Strategy Pause after a text chunk (a paragraph, a small section, a page). Identify the structure of that chunk. State a main idea with that structure in mind. Jot it. Continue reading, pausing, jotting main idea(s). Look back across them to put the main ideas together into one overarching main idea.

Lesson Language *You know several strategies for using a text's structure to help articulate a main idea. If the text contains cause(s) and effect(s), then your statement should, too. If there's a problem and solution, you need both in your main idea statement. But what do you do when the author uses a variety of structures within the same book—or even on the same page? The truth is, most authors will! For example, in the second chapter of* The Secret of the Scuba Diving Spider . . . and More! *(Rodríguez, 2018), we learn about caterpillars. The chapter begins with a short narrative about a scientist who became interested in studying caterpillars because of the sounds they make. Next, the author* compares *the caterpillar to other noise-making insects. In the next section, we learn about* problems *(predators) and* solutions *(defenses). Then, the next section uses a* cause-and-effect *structure to describe an experiment (scientists observed X, so they studied Y). If I had tried to identify the structure of the entire chapter, I couldn't have done it because it changes. I had to go part by part. And now that I have jotted a few main ideas— caterpillars can make sounds, some scientists are fascinated by how and why some caterpillars whistle, whistling is one of the several defenses caterpillars use to survive—I can combine them into one overarching main idea by considering what they all have in common. I could say something like this: "Like many animals, caterpillars have unique defenses to keep themselves safe from predators, one of which (whistling) scientists have only begun to study."*

Prompts

- Chunk up the text so that you can consider it slowly, part by part.
- Remember that different parts might follow different structures.
- State a main idea of this part, using what you know about structure to help, before moving on to the next part.
- Now that you have main ideas for each part, try to put them together into one overarching, complex main idea.

Skills
- **inferring**
- **synthesizing**
- **analyzing**

Progression

Is able to synthesize information to state or infer a main idea and is ready to consider structure to determine multiple main ideas or a main idea with complexity.

Research Link

When reading a text containing various structures, Meyer, Brandt, and Bluth (1980) found that students with solid vocabulary knowledge but below-average comprehension scores benefitted from instruction in signal words that cued them at key points to use a "structure strategy" to map the text onto a known structure (e.g., compare/contrast, cause/effect, problem/solution).

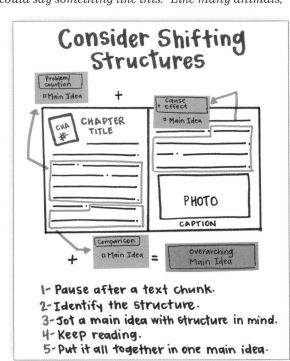

8.18 Notice the What and the How of Information

Skills

- analyzing
- synthesizing
- inferring

Progression

Is able to identify complex main ideas and is ready to read critically to analyze an author's craft, authority, or bias, or compare and contrast main ideas from different books on the same topic(s).

Research Link

Through the use of close reading (Brown & Kappes, 2012) and text-based questioning (Fisher & Frey, 2012), readers can be supported to identify techniques that authors employ to move their audience emotionally. Close reading techniques may improve both academic performance and self-perception, especially among struggling readers (Fisher & Frey, 2014).

Strategy Pay close attention to *what* information the author shares and also *how* the author shares it. For example, note word choices, opinion words or other strong language, point of view (*you/your* versus *we/our*), and use of repetition. As you put it all together, think, "What main idea is the author trying to get across based on *what* they shared and *how* they shared it?"

Lesson Language *What is the main idea of* We Are Water Protectors (*Lindstrom, 2020*)? *Now that we've read the whole book, here are some things I noticed about the author's choices. In the author's note she says, "Water is sacred"—* sacred *is a very strong word. She uses an analogy of a "black snake" to represent the oil pipeline. She chose to write using* we *and* I, *maybe to bring the reader closer to the topic and help us care more. She says that "leaks cause tremendous damage"—the use of the word* tremendous *adds extra emphasis. The word* protect *is repeated again and again throughout the book and even in the author's note. Adding all of this up, turn and tell your partner, what do you think she's trying to convince us of? What's her main idea?*

Teaching Tip You might also make note of an author's persuasive techniques *as* you are reading a text (rather than at the end) so students see how these choices add up across the text.

Prompts

- That's the information, but consider *how* the author presents this information.
- Look at the choice of words.
- That's the fact. Name the *idea* the author has about the topic.
- Which side does it seem the author is taking?

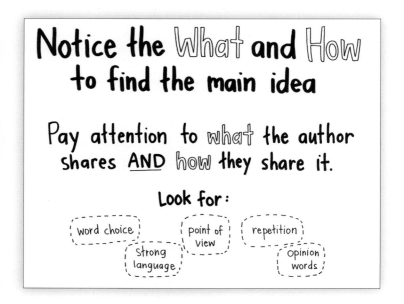

Research and Recognize the Author's Authority and Bias

Strategy First, learn about who the author is from the author bio included in the book. Then, consider what stake the author has in the topic based on their credentials and experience. As you read, consider what information is being included and what is being excluded. Consider if the author is conveying their personal opinions (through language choices) alongside the factual information.

Lesson Language *Always consider not only the information in a book, but also who wrote it. An author made decisions about what to include (and how to include it) and what to leave out. Knowing about the author can hint at their possible angle on the topic, which may help you figure out a main idea. For example, Andrea Wang's bio reveals she was an environmental consultant who worked to clean up hazardous materials and assess their impact on people's health and the environment. Knowing this, it stands to reason that in* The Science of an Oil Spill *(Wang, 2015), she will communicate her perspective that oil spills are harmful and disastrous with serious consequences.*

Teaching Tip Although the strategy is written to direct readers to consider the perspective of an author within a *single* text, it could also be used to help readers consider different treatments of the same topic written by different authors. In addition, this strategy is vitally important to teach readers as they analyze news articles for potential bias and to evaluate sources when researching, especially online. If students are reading these types of texts, you may point them to some practical ways to learn more about the author: click on a hyperlinked name to visit a website with their bio, scroll to the bottom to find a bio, or Google search to find out about other pieces the author has written.

Prompts

- What do you know about the author?
- What does the author's background tell you about any potential opinions they may have about the topic?
- What's the slant?
- Which information goes with that slant?

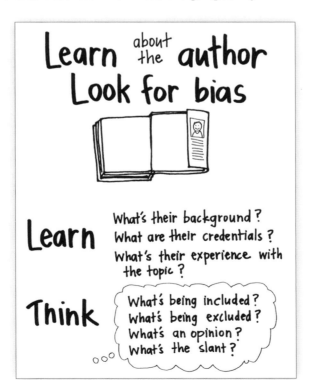

Learn about the author
Look for bias

Learn
What's their background?
What are their credentials?
What's their experience with the topic?

Think
What's being included?
What's being excluded?
What's an opinion?
What's the slant?

Skills

- **analyzing**
- **inferring**

Progression

Is able to identify complex main ideas and is ready to read critically to analyze an author's craft, authority, or bias, or compare and contrast main ideas from different books on the same topic(s).

Research Link

McGrew and colleagues (2018) created a bank of 15 tasks to measure *civic online reasoning* for students in middle school through college. Consistent with prior research, they found that participants struggled to determine the source of the text, who was behind the information, and other tasks that involved critical literacy skills.

Skills

- **synthesizing**
- **analyzing**
- **inferring**

Progression

Is able to identify complex main ideas and is ready to read critically to analyze an author's craft, authority, or bias, or compare and contrast main ideas from different books on the same topic(s).

Research Link

In a small study situated in a single sixth-grade classroom (Tracy, Menickelli, & Scales, 2017), researchers observed a thematic unit on "courage" that included newspaper articles, songs, videos, and infographics, among other types of texts, and documented how students organically built a multifaceted perspective around the topic of courage from these varied sources.

Strategy Read a set of texts on the same topic or related topic(s). Articulate the main idea(s) of each individual text. Consider if there is a main idea that threads across all the texts. Consider how the main idea(s) in each text (or portions of each of the texts) differ.

Lesson Language *I've been reading about environmental issues. My text set includes* Climate Change and How We'll Fix It *(Harman, 2020),* Can We Save the Tiger? *(Jenkins, 2011),* Every Breath We Take: A Book About Air *(Ajmera & Browning, 2016), and* The Science of an Oil Spill *(Wang, 2015). These books are about different topics—climate change, animal extinction, air (and air pollution), and oil spills, but they all connect under the same broad topic of environmental issues. I'm going to first think if there is any idea that is the same in all of them. I think one similar idea is that people have the ability, and a responsibility, to do what they can to protect the planet and the creatures living here. It's not the only main idea in each book, but it is one idea. There are some differences though, too. The climate change and oil spill books position companies, lawmakers, and systems at the root of the problems and argue they are responsible for solutions. In* Can We Save the Tiger?, *the author doesn't offer a concrete solution, though it's clear that animals are in danger because of people's actions. And in the book about air, it seems the author is speaking to the reader and giving advice for what they personally can do to help keep air clean—turn off lights, heat your home with clean energy, ride bikes or walk. However, reading a more detailed book about climate change has me thinking this author simplified the solution for younger readers.*

Prompts

- What's the main idea on the topic in this book? How about in that one?
- What's different about the ideas the authors are presenting in each?
- Which idea do you think is more logical, persuasive, or compelling?
- Name one main idea that seems to be a thread across all the books in your text set.

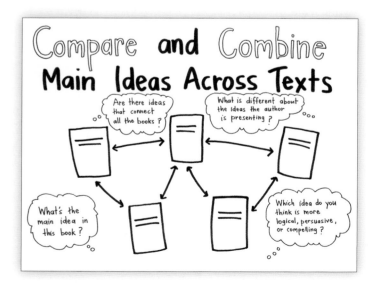

Young children can be taught to recognize an author's voice, point of view, and perspective, and that they have the agency to respond to that voice with their own ideas.

—Jennifer Serravallo

Comprehending Key Details

◎ Why is this goal important?

Readers need to monitor for meaning and keep track of details along the way, tasks made more challenging as they read texts that can be dense with information. Slowing down to process information is critical (Carver, 1992). In addition, readers may come to a text with misunderstandings or gaps in their knowledge about a topic, and when they learn new information, they need to be flexible to learn and/or change their thinking (Guzzetti, 2000; Tippett, 2010; Zengilowski et al., 2021).

Readers also need to understand the difference between details and *key details*—the information that is important and connected to the main idea(s) (Winograd, 1984). Determining key details is the difference between taking a highlighter to every single word in a textbook and highlighting just the information that aligns to your purpose for reading or to the topics and main idea(s) of the text. Books for beginning readers tend to be very cohesive, and it's rare to find a tangential detail, but as texts get more complex, supporting a topic or main idea with related details becomes more challenging. Every page contains more information, and not all the details align with the main idea (Garner, Gillingham, & White, 1989). In addition, text features—rich with information—become more plentiful, and readers must develop skills to mine these features for details as well (see Strategies 10.16–10.21, for examples).

Readers connect details with main ideas in different ways. Some think whole to part. They step away from their reading and can state a main idea in a sentence. With prompting, they offer details from the text as evidence to back up the idea. Other students start with the parts: they tell you a variety of details, and in the telling they come to understand a main idea, "So I guess it's about . . ." But regardless of how they get there, students need to use reasoning to connect main ideas and details (Williams, 1988).

Eventually, readers will encounter texts complex enough to have multiple main ideas with even more words and features on each page, and the ability to sort and match details to each idea becomes more challenging. In addition, sections or chapters in these complex texts can be quite long, requiring the reader to sort through even more information and details from across many pages to figure out what is most important.

Skills a reader might work on as part of this goal

Activating prior knowledge
Remembering and applying relevant information before, during, and after reading a text.

Questioning
Reading with a focus based on curiosity, and seeking out answers from within the section.

Summarizing
Speaking or writing a succinct summary that incorporates the topic(s) and/or main idea(s) and related information (key details).

Self-monitoring
Being aware of one's understanding and using strategies to fix up confusions, learn new information, or adjust reading rate to maintain comprehension.

Analyzing
Identifying categories of information to compare and contrast details. Considering *how* an author develops a main idea with details.

Synthesizing
Recognizing how details fit together across the text.

Determining importance
Identifying key details from the text and features that relate to the topic(s) and/or main idea(s) in a text.

Visualizing
Creating mental images to better understand information.

Building knowledge
Searching out information beyond the text to add to the details an author provides.

◎ How do I know if this goal is right for my student?

To assess a reader's ability to understand details and match key details with a main idea, ask students to respond to prompts and questions about a text or excerpt, and then evaluate the quality of their responses. The text can be short (e.g., an article, a portion of a textbook, or chapter from a longer work) or long (e.g., an entire informational picture book); it can be one you choose or they choose; and you can decide to read it aloud or have them read it independently. Plant questions at key points in the text, or ask them to read the whole text and respond by jotting or talking about the text when they're done.

Here are some prompts and questions you can use that align to this goal:

- What details support [name a main idea]?
- What details connect to the main idea?
- Describe what you picture when you read the details in this part.
- Summarize the text.

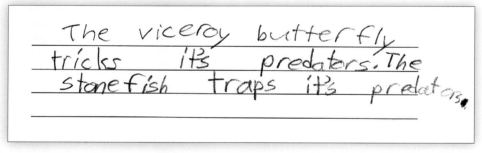

The viceroy butterfly tricks it's predators. The stonefish traps it's predators.

This reader lists two facts about two different subtopics in his book. He could work on visualizing and describing what he's reading about (Strategies 9.6–9.8) or determining which details are related to which main idea or topic to summarize the text (Strategies 9.9–9.13).

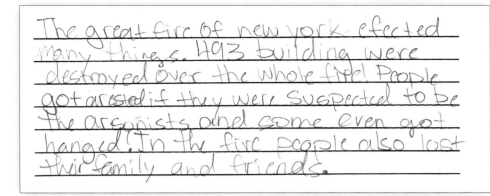

The great fire of new york efected many things. 493 building were destroyed over the whole fire! People got arested if they were suspected to be the arsonists and some even got hanged! In the fire people also lost thir family and friends.

This reader is able to name several specific key details from the article she read that supports a main idea. Right now, she is listing the details and could learn to *explain* how the details support the main idea (Strategies 9.14–9.17).

What Texts Might Students Use When Practicing Strategies from This Chapter?

All texts include details that elaborate on events, topics, and/or ideas. The strategies in this chapter, however, are most helpful for students who are reading informational, persuasive, or procedural texts. Here are a few examples:

Informational picture books. Short texts that use both pictures and words to tell about a topic such as the Bill of Rights, the solar system, gorillas, and so on.

Textbooks. Subject-area (science, history) course book.

Feature articles and op-eds. Short articles, such as those found in popular children's magazines, centered on a topic, often with some slant, perspective, or angle.

Procedural/how-to texts. Texts written to teach the reader how to do or make something (e.g., recipes, craft books, owner's manuals, and so on), which often include lists of materials and explanatory steps.

Narrative nonfiction. Texts that teach about a person (e.g., biographies) or events (e.g., historical accounts) or books that teach about a topic but are organized chronologically, such as the story of bird migration.

◎ How do I support students as they work to connect topic(s) and main idea(s) with key details?

After evaluating a student's verbal or written responses about the topic(s), main idea(s), and key details in their reading, select strategies that you can model, that they can practice with you, and that they can use independently to increase their skills.

Although development is rarely perfectly linear, skill progressions can help us pinpoint where a student is now and what might come next. Use the if–then chart on page 299 to evaluate your students' reading and find strategies that will support their growth.

A Progression of Skills: *Comprehending Key Details*

If a student . . .

Recalls few details and needs support remembering more of what they read by connecting what's in the text to prior knowledge, and self-monitoring during reading.

Is able to list facts and information and is ready to practice visualizing information.

Is able to remember and visualize details and is ready to determine important details related to a topic, subtopic, and/or main idea and use those details to summarize information within or across texts.

Identifies key details from across a text and is ready to learn to explain *how* **those details support a main idea by providing a strong summary, categorizing similar information, and/or analyzing how an author develops the main idea.**

Then you might teach . . .

9.1   **Read with a Sense of "Wow"**

9.2   **Move from What You Know to What's New**

9.3   **Check Yourself**

9.4   **Monitor for Clicks and Clunks**

9.5   **Read, Cover, Remember, Retell**

9.6   **Slow Down for Numbers**

9.7   **Visualize with Comparisons**

9.8   **Look for Comparatives and Superlatives**

9.9   **Build Knowledge with a Text Set**

9.10 **Ask: How Do I Know?**

9.11 **Distinguish Important from Interesting**

9.12 **Frame Your Reading with a Question**

9.13 **Follow the Details in Procedures and Lists**

9.14 **Categorize to Compare**

9.15 **Find Contradictions**

9.16 **Summarize with Explanations**

9.17 **Analyze the Development of an Idea with Details**

Strategy Approach the text expecting to learn. As you read new-to-you information (facts, figures) or see something new (photographs, diagrams), pause and let the information sink in. React and respond with "Wow, I never knew . . ."

Lesson Language *When you read with curiosity and interest, you're more likely to learn and remember the new information you encounter. As you read, try to let the information "sink in," thinking about how it answers questions, satiates your curiosity, or surprises you. You may even react to new information you encounter by saying "wow" and adding on to what's so interesting about what you just read. Watch me read a bit from* Nano: The Spectacular Science of the Very (Very) Small *(Wade, 2021). "Every single thing on this planet is made from atoms. The air you breathe? Atoms. The water you drink? Atoms. Your home and all your things? Atoms. And each and every living thing, including YOU—atoms. Atoms. Atoms." OK, wow. I knew that atoms are small and that they make up a lot of things, but I didn't realize they make up everything—even me! Wow.*

Prompts
- Read as if you're expecting to learn something. Read for the new, wow-worthy info.
- What did you learn that's new to you?
- Say back what you learned. Start with, "Wow, I never knew . . ."
- If you can't say it back, reread until you can.

Read for the new **WoW-worthy info!**
What did you read that's new to you?

Wow! I never knew...   Wow! I never knew...   Wow! I never knew...   Wow! I never knew...

Skills
- self-monitoring
- determining importance

Progression
Recalls few details and needs support remembering more of what they read by connecting what's in the text to prior knowledge, and self-monitoring during reading.

Research Link
In a number of studies (e.g., Mason, 2013), researchers explored TWA, a set of nine guided questions divided into three phases: *T*hink Before Reading, *W*hile Reading, and *A*fter Reading (Mason, 2004). Each question prompts a specific metacognitive strategy, including reflecting on new information. The TWA intervention improved reading comprehension among fifth-grade students who struggled with reading (Mason, 2004), and has shown similar promise with fourth graders (Mason et al., 2006).

Move from What You Know to What's New

Skills

- **activating prior knowledge**
- **determining importance**
- **self-monitoring**
- **questioning**

Progression

Recalls few details and needs support remembering more of what they read by connecting what's in the text to prior knowledge, and self-monitoring during reading.

Research Link

For many decades, researchers have written about the connection between background knowledge and comprehension (e.g., Tierney & Cunningham, 1984). However, because misconceptions can be incredibly persistent (Lipson, 1982), especially when new text is incompatible with existing thinking (Alvermann, Smith, & Readence, 1985), readers may need additional support to integrate their existing knowledge with new knowledge.

Strategy Before reading, talk or write about what you know for sure about the topic, what you think you know, and what you wonder. As you read, add new information, clear up your misunderstandings, and answer your questions.

Lesson Language *Before I read* Bei Bei Goes Home: A Panda Story *(Bardoe, 2021), I thought about what I know for sure: pandas are black and white. I've seen them at the zoo and I know they like bamboo. They are native to China. I think that's about it! What do I think I know? I think they are endangered but I'm not sure. I also think that even though they are cute and cuddly looking, they can be dangerous, like other kinds of bears. What am I curious about? I'm wondering about how they care for their young, and I'm also curious if what I think I know about them is true, and if so, what people might be doing to try to protect the animals from becoming extinct. Now it's time to read to check myself—am I correct about what I know (and what I think I know)? What will the answers to my questions be? What else might I learn that I wasn't expecting?*

Prompts

- You can start with, "I'm not sure, but I think . . ."
- What's something you're sure you know? How are you sure?
- What are you wondering about your topic?
- What are you learning, now that you've read this part?

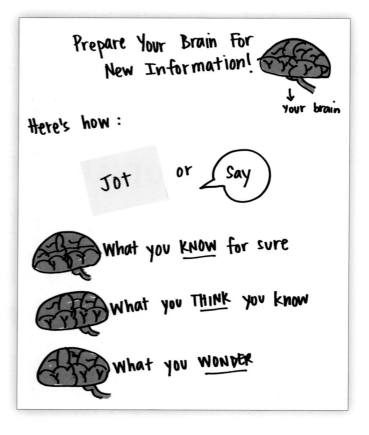

Strategy When the information you read feels confusing, stop and say, "Huh?" Slow down, reread, consider why you're confused. Did you misread the information? Did the information contradict something you thought you already knew about the topic? As you reread, be prepared to revise your thinking or learn something new.

Lesson Language *Let me tell you about some of the moments I had to pause and say, "Huh?" and fix up confusion when I was reading* Climate Change and How We'll Fix It *(Harman, 2020). In the section "Too Much Stuff," I came to the discussion of greenhouse gases such as methane. I read the paragraph, but there was information in there that surprised me. I knew that cows produce methane, but I didn't realize a sitting pile of garbage in a landfill also produces methane. So I reread to make sure I really understood what the text said and didn't confuse it with something I thought I knew. When I got to the inset box "Plastic Problem," I had to slow way down because I wasn't sure how to read the graphic, until I realized the paragraph on the upper left introduces the section, and then I should read the diagram top to bottom. When I read that "waste plastic ends up in the ocean, making the water more* **acidic***" (p. 13), I said, "Huh?" I needed more information about that word in bold, so I paused my reading to look it up in the glossary.*

Prompts

- What was confusing here?
- What made that part confusing?
- Go back and reread to revise your thinking.
- Based on what you just read, do you think you misunderstood the first time?

Skills

- **self-monitoring**
- **activating prior knowledge**

Progression

Recalls few details and needs support remembering more of what they read by connecting what's in the text to prior knowledge, and self-monitoring during reading.

Research Link

Among elementary school students in particular, the hesitation to slow down and monitor for meaning may be due to an overemphasis on reading rate as a proxy for reading ability (Kucer, 2017), but strategies can help. Researchers working with a large group of middle school students found that students with learning disabilities particularly benefited from a five-step self-questioning protocol to support self-monitoring (Wong & Jones, 1982).

Progression

Recalls few details and needs support remembering more of what they read by connecting what's in the text to prior knowledge, and self-monitoring during reading.

Hat Tip

Reading & Writing Informational Text in the Primary Grades (Duke & Bennett-Armistead, 2003)

Research Link

"Click and Clunk" is one of four components of Collaborative Strategic Reading (CSR; Klingner & Vaughn, 1998), inspired by the reciprocal teaching comprehension strategies of Palincsar and Brown (1984) and cooperative learning techniques suggested by Johnson and Johnson (1989). In numerous studies (Klingner, Vaughn, & Schumm, 1998; Vaughn et al., 2011), students in the CSR groups made greater gains in reading comprehension than their peers in the control groups.

Strategy After reading each sentence, think about whether you get it ("click!") or it's confusing ("clunk!"). As you read it should feel like "Click, click, click." When you hit a "clunk," go back and reread, or seek out information you need to understand from outside the text before continuing on.

Lesson Language *Let's read a section from* Art of Protest *(Nichols, 2021) and see what "clicks" and what "clunks." OK. "A Visit to South Africa" What do you think? Click? We know South Africa is a country in the continent of Africa. The author visited there. OK, let's continue. "I got the chance to visit the home of former South African president Nelson Mandela during a solo adventure to Africa a few years ago" (p. 46). Click or clunk? Even if you don't know who Nelson Mandela is, can you follow what the author is writing about? Sure. She tells us he was a president of the country. We know what a president is. OK, let's continue. "Upon visiting the Apartheid Museum, which chronicles the history of ending apartheid rule in the nation, I was struck by the ways that art and graphics had influenced the social movement" (p. 46). OK, before we even finish that sentence, click or clunk so far? We know what a museum is, but have you ever heard of* apartheid? *No, huh? OK, that's a clunk, and we need to figure out what to do. It seems important enough not to just breeze past it. We can read on a bit and see if there's more support to help us understand, and if not, we can look it up.*

Prompts

- Did you understand that? *Click?*
- Check yourself before moving on.
- You didn't understand? *Clunk?* Go back and reread.
- Pause and think, *click or clunk?*

Strategy Read as much as you can cover with your hand or a sticky note. Cover the text you just read. Focus on remembering what you read (it's OK take a moment!). Say back what you remember (it's OK to peek back!). Repeat.

Teaching Tip This strategy is one of my favorite strategies to teach when students are first learning how to research (without plagiarizing), although it works any time you want to slow readers down to monitor their comprehension. When researching, students often copy down information without really understanding it. Covering up the information before retelling (or taking notes) requires students to understand it well enough to put it into their own words. I also find that students read more attentively when they know they have to say back what they learned without reading it from the text.

Prompts
- Read. Now cover.
- Say back what you read.
- Not sure? Uncover the text and reread. When you think you have it, cover it again.
- Make sure you think as you read, to make sure you "get" it.

Know What You're Reading!

Here's how:

step 1: READ!

step 2: COVER!

step 3: REMEMBER!

step 4: RETELL!

Skills
- **summarizing**
- **self-monitoring**

Progression

Recalls few details and needs support remembering more of what they read by connecting what's in the text to prior knowledge, and self-monitoring during reading.

● ○ ○ ○

Research Link

In a synthesis of studies that explored ways to improve comprehension of expository texts for students with learning disabilities (Gajria et al., 2007), paraphrasing had a larger effect size than other cognitive strategies. Ellis and Graves (1990) found that paraphrasing each paragraph supported comprehension more effectively than repeated readings, combining paraphrasing with repeated reading, or simply providing readers with a brief definition of "main idea."

Skills

- **visualizing**
- **self-monitoring**

Progression

Is able to list facts and information and is ready to practice visualizing information.

Hat Tip

Inside Information: Developing Powerful Readers and Writers of Informational Text Through Project-Based Instruction (Duke, 2014b)

Research Link

In a study with adults, about a third of the participants made errors when visualizing and estimating the change in quantity from *thousand* to *million* to *billion* to *trillion*: the similar words for these large numbers tend to disguise the magnitude of their differences (Landy, Silbert, & Goldin, 2013). Providing readers with concrete comparisons to put numbers into perspective may assist comprehension (Barrio, Goldstein, & Hofman, 2016).

Strategy When you read a sentence containing details with numbers, stop and think, "How is this number being used? What is the detail with the number trying to teach me?" Pause to visualize.

Lesson Language *Numbers can teach us about all kinds of things including size, scale, distance, quantity, age, dates, and more. Consider this from* Nano *(Wade, 2021): "'Tiny' doesn't just mean "little"—it means more than a quintillion times smaller than a grain of sand" (unpaginated). How's that number being used? The author is making the point that atoms are very, very, very, very tiny. I am not even sure I can visualize* quintillion *but I know it's got to be more than a* billion *and I can imagine even something a* billion *times smaller than a grain of sand is absolutely microscopic and this is even smaller. Let's peek in another book,* Little Killers: The Ferocious Lives of Puny Predators *(Collard, 2022): "In France, scientists discovered that at least five species of turbellarians have invaded their country—including two that can grow to more than 18 inches (45cm) long!" (p. 20) OK, what else do I know that's 18 inches? Well my ruler is 12 so that's one and a half rulers long. (Show the length with your hands.) Now, since these are flatworms, that's pretty gross!*

Prompts

- How is the number being used (length, weight, size, number of years, etc.)?
- What do you picture in your mind?
- How does that number help you understand the information?
- To understand that number, you can think of what else you know with the same measurement (or size, age, etc.).

Strategy Sometimes an author will compare information to something else, to help you better understand the information. Be on the lookout for words such as *like*, *as*, or *than*. Think about how the two things are similar and different and how the comparison helps you visualize and understand the information.

Lesson Language *In* The Science of an Oil Spill, *Wang (2015) describes what happened during the Deepwater Horizon disaster. She writes, "Flammable [natural] gas flowed out of the well pipe and covered the rig. Since the [natural] gas was heavier than air, it settled on the deck like an eerie fog" (p. 7). That second sentence has two comparisons—gas heavier* than *air, settled . . . like an eerie fog. Let's start with the first one. What's similar about natural gas and air? They are both types of gases. What's different? Natural gas is heavier. It can settle on a surface. Comparing its heaviness to air helps us understand why it settled on the deck and how it could lead to the explosion. Now let's look at the next one. Tell your partner what's being compared with "like an eerie fog" and how the comparison helps you understand the information.*

Prompts
- What's being compared?
- Say what's the same about the two things.
- How does that comparison help you understand the topic?

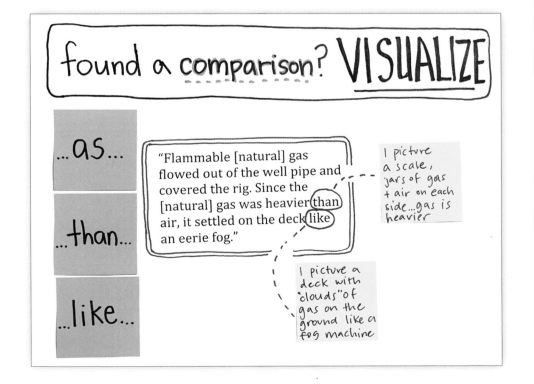

Skills
- **inferring**
- **visualizing**

Progression

Is able to list facts and information and is ready to practice visualizing information.

● ● ○ ○

Research Link

Glynn and Takahashi (1998) conducted a two-part study into teaching with analogies. In the first study, eighth graders who learned from an analogy-enhanced text remembered more content than their peers in the control group. In the second study, sixth graders reported that an analogy-enhanced text made the material easier to understand, suggesting that analogies activate students' background knowledge, allowing them to relate new knowledge to familiar concepts.

Skills

- **inferring**
- **visualizing**

Progression

Is able to list facts and information and is ready to practice visualizing information.

● ● ○ ○ ○

Research Link

Research has shown that grammatical knowledge and awareness of comparative signals in morphology (e.g., inflectional endings like *-er* and *-est*) and syntax (e.g., words such as *more, most, less, least*) not only assist with reading comprehension (Carlisle, 2010) but also play a crucial role in approaching and solving math word problems that involve comparisons (Knight & Hargis, 1977).

Strategy Notice when two or more things are being compared using words ending in *-er* or *-est* or with words such as *more, most, least*. Identify and name what the author is comparing. Read carefully for details that tell you how these things are different.

Lesson Language *In one section of* Climate Change and How We'll Fix It *(Harman, 2020), the author discusses how businesses are under pressure to increase profits, often at the expense of harming the environment. Consider these sentences: "Some companies accept making small**er** profits in order to be **more** eco-friendly, but they often operate on a **much** small**er** scale" [emphasis mine] (p. 21). First we have to figure out what is being compared—companies that use eco-friendly practices and those that do not. Now we need to think: What does this tell us about each company being compared? Well, the ones that are eco-friendly are smaller and often end up making less money. That means bigger companies that make bigger profits might not make decisions based on protecting the environment.*

Prompts

- Do you see any words that end in *-er* or *-est* that could hint at comparisons?
- What two (or more) things are being compared?
- What details do you know about each of those things?
- Name any details you can figure out based on what is explicitly stated about one.

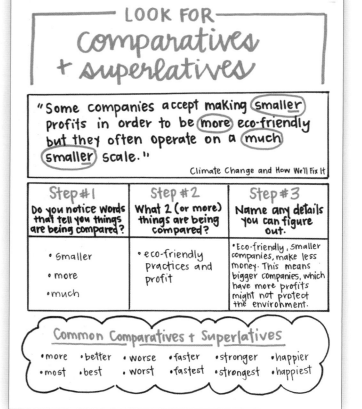

Strategy Collect a set of texts on the same topic. Find the text that seems the least complex. As you read it, collect information (in your mind, or by jotting notes). As you read each additional text, notice when the information is new and adds on to what you already learned, or when information is the same and reinforces what you already learned.

Lesson Language *I have three books that focus on the environment and climate:* The Science of an Oil Spill *(Wang, 2015),* Climate Change and How We'll Fix It *(Harman, 2020), and* Every Breath We Take *(Ajmera & Browning, 2016). I read* Every Breath We Take *first, since it's the simplest of the three. Then, I went to* Climate Change *and read more about air pollution. When I got to the section titled* "Energy and Fuel," *I had to think about what was new information and what was the same as in the first book I read. For example, when I read that* "burning 'dirty' fossil fuels . . . releases huge amounts of greenhouse gases into the atmosphere, as well as other forms of dangerous air pollution that harm people's health" *(p. 8), I remembered reading* "dirty air can make us sick" *(unpaginated) from* Every Breath. *So that part* repeats *or* reinforces *the same information. But the part about the atmosphere and burning fossil fuels? That's new information that adds on to what I already learned to explain why and how the air becomes dirty and unhealthy.*

Teaching Tip While reading across a text set, in addition to discovering information that adds to or reinforces what they read in previous books, readers will sometimes encounter information that may *contradict* another book in the set. See Strategy 9.15 for an example of language to use when helping children think through contradictions.

Prompts
- What is the topic(s) that connects all these books?
- Pause there. Does what you just read repeat something you learned in another text, or add on?
- How does that information add to your understanding about [topic]?
- Say, "This information repeats what I learned in the other text because . . . This information is new/adds on because . . ."

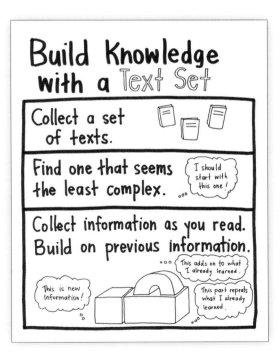

Skills
- **building knowledge**
- **activating prior knowledge**
- **synthesizing**

Progression

Is able to remember and visualize details and is ready to determine important details related to a topic, subtopic, and/or main idea and use those details to summarize information within or across texts.

Research Link

In a study with fourth graders, participants who read a set of conceptually coherent texts demonstrated greater knowledge of the topics and related vocabulary, and were better able to remember the content of the texts, than their peers who read a group of unrelated texts (Cervetti, Wright, & Hwang, 2016).

Progression

Is able to remember and visualize details and is ready to determine important details related to a topic, subtopic, and/or main idea and use those details to summarize information within or across texts.

Hat Tip

Inside Information: Developing Powerful Readers and Writers of Informational Text Through Project-Based Instruction (Duke, 2014b)

Research Link

In a large study, seventh-grade students who received RAP strategy instruction (*R*ead a paragraph, *A*sk yourself, "What were the main idea and details in this paragraph?," and *P*ut the main idea and details into your own words [Schumaker, Denton, & Deshler, 1984]) received higher reading comprehension scores than their peers who did not, including double the percent gain for students with learning disabilities (Katims & Harris, 1997).

Strategy After reading a section or whole book, state what it was mostly about as you touch your palm. Then, ask yourself, "How do I know?" Say back the information that is most connected to or best supports the idea, listing it across your fingers.

Lesson Language *I think the fifth chapter in* The Secret of the Scuba Diving Spider . . . and More! *(Rodríguez, 2018) is mostly about* (touch palm) *how cockroaches are amazing creatures that are also very useful to scientists. How do I know? Well, I know because* (touch one finger) *it says in the book that roach biologist Robert Full uses them every day to begin experiments. It also said that* (touch another finger) *they use the roaches to learn how to build better robots. Also* (touch a third finger) *the section describes all the interesting parts of the cockroach such as their exoskeleton and their ability to fit through tight spaces, their flexible joints, and the sensors they have all over their bodies that make their design so special and interesting to researchers. All this information connects to that one main idea.*

Prompts

• State the main topic or idea of what you just read.
• Name detail(s) that match that idea.
• How do you know that main idea is accurate? List the information.
• Touch your palm and say the main idea. Touch each finger as you list out the information that supports the main idea.

Strategy After reading a sentence or looking at a visual, stop and think: "Does this information or detail support the main idea of this page (or section or book)?" If it doesn't, it may be that the author included something interesting, but that isn't necessarily important for understanding the main idea of the page (or section or book) or for writing a concise summary.

Lesson Language *In informational texts, we'll find facts that the author included to wow, amaze, gross out, or otherwise keep the reader reading. It's all related in some way to the topic. However, when we go to summarize a text, we need to sort through all the information and choose only what's most connected to the* main idea. *For example, after reading the section "Cave of the Sleeping Lady" in* All Thirteen *(Soontornvat, 2020), a book about the Thai boys' soccer team that got trapped in and then rescued from a cave, I understand that the chapter is mostly about the serpentine cave system, how it formed, what it's like to be inside, and the first moments when the team decided to explore the cave the day they got trapped. An entire page at the end is devoted to a photograph of two abandoned bicycles. What does that have to do with the rest of this chapter? The photograph is* interesting *because it helps us imagine being there and to relate to the boys (we may have bikes just like this). Seeing two bikes in the dark also sets an eerie mood because we know the boys have gone in the cave and are about to be trapped. But does this photo help us understand the cave system, the main point of this chapter? Is it* important*? No. It's an interesting detail, but not essential to understanding the main idea.*

Prompts
- Interesting or important? How do you know?
- Does it connect to the main idea? If not, file it away as interesting, but not necessarily important to the main idea.
- Yes, you're right that's an interesting bit of additional information because it doesn't connect to the main idea.
- Say, "I know this information is important to the main idea because . . ."

Progression

Is able to remember and visualize details and is ready to determine important details related to a topic, subtopic, and/or main idea and use those details to summarize information within or across texts.

Research Link

Winograd (1984) found that when eighth graders were asked to identify important information, less skilled readers were apt to choose inherently interesting sentences full of rich visual detail, regardless of how they related to the main idea. As a result, Winograd and Bridge (1986) suggest that identifying important facts is an active, metacognitive skill readers need to develop to see how facts relate to support a main idea.

Skills

- **questioning**
- **determining importance**

Progression

Is able to remember and visualize details and is ready to determine important details related to a topic, subtopic, and/or main idea and use those details to summarize information within or across texts.

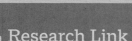

Research Link

Researchers explored the role of headings and whether their presence, location, or form (as a statement or a question) influenced memory, comprehension, information retrieval, or other aspects of reading (Hartley et al., 1980; Hartley & Trueman, 1985). They found that, overall, headings were a beneficial feature. Although inconsistent, they also found evidence that headings written in the form of questions were particularly supportive of students who began with the lowest comprehension.

Strategy Turn the heading into a question. Read the section trying to answer the question. When you finish reading a section, pause to think about what information best answered the question.

Lesson Language *When a heading is phrased as a question, it sets you up to read on and search for information that answers the question. But you can set yourself up the same way even when the headings are just labels, phrases, or statements. You just have to rephrase them as questions! For example, in* The Science of an Oil Spill *(Wang, 2015), some of the headings are already framed as questions ("What Is Oil?" and "What Causes an Oil Spill?"), but others aren't. Let's practice turning the non-question headings into questions. The first one is "Blowout in the Gulf." That could be changed to "What Was the Blowout in the Gulf?" or "What Caused a Blowout in the Gulf?" The next one is "Oil Spill Impacts." We could change that to "What Are the Impacts of Oil Spills?" Last one, your turn: "Oil Spill Response and Prevention." How could you phrase that as a question to set you up to read information to answer it?*

Prompts

- Read the heading. Turn the phrase into a question.
- What information answers that question?
- Read a bit to see if you can find any information that fits with your question.
- Now that you finished reading the section, what information best answers the question?

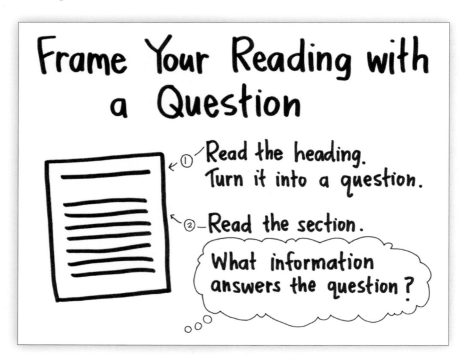

Strategy Whenever you see steps in a procedure or items in a bulleted list that have multiple details, think of each step/item as its own section. Be clear about what the topic/main idea of the step/item is and what the details are that go with each.

Lesson Language *When you see detailed information that's presented as a list, remember that every item on the list is there for a reason, and in a sense, each has its own topic/main idea and details. For example, in* Art of Protest *(Nichols, 2021) several pages are titled "Try This" with a series of numbered items that follow the heading. As I read, I need to think, "What's the main thing this (step/ numbered item) is about?" and then be clear on the details the author uses to elaborate. On page 16, the first numbered item teaches a practical way to use art in protests related to social movements. Specifically, the author suggests listing social issues, circling those that matter most, and brainstorming how to use art to solve problems or protest the issue. Let's look down at the third numbered item. It says, "Create a protest sign. Write or draw a sketch of what your sign will say. Then gather materials around your home like markers and cardboard to create your sign." Turn and tell your partner what that item is mostly about, and what specific details go with it.*

Prompts
- Say back what's most important in this step/item.
- What are some of the details or specific information that goes with that step/item?
- Yes, you're basically summarizing each step. Say what it's mostly about, and then the details.
- Make sure you understand that step before moving on to the next one.

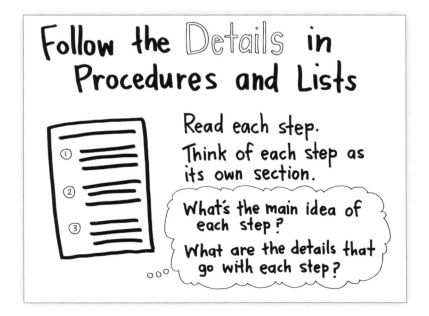

Skills
- **self-monitoring**
- **determining importance**
- **synthesizing**

Progression

Is able to remember and visualize details and is ready to determine important details related to a topic, subtopic, and/or main idea and use those details to summarize information within or across texts.

Research Link

According to observations made in a dissertation study (Martin, 2011), students approach procedural texts in fundamentally different ways than they do other genres of informational texts. As a result, students need explicit instruction to support them in identifying the features of the procedural genre and how the strategies they use for comprehending other types of informational texts apply (or do not apply) to procedural texts.

Skills

- **analyzing**
- **determining importance**

Progression

Identifies key details from across a text and is ready to learn to explain *how* those details support a main idea by providing a strong summary, categorizing similar information, and/or analyzing how an author develops the main idea.

Strategy Decide on two related topics to compare (in the same book or across a text set). Organize information into categories as you read. Compare the related topics using the categories.

Lesson Language *In* Africa, Amazing Africa: Country by Country *(Atinuke, 2019), the author teaches about each African country region by region. To compare countries (and the information you learn about each one), it can be helpful to put the information you learn about each country into categories. For example, when I read a fact like "Angola's capital city, Luanada, is right on the beach, where skyscrapers overlook palm trees" (p. 10), I can name the category "geography." As I read on, I'll look for more details about geography, and I'll make categories for the other kinds of information I'm learning such as how people live, what the cities are like, what resources or exports come from the country, and so on. Once I have categories in mind, I can compare across them. For example, I notice details about sports: basketball is very popular in Angola, but soccer (which they call* football*) is the most popular sport in Mozambique.*

Teaching Tip If they have enough background knowledge, students can also decide on categories *before* they begin reading. For example, when comparing water pollution with air pollution, they might decide to look for information related to categories such as locations, causes, solutions, and so on.

Prompts

- Read a sentence. What category connects to the information in that sentence?
- Do you see information in this other section/book that fits with that category?
- List the information that is the same and different within the category.
- Say the category. Now say the information about each topic that's the same and different.

Research Link

In a study with eighth graders, researchers found that instruction about compare-contrast structure, including the identification of topics, looking for points of comparison, and identifying signal words, helped students write more effective compare-contrast essays when they were relatively unfamiliar with a topic. The instruction was less effective when students had more prior knowledge, suggesting readers may forgo using an organizational strategy in favor of existing mental categories (Hammann & Stevens, 2003).

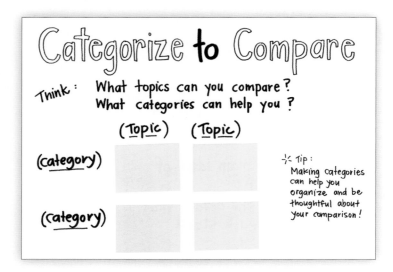

Strategy Find related information in two (or more) texts on the same topic. Identify consistent information across the texts. Identify the information that is contradictory. Consider why the information might be different (see chart).

Lesson Language *In my text set about environmental issues, I found a bit of information that seems contradictory. In* Every Breath We Take, *Ajmera and Browning (2016) write that a solution to having clean, breathable air is for each of us to make changes—turning off lights and heating our homes with clean energy, riding bikes more often, or walking rather than using a car. In* Climate Change and How We'll Fix It, *however, although Harman (2020) does mention that cars and trucks burn fuel that leads to air pollution, she offers more complex solutions. She argues that companies and lawmakers are responsible for making sure we all have cleaner air (though she does also mention individual efforts). Why would the first author make it seem like it's up to us as individuals and the second author make it seem bigger? I checked the publication dates and they are similar. The authors' bios suggest they both care about the environment and are clearly informed about the topic, so it's not that. I think it may have something to do with their intended audiences:* Every Breath *is really meant to be a simple introduction to the topic for younger children, so maybe the author kept solutions simple and concrete for that audience.*

Prompts

- Does any information in one book disagree with or contradict information in the other?
- Consider why the information might be contradictory (check the chart).
- Check out the author. Would they have a reason to mislead? Be misinformed?
- Check out the publication date. Has knowledge about this topic evolved since then?

Skill
- analyzing

Progression

Identifies key details from across a text and is ready to learn to explain *how* those details support a main idea by providing a strong summary, categorizing similar information, and/or analyzing how an author develops the main idea.

Research Link

Although this strategy is appropriate for science, which is revised over time based on new discoveries and the capabilities of new technologies, identifying and analyzing contradictions is especially critical for social studies, history, and other topics that are vulnerable to misrepresentation, may only present one perspective, or may omit marginalized voices (Pennington & Tackett, 2021).

Considering Contradictions

- Is one of the book's publication dates older making the information outdated?
- Is one text simplifying the information because of its intended audience?
- Did one author make an "error of omission" by leaving out a piece of key information?
- Does it seem like one author is trying to deceive the reader?

Summarize with Explanations

Skills

- **summarizing**
- **determining importance**
- **synthesizing**
- **analyzing**

Progression

Identifies key details from across a text and is ready to learn to explain *how* those details support a main idea by providing a strong summary, categorizing similar information, and/or analyzing how an author develops the main idea.

●●●●

Research Link

In a classic study (Armbruster, Anderson, & Ostertag, 1987), researchers provided fifth graders with explicit instruction in text structure, along with graphic organizers for summarizing and organizing the text's main ideas and details. They found that readers who received the intervention had access to a useful mental frame for recalling and organizing the main ideas and details from the text (Meyer, 1985).

Strategy After reading a section, state or jot the section's main idea. Next, reread to find information that goes with the idea. To summarize, share the main idea and then after each piece of information from the text, use your own words to explain *how* the information supports, extends, or backs up the main idea.

Lesson Language *The first part of* Can We Save the Tiger? *(Jenkins, 2011) introduces the idea that peoples' actions and the ways we've changed the planet have impacted animals to the point that they are extinct or endangered. With that main idea in mind, I can reread the section and find the information that fits with it. One thing I read is that there are billions of people. Does that support the idea? Not exactly by itself. You could add onto it by saying that each one of those people has a negative impact on animals, but I am not sure that's even true because it doesn't say it in the text and I don't want to make stuff up. Let me keep reading. Here's some information, "We've turned forests into farmland, dammed rivers, and built towns and cities to live in" (p. 6). Does that fit with what I think this section is mostly about? Yes, absolutely. How so? Well, damming rivers and cutting down forests changes animal habitats and makes it harder for them to make shelters or find food. The answer to "How so?" is in my own words, it's my own explanation, it's not something from the text.*

Prompts

- Keep the main idea in mind as you reread this section to find related information.
- Explain how that information backs up the main idea.
- Yes, that's the main idea and one piece of information. Now explain: "This information fits with the main idea because . . ."
- Yes! All the information you listed is from this part and fits with the main idea.

Summarize with **Explanations**

① Read
② State or jot the main idea

The main idea here is . . .

③ Reread for info that goes with the idea

(In Your Own Words) Explain how the info backs up or extends the main idea

Analyze the Development of an Idea with Details

Strategy Name the main idea(s) of the text. Ask yourself, "*How* does the author develop this idea?" Notice the information an author includes in each part of the text that aligns to the idea.

Lesson Language *Throughout the book* Climate Change and How We'll Fix It, *Harman (2020) informs us about the dangers of climate change and convinces readers that we need to make changes—individually and systemically—to save the planet. I figured out that main idea by putting the information across the text together; now I can analyze how she did it. I'll have to think about where the idea shows up in each part of the book and also consider what information she includes and why it supports the idea. For example, in the section on energy and fuel, she develops the book's main idea by comparing different energy sources (renewable and nonrenewable, clean and dirty) and gives specific details about how fossil fuels cause problems by producing greenhouse gases. The details she includes clearly show what we need to change and why. She didn't focus on costs to consumers or profits to companies or jobs or any other details that go against the main idea. Let's look at the next section and see what information she's included to back up the main idea.*

Prompts

- What information does the author include to support that idea?
- Look across the text at each part. Explain how the idea is developed.
- Consider why the author included the information they did.
- What information in each part supports the main idea?

Skills

- **determining importance**
- **analyzing**

Progression

Identifies key details from across a text and is ready to learn to explain *how* those details support a main idea by providing a strong summary, categorizing similar information, and/or analyzing how an author develops the main idea.

Research Link

In a review of research on *scientific literacy*, Britt, Richter, and Rouet (2014) outline the challenges faced by laypeople who read about science, including navigating the author's choices of both genre (e.g., explanatory, persuasive, a combination) and text structure (e.g., collection, description, problem/solution, compare/contrast), as well as decisions about organization, word choice, and audience, all of which the reader can infer, but will never know with certainty.

Comprehending Text Features

◎ Why is this goal important?

Making sense of text features is essential to reading and understanding informational texts. Authors use a wide variety of text features—photographs, illustrations, maps, charts, graphs, headings, sidebars, tables of contents, indexes, and so on—to support the main text, to add extra information, and/or to help readers navigate the content. Text features help readers identify main ideas (see more in Chapter 8), understand key details (see more in Chapter 9), and learn new vocabulary (see more in Chapter 11). However, each type of feature requires readers to unpack key information in specific ways, and for that reason, learning to read features is an important goal on its own.

Despite their central role in informational texts, researchers have found that teaching text features in isolation may not be effective (Duke, 2014b; Purcell-Gates, Duke, & Martineau, 2007). To really treat these features as the information-rich resources they are, we need to make sure that the strategies we offer students go beyond simply *identifying* the features (e.g., "That's a map") and instead teach them how to *use* features: reading them carefully and synthesizing information from the features with information in the main text (Maloch, 2008). Readers can also learn to consider the purpose(s) and function(s) of features, and consider why the author may have included them (Kelley & Clausen-Grace, 2008, 2010).

When children first read texts with features, they'll often find photographs and illustrations that directly correspond to the straightforward text on the page. In these beginning texts, the illustrations and photographs may even offer more information than the written text. For example, a text may have a diagram of germs that shows the specific shapes of various bacteria and viruses, when the text simply states that germs come in different shapes. As texts get more complex, so do the types of features and quantity of features readers encounter. Eventually, text features become more text heavy (e.g., side-bars, timelines, detailed inset boxes, graphs) and function almost like sections with their own main idea(s) and detail(s). Readers need strategies that help them get information from these more complex features and explain how they relate to one another, as well as to the main text.

Visualizing
Creating mental images beyond what's explicitly shown or described in the features and text.

Determining importance
Identifying key details from features that relate to the topic(s) and/or main idea(s) in a text.

Analyzing
Identifying categories of information to compare and contrast details from within features. Considering *how* an author develops a main idea with details.

Skills a reader might work on as part of this goal

Self-monitoring
Being aware of one's understanding and using strategies to fix up confusion, learn new information, or adjust reading rate to maintain comprehension.

Building knowledge
Reading relevant information beyond the main text to add to the details an author provides.

Summarizing
Speaking or writing a succinct summary of a feature, and/or including features in a summary of the whole section or text.

Synthesizing
Matching information from features with the key details, topic(s), and/or main idea(s) in the rest of the text.

Planning
Preparing to read a page or section that includes both text and features.

◎ How do I know if this goal is right for my student?

To assess students' ability to understand information from text features, observe children while they read informational texts to notice if their attention is on the text, features, or both. Ask them about their plans for how they would approach a "busy" page, filled with various features and sections of text. Ask students to respond to prompts and questions about feature(s) in a text or excerpt, and then evaluate the quality of their responses. The text can be short (e.g., an article, a portion of a textbook, or chapter from a longer work) or long (e.g., a complete book); can be one you choose or they choose; and you can decide to read it aloud or have them read it independently. Plant questions at key points in the text, or ask them to read the whole text and respond by jotting or talking about the text when they're finished.

Here are some prompts and questions you can use that align to this goal:

- What details can you learn about [topic] from [feature]?
- What does the [feature] teach you?
- How does the [feature] fit with the information in this section?

I can learn that the spot is moving in a diagnol and it looks like its orbiting around somthing.

This student's jot about a photograph shows she's paying attention to the feature and can list a few vague details. As a next step, she could learn to study the photo more closely to be more specific about what it is teaching, and she can work to connect relevant information from the main text with the feature (Strategies 10.3–10.7).

> This image teaches me that a planet orbiting can make the star wobble because the star's and panet's gravation pull one another.

This student's jot about an image shows that she's able to get details not only from the photograph, but also from the surrounding text (words and concepts like "planet orbiting" and "gravitational pull" and "make the star wobble" aren't explicitly stated anywhere on the image, only in the surrounding text). She is ready to learn to study more complex types of features to do the same (Strategies 10.8–10.25).

What Texts Might Students Use When Practicing Strategies from This Chapter?

Any text containing graphic features (maps, charts, tables, and so on), headings or subheadings, or visuals (photographs, illustrations), For example:

Informational picture books. Short texts that use both pictures and words to tell about a topic such as the Bill of Rights, the solar system, gorillas, and so on.

Articles. Short articles, such as those found in popular children's magazines.

Textbooks. Subject-area (science, history) course books.

Procedural/how-to texts. Texts written to teach the reader how to do or make something (e.g., recipes, craft books, owner's manuals, and so on), which often include lists of materials and explanatory steps.

Narrative nonfiction. Texts that teach about a person (e.g., biographies), or events (e.g., historical accounts), or books that teach about a topic but are organized chronologically, such as the story of bird migration.

◎ How do I support students as they work to understand information from text features?

After evaluating a student's verbal or written responses about the text features in their reading, select strategies that you can model, that they can practice with you, and that they can use independently to increase their skills.

Although development is rarely perfectly linear, skill progressions can help us pinpoint where a student is now and what might come next. Use the if-then chart on page 323 to evaluate your students' reading and find strategies that will support their growth.

A Progression of Skills: Comprehending Text Features

If a student . . .

Needs to attend to all the information in every part of a text—both the main text and features—and make plans for how to read the page or spread.

Recognizes common features such as photos and illustrations and is ready to study them more closely to visualize, determine important information, and synthesize what's in the feature with what's in the main text.

Is reading texts with complex features (map, graph, table, sidebar, glossary, and so on) and needs to study them more closely to visualize, determine important information, and synthesize information from the feature with that in the main text.

Is reading texts with multiple features. Is ready to analyze an author's intent regarding text features, synthesize the information in multiple features and text, and/or compare and contrast information from across features.

Then you might teach . . .

10.1   **Scan and Plan**

10.2   **Scan Before You Turn**

10.3   **Turn the 2D into 3D**

10.4   **Bring Pictures to Life**

10.5   **Cover Up Then Zoom In**

10.6   **Get More from Photographs**

10.7   **Caption It!**

10.8   **Be Alert to Bold Words**

10.9   **Preview Important Words**

10.10   **Use Text Features to Learn New Words**

10.11   **PREview with the Table of Contents**

10.12   **REview with the Table of Contents**

10.13   **Find Just the Information You Need**

10.14   **Get a Heads Up with Headings**

10.15   **Crack Open Crafty Headings**

10.16   **Explore Maps**

10.17   **Go with the Flow(Chart)**

10.18   **Consider Sidebars as Sections**

10.19   **Study Charts and Tables**

10.20   **Take Time with Timelines**

10.21   **Summarize Information in Graphs**

10.22   **Use Context to Understand Fact Lists**

10.23   **Study What Diagrams Show and Tell**

10.24   **Consider Primary Sources**

10.25   **Continue Your Reading After the End**

10.26   **Compare and Contrast with Images**

10.27   **Ask: Why a Text Feature?**

10.28   **Fit the Features and the Text Together**

10.1 Scan and Plan

Strategy First, scan the page or section to notice the text layout and organization. Then, make a plan for how you'll read the information from the text and features. Read it according to your plan.

Lesson Language *Sometimes the pages in the informational books we read are just busy! There may be words in one place, pictures in another, a diagram over here, a map over there. It can feel like you're inside a maze, trying to find your way through, unless you have some plan for how you'll approach it all. For example, look with me at this spread from* Nano *(Wade, 2021). Let's name what we see—main text on the upper left side. A footnote at the bottom of that page. On the right-hand page, there's a large box with a key detailing the color coding for elements. There are bubbles above showing diagrams of molecular structures for rocks, salt, and cotton. This is a lot of information to take in. Let's make a plan. What will we read first? After that?*

Teaching Tip Some books utilize predictable, repetitive layouts (like this one!) where a reader can reflect after using a plan for one page or spread to decide if it worked well, and if so, use the same plan to read each similar page. In other cases, structures and layouts vary from spread to spread or chapter to chapter, and readers will need to be flexible and use this strategy at many points throughout the book.

Prompts

- What will you read first? Why?
- You planned to look at all the features first.
  Now, as you read the words, check back with the features.
- Read this first part. Let's see how your plan works out for you.
- Now that you've finished this section, will you read the next section the same way?

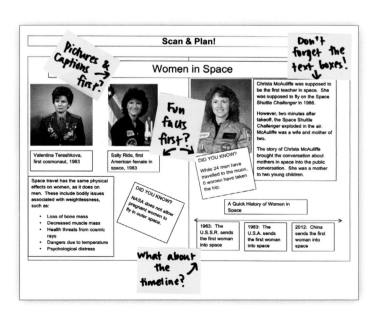

Skill

- planning

Progression

Needs to attend to all the information in every part of a text—both the main text and features—and make plans for how to read the page or spread.

Research Link

From a series of studies observing how elementary school students make sense of visually rich informational texts, researchers found that readers referred to some visuals or features multiple times. Others were overlooked entirely or were given a cursory glance without thought as to how they contributed meaning to the whole (Norman, 2012; Norman & Roberts, 2015; Roberts & Brugar, 2017).

Skill

- **self-monitoring**

Progression

Needs to attend to all the information in every part of a text—both the main text and features—and make plans for how to read the page or spread.

● ○ ○ ○

Research Link

In a classic study with college students, Mayer and colleagues (1995) found that when readers could view corresponding text, illustrations, and captions together on the same page in a science textbook (versus on separate pages), they had a much deeper understanding of the concepts.

Strategy Read the information from the text and features in an order that makes sense to you. However, make sure you've read everything—both the features and the text—by doing one last scan before turning the page.

Teaching Tip Some students gravitate toward text features and may skim or ignore the main text on the page. Others will focus on the text and skip right past the text features. Reading everything on the page requires readers to slow down their pace, concentrate on details they get from each part of every page, and synthesize the information. Teach them to check that they've read and thought about it all before turning the page.

Prompts

- I think you skipped something. Scan the page again to see if you can find it.
- Before you turn the page, look around the spread one more time to make sure you haven't missed anything.
- Yes, you read all the text and you read and studied all the features. Go ahead and turn the page.
- Check yourself. Did you read it all?

Strategy Look closely at the two dimensional (2D), or flat, photograph, illustration, or diagram. Imagine it in three dimensions (3D), like it is in real life. Read the words in the caption and in the surrounding text to help you imagine.

Lesson Language *In* Every Breath We Take *(Ajmera & Browning, 2016), on the page about how air moves and things can ride on the wind, there's a photograph of hot air balloons. In the photo, they look like balloons of different sizes pasted sort of randomly against a blue sky. But if I imagine myself being there, in the actual place and at the moment the photo was taken, I can see them in 3D. I realize they are not different sizes. The larger ones are just closer to me and the smaller ones are farther away. I can also sense the ground and that helps me see that some are quite a bit higher in the sky than others. And even though they* look *like they are very close and about to run into each other in the photo, my 3D view helps me see that there is, in fact, plenty of space between them.*

Teaching Tip Understanding the concept of *dimensions* and the difference between 2D and 3D is key to being able to use this strategy. Check your readers' understanding of these concepts, and provide support as needed.

Prompts
- Look at the illustration/picture. Read the caption to understand it better.
- What do you imagine, beyond just the flat picture?
- Describe what it's like in three dimensions (3D).
- What's it like in real life?

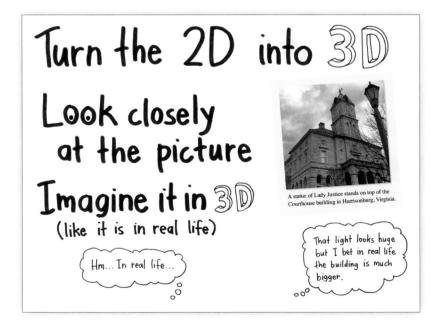

Skill
- **visualizing**

Progression

Recognizes common features such as photos and illustrations and is ready to study them more closely to visualize, determine important information, and synthesize what's in the feature with what's in the main text.

Research Link

Study participants read a sentence describing an object with an implied orientation (e.g., "John put the pencil in a cup" = vertical pencil). When presented with images of the objects, participants responded more quickly to images that matched the orientation they had read, providing evidence that readers store information in a perceptual system that is sensitive to three-dimensionality and that textual information influences how images are perceived (Stanfield & Zwaan, 2001).

Skill

• **visualizing**

Progression

Recognizes common features such as photos and illustrations and is ready to study them more closely to visualize, determine important information, and synthesize what's in the feature with what's in the main text.

Research Link

According to theories of *embedded cognition* (e.g., Barsalou, 2008), readers construct mental representations using information from all their senses through a similar process, whether the source information is directly experienced or encountered in a text. When readers have lived experiences that correspond with textual information, they can generate a more realistic and accurate mental model (e.g., Zwaan, 1999).

Strategy Look closely at the photograph or illustration and any accompanying caption. Imagine it in real life: How does it move? What does it feel like? Smell like? Sound like?

Lesson Language *On page 7 of* The Science of an Oil Spill *(Wang, 2015), there's a photograph of a huge structure in the middle of the ocean and it's on fire. The boats surrounding it are spraying the fire with water. The caption says, "Leaks from the oil well led to huge explosions on the Deepwater Horizon." If I take a moment with the photo and imagine movement and use all my senses, the picture comes to life. I can* see *the movement of the smoke billowing and the flames getting bigger, and then smaller as the spraying water eventually puts the fire out. I can* feel *the heat generated by the inferno. I can* smell *the horrible fumes of the oil burning. I can* hear *the sounds of explosions and the water spraying from the boats. When I visualize like this, it helps me get more details from the picture, and helps me understand it better.*

Prompts

• Read the caption. Now look at the picture. Use your senses to describe what you see.
• Describe how it moves, or what it does.
• Use your senses.
• Say, "I see . . . I feel . . . I smell . . . I hear . . ."

Strategy When you come upon a detailed image, look at it first as a whole. Say what you see. Use sticky notes to cover up quadrants. Uncover one part of the image and zoom in. Name some new details you notice. Repeat with each quadrant.

Lesson Language *When I came to the photograph of two scientists with a panda on page 43 of* Bei Bei Goes Home: A Panda Story *(Bardoe, 2021), I knew I wanted to spend a bit of time with it. The foreground is simple: I see two men holding a panda. But the background has lots of detail that I didn't want to miss. With four sticky notes, I created a grid. Peeling off the one in the upper right-hand corner helped me to zoom in and see closely. When I looked at the details, I noticed multiple hands with latex gloves, bodies in blue gowns, and a vitals monitor. It looks as if they are performing surgery. After I put the sticky note back in place and peeled off the one in the lower left-hand corner, I noticed a sign that says "Processed Poop"! I didn't see that before I looked closely. I can also make out some of the rest of the sign that mentions that scientists dry out the panda poop before analyzing it. On the lower right-hand side I see a microscope. It looks like a really powerful one. So, if I put all these details together, I can say more about the photo: Scientists do many things to study pandas, such as observing live pandas, looking at things they collect from the pandas, and maybe even operating on them.*

Prompts
- Look at it as a whole. What do you notice?
- Cover it up first. Now zoom in.
- Really look closely, part by part. Try to say more.
- You learned something from the picture because you looked closely.

Skill
- determining importance

Progression

Recognizes common features such as photos and illustrations and is ready to study them more closely to visualize, determine important information, and synthesize what's in the feature with what's in the main text.

⬤⬤◯◯

Research Link

One principle of the Cognitive Theory of Multimedia Learning (Mayer, 2005) is that a reader-viewer has a limited capacity for processing information, so it can be helpful to reduce the amount of information presented. Another principle is that the reader-viewer doesn't passively learn from images and text, so instruction needs to support *generative processing* that helps students see material as a coherent whole.

1. Look at the whole   *2. Zoom in*

Progression

Recognizes common features such as photos and illustrations and is ready to study them more closely to visualize, determine important information, and synthesize what's in the feature with what's in the main text.

● ● ○ ○

Research Link

In one study, college students in a geology class (Dean & Enemoh, 1983) were asked to view a photograph of a meandering river before reading a complex text about rivers. Researchers found that the picture served as a sort of "mental organizer" for readers with low prior knowledge, providing them with sufficient background knowledge to better comprehend the text.

Strategy Look at the photographs. Read the main text and/or captions. Go back to study each photo and think, "What do I see in the image that is the same as what's explained in the words? What information do I get from the photo that goes beyond what is in the written text?"

Lesson Language *Photographs often contain more information than what you read in the text. For example, in* Secret of the Scuba Diving Spider . . . and More! *(Rodríguez, 2019), let's look closely at the photo on page 9 and say what we see: a spider in the center of a web. There's dew on the web. The spider is striped. Now I can read the caption.* (Read aloud.) *Now I can go back to the image to say what's the same and what's new. Well, in the caption I read that spiders sit and wait to capture prey. I also read that this is called a "striped spider" and that the web is covered with "morning dew." Now let me look back at the image and study it. What other information can I add based on what I see? Well, it's kind of cool how I can see the underside of the spider. If I look closely, I can see its pincers . . . or maybe that's its mouth? I can see that the spider has eight legs—I didn't read that in the text—and it seems like it positions itself upside down to wait in the web. I can also understand how complex the web is. The spider has set up a tight grid of lines that is sure to trap an insect!*

Prompts

- Look at the photo. Say what you see. Now read the caption or text.
- Point around the image. List information you can learn from looking closely.
- What can you learn from the photo that's not in the words?
- That's something you learned from the words. What can you learn from the photo?

Strategy Read the text. Look at the image. Think, "What is one sentence that summarizes what this image is teaching me?" Use the information from the image and the main text to help you.

Lesson Language *When photographs or illustrations don't have captions, you can try writing a caption (actually writing it on a sticky note, or just "writing it" in your head). For example, in the section on Tanzania in* Africa, Amazing Africa *(Atinuke, 2019), there is a large illustration that takes up one-third of the page, but doesn't have a caption. When I look at it, I see a person surrounded by baskets of various things, hanging fruit, and tables with items on display. But what is the image trying to teach me? To know, I need to read the section.* (Read aloud.) *Ah, so the illustration must have something to do with this statement, "Zanzibar is famous for its busy markets, which are rich with the scents of spices and the voices of merchants from all around the world" (p. 34). Looking back at the image, what's a caption we can create to explain what the image is showing? Maybe, "A merchant sells fruit and other items from inside a tent in the Zanzibar market."*

Prompts
- Use your own words in the caption, not just a fact you read.
- Make a one-sentence caption.
- What do you see in this image? Now write a caption.
- What information does this image show?

Skills
- **summarizing**
- **synthesizing**
- **determining importance**

Progression

Recognizes common features such as photos and illustrations and is ready to study them more closely to visualize, determine important information, and synthesize what's in the feature with what's in the main text.

● ● ○ ○

Research Link

Translating between written and visual modalities, and making sense of the two when combined (e.g., a captioned illustration), is not automatic, nor is it easy. However, through explicit instruction in visual literacy, even students in early elementary can successfully understand, and compose, multimodal informational texts (Coleman, Bradley, & Donovan, 2012; Varelas et al., 2008).

Be Alert to Bold Words

Progression

Is reading texts with complex features (map, graph, table, sidebar, glossary, and so on) and needs to study them more closely to visualize, determine important information, and synthesize information from the feature with that in the main text.

Research Link

In a review of previous research, Lorch (1989) reported consistent findings that the use of *typographical cues* (e.g., boldface, italics, underlining), an unambiguous way for an author to signal that information is important, improved memory for the signaled content.

Strategy Notice when a word is in bold. Ask yourself, "Would a definition or more information about this important word help me to better understand?" If so, check to see if there's a glossary. Locate the word (the glossary is in alphabetical order). Read the definition. Turn back to the sentence where you first read the word. Incorporate the definition as you reread the sentence.

Lesson Language *Authors use bold words to alert us to their importance. Sometimes, the bold print just means, "Hey, pay attention! This word matters!" For example, in* Nano *(Wade, 2021), the author uses bold print here, for the word* atoms *(point to word on page 6) and here for the word* molecules *(point to word on page 7). When I was first reading this book, I checked to see if there was a glossary and there wasn't, so I reread the context around the words carefully to learn what I could about their meanings. In some books, however, like* The Science of an Oil Spill *(Wang, 2015), bold print signals a connection to a glossary. Let's look on page 22 where the word* toxic *is in bold: "Oil is **toxic** and causes many serious health problems." From the sentence we can figure out that* toxic *has to do with causing health problems. But if we want to know more, we can look in the glossary. Let's see what it says, "Toxic: Poisonous." Ah, so I can go back and reread the sentence with that definition tucked in to help me understand it. It would sound like this, "Oil is toxic, or poisonous, and causes many serious health problems."*

Teaching Tip This strategy would also be helpful for students who are working on a goal of understanding vocabulary (see more strategies for this goal in Chapter 11).

Prompts

- Do you see any bold words on this page?
- Check to see if there is a glossary.
- Do you need more information about this word?
- Reread the sentence and incorporate the definition from the glossary into it.

Strategy Preview important words and their definitions by reading a key terms/ words box or by skimming the chapter for bold words and then reading their definitions in the glossary. Get a basic understanding of the word(s) from the definition(s). Read the section or chapter. When you come to a word whose definition you previewed, add to that definition based on your understanding of what's in the text.

Lesson Language *Before we start reading this section on page 8 from* Climate Change and How We'll Fix It *(Harman, 2020), let's preview key vocabulary by looking for words in bold. Ah, there's* renewable, fossil fuels, *and* crude oil. *Let's read their definitions in the glossary quickly before reading the section. (Read definitions.) OK, those definitions are helpful and give us a basic gist. Now, let's read the section expecting to learn more about each word. First up is* renewable, *which we learned from the glossary means that it won't run out. Ah, it says here that examples of renewable sources are the sun, wind, ocean, and underground heat. It also says renewable energy is "clean" and that renewable energy doesn't produce greenhouse gases or other pollution. The illustration below shows examples—wind turbines, solar panels, something in the water that must help capture energy created by waves. So do you see how the glossary definition got us started, but from reading the text we got much more information?*

Teaching Tip This strategy would also be helpful for students who are working on a goal of understanding vocabulary (see more strategies for this goal in Chapter 11).

Prompts
- Preview the important words and their definitions from this section.
- That glossary definition gives a gist, but after you read more in the main text, can you add to it?
- Read the words and their definitions in this key terms/ words box before reading the section.
- Put the information you learned about this word in the text together with the information you learned from the glossary/key word box.

Skills
- **building knowledge**
- **synthesizing**

Progression
Is reading texts with complex features (map, graph, table, sidebar, glossary, and so on) and needs to study them more closely to visualize, determine important information, and synthesize information from the feature with that in the main text.

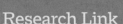

Research Link
In a study using the THIEVES strategy (Manz, 2002) to preview texts with English learners in Iran, all the readers in a control group reported that unknown vocabulary was a major hurdle to their comprehension. However, only 72% of readers in an experimental group who were cued to look for boldface words and check definitions in a list of key terms or glossary reported struggling with unknown words (Khataee, 2019).

Skills

- **synthesizing**
- **self-monitoring**
- **building knowledge**

Progression

Is reading texts with complex features (map, graph, table, sidebar, glossary, and so on) and needs to study them more closely to visualize, determine important information, and synthesize information from the feature with that in the main text.

Research Link

Readers learn new vocabulary incidentally, and research has shown that encountering new words frequently in a variety of contexts improves vocabulary acquisition (Jenkins, Stein, & Wysocki, 1984). However, comprehensive definitions and relationships between concepts are not always clear from context alone (Herman et al., 1987), so readers may need support to connect information in text features to word learning.

Strategy When you come to a word and you don't know its meaning, check the features on the page, in the section, and across the book (for example: a word bank, a chart, a map, a picture, a glossary). Find information that teaches you about the word. Go back to the sentence and try to use the definition in the context.

Lesson Language *When you're learning about a new topic, you'll likely also be learning new words that are specific to the topic. In many cases, the author won't leave you high and dry, grasping at the meaning of those important words. In addition to looking at the sentences on the page, you can look to text features for support. For example, in* Pink Is for Blobfish *(Keating, 2016), the blobfish is described as being "made of gelatinous goo" (unpaginated). I can look at the photo to see what "gelatinous" looks like—a big squishy shiny blob! It's also in bold print so I can get the definition from the glossary, "having a jelly-like consistency." If I put those two bits of information together, I can go back to the sentence to read it again and learn that new word.*

Teaching Tip This strategy would also be helpful for students who are working on a goal of understanding vocabulary (see more strategies for this goal in Chapter 11).

Prompts

- Are there any features that would help you understand that word?
- Based on this picture (or sidebar or map or so on), what might the word mean?
- Is it bold? If so, check the glossary.
- You used the picture *and* the glossary to understand the word more completely!

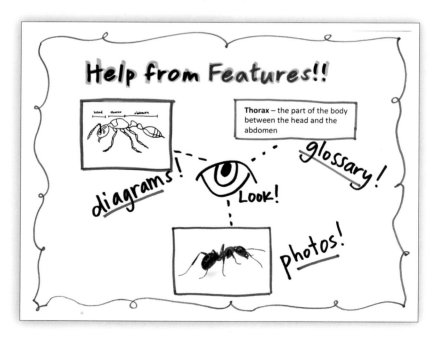

Strategy To preview the text, read through the chapter and/or section titles in the table of contents. Think, "How is this book organized? What are some of the main ideas (or topics) in the book?" Prime your brain to create "file folders" that will help you to organize information as you read.

Lesson Language *Some books have tables of contents and some don't. When they do, don't skip over this helpful text feature! Let's look at a book we haven't yet read:* Africa, Amazing Africa *(Atinuke, 2019). Just from a quick skim of the table of contents, I can see how it will really help us get oriented to the book. We can see there is a short introduction, and then the book is broken up into five big sections—Southern, East, West, Central, and North Africa—and then there are several countries listed underneath each section, each with its own heading. I can get ready to read by creating mental file folders to organize the information country by country.*

Teaching Tip This strategy would be helpful for students who are working on a goal of understanding main idea (see Chapter 8 for more strategies related to that goal).

Prompts
- Spend a little time with the table of contents. Read through each chapter title.
- After previewing the book with the table of contents, what are some topics you expect to learn about across this book?
- Based on what you see in the table of contents, how did the author organize the information in this book? Why organize the information in that way?
- What "folder" will you need to make in your brain for this chapter?

Use the **Table of Contents**

(Think) **How is the book organized?**
What are some topics in the book?
Create mental file folders to help you organize information.

TOPIC TOPIC Oh... That fits with this topic! TOPIC

Progression

Is reading texts with complex features (map, graph, table, sidebar, glossary, and so on) and needs to study them more closely to visualize, determine important information, and synthesize information from the feature with that in the main text.

Research Link

The table of contents is one way of signaling the top-level organization of a text (Armbruster, 1984). Using the table of contents to preview the text has been shown to improve comprehension and recall (e.g., Meyer & Ray, 2011).

REview with the Table of Contents

Skills

- **summarizing**
- **determining importance**

Progression

Is reading texts with complex features (map, graph, table, sidebar, glossary, and so on) and needs to study them more closely to visualize, determine important information, and synthesize information from the feature with that in the main text.

Research Link

In a series of experiments with college-age readers (Krug et al., 1989), researchers found that using an outline (which functions like a table of contents) improved readers' recall of information, especially when it matched headings found within the text.

Strategy To use the table of contents to review the text you just read, read back over it to remind yourself of the main idea(s) and topic(s) you read about. You could even quiz yourself by asking, "What did I read about in that section?" and recounting the key details.

Lesson Language *Let's look at a book we read recently to see how the table of contents can help us remember some of what we learned. In* The Secret of the Scuba Diving Spider . . . and More! *(Rodríguez, 2018), we see the titles of five chapters. Do the titles jog your memory? What was the chapter "A Caterpillar's Emergency Whistle" mostly about? Can you remember some details from the chapter? Turn and tell your partner.*

Teaching Tip This strategy would also be helpful for students who are working on a goal of understanding key details (see Chapter 9 for more strategies related to that goal).

Prompts

- Use the table of contents to review. Read a chapter title, and give a quick summary of what you read about in that chapter.
- You can say, "In this chapter, I remember I learned . . ."
- What do you remember about this chapter?
- Why do you think these chapters were grouped together in this section?

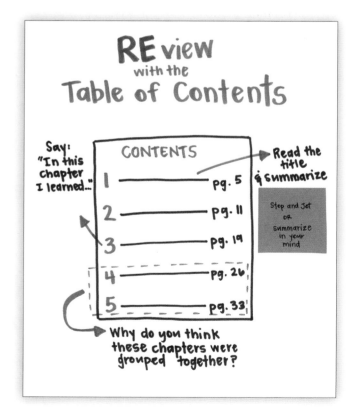

Strategy Have your research question(s) in mind. Scan through the table of contents thinking, "Which chapter(s) might contain the information I'm looking for?" or through the index looking for key words related to your question(s). Turn to the related pages and read.

Lesson Language *You know that I typically encourage you to read a whole text—beginning to end—so you understand all the information the author included and carefully ordered. However, when you're doing a research project, or when you just need specific information to answer a question, you may not want to read the whole text. A table of contents and/or an index can help you quickly find the information you need. For example, if I'm looking in* Can We Save The Tiger? *(Jenkins, 2011) to see how information about endangered animals relates to what I'm reading about climate change in my text set, I might go to page 50, the page number listed next to the key word* climate *in the index. Or in* All Thirteen *(Soontornvat, 2020), this is a biiiiiig book, so searching for specific information can be challenging. But if I take a look at the table of contents, it can help me narrow down which chapter to turn to to learn about, say, how they were trapped in the caves—I think I'd turn to Chapter 5, titled "Trapped," to get that information.*

Teaching Tip This strategy would be also be helpful for students who are working on a goal of understanding key details (see Chapter 9 for more strategies related to that goal).

Prompts
- What are you hoping to learn?
- Look at the table of contents with your question in mind.
- What made you pick that chapter?
- What key words will you search for in the index to find information related to your topic?

Find Just the Information you need

1 What are you hoping to learn?

2 Think of **key words** that could help you.

3 Look at the Table of Contents or Index for **key words** related to your question.

Skills
- **determining importance**
- **planning**

Progression

Is reading texts with complex features (map, graph, table, sidebar, glossary, and so on) and needs to study them more closely to visualize, determine important information, and synthesize information from the feature with that in the main text.

Research Link

In a small experiment (Dreher & Sammons, 1994), fifth graders were asked to research answers to three questions in an unfamiliar informational text. Students who used guiding questions were more successful than the students who were not. The guiding questions seemed to cue students to make use of the index.

Skills

- **inferring**
- **synthesizing**

Progression

Is reading texts with complex features (map, graph, table, sidebar, glossary, and so on) and needs to study them more closely to visualize, determine important information, and synthesize information from the feature with that in the main text.

Research Link

Headings are a common text feature that may signal important content, text organization (hierarchical or sequential), or both (Lorch, 1989). Headings that signal hierarchical organization support readers to produce more complete and accurate outlines of the text, while sequential organization support faster searches of the text (Lorch, Lemarié, & Grant, 2011).

Strategy When you come to a heading or subheading, stop to read and consider it carefully. Think, "What do I expect to learn about in this section or subsection? How might it relate to what I've read so far about this topic?"

Lesson Language *A heading is a text feature that is sort of like a road sign— it gives us a heads up about what's coming and helps us see how the content is organized. Subheadings are smaller headings that are beneath or below the main headings (notice the prefix sub-). It's important not to skip over any of them. To see how this works, let's look at* Little Killers: The Ferocious Lives of Puny Predators *(Collard, 2022). The title of Chapter 7 is "Swarming Spiders," and from the topic of the book, I can figure out that this chapter must be about one specific little killer— some kind of spider. If I were reading through the chapter, the first heading I would come to is "Spider Societies." If I stop to think about it, I predict this section is going to be about how the spiders live their "ferocious lives" in groups. (Read the section.) The next heading is "Tremendous Traps," and I know it's a new heading and not a subheading because the font size and color are the same as the one before. I'm pretty sure this section is going to explain how the spiders catch their prey—since I also know they are predators from the book's title. Let's read and find out. (Read the section.) The last heading is "Social Advantages," and I bet it's going to answer the question from the very end of the section just before it, "Why work together?" See how I thought across and between the headings and text to make predictions?*

Teaching Tip This strategy would also be helpful for students who are working on a goal of determining main idea (see Chapter 8 for more strategies related to that goal).

Prompts

- Check for headings. They'll be written in a larger, often differently colored font than the main text—headings are typically larger than subheadings.
- What do you think this section will be about? Why?
- Are there any subheadings—sections within sections?
- How does the information in this section fit with the topic (of the book)?

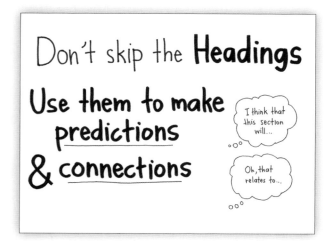

Crack Open Crafty Headings

Strategy Notice when a heading doesn't explicitly say what the section is about, perhaps because the writer is trying to be engaging, humorous, or clever. Think, "What can I infer this section *might* be about, based on what I've read so far?" Read on to gather information from that section. Go back and reword the heading in a way that captures the main idea of the section.

Lesson Language *Some headings and subheadings are like the boldest, clearest traffic signs: They tell us exactly what's to come and help us navigate the text. Others, however, aren't so clear. Sometimes the author crafts a heading that's clever and makes you want to read to figure it out, but at first, it can be a little confusing! When you notice a heading or subheading that you know is not meant to be taken literally, you'll have to infer the meaning. Often, you'll need to read the whole section and then go back to the heading to infer its meaning. For example, in* Climate Change and How We'll Fix It *(Harman, 2020), there's a subheading that says, "Attack of the killer cow farts!" It's under the heading "Food and farming" in Part 1 of the book, "What We Know," so I'm guessing it has something to do with how raising cows for food impacts the climate. Now I need to read the section to see exactly what it says, and then I can go back and revise the heading into something more literal to help me remember.*

Teaching Tip This strategy would also be helpful for students who are working on a goal of determining main idea (see Chapter 8 for more strategies related to that goal).

Prompts

- Read the heading. What do you think it means?
- Based on what you read in this section, try rewording the heading.
- List back what you learned. Now can you explain the heading?
- The way you just said that heading was simple and clear!

CLEVER HEADING:	SECTION IS ABOUT:	my NEW HEADING
Ready for Action	moving... how our bodies move when we play sports	MUSCLES
Power Up	how we get more energy or more power when we play sports	STRENGTH, POWER, ENDURANCE, SPEED
Dressed for Success	clothing, or... uniforms that people wear when playing sports	INCREASING SPEED, PREVENTING AIR RESISTANCE

from: Spring Into Action

Skills

- **inferring**
- **determining importance**

Progression

Is reading texts with complex features (map, graph, table, sidebar, glossary, and so on) and needs to study them more closely to visualize, determine important information, and synthesize information from the feature with that in the main text.

Research Link

Anderson and Armbruster (1984) cited a large body of research that a well-organized text influences the amount and types of knowledge that a reader acquires. Although "clever" headings may be entertaining and/or foster interest, Anderson and Armbruster caution that headings that obscure the author's topic, purpose, or question can lead to confusion, and they provide guidelines for rewording headings to clarify the author's intentions.

Skills

- **determining importance**
- **synthesizing**
- **summarizing**

Progression

Is reading texts with complex features (map, graph, table, sidebar, glossary, and so on) and needs to study them more closely to visualize, determine important information, and synthesize information from the feature with that in the main text.

● ● ● ○

Research Link

In one study (Brugar & Roberts, 2017), researchers found that 80% of a large group of third-through fifth-grade students could identify a map by name, but they struggled to identify the purpose, rarely made use of the legend, and therefore could not make sense of the symbolic information on the map.

Strategy Read information about the map: the title, symbols, key, scale, legend, or caption. Read any labels you see on the map itself. If there is color-coding, consider what those colors are trying to show. Study the map. Summarize what you learn from the map, and think about how it connects to the rest of the section.

Lesson Language *On page 21 of* The Science of an Oil Spill *(Wang, 2015), I notice a map of the southeastern United States. The title is "Impacts on Gulf Birds." There is no map key, but the areas of land are labeled (Alabama, Mississippi, Louisiana) and the areas of water are as well (Atlantic Ocean, Gulf of Mexico). There are also a bunch of dots of different sizes and in different colors. The caption explains that the map shows "where dead seabirds were collected along the northern Gulf Coast after the Deepwater Horizon spill." It goes on to say that the larger dots mean more dead birds. So it seems like the colors don't mean anything, but they help us see the larger and smaller dots. OK, with that to guide me, let me study the map. I'm noticing that most of the largest dots are north and a little west of the spill site, on the Gulf Coast in Louisiana and Mississippi. However, I also see tiny dots much farther east and west into Texas and Florida. This makes me think that the oil spread very far and had a terrible impact on many types of seabirds.*

Teaching Tip This strategy would also be helpful for students who are working on a goal of understanding key details (see Chapter 9 for more strategies related to that goal).

Prompts

- Check the title first.
- Connect the symbols to what you see in the rest of the map.
- Using the information from the map key really helped you understand what the author is teaching with this map.
- How does this map help you learn about the other information in the section?

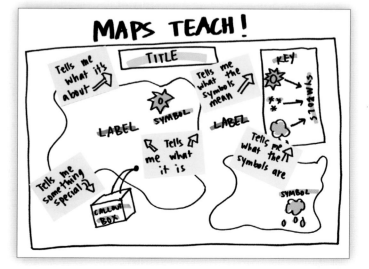

Strategy Read the title to understand what the flowchart is mostly about. Then, follow the arrows and/or numbers to understand how each part fits with the others. Make sure you understand each part before you move on to a new one. Summarize what you learned from the entire chart, and think about how it connects to the rest of the section.

Lesson Language *In* Climate Change and How We'll Fix It *(Harman, 2020), the flowchart "Plastic Problem" on page 13 requires some close study. I see an introductory paragraph, six images, captions to go with each image, and many arrows. Let me start at the top and read the introductory paragraph. (Read aloud.) OK, so from that I understand that plastics cause problems "at every stage," so this flowchart must be showing me different stages of plastic and explaining what the problem is, exactly. Let me start at the top and look at the image and caption, and then follow the arrow to the next one. This first one shows a rig and says that "fossil fuels are extracted, transported and processed to make plastics." That makes sense—the first step is getting the raw materials. Let's follow the arrow to the next image: a truck. I need the caption to help me understand how the truck relates to plastic problems. (Read caption.) Ah, I see. So this is showing transportation and the greenhouse gases that come from trucks carrying plastic goods around. Now I see four arrows coming from that one, as well as one coming back to that one. Let's take it one at a time . . .*

Teaching Tip This strategy would also be helpful for students who are working on a goal of understanding key details (see Chapter 9 for more strategies related to that goal).

Prompts
- Show me what you'll read first. What will you read next?
- Make sure you go in order—left to right or top to bottom. Follow the arrows.
- Did you understand what you learned from that step? Retell the most important information.
- Summarize what you learned from this whole flowchart.

Skills
- **synthesizing**
- **self-monitoring**

Progression
Is reading texts with complex features (map, graph, table, sidebar, glossary, and so on) and needs to study them more closely to visualize, determine important information, and synthesize information from the feature with that in the main text.

Research Link
In a review of four textbooks for grade 6 science (Slough et al., 2010), researchers identified 514 graphical representations, of which only 10 were flowcharts (2% of total graphics). Although readers do not encounter them often, practice interpreting flowcharts is especially necessary because of their abstract, and potentially ambiguous, symbolic representations (Henderson, 1999).

Skills

- **summarizing**
- **synthesizing**
- **determining importance**

Progression

Is reading texts with complex features (map, graph, table, sidebar, glossary, and so on) and needs to study them more closely to visualize, determine important information, and synthesize information from the feature with that in the main text.

Research Link

Kucan and Palincsar (2018) developed the *Text Analysis Tool* to support text-based discussions. One set of questions in the tool address text organization, including the content and function of sidebars. In a study piloting the tool, participants noted that sidebar information, while interesting, was potentially distracting because it was sometimes tangentially related to the information in the main section.

Strategy Read the sidebar. Think of it like a section. Ask yourself, "What's the main idea?" and "What details support it?" Summarize the key information you learn in a few sentences. Then think, "What does the information in the sidebar have to do with the rest of the section?"

Lesson Language *In more complex texts, the features can have a lot of words! For example,* All Thirteen *(Soontornvat, 2020) is filled with sidebars—let's look together at the one titled "This is Mae Sai" on pages 4-5. I'm going to read it aloud to you and I want you to think about what the whole thing is mostly about and the details that support that main idea. (Read aloud.) So we read information about this town: about the variety of languages spoken, religions practiced; that tourists from all over travel here; the kinds of jobs people have here; the kinds of things that take place in this region. Putting all this together, it seems like this section is trying to give us a flavor of this place and is making the point that it's diverse in many ways. The chapter in which this sidebar sits is all about the boys' soccer team and what life is like for them on a typical Saturday with soccer practice. So how does this sidebar fit? I think the author is trying to set the stage for the main event by giving us background about the boys, and about where they live, and what life is like for them.*

Teaching Tip This strategy would be helpful for students who are working on goals of determining main idea (find more strategies in Chapter 8) and understanding key details (find more strategies in Chapter 9).

Prompts

- Think about what strategy you'll use to help you find the main idea.
- What's the purpose of this sidebar? What's it mostly about?
- How would you summarize what you read?
- Now consider how the sidebar fits with the information in the rest of the section.

Sidebars Hold Meaning

HEADING

photo

side-bar

side-bar

1. **Read** the sidebar.
2. **Ask:** What's the main idea? What details support it?
3. **Summarize** key information.
4. **Think:** How does the sidebar connect with the section?

10.19 Study Charts and Tables

Strategy Get oriented to the chart or table: read the title, headings, and any caption. First, consider how the information in a chart is organized to make a plan to read it. Read through the information slowly, pausing to process as you go. Sum up what you learned and how it connects to the rest of the section.

Lesson Language *Page 162 in* All Thirteen *(Soontornvat, 2020) has a table titled "Human Responses to Levels of Oxygen Concentration" that is filled with numbers and bulleted facts. I'm going to get oriented: I see two columns and the headings say "Oxygen Level" and "Body's Responses," so I'll read it one row at a time and consider those headings as I go. The first row says "21%" under the Oxygen Level column and "normal" under the Body Responses column. As I read down the table, I see the numbers decrease: the next row says 15 to 19% and "unable to exert strenuous energy" and "impaired coordination." As I read down further, I see the oxygen percentages are lower and the body's response becomes more drastic—all the way to fainting, unconsciousness, and then death. So why is this chart here? Well, from the main text in the chapter we just learned that the boys' oxygen levels are "dipping dangerously low" (p. 161) in the cave, making the rescue even more urgent. This table shows us what might happen to the children over time as they use up the oxygen.*

Teaching Tip This strategy would also be helpful for students who are working on a goal of understanding key details (see Chapter 9 for more strategies related to that goal).

Prompts

- Get oriented and make a plan: How will you read this table/ chart?
- Consider how the information is organized to understand how it's related.
- Read through the information in the chart part by part. Pause to think about it before reading on.
- Now consider: How does this information relate to what's in the main section?

— STUDY —
Charts and Tables

·TABLE·

·CHART·

Steps to Understanding the Chart or Table:
- ☐ Make a plan for reading.
- ☐ Read the title, headings, and captions.
- ☐ Read information slowly. Part by part.
- ☐ Ask: How does this information relate to the main section.

Skills
- **planning**
- **self-monitoring**
- **summarizing**

Progression

Is reading texts with complex features (map, graph, table, sidebar, glossary, and so on) and needs to study them more closely to visualize, determine important information, and synthesize information from the feature with that in the main text.

● ● ● ○

Research Link

In a study exploring how upper elementary students interpret graphical devices in social studies (Brugar & Roberts, 2017), results indicate that readers need significant support to interpret the information presented in charts and tables, including being able to distinguish between them.

Skills

- **synthesizing**
- **inferring**

Progression

Is reading texts with complex features (map, graph, table, sidebar, glossary, and so on) and needs to study them more closely to visualize, determine important information, and synthesize information from the feature with that in the main text.

Research Link

In a study exploring how upper elementary students interpret graphical devices in social studies (Brugar & Roberts, 2017), researchers found that students were more familiar with timelines compared with features like captions and tables, that understanding the information on a timeline seems to improve with age, and that students were responsive to instruction regarding timelines, improving their scores on a visual literacy assessment.

Strategy Read the title of the timeline and any introductory information that's included. Read the text connected to each date. Think about how the dates and the information connect to the topic and what you've read. Ask yourself, "What does this timeline help me understand?"

Lesson Language *Across pages 26–29 in* Art of Protest *(Nichols, 2021), the author offers a timeline titled "A Brief History" detailing how art has been used as protest throughout history. Let's read the paragraph next to the first event. (Read aloud.) OK, so these dates in the 1800s in Spain occurred before anything else we've read in this book so far—mostly we've been reading about art used in the 1960s in the United States. In what ways does it connect to what we have read, though? Well, earlier on page 14 we learned about purposes for protest art and some of them seem relevant here. It seems like Goya was informing the public and also trying to influence action with his eighty-two etchings depicting the horrors of war. The description says that Goya's art was "politically charged," so that also kind of connects to the mention of "political art" on page 23, though that discussion focuses more on cartoons and satire. Let's move on to the next date on the timeline and its paragraph, and see what we can learn from it, and how it connects to the rest of the text we've read so far . . .*

Teaching Tip This strategy would also be helpful for students who are working on a goal of understanding key details (see Chapter 9 for more strategies related to that goal).

Prompts

- What do you remember reading about that connects to this event?
- Show me how you're going to study this timeline.
- I like how you're thinking about the information from the book to help you understand each event on the timeline.
- Try to summarize what you learned.

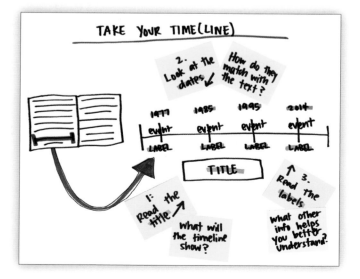

Strategy Read the title of the graph to understand what it's mostly about. Then, read labels to understand what each dot, bar, pie slice, or line shows. Say back what you learned. Then, consider how the information in the graph connects to what you read in the section.

Lesson Language *Graphs—line, pie, or bar—pack a lot of information into one feature. Take a look at the bar graph titled "Daily Rainfall Amounts at Tham Luang Nang Non" in the book* All Thirteen *(Soontornvat, 2020). From the title we know the graph will teach us about how much rain falls each day. Let's look at the labels. The y-axis shows us the amount of rain each day in inches and millimeters. The x-axis shows us time—specifically June and July of 2018. Now let's look at the data. We can see the bars increase quickly and dramatically in late June, then plummet in early July and stay low throughout the month of July. So how does this connect? Well, in the main text we learned that the boys have been trapped in the cave for a while due to heavy rainfalls and flooding. That aligns to the part of the bar graph showing lots of rain in a short period of time. I just read that the rescue will begin on July 8, so if I match that date up to the bar graph, I can see that the rainfall amounts have been low for at least a week and what the estimated rainfall will be in the days when they are attempting the rescue.*

Teaching Tip Articles in magazines for children such as *Time for Kids* or *Scholastic News* regularly include graphs filled with interesting information.

Prompts

- After reading the title, what do you think this graph will teach?
- Don't skip the labels—they're important.
- Say back what you learned from the graph.
- Explain how what you read here fits with the rest of the section.

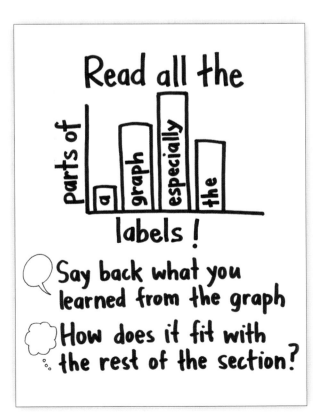

Skills

- **synthesizing**
- **summarizing**

Progression

Is reading texts with complex features (map, graph, table, sidebar, glossary, and so on) and needs to study them more closely to visualize, determine important information, and synthesize information from the feature with that in the main text.

Research Link

In an oft-cited review of studies on graph comprehension (Friel, Curcio, & Bright, 2001), the authors specify that to make sense of a graph, a reader must develop *graph comprehension*, which involves *translation* (i.e., moving from symbolic representation to words), *interpretation* (i.e., identifying patterns within the graph), and *extrapolation/interpolation* (i.e., thinking about trends in the data, or hypothesizing about possible causes).

Skill

- **synthesizing**

Progression

Is reading texts with complex features (map, graph, table, sidebar, glossary, and so on) and needs to study them more closely to visualize, determine important information, and synthesize information from the feature with that in the main text.

● ● ● ○

Research Link

In one study of the impact of "seductive details" (interesting but irrelevant information) on comprehension, researchers found that, contrary to the distraction mentioned in most previous studies, learners did not experience negative effects on comprehension outcomes if they were explicitly told that certain seductive details were not essential to understanding the main text (Eitel, Bender, & Renkl, 2019).

Strategy Read the section. Turn to the fact list, reading each fact carefully. After each one, pause to think about what you already read (and perhaps saw in graphical features). Think, "How do these facts help me know more about what I just read?"

Lesson Language *Be on the lookout for "fast facts," "fun facts," "surprising facts," or other sidebars filled with extras. Authors use these features to quickly add some information or to include facts that are interesting but don't really fit into the main flow of text. You'll need to read them carefully and consider how they expand upon or extend the information in the rest of the section. For example, in* Africa, Amazing Africa *(Atinuke, 2019), each page features a paragraph or two of main text, an illustration, and a few extra facts on the bottom or side of the page. For example, on the page about the country Burundi, the main text teaches about how boys are taught to become drummers and a bit about the rhythms they play. The illustration shows a group of men playing drums of different shapes and sizes. The facts in the bottom teach about the materials used to make drums (wood from the umuvugangoma tree) and recommends listening to a specific drumming group from Burundi online. All the information relates to drumming in this country, and the extra facts give more background.*

Teaching Tip This strategy would also be helpful for students who are working on a goal of understanding key details (see Chapter 9 for more strategies related to that goal).

Prompts

- Think about what you already know about the topic before you read the extra facts.
- Read the main text first, and then turn to the extra facts.
- Does this fact feature give you extra information? Or does it summarize information from the text?
- Keep the information from the rest of the section in your mind as you read the extra facts.

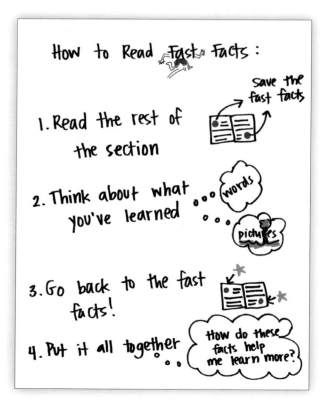

Study What Diagrams Show and Tell

Strategy Read the diagram's title. Look at what the diagram is showing. Read the labels to understand what the diagram is showing and telling. Finally, think about how the diagram connects to the information in the text.

Lesson Language *Let's study the diagram on page 6 of* The Science of an Oil Spill *(Wang, 2015) to see what we can learn from it. First, the title is "Oil Rigs." I see a drawing of an oil rig, the ocean, and earth below it. Let's read the labels to see what we're looking at here. So the big thing at the top of the image is the rig. The long line is labeled as the "drill pipe and well." The blue represents the ocean, and the brown represents the seafloor and all the earth underneath it. I see the "oil reservoir" labeled, as well as measurements showing how deep it is. Let's now read the caption. (Read aloud.) OK, so the diagram is showing how deep it is, and the caption is making a point about how much weight the water and rock forces upon the oil reservoir. I think this diagram is in the section on the* Deepwater Horizon *blowout because it shows how risky drilling for oil is due to the pressure below the rigs.*

Prompts
- Read all the parts of the diagram, including the labels.
- Now that you've read the labels and looked closely at the images, explain what you're learning.
- How does this diagram help you learn more about what you read in the section?
- Now that you're seeing it in a diagram, what else are you learning?

Skills
- **summarizing**
- **synthesizing**

Progression

Is reading texts with complex features (map, graph, table, sidebar, glossary, and so on) and needs to study them more closely to visualize, determine important information, and synthesize information from the feature with that in the main text.

●●●○

Research Link

Although visuals are intended to support readers, misinterpretations of abstract graphics, such as diagrams, can interfere with learning. Researchers who had students in grades 2–8 sort four diagrams of the water cycle found that participants were confused about the function of symbols, overlooked key relationships among components of the diagram, and/or failed to check that their interpretations were consistent with information in the main text (McTigue & Flowers, 2011).

10.24 *Consider Primary Sources*

Skills

- **synthesizing**
- **determining importance**
- **analyzing**

Progression

Is reading texts with complex features (map, graph, table, sidebar, glossary, and so on) and needs to study them more closely to visualize, determine important information, and synthesize information from the feature with that in the main text.

Research Link

Drawing on research in comprehension, Neumann, Gilbertson, and Hutton (2014) argue that primary sources often come from a time and place that is unfamiliar to students, so building background knowledge is necessary to promote meaning-making.

Strategy Identify the author of the primary source and their perspective. Read it to learn its main idea(s) and key details. Then think, "How is this document connected to the main text? How did what I just learn give me extra information about the topic?"

Lesson Language *In* Soontornvat's All Thirteen: The Incredible Cave Rescue of the Thai Boys' Soccer Team, *we come across a collection of primary source documents—letters written by the boys to their families from inside the cave. The letters are in the chapter titled "Panic." As I read the typed translation of the notes, I notice a main idea—all the boys seem to be reassuring their families. They tell them not to worry. That they are safe. That the Navy SEALS are taking good care of them. They ask their families to reassure their teachers that they are just fine. The coach also writes a letter with a similar message: the kids are OK and I'm taking good care of them. So, now that we've identified the main idea across these documents, let's think about how they connect to the main text. Well, at this point the boys have been trapped for two weeks already. They are down to their "last option" for rescue, something so dangerous the rescue teams have saved it as a last resort: the boys will have to swim out. If we put what we are learning in the main text together with what we see in these primary sources, what are you understanding? What are you thinking about?*

Prompts

- Explain what you learned from the primary source by itself.
- How does the primary source help you understand the rest of the text?
- Talk to me about who wrote the document and what you know about their perspective.
- You can say, "In the text I learned . . . and when I read the primary source I learned . . ."

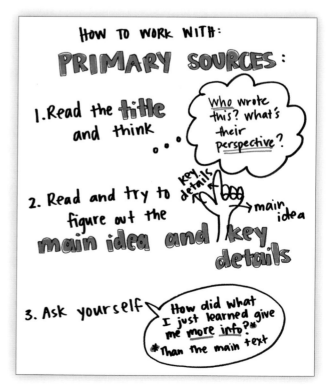

Strategy After you reach the end of the main text, be on the lookout for features that help you learn more: endnotes, citations of books the author used when writing the text, lists of other recommended reading (websites, books, articles), or even additional sections with more information, like appendices or an author's note. Make a plan for how you might continue your study of the topic.

Teaching Tip Explore material in the back of various books in your collection with students. For example, the sections "More About Nanoscience" in the back of *Nano* (Wade, 2021) and "More on Water Protectors" in the back of *We Are Water Protectors* (Lindstrom, 2020) offer several paragraphs of detailed information that expands upon what's in the text. This shift in style in supplementary material to present facts in a more straightforward way is common in more lyrically written informational texts and in narrative nonfiction. Readers may need to slow their pace and read strategically to understand the main ideas, key details, and vocabulary in these more complex sections. In addition to extra information, show students how authors sometimes include references they used for research (something students can be encouraged to do!) and/or recommendations for further reading. You'll find notes like these (labeled in different ways) in *Africa, Amazing Africa* (Atinuke, 2019), *Art of Protest* (Nichols, 2021), *All Thirteen* (Soontornvat, 2020), and *The Secret of a Scuba Diving Spider . . . and More!* (Rodríguez, 2018).

Prompts
- Before you're finished, check the back of the book to see if you find any additional information you might want to explore.
- Which books or websites look interesting to continue your reading?
- These are references the author used. Are you interested in reading any?

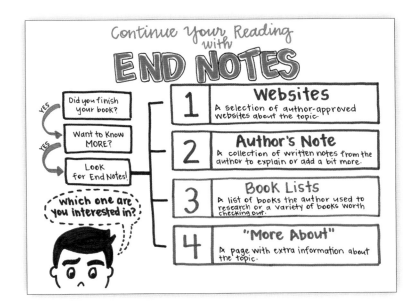

Progression

Is reading texts with complex features (map, graph, table, sidebar, glossary, and so on) and needs to study them more closely to visualize, determine important information, and synthesize information from the feature with that in the main text.

Research Link

In a small study, a middle school book club focused on understanding *peritext* (i.e., features other than the body text). After 5 months, the participants were better able to discuss the functions of peritext and how the inclusion of *intratextual* (e.g., afterword), *supplemental* (e.g., glossary, timelines), and *documentary* (e.g., bibliography, source notes) features can help determine the credibility of an informational text (Gross et al., 2016).

Compare and Contrast with Images

Skill

- analyzing

Progression

Is reading texts with multiple features. Is ready to analyze an author's intent regarding text features, synthesize the information in multiple features and text, and/or compare and contrast information from across features.

● ● ● ●

Research Link

In a meta-analysis of the effects of graphics on reading comprehension (Guo et al., 2020), researchers found that graphics included in a text had a moderate positive effect on reading comprehension. This effect was more pronounced when the graphics were all the same type (e.g., all photographs).

Strategy Look closely at images and other visual features within a section and find two or more that relate to the same topic. Look for details within each feature, and compare what you learn in each. Think, "What similar information do you learn from two images or features? What information is different?"

Lesson Language *The information in* All Thirteen: The Incredible Cave Rescue of the Thai Boys' Soccer Team *(Soontornvat, 2020) is densely packed in the text with just a few visuals along the way. But when we do come upon photographs, we need to study them and compare them to help us understand the information. For example, across pages 117–119, there are three photos of the water diversion team at work, trying to keep more water from flooding the cave. Let's look closely at the first image. What do we see? There are several people in uniforms. They seem to be setting up what look like dams made from bamboo and wood. It looks like the purpose is to hold back a stream. Let's look at the second photograph. What's similar and what's different? In this photo, a group of people is also working together and trying to divert water. But they are in different uniforms (blue with patches instead of camo), they are using different materials (a blue tube and sandbags), and they seem to be working on a different type of waterway (a waterfall rather than a stream). By comparing these two images, I found specific details I may have otherwise overlooked.*

Teaching Tip As an extension, you could teach children to synthesize what they notice across multiple visuals to draw conclusions and come up with big ideas. For example, from these photos you might conclude that different groups of people worked in different ways toward the same goal. Or that the water was such a massive problem that they had to have multiple strategies for holding it back. Or that different types of water sources required different solutions.

Prompts

- Can you find two or more images that teach about the same topic?
- Name what details you can learn from closely studying each individual image.
- Compare—what information is the same between these two photos?
- Contrast—what different or new information can you learn from each?

THE READING STRATEGIES BOOK 2.0

Strategy When you encounter a text feature (graph, chart, picture, diagram, and so on), stop and think: "What information is it giving me? How does it connect to what else is on the page?" Then consider, "Why might the author have chosen to include this information in a feature instead of the main text?"

Teaching Tip This more advanced strategy asks readers to infer reasons why an author would choose to present information in a particular way. Ask students to imagine what it would take to convey the information in the visual or graphic feature using only text. This will help them see that some details and information are much more effectively and efficiently communicated through text features. For example, to describe the cave system in *All Thirteen* (Soontornvat, 2020) would take many words and the reader still may not be able to understand how serpentine and complex each opening is and how interconnected and complicated the entire system is. In this case, the picture (diagram) is easily worth a thousand words. This strategy helps students not only comprehend the text, it also serves them well when they write their own informational texts and need to consider how best to present their information.

Prompts

- Why might the author have chosen a feature to show this information?
- How does the feature share the information differently than if it were just words?
- How is the information well suited to this feature?
- Say, "The feature . . . but if it was just plain text . . . "

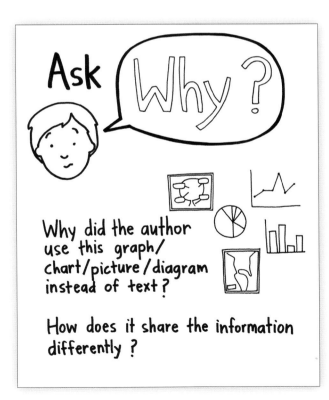

Skill
- analyzing

Progression

Is reading texts with multiple features. Is ready to analyze an author's intent regarding text features, synthesize the information in multiple features and text, and/or compare and contrast information from across features.

Research Link

In a study of 25 expert teachers of grades 3–8 (Fisher, Frey, & Lapp, 2008), researchers observed that when discussing text features, teachers often invoked the author's purpose for including specific text features, including figures, photographs, highlighted words, and headings.

Skills

- **planning**
- **synthesizing**

Progression

Is reading texts with multiple features. Is ready to analyze an author's intent regarding text features, synthesize the information in multiple features and text, and/or compare and contrast information from across features.

● ● ● ●

Research Link

In a small study (Norman & Roberts, 2015), researchers examined how second graders paid attention to graphics and their extensions (e.g., captions, labels, keys, and other accompanying text) and how they made sense of them in the context of the informational text as a whole. Their findings suggest that younger students in particular need extensive support with integrating features with the main text.

Strategy Scan busy page(s) to make a plan for how to read each section and feature. As you read, pause often to check across and between the information in the text and features, actively finding connections. Think again and again, "How does this all fit together?"

Lesson Language *As we read the spread titled "Evidence of Climate Change" (pages 14–15) in* Climate Change and How We'll Fix it *(Harman, 2020), we will need to make active connections between a lot of elements: there's a title, a bolded introduction, two subsections with their own titles, a small inset box, four separate illustrations, and a speech bubble! What's the plan? Let's quickly glance at the illustrations—there's an earth with some things flying around it, some people standing on ice (but it's hard to tell what they are doing exactly), and a dinosaur and a wooly mammoth. On their own, it's hard to tell what these images are meant to teach us about climate change, but let's read and go back and forth between the text and these illustrations as we go. We can save the inset box on the right-hand page until the end.* (Read from the top, pausing after a small chunk of text to cross-reference features.) *OK, let's pause here. Does what we read connect to any of these illustrations? How? Please turn to your partner and explain the connections you see.* (Read aloud section titled "Satellite Science.") *Ah, so it seems like this section likely goes with the illustration of the earth that we looked at before. How does it connect? Share your thoughts with a partner. Let's move on now to the next section, "Still Not Convinced?" and as we do, let's consider if either of the other two illustrations have information that fits with it.*

Prompts

- Stop there. Which text feature should you look at to go with this text?
- Remember to go back and forth between features and text, actively connecting the information.
- Read a little more slowly. Connect to features as you go.
- How does [feature] fit with [text]?

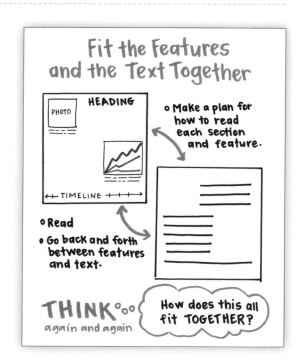

Despite their central role in informational texts, researchers have found that teaching text features in isolation may not be effective. Readers need to learn to go beyond identifying features and instead need to learn to use them.

—Jennifer Serravallo

Comprehending Vocabulary and Figurative Language

◎ Why is this goal important?

A reader's ability to understand vocabulary and language in a text has been empirically linked to reading comprehension, which is why instruction around words and language deserves such a prominent place in our classrooms (Beck, McKeown, & Kucan, 2013; Logan & Kieffer, 2017; Mancilla-Martinez & McClain, 2020; Stanovich, 1986; Watts-Taffe, Fisher, & Blachowicz, 2017). Vocabulary is one of five core components of reading instruction that are essential for successfully teaching children how to read (National Reading Panel, 2000). Vocabulary knowledge helps students access background knowledge, express ideas, communicate effectively, and learn about new concepts. "Vocabulary is the glue that holds stories, ideas, and content together . . . making comprehension accessible for children" (Rupley, Logan, & Nichols, 1998, p. 339). In fact, many researchers have found a relationship between increasing comprehension and increasing vocabulary knowledge (e.g., Carver, 1994; Schmitt, Jiang, &

Grabe, 2011). Knowledge development, which could be considered the "sixth pillar of reading instruction" (Cervetti & Hiebert, 2015, p. 548), is essential for comprehension, with ample research showing the reciprocal relationship between knowledge building and vocabulary development (Cervetti, Wright, & Hwang, 2016; Wright et al., 2022).

Given the research on the many links between comprehension and vocabulary knowledge, many schools have rushed to implement vocabulary programs. Although some students learn words this way, research actually suggests that most word learning occurs through reading, writing, speaking, and listening (Baumann, Kame'enui, & Ash, 2003; Krashen, 2004; Miller, 1999; Nagy, Anderson, & Herman, 1987; Wright & Cervetti, 2017). In particular, scholars have highlighted the difference between "book language" and oral language: the words and language that readers encounter in books are often more complex, and appear less frequently, that what they find in everyday language (Castles, Rastle, & Nation, 2018; Montag, Jones, & Smith, 2015). Therefore, teachers can do a lot to support their students' vocabulary and figurative language learning goals by creating a classroom in which children read voluminously from a wide range of texts, listen to content-rich books read aloud, engage in discussions about texts, are encouraged to notice when words and phrases are new, learn strategies for figuring out what they mean, and are encouraged to use those words when they write and speak.

In Chapter 3, you read about what it takes for a reader to *orthographically map* a word—they must link a word's spelling, pronunciation, and meaning in their minds. There are times when a child will encounter a word they can decode but are unaware of its meaning. Other times, a child may not be able to decode a word accurately but can still figure out a likely meaning from context so as not to interrupt their overall comprehension. The strategies in this chapter will help students in either case, as they focus on both word consciousness and learning new words and phrases. Cobb and Blachowicz (2014) note that these are two of many aspects of comprehensive vocabulary instruction, which may also include teaching individual words and providing rich and varied language experiences.

Skills a reader might work on as part of this goal

Building knowledge
Using within-text or outside-of-the-text resources (e.g., glossaries, dictionaries, adults, or peers) to understand words and phrases.

Self-monitoring
Developing an awareness (i.e., word consciousness) of when a word or phrase is familiar or unfamiliar, and pausing to utilize strategies to understand its meaning.

Synthesizing
Putting relevant information from across pages or chapter/section or text features together to explain a word or phrase.

Activating prior knowledge
Remembering where or in what contexts the reader has encountered the word part, word, or phrase (or similar words or phrases) in the past, and applying relevant background knowledge to figure =out the word in a current context.

Inferring
Using relevant information from prior knowledge together with context to figure out a probable meaning of the word or phrase.

Determining importance
Using relevant information from context to better understand the meaning of the word or phrase.

Visualizing
Using mental imagery to understand what a word or phrase means.

Analyzing
Using a knowledge of morphology, etymology, or grammar to determine a probable meaning of the word, *or* considering authorial intent to interpret layers of meaning.

◎ How do I know if this goal is right for my student?

There are several ways you can determine that a focus on vocabulary and figurative language would best benefit a given student.

You might use a standardized word knowledge assessment to gather whether the student's word knowledge is appropriate for his or her age or grade. If this assessment reveals a student could use support, teaching strategies from this chapter to help them be alert to new words and figure out meanings from context could be helpful to their overall vocabulary development.

You might also ask a child to read aloud to you and ask them to define words they come upon in the course of their reading. After they read aloud or silently, you may also ask, "Were there any words you just read in that last section that you could *decode* but *didn't know the meaning of*? What did you do in those situations?"

You might also determine this is a worthy goal by asking a student to identify a word or phrase they don't know and then to *define* and/or *explain* the meaning of it based on context.. You could also choose words and/or phrases with appropriate contextual support—words that are defined within the text or words whose meaning can be figured out by looking closely at or reading an illustration or text feature—and ask students to figure out their meaning from context. The intention here is not to assess a child's *existing* vocabulary knowledge, but rather his or her ability to read for clues and details, and to infer or deduce the meaning of the word. After they provide you with a definition or explanation, you could further prompt them by asking, "What did you do to determine that's what the word/phrase means?" to better understand what strategy(ies) they are able to use with independence.

> I think being an individualist means you relay on yourself like a lone wolf.

This student jotted about the word *individualist* when reading a fiction chapter book. He provides both a simple definition he inferred from context and an analogy that a character used. He could learn some strategies to help him use word parts (morphology, etymology) to help him figure out word meanings as well (Strategies 11.11–11.14).

In an informational text about the ocean, this reader encountered the term *tide pool* and jotted his attempt at a definition, which shows he's monitoring his reading and paying attention to new words. Although he's correct that fish go in along with the tide, his understanding is still more of a gist. There are more details in the text he could have used to help him articulate a complete definition (Strategies 11.7–11.10).

> Every time the tide came out More fish would go in.

What Texts Might Students Use When Practicing Strategies from This Chapter?

The strategies in this chapter can be used when students are reading any type of text, in any genre or format. However, it's essential to remember that for children to *learn* new words from texts, they need to *encounter* new words! This means that the texts they read when practicing their vocabulary and figurative language strategies should be challenging enough to include new words and phrases or familiar words and phrases used in new ways.

Note that some of the strategies in this chapter guide children to use resources that are only available in digital texts such as e-readers.

◎ How do I support students as they understand vocabulary and figurative language?

After evaluating samples of your students' written or verbal definitions, explanations, and/or descriptions of words and phrases in their reading, select strategies that you can model, that they can practice with you, and that they can use independently to increase their skills.

Although development is rarely perfectly linear, skill progressions can help us pinpoint where a student is now and what might come next. Use the if–then chart on page 359 to evaluate your students' reading and find strategies that will support their growth.

A Progression of Skills: *Comprehending Vocabulary and Figurative Language*

If a student . . .	Then you might teach . . .
Skips over or ignores unfamiliar words and needs support to self-monitor and approach word learning with consciousness and curiosity.	11.1 Be Word Conscious and Curious 11.2 Say It Out Loud
Is aware when a word is unfamiliar and is ready to learn to infer a gist or definition from prior knowledge and/or sentence-level context.	11.3 Monitor for Sound-Alikes 11.4 Mine Your Memory 11.5 Insert a Synonym 11.6 Use Part of Speech as a Clue 11.7 Consider Topic-Specific Meanings 11.8 Look to See If It's Right There in the Sentence! 11.9 Consider Sentence Structure 11.10 Consider Cohesion and Conjunctions
Is able to use context and prior knowledge to infer and is ready to learn to analyze word parts and apply a knowledge of grammar, morphology, and/or etymology.	11.11 Use Individual Words to Figure Out Compound Words 11.12 Look for Word Part Clues: Prefixes and Suffixes 11.13 Look for Word Part Clues: Roots and Bases 11.14 Get Help from Cognates
Is confidently and independently using a variety of strategies to figure out unfamiliar words and is ready to supplement word learning using outside resources.	11.15 Use a Reference and Explain It 11.16 Look It Up Within an E-Book 11.17 Phone a Friend 11.18 Read Up a Ladder 11.19 Listen or Watch to Learn
Is able to understand and/or figure out the meanings of words and is ready to consider words within a larger context and analyze an author's word choice for a deeper understanding and interpretation.	11.20 Use Mood as a Clue to Meaning 11.21 Stick to Your Story 11.22 Consider the Type of Figurative Language 11.23 Picture It 11.24 Be Alert to Word Choice

359

Strategy Expect to learn new words (or encounter words you know used in a different way) as you read; read with awareness. When you come to a word or phrase that's new to you, approach it with curiosity. Take time to use strategies to try to figure out what the word or phrase might mean, or keep track of it to learn more about it (from a resource or friend) later.

Lesson Language *It's fun to be word conscious and curious. When you are, it's as if you have a little radar that goes off when you come to a word that's new or to one that's familiar but being used in a whole new way. Whenever your understanding gets interrupted by a word you don't know, or by a familiar word that's used in a different way, it's important to stop and apply a strategy to figure it out. As you read, learn to know what you know—and what you don't!*

Teaching Tip Consider creating a space in your classroom where children can post and collect words and phrases they find and marvel over. Encourage them to use the words and phrases when they speak and write.

Prompts
* You said you know all these words? Tell me about this one.
* Think about how the word is being used. Do you know the word in this context?
* You realized you didn't know that word. That's a first step!
* Now that you figured out you know this word, but not how it's used in this phrase, what will you do?

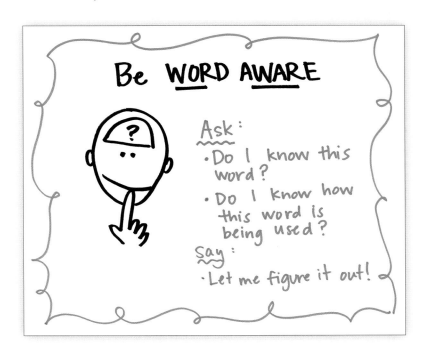

Skill
* **self-monitoring**

Progression

Skips over or ignores unfamiliar words and needs support to self-monitor and approach word learning with consciousness and curiosity.

Hat Tip

No More "Look Up the List" Vocabulary Instruction (Cobb & Blachowicz, 2014)

Research Link

One study found that, with instruction, second graders became better at noticing when they didn't understand a word (Wise, 2019), and another found that word consciousness instruction led to accelerated word learning for fourth graders in linguistically diverse classrooms (Scott, Miller, & Flinspach, 2012). Similarly, researchers found that encouragement to be "tuned in" to new words accounted for a difference in word learning in middle-grade classrooms (Beck, Perfetti, & McKeown, 1982).

Say It Out Loud

Skills

- **self-monitoring**
- **activating prior knowledge**

Progression

Skips over or ignores unfamiliar words and needs support to self-monitor and approach word learning with consciousness and curiosity.

Research Link

After decoding, if a word does not make sense, checking context is an appropriate method to decide on a meaning or pronunciation (Mesmer & Kambach, 2022; Pressley & Allington, 2014). Readers can try different vowel sounds to test pronunciations of a written word with multiple potential pronunciations (e.g., *field*) to see if any match words in their oral vocabulary (Lovett et al., 2000; Meese, 2016; Steacy et al., 2016).

Strategy When you come to an unfamiliar word, there's a chance you know it but just haven't seen it written down before. First, try saying it out loud. Ask yourself, "Is it a word I know?" If not, try changing the pronunciation by stressing a different part of the word and see if it sounds familiar.

Lesson Language *English can seem like a funny language because it's* morphophonemic. *That means sometimes words change spellings in a predictable way even when that change sounds a little different (for example, adding -ed to a verb signals past tense, although the -ed may sound different:* walked, smiled, predicted*), and other times the spellings are what they are because the words have roots in other languages. Although there are many words that follow predictable patterns, there are also words spelled the same way with different pronunciations (for example, "tear a piece of paper" versus "a tear streamed down my face"), and words where the same combination of letters can represent different sounds (consider* ough *in* cough, bough, through, rough*). Sometimes you will know a word because you've heard it spoken, or even used it yourself, but never encountered it in print and therefore don't recognize it right away. To really know the word, you need to connect its meaning with its spelling with how it sounds when you say it. To help you recognize the word, you can pause your reading and try to say the word aloud—perhaps even trying different pronunciations that match the spelling of the word. You may surprise yourself and say it in a way that makes you think, "Oh, I do know that word!"*

Teaching Tip This strategy is a good choice when you have a strong sense that the word is part of a child's speaking vocabulary but will be less helpful if both its pronunciation *and* meaning are new. Keep in mind this strategy calls for decoding flexibility—for more support with this, see the strategies in Chapter 3.

Prompts

- Try a different vowel sound *here* and *here*.
- Put an emphasis on the first part of the word instead of the last.
- Is there a different way to pronounce those spelling patterns?
- Does that sound like a word you've heard?

Strategy If you can decode a word but it doesn't make sense, it might be that it's a *homophone*—words that are pronounced the same but have different meanings. Think about how the word is used in the sentence to figure out its meaning. To remember it, take note of the meaning and spelling of the new word and how those differ from the word you already know that's pronounced the same way.

Lesson Language *In this sentence, "The cellar is dark. When I went down there, I heard a rumbling noise." I can decode* cellar. *I know the word that means "someone who sells things," but that doesn't make sense in this context, and this word is spelled differently, too:* c-e-l-l-a-r *versus* s-e-l-l-e-r. *So this word must be something different. From the context I can tell that* c-e-l-l-a-r *is a place and I can infer that it is another word for a basement.*

Teaching Tip A quick online search will help you find the 100 most common homophone pairs in English. These are tricky for all beginning readers, but especially children who are bilingual and/or dyslexic. Outside of reading time, consider playing games to help children become familiar with them, encourage them to draw picture clues to help them remember the differences and create a word bank in the classroom for reference, or challenge children to make up silly sentences with pairs in a sentence together ("They're going to the sea to see which witch had flown there"). For more information on teaching homophones, homonyms, and homographs to English language learners, see the seven-step instructional plan developed by Jacobson, Lapp, and Flood (2007).

Prompts
- What are the different ways you know to spell a word with this pronunciation? What does *this* one mean?
- You pronounced it correctly, but there are two words with two different spellings that sound the same. *This* spelling means ___. The other spelling means ___.
- Look closely at how it's spelled. Does that help you figure out what it means?
- Use the context to check if you have attached the correct meaning to that word, based on how it's spelled.

Skills
- **self-monitoring**
- **activating prior knowledge**

Progression
Is aware when a word is unfamiliar and is ready to learn to infer a gist or definition from prior knowledge and/or sentence-level context.

Research Link
Research suggests that, compared with readers of the same age and level, dyslexic readers have difficulty recognizing that a word with a plausible pronunciation is, in fact, misspelled (e.g., *roze* versus *rose*). This challenge is especially complicated by homophones (e.g., *rows* versus *rose*), as dyslexic readers may have trouble connecting the different spellings with different meanings (O'Brien, Van Orden, & Pennington, 2013).

Skills

- **activating prior knowledge**
- **inferring**

Progression

Is aware when a word is unfamiliar and is ready to learn to infer a gist or definition from prior knowledge and/or sentence-level context.

Hat Tip

A Practical Guide to Reciprocal Teaching
(Lubliner, 2001)

Research Link

When their teachers used a Comprehensive Vocabulary Development program including a suite of "metacognitive word-learning tasks," fifth graders in one study reported that using their memory of a word was the strategy they found most accessible and the one they used the most (Lubliner & Smetana, 2005).

Strategy If you read a word and don't know its meaning right away, pause. Think, "Have I ever seen this word before?" Say it aloud and think, "Have I ever heard this word before?" Even if you can't articulate an exact definition, see if you can get a gist based on your memory of how or where you've heard the word used before in books, TV shows, or conversations with adults or friends. Then think, "What could it mean in this context?"

Lesson Language *I was conferring with Jayda yesterday and she was reading Grace Lin's* Where the Mountain Meets the Moon *(2009). She came to this sentence, "To coax rice out of the stubborn land, the fields had to be flooded with water" (p. 1). She identified* coax *as a word that she didn't immediately understand. I asked her if she'd ever seen or heard the word before. She said, "I've never seen it before, but I can read it. I think I heard my mom use it, though. When we first adopted our dog. Our dog was nervous and wouldn't come out of her crate, and my mom said something like, 'We'll have to coax her out,' and we got a piece of bacon and she came out and let us pet her. So I think it's something like 'come out,' and that makes sense here. They are trying to get the rice to grow, or come out, of the land." Jayda took time to think about the word and worked to activate some prior knowledge she had about the word. You won't always have heard or seen the word before, of course, but it's one strategy you can use to help you.*

Prompts

- Have you seen the word written before?
- Say it aloud. Have you heard anyone use the word?
- Does the way you remember it being used help you figure out its meaning here?
- Now that you have the gist, see if your sense of the word fits with what you read.

Strategy When you come across an unfamiliar word or phrase, insert a word or phrase you know that would fit the meaning and structure of the sentence and makes sense with the overall context. Use your knowledge of the familiar word to help you understand (and learn!) the new word.

Lesson Language *I was reading this section, "Get My Message?" from* What Is a Primate? *(Kalman, 1999). When I came to a sentence with a word that was new to me, I had to temporarily stick in a synonym to help me understand and learn the new word. Here's the sentence: "Gorillas use many sounds to 'talk' to one another. Female gorillas grunt to scold their young" (p. 10). That word: g-r-u-n-t. I didn't know what it means, even though I could pronounce it. But based on what I'm learning about in this part, I think* grunt *means to make some kind of sound. Female gorillas make a sound to scold their young. Yes, that makes sense in the context.* Grunt *is a kind of sound gorillas make.*

Prompts
- Temporarily stick in a word or phrase that you know that would make sense here.
- Now that you found a synonym, connect that word's meaning to the word the author used.
- You can decode the word but don't know its meaning. Is there another word that might fit there? That could be a synonym.
- You're not sure what that phrase means. Can you say a word or phrase that makes sense that may be a synonym?

Insert a **SYNONYM**

angry? mad?

When her best friend grabbed her toy, she was furious with him.

by? next to? near?

He placed the glass of orange juice alongside his plate.

Skills
- **activating prior knowledge**
- **inferring**
- **self-monitoring**

Progression

Is aware when a word is unfamiliar and is ready to learn to infer a gist or definition from prior knowledge and/or sentence-level context.

Research Link

In a systematic review of 36 studies on vocabulary instruction, Wright and Cervetti (2017) found evidence that helping students connect words to semantic categories of synonyms supported their word learning. In one of the studies, Lubliner and Smetana (2005) found that "insert a synonym" was a successful strategy to help students monitor whether their inferred meaning of a word made sense in context.

Use Part of Speech as a Clue

- **inferring**
- **analyzing**

Progression

Is aware when a word is unfamiliar and is ready to learn to infer a gist or definition from prior knowledge and/or sentence-level context.

Research Link

For 15 weeks, third graders in one study engaged in regular practice with a cloze activity that emphasized syntax and parts of speech to determine unknown words (Sampson, Valmont, & Van Allen, 1982). The students showed improvements in reading comprehension, but they did not outperform their peers (in a control group) in vocabulary development, suggesting that this strategy helps readers use their existing vocabularies more than learning new words.

Strategy When you come to an unfamiliar word, think about the "job" the word has in a sentence. Use your knowledge of the word's job to help you figure out what the word might mean.

Lesson Language *Let's look at a few sentences from* The Secret of the Scuba Diving Spider . . . and More! *(Rodríguez, 2018) to see if this strategy can help. "The bats chat constantly during their nocturnal outings" (p. 20). If I'm trying to figure out* nocturnal, *I can first think, "What job does the word have?"* Nocturnal *is a describing word (or adjective) that provides more detail about the kind of outings that bats go on. If I think about bats, I know they go out at night, so* nocturnal *might mean nighttime. Let's look at another: "The roach lifted the rest of its body and pushed the surrounding walls with the middle and hind legs to get across the crevice" (p. 37). In this sentence,* crevice *has to be a word for a place or thing (or noun) that the roach has to crawl across. Roaches aren't very big, so the type of thing it has to crawl across can't be very big either. In this case, maybe it means a narrow crack or gap or bump. It's hard to know exactly from just this sentence, but I can read on to see if I get more information. The part of speech helped me at least get a gist.*

Teaching Tip Readers can't make an inference about *which* job a word is doing in a sentence until they understand that words *have* different jobs, so be sure that you've taught basic parts of speech before sharing this strategy. You may even teach students the terms for these "jobs" (e.g., nouns, verbs, adjectives, and so on), but this isn't essential. Although this strategy can help children with any word, it may be especially helpful for homographs as the different meanings are often tied to parts of speech. Consider, for example, the word *compact*, which could mean a makeup holder (noun); to press together (verb); or small, dense, or tightly packed (adjective). See Strategy 11.7 for more on multiple meaning words.

Prompts

- What job does that word have in this sentence?
- Think about what kind of word it comes after (or before). Does that help you figure out the job it has?
- Now that you know the job of the word, what might it mean?
- Is that word a thing? Action? Describing word?

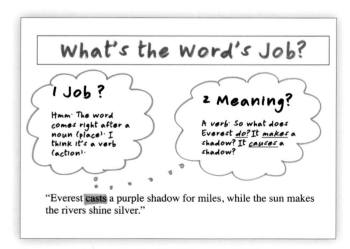

Text excerpt from *To the Top!* (Kramer, 1993).

Strategy When you come to a word you know, but it isn't making sense, it may be because it's being used in a topic-specific way that's new to you. Think about the topic you're reading about and the specific context where the word is used, and see if that helps you figure out how the familiar word is being used in a different way.

Lesson Language *You know that the same word can do different jobs in a sentence and that this changes the meaning of the word—you can* dress *yourself for school or wear a* dress *to a party. But sometimes a word means something completely different even when it's doing the same job in a sentence because it has a different topic-specific meaning. For example:*

- *A* trunk *if you're reading about trees and a* trunk *if you're reading about luggage (not to mention a* trunk *if you are reading about elephants!)*
- *Running if you're reading about a car's motor and* running *if you're reading about sports*
- *Blue if it describes the color of your walls and* blue *if it describes the way you're feeling*

Other times, a word's most basic meaning is the same, but the topic-specific meaning can be very different.

- *A* shuttle *that carries astronauts is different than a* shuttle *to the rental cars at the airport. They both move people, but one's a spaceship and the other is a bus.*
- *A* plate *in your kitchen is different than a* plate *in the earth's crust. They're both flat, but one's a round piece of paper, plastic, or ceramic small enough to hold, the other is a piece of the outer layer of the earth so big that it can fit an entire continent.*
- *An* adaptation *in biology is different than an* adaptation *in theater. They're both changes, but one is a new structure or feature that has evolved in a living thing and the other is a new movie or a play based on a book.*

Prompts

- What meanings do you know for that word? Think of the topic you're reading about.
- How do you know it can't be *that* meaning in *this* context?
- What's another meaning that might make sense here?
- That's one meaning of the word, but does that make sense here?

Progression

Is aware when a word is unfamiliar and is ready to learn to infer a gist or definition from prior knowledge and/or sentence-level context.

Research Link

In a series of experiments, Klein and Murphy (2001) explored *polysemous words* (those with different, but related, meanings [e.g., *paper, film, copy*]) and *homonyms* (words with the same spelling but no related meaning [e.g., *bank, right, tire*]) and found evidence that these words are stored separately in memory. Readers can quickly access meaning if the word is used in a familiar sense, but comprehension is slowed when the word is used in an unfamiliar way.

Look to See If It's Right There in the Sentence!

Progression

Is aware when a word is unfamiliar and is ready to learn to infer a gist or definition from prior knowledge and/or sentence-level context.

Strategy When you encounter a topic-specific word, look before the word and after the word to see if it is defined. Seeing words like *are*, *or*, and *called*, or punctuation like commas or dashes, will sometimes give you a clue that the definition is right there!

Lesson Language *Let's look at three examples of sentences in the book* Penguins *(Arlon & Gordon-Harris, 2012) where the authors used a word that is important for learning about the content, and then gave us the definition right there in the same sentence. As we look at these examples, let's think about the clues that let us know the definition is there.*

1. "So each year penguins molt—their feathers fall out." (p. 21)
2. "Krill are like tiny shrimps." (p. 22)
3. "These penguins used to make their nests out of their own poop, called guano!" (p. 41)

In the first example, we can figure out the word molt *because the definition follows a dash. Authors often use dashes and commas to insert a definition right there in the sentence, so make sure you watch out for that. The second sentence has the word* krill, *which we can figure out because we see the words* are like. *And the last sentence has the word* guano. *How can we figure that one out? There's that key word:* called!

Prompts

- Can you find a word the author may have defined for you?
- Do you see any key words that tell you the definition is in the sentence?
- Look at the punctuation. I think I see something that could help you find the definition right in the sentence.
- Yes, the definition is right there. You saw the commas/key words and knew that.

Look, the definition might be **right** **there** in the sentence!

- Watch for [are] [or] [called]
- Look for punctuation , -

For example: Some bird eggs have markings that help them camouflage, or blend into their surroundings.

Strategy Sometimes the way a sentence is structured can help you figure out what an unfamiliar word means. First, identify the sentence structure. Then, ask yourself, "Does this mean these things are alike? Are they opposites? Does one cause the other?" Infer the meaning based on the relationship.

Lesson Language *I'm going to share a few sentences and think aloud about how I notice the way the information in the sentence fits together and how that helps me think about what a word might mean. It doesn't always get me to an exact definition, but it gets me a sense of the word so that my overall comprehension isn't interrupted.*

"Unlike Melissa who was patient and kind, her mother had a quick temper." *In this sentence, Melissa and her mother are being compared. I understand what* patient *and* kind *mean, so "a quick temper" must mean the opposite of that since it says* unlike.

"If we want to win, then we have to persevere." This is an if-then or cause-effect sentence. So persevere *means something that you have to do to win. Work hard? Keep going?*

"Being in the mountains made her feel a sense of relaxation and tranquility, as if she didn't have a care in the world." The second part of the sentence gives more information. Relaxed *goes with not having a care. So* tranquility *must mean something similar to relaxation.*

Prompts

- Pause to figure out how the words in the sentence work together. What's the relationship between the information?
- How would you describe the relationship between the information in the first part and the second part?
- Now that you paid attention to structure, can you figure out what this word might mean?

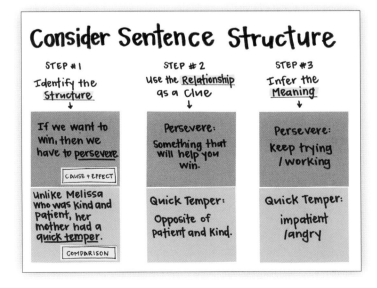

Progression

Is aware when a word is unfamiliar and is ready to learn to infer a gist or definition from prior knowledge and/or sentence-level context.

⬤⬤◯◯◯◯

Research Link

According to research summarized by Kintsch and Mangalath (2011), word meanings are not stored ready-made in our memories—they only take on meaning in the interaction with their context. Consequently, meaning is constructed for a word every time that word is encountered. Signal words for different text structures can help strengthen networks of meanings among words, allowing for easier mental access the next time those words are encountered (Ericsson & Kintsch, 1995).

Skills

- **analyzing**
- **inferring**

Progression

Is aware when a word is unfamiliar and is ready to learn to infer a gist or definition from prior knowledge and/or sentence-level context.

●●○○○

Hat Tip

Learning to Learn in a Second Language (Gibbons, 1993)

Research Link

In a pair of studies, researchers asked children of varying ages and comprehension abilities to complete cloze tasks using conjunctions. They found that younger children and those the researchers termed "poor comprehenders" were less able to choose appropriate conjunctions to complete the task. Adult proficient readers, they found, use conjunctions for comprehension and to remember information (Cain, Patson, & Andrews, 2005).

Strategy Look for conjunctions (e.g., *but, or, yet, so, for, and, nor, after, before*) that can help you understand how the information in a sentence is related. Consider how the word you're trying to figure out relates to the rest of the information in the sentence.

Lesson Language *Don't underestimate the power of little words to lead you to big meanings. Conjunctions always signal a relationship between information in a sentence, and sometimes that relationship offers a clue that helps you understand an unfamiliar word or phrase. For example,* so *usually means that one thing is causing another—"She never brushed her teeth,* so *she got a cavity." If I'm trying to understand what a* cavity *is, I can think about what would happen as a result of someone not brushing their teeth. Words such as* after, before, *and* while *indicate some kind of time relationship—"She brushed her teeth* before *she called it a night." If I want to understand the meaning of the figurative phrase "call it a night," I could think about what people usually do after they brush their teeth to infer what would make sense in the context.*

Prompts

- Check the conjunction—how does the information in the sentence fit together?
- Now that you've thought about how the parts of the sentence go together, what might this word/phrase mean?
- Does the meaning you inferred fit in the context? Consider the conjunction.
- Since that word is showing an order of events, what are you thinking now about that word/phrase?

CONSIDER
conjunctions

She never brushed her teeth [so] she got a cavity.?

✓ Check the conjunction and its relationship.

✓ How do the two parts go together?

✓ What might the word mean?

✓ Does it fit?

Use Individual Words to Figure Out Compound Words

Strategy Notice if the long word you're trying to understand is a *compound* word: a longer word made up of two shorter words. Split the word into two parts. Think, "What does each of these words mean on its own?" and then think, "What might this whole word mean with these two parts together?"

Lesson Language *Hundreds of words in English are known as* compound *words, words that are made by combining two shorter words. Each shorter word has a meaning on its own, and when combined together, they make a new word with its own meaning. Let's look at a few examples. I'll start with one you all know:* airport. *We can break it up into* air *and* port. Air *is the gas that surrounds the earth. A* port *is a place where transportation vehicles dock. So an* airport *is a place where transportation vehicles that travel by air (airplanes) dock. Here's one you may not know:* careworn. *First, what are the two shorter words? Right—*care *and* worn. *We know what each word means by itself.* Care *means you're paying attention, giving someone what they need, or concerned.* Worn *means damaged or shabby, usually because it gets too much use. So what might* careworn *mean, then? It could describe someone who is worn out from caring too much.*

Prompts

- Can you break this word into two parts, where each part is a word by itself?
- Define each shorter word.
- Now put the two parts together—what would this compound word mean?
- Does one part of the word modify or describe the other part?

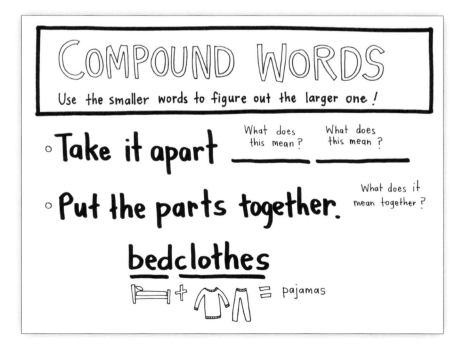

Skills

- **analyzing**
- **inferring**
- **activating prior knowledge**

Progression

Is able to use context and prior knowledge to infer and is ready to learn to analyze word parts and apply a knowledge of grammar, morphology, and/or etymology.

●●●○○

Research Link

In a pair of experiments, researchers found that it took skilled readers longer to process new compound words. Even when the new word was a combination of familiar words, readers still processed it as an unknown word and reread the sentence searching for context clues. They also found evidence that readers remembered the meaning of the new compound word after a single exposure (Brusnighan & Folk, 2012).

Skills

- **analyzing**
- **inferring**
- **self-monitoring**
- **activating prior knowledge**

Progression

Is able to use context and prior knowledge to infer and is ready to learn to analyze word parts and apply a knowledge of grammar, morphology, and/or etymology.

Hat Tip

Spelling K–8: Planning and Teaching (Snowball & Bolton, 1999)

Research Link

In a meta-analysis of studies of the effects of morphology instruction, researchers concluded that morphological knowledge supports vocabulary knowledge, and that "knowledge of roots and affixes provides students with knowledge to support accessing the meanings of words" (Goodwin & Ahn, 2013, p. 278).

Strategy Identify the parts of a longer word you know: the prefixes and suffixes. Think about what each part means, and then put the word back together. Check to make sure the meaning you came up with makes sense in the sentence.

Teaching Tip Create word family charts with your students and have them up as resources in the classroom. During read-alouds or minilessons, when you come to complex, long words that have familiar word parts, show students how to use the charts as resources to figure out the word. Part of the usefulness of this strategy is in knowing what the word parts mean, the other is in actually going through the steps of deconstructing and reconstructing the word. This strategy can be modified depending on the text complexity and grade level—choose prefixes and suffixes your students are most likely to encounter based on the texts they're reading.

Family	Prefix	Examples	Meanings
"not"	dis-	disobedient disagree	not obedient, misbehaved don't agree, different opinions
	un-	unhelpful unlock	not helpful not locked
	in-	incomplete independent	not complete/finished don't depend on others, can do it by yourself
	im-	imperfect immature	not perfect, has flaws not mature, juvenile
	non-	nonfiction nonliving	not fiction, real not alive
	ir-	irresponsible irregular	not responsible not regular
	il-	illegal illiterate	not legal not literate, can't read or write

Prompts

- What part do you see? What does that part mean?
- Put that together with the rest of the word. What does the entire word mean?
- You know that part.
- What other words do you know with that same prefix (or suffix)?

Strategy Within a longer word, look for a meaningful part (a root or a base) you might know. Think about where you've seen or heard the root in a different word, and use that to help you remember, or figure out, what this one means. Notice the other parts of the word that modify the meaning of the root or base. Then, think about how the word is being used to figure out its meaning in this context.

Teaching Tip A word root is a part that comes from Latin, Greek, or Indo-European languages to which other affixes can be added. Without the rest of the word, the root cannot stand on its own (e.g., *struct* in *construct, reconstruct, construction).* This is sometimes confused with a *base word*, which *is* a word on its own (e.g., *teach* in *teachable, unteachable, reteach*). However, this distinction doesn't really matter when using the strategy. If a student recognizes a familiar part of a longer word, they can use that knowledge to figure out the new word. For more information on affixes, see Strategy 11.12.

Prompts

- This part is a root. Do you know another word with the same root that can help you figure out what this part means?
- Is there a root or base word you know?
- Put the root together with the rest of the word. What do you think it means?
- Check the beginning and ending of the word, too.

Skills

- **analyzing**
- **inferring**
- **activating prior knowledge**

Progression

Is able to use context and prior knowledge to infer and is ready to learn to analyze word parts and apply a knowledge of grammar, morphology, and/or etymology.

Research Link

Sixth- and seventh-grade students who were given minimal instruction about bound Latin roots (e.g., *spect* as in *spectator, inspect, spectacle*) were able to comprehend words containing those roots when they encountered them in their reading (Crosson & McKeown, 2016). More advanced readers tend to benefit more from word-level analysis since they encounter more complex words on which to apply their learning (Castles, Rastle, & Nation, 2018).

— Get to the BASE —

BASE WORDS WE KNOW	WORDS WITH THAT BASE	WHAT WHOLE WORD MEANS
teach	teacher	→ person who teaches
	teachable	→ person ready to learn
cycle	bicycle	→ a bike or vehicle with 2 wheels
	motorcycle	→ 2-wheeled bike powered by a motor
	cyclist	→ person who rides a bike
transport	transportation	→ the movement of goods or people from place to place
	transporting	→ the action of moving

Skills

- **analyzing**
- **inferring**
- **activating prior knowledge**

Progression

Is able to use context and prior knowledge to infer and is ready to learn to analyze word parts and apply a knowledge of grammar, morphology, and/or etymology.

Hat Tip

No More "Look Up the List" Vocabulary Instruction (Cobb & Blachowicz, 2014)

Research Link

In a study of Spanish-English bilingual kindergarteners and first graders, researchers found that children who were exposed to more Spanish knew more English cognates than those who received balanced amounts of Spanish and English or who were exposed to more English (Pérez, Peña, & Bedore, 2010). A speaker of two (or more) languages has an expanded repertoire of linguistic resources, with particular word-learning benefits when languages have related origins.

Strategy If the word looks, or is pronounced, like a word you know from another language, think about what the word means in the other language. See if a similar meaning would fit in the context in which you encountered the English word.

Teaching Tip This strategy would be best for a student who is bi- or multilingual or who is studying another language. Be aware that there are many types of cognates. Some are phonologically similar and orthographically identical and are known as "perfect cognates" (e.g., *animal* [English]—*animal* [Spanish]); others are phonologically similar and orthographically similar (e.g., *accident* [English]—*accidente* [Spanish]). Especially tricky are "false cognates" which are word pairs that are phonologically and/ or orthographically similar but not related in meaning, such as *pie* ("food with a crust" [English]—"foot" [Spanish]) or *recorder,* which looks like the English word *record* but means "to remember or remind" in Spanish (Rodríguez, 2001).

Prompts

- Do you know a word in another language that looks like this?
- Think about what the word means in the other language(s) you know.
- What might this word mean in English?
- Think about how it's used here—does the word you matched with this word fit here?

Hey! That Sounds Just Like a Word I Know...

In English...	In Spanish...
Abuse	Abuso
Abbreviate	Abreviar
Accept	Aceptar
Majority	Mayoría
Realization	Realización

① THINK of a word you know in another language that looks +/or sounds like the word.

② THINK what does the word mean in the other language?

③ CHECK does the word in this book mean the same?

"cognates" — there are hundreds + hundreds!

THE READING STRATEGIES BOOK 2.0

Strategy If you can't figure out a word from context, and not knowing is getting in the way of your understanding, find a definition (or definitions) by consulting a reference within or outside of the book. Go back to the sentence where the word appears to see how the word is being used, then choose the definition that best fits the context. Explain what the word means in your own words based on how it's being used.

Lesson Language *When you've found that you've tried your go-to strategies and you still can't figure out the word, you may choose to look it up. You don't want to interrupt your reading on every page to run to a reference, but if you find that not knowing the word interferes with understanding what you're reading, or if you are just really curious about what the word might mean, you may choose to find a definition. Whether you use an online dictionary, a printed dictionary, or a glossary within the text, the important thing to remember is that a simple definition is rarely enough to really help you understand the word. Always think about the context in which the word appears to make sure you're choosing the right definition (as we know many words have multiple meanings!).*

Teaching Tip As standard dictionaries assume an adult audience, be sure to have children's dictionaries available, physically or online, for younger learners. For quick access with older learners, let them know they can type *define* plus any word into Google, which displays definition(s) from the Oxford Dictionary, plus other useful information, like audio pronunciations and synonyms. You might also consider various browser extensions, such as Google Dictionary, which can display the definition of any word encountered online with a simple click. These and similar digital tools are particularly useful for English language learners.

Prompts

- What resource can you check to help you?
- You found a few definitions. How can you figure out which is correct in this context?
- Which definition applies in this case?
- You figured out that it was the second definition, not the first, that works in this context. You're really thinking about the meaning!

Skills
- **building knowledge**
- **self-monitoring**
- **synthesizing**

Progression
Is confidently and independently using a variety of strategies to figure out unfamiliar words and is ready to supplement word learning using outside resources.

Skills

- **building knowledge**
- **self-monitoring**
- **synthesizing**

Progression

Is confidently and independently using a variety of strategies to figure out unfamiliar words and is ready to supplement word learning using outside resources.

Research Link

In a study with bilingual and monolingual fourth graders (Proctor, Dalton, & Grisham, 2007), researchers found that multimedia features, including on-demand definitions and Spanish translations, improved students' receptive vocabulary knowledge.

Strategy If you are reading an e-book on a tablet or other device and you encounter an unknown word, infer a meaning using word- and sentence-based strategies (e.g., morphology, context). Hover your cursor over the word until the definition pops up. Read the definition to confirm or revise your understanding of the word. Reread the sentence to notice how the word is being used and connect the definition to context.

Teaching Tip The look-it-up feature for e-books, found on most tablets and other digital devices, is really a game changer because it takes so little time away from reading to find out the meaning of an unfamiliar word. Although students still need to keep an eye on their engagement and pace to make sure they aren't stopping so often it gets in the way of comprehension, you can encourage them to be more curious about words when they are reading electronically. After all, the process of inferring a word's meaning then quickly checking its definition (to verify the accuracy of an inference) is a powerful way to learn new words.

Prompts

- If you're not sure what it means, you can use the built-in dictionary to get a definition quickly!
- Now that you've read the definition, reread the context in which it's being used.
- How does that definition fit with what's happening in the text?
- Remember, you're reading an e-book, so you can view the definition of the word instantaneously!

Strategy Ask yourself, "Do I know anyone who might know what this word means?" Ask a friend, parent, or teacher for a quick definition (or if it's not a good time to interrupt, jot a note to ask them later). Once you get their definition or explanation, reread the sentence to consider if what they said fits with the context.

Teaching Tip Although students may have easy access to e-book look-it-up features, online dictionaries, or a physical dictionary or glossary, there may be times when asking another person is preferable. Sometimes it's about convenience and efficiency—a friend with a good vocabulary is sitting right there and the dictionary is across the room. But, it's also true that when you talk to people about words, the conversation you have can lead to deeper understanding—something you can't get from a dictionary. If, however, you notice a student typically uses this strategy *first*, then modify the strategy language and encourage them to infer a meaning first and then use a friend to confirm or revise their inference.

Prompts
- Who might you ask for help?
- They gave you a definition. Let's see if the definition fits the context.
- Provide them with the context in the sentence so they give you the definition of the word that fits here.
- Have you tried your other strategies? OK, then you can ask a friend or grown-up!

Skills
- **building knowledge**
- **self-monitoring**
- **synthesizing**

Progression

Is confidently and independently using a variety of strategies to figure out unfamiliar words and is ready to supplement word learning using outside resources.

● ● ● ● ○

Research Link

In a study with first graders of various reading abilities (Lee, 2017), participants read e-books with audio support, with and without additional word explanations provided by the teacher. Overall, having the teacher's support resulted in more word learning, especially for students with higher reading abilities. Simply hearing new words once in the audio narration did not result in incidental word learning.

Strategy Collect several books on the same topic. Read the easiest of the books first, collecting words and definitions in your notebook or on sticky notes that are important to the topic. Read the next most challenging book, using the prior book and your notes to remember word meanings. Collect new words and meanings as you read. Continue until you can read the most challenging book you chose.

Teaching Tip This strategy will work very well for informational texts, where most of the vocabulary that students will encounter will be content-specific and will likely overlap with other books at various levels. It also helps children reading "up ladders" to have prior knowledge so they can better use the context when they get to a more challenging text. Some types of fiction lend themselves to this strategy, such as historical fiction, where gaining familiarity with the setting or time period makes it easier to read other books set in a similar place or time. It is important to note that most of the challenging vocabulary students encounter will be what Beck, McKeown, and Kucan (2013) term "tier 2" vocabulary—words that are less frequent, but may be found and used across a variety of contexts, such as *bewildered*, *ceased*, or *embraces*. This strategy will be most helpful for learning "tier 3" vocabulary—words that are content-specific, and much less likely to be encountered in everyday speech, such as *pharaoh*, *tomb*, *sarcophagus*, or *hieroglyphics*.

Prompts

- Which books can you find that deal with the same topic?
- Those texts are all broadly connected by topic, but you'll want your text set to be a little more focused for this strategy to work.
- You collected several books about ___. Which looks easiest?
- What words did you learn from this first book that might help you as you read the next one?

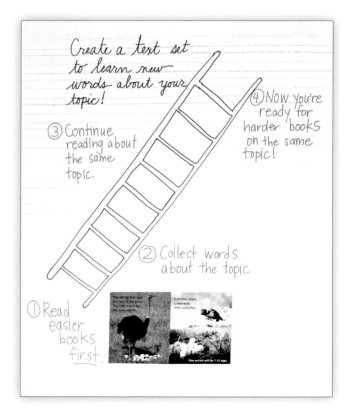

Strategy Think about the key topic(s) in the book you've chosen. Find an audio/visual source on the same topic(s). Watch or listen for information and for key vocabulary. Jot down words you learn that connect to your topic(s).

Lesson Language *If you're finding a book you're reading (or that you want to read) is too challenging because of the vocabulary, you could study up, priming yourself with information (and relevant words!) before trying it. Searching for audiobooks (on Epic! [www.getepic.com] or from your public library's access to Libby, Overdrive, or Hoopla, for example), podcasts, or even a YouTube video about the topic you want to read about will help you learn background information and key vocabulary words you're likely to encounter and need to know when you read the book.*

Prompts
- So you know what this book is about. What topics could you search for that would help you understand it better?
- You found a video on that topic. As you watch, jot down some words you hear that you think are important to your topic. Define them based on how they are used in the video.
- What words did you hear in the podcast that you think might help you in this book?
- I see that you've jotted down important words and what you think they mean based on how they were used in the video!

To get - READY for a topic use audiobooks, podcasts, or youtube videos.

They can help you with background information and vocabulary.

> The oldest trees make up the highest canopy.

> Tree roots work with symbiotic fungi called mycorrhizae.

> Fungi networks spread further than tree roots and connect different tree roots together.

> Fungi connections are called mycorrhizal networks.

⚹ Use sticky notes to help you keep track of info!

Now you're ready to read!

Skill
- **building knowledge**

Progression
Is confidently and independently using a variety of strategies to figure out unfamiliar words and is ready to supplement word learning using outside resources.

● ● ● ● ○

Research Link
In a review of research, Cervetti and Wright (2020) provide ample evidence that knowledge supports comprehension and comprehension builds new knowledge. Studies have found that knowledge can support vocabulary development as well by supporting readers to make informed inferences about the meanings of unknown words (e.g., Barnes, Ginther, & Cochran, 1989; Kaefer, Neuman, & Pinkham, 2015).

Skills
- **self-monitoring**
- **inferring**
- **synthesizing**

Progression

Is able to understand and/ or figure out the meanings of words and is ready to consider words within a larger context and analyze an author's word choice for a deeper understanding and interpretation.

● ● ● ● ●

Research Link

Researchers compared instruction in morphemic analysis (e.g., prefixes) with instruction in contextual analysis (e.g., clue types including mood and tone) with fifth graders. Both of the strategies, individually or in combination, supported students to remember the meanings of words included in the lessons and to infer unknown words that had similar context clues to those featured in the intervention instruction (Baumann et al., 2002).

Strategy When you come to an unfamiliar word or phrase, think about what's happening and what the mood or feeling is at that moment in the text. Is it scary? Sad? Happy? Suspenseful? Knowing the mood might help you infer about the word or phrase's meaning. Try to explain or define it, keeping the mood, and what's happening, in mind.

Lesson Language *When we read the book* My Footprints *(Phi, 2019) as a class, we noticed the author uses such rich, descriptive language. For example, on the first page Phi writes, "new snow cracks like eggshells," and we can see from the photo that there are no eggs at all. What does that phrase mean? Well, we can start by thinking, what's happening? What's the mood? Thuy is being laughed at, and she's feeling nervous and upset. The author is comparing the snow's crunch to eggshells cracking because she's feeling tense. Later, when she's home, Momma Ngoc's and Momma Arti's smiles "feel like a heater that warms . . . [her] toes." Not literally a heater, but what could this mean? What's happening? What's the mood? Well, Thuy is home and feels safe with her moms and loved. The mood is happy, peaceful. She's warmed from the inside out.*

Prompts
- What's the mood?
- That's what is *happening*. What is the *feeling*? Now what might that word or phrase mean?
- You figured out a feeling from the sentence. Based on that feeling, what can you infer this word means?

"The morning of June 27th was clear and sunny, with the fresh warmth of a full-summer day; the flowers were blossoming **profusely** and the grass was richly green." -"The Lottery" (Jackson, 1948)	joyful beautiful happy	profusely—a lot of flowers? Blooming a lot?
"Never before that night had I felt the extent of my own powers—of my **sagacity**. I could scarcely contain my feelings of triumph." -"The Telltale Heart" (Poe, 1843)	powerful strong	sagacity—something positive about his mind that makes him feel strong.
"But the wet, dirty environment of the cave **wreaks havoc** on the skin, where any scrape or blister can become easily infected." -*All Thirteen* (Soontornvat, 2020)	scary gloomy	wreaks havoc—causes harm or hurt or problems.

Strategy Think about what's happening in the larger context, not just the sentence where the word or phrase appears. Come up with a definition. Explain why that meaning for the word or phrase works using specific details from the story.

Lesson Language *It's important to stick close to the details of a story when you're figuring out an unfamiliar word or phrase. For example, when we came to this sentence in Erdrich's* The Birchbark House *(1999), we knew there was some language we should take a bit of time to figure out: "Omakayas helped her, threading the tough basswood strands through holes punched by Grandma's awl."* Basswood? Awl? *We know a* bass *is a kind of fish, but that meaning doesn't fit the details—they're not anywhere near water or fish in this part of the book. So let's think: What is happening here? This is the part of the story where they have just peeled bark away and she says, "[W]e need your bark for our shelter." They are building a house. So this sentence gives us some details about them doing that. In the sentence before, she mentions sewing pieces of bark together. So the* basswood *must be some kind of material—maybe from a tree, since "wood" is also part of the word—that's being used to bind the pieces of bark together. And an* awl *must be a tool of some kind that can put holes in the bark to make the threading go easier.*

Prompts
- Think about the whole context, not just the sentence.
- Explain why you think that's the meaning.
- Does the way you explained it fit with the details of the whole story?
- I notice you thought about what was happening in the story to figure out what that word means.

Skills
- **inferring**
- **synthesizing**

Progression

Is able to understand and/or figure out the meanings of words and is ready to consider words within a larger context and analyze an author's word choice for a deeper understanding and interpretation.

Hat Tip

Bringing Words to Life: Robust Vocabulary Instruction, **second edition** (Beck, McKeown, & Kucan, 2013)

Research Link

In a classic study, Nagy, Herman, and Anderson (1985) had eighth graders read texts of about 1,000 words, testing them on the meanings of 15 target words. Their findings (confirmed by a larger subsequent study [Nagy, Anderson, & Herman, 1987]) revealed small, but statistically significant, gains in vocabulary knowledge. Extrapolating those findings over time, the researchers concluded that readers acquire a substantial amount of word learning incidentally, using context.

Consider the Type of Figurative Language

Strategy If you suspect you've come across some figurative language, think about the different types of that kind of language that you know. Ask yourself, "Could this be ___ [metaphor, hyperbole, an idiom, etc.]?" With the chart as a reference, use what you know about the type of figurative language to try to figure out the author's intended meaning. Once you think you have an idea of what it means, consider it in context.

Teaching Tip You spend so much time teaching students to figure out what words mean, it can be challenging to help them understand that, sometimes, words *don't mean* exactly, literally, what they say. Teach students that when they encounter a phrase where they understand the words individually, but the phrase isn't making sense, it might be because the author is using the words figuratively instead of literally. Then, work together to build a knowledge base about different kinds of figurative language so students will be able to use this strategy when they encounter new figures of speech. The chart provided on this page is meant to be an example. If you create a similar chart using examples your students provide, it will be more meaningful and your students will be more likely to reference it as they practice. Keep in mind that figurative language can be particularly confusing for students who do not speak English as their first language, as direct translations will make no sense, and figurative phrases vary depending on the language.

Relationship	What Is It?	Example
Oxymoron	Words that are put together that have very different, sometimes opposite, meanings	Sound of silence Living dead Accurate estimate
Pun	Humorous use of words because at least one word in the phrase sounds like another word but has a different meaning	I'm so board. I wish something fun wood come around.
Metaphor	Comparing without using *like* or *as*	That desk is such a pigsty.
Hyperbole	Exaggeration	I've been waiting in line forever. I told you a thousand times!
Idiom	A saying that doesn't mean what the words in the phrase literally mean	Let's hit the road. You're driving me up the wall.

Prompts

- What type of figurative language do you think this might be?
- That's hyperbole. Remember what you know about hyperbole to figure out what the author means in this story.
- Yes, that's a pun! Does that help you figure out what it might mean?
- Instead of taking it literally, think about what else the author might mean in this context.

Strategy For certain types of figurative language (metaphor, simile, hyperbole), it can be helpful to picture what the phrase would mean if the author meant it *literally*, and then think, "What does it mean knowing the author means it *figuratively*?"

Lesson Language *You'll understand plenty of common examples of figurative language as soon as you hear them—you know what it means to call someone a couch potato or to be busy as a bee. When your mom says, "I told you a million times to clean your room," you know she just means that the three or four times she mentioned it were enough to really annoy her! But sometimes you'll discover figurative language while you are reading that is so original you'll have to pause for a moment and think about what it means. One strategy you can try is to picture the words literally and then think about what they mean figuratively. For example, the first line in Oge Mora's picture book Saturday (2019) reads, "This morning Ava and her mother were all smiles." I can picture that literally—both of them with faces covered with huge smiles—and then think what it means figuratively, this means they were happy.*

Teaching Tip Keep in mind that some students (and adults) misuse the word *literally* as a qualifier in their colloquial speech to refer to things that aren't literal at all! For example, "It's so hot out here, I'm literally melting." This common use of the word *literally* can be confusing for students who are just learning the difference between literal and figurative language, so be sure to talk about it as you're helping them to understand the concept.

Prompts
- Tell me what you picture if this phrase was meant to be taken literally.
- That's the literal meaning. What does it mean as figurative language?
- I can tell you pictured it to see that it can't literally mean that. What do you think the author is trying to say?
- Does your inferred meaning fit with the rest of the text?

Skills
- **visualizing**
- **inferring**

Progression

Is able to understand and/or figure out the meanings of words and is ready to consider words within a larger context and analyze an author's word choice for a deeper understanding and interpretation.

Hat Tip

Reading with Meaning: Teaching Comprehension in the Primary Grades, **second edition** (Miller, 2012)

Research Link

In an expansive review of figurative language and mental imagery that touches on psychology, philosophy, and literary theory, Carston (2018) concludes that many people spontaneously generate mental images when hearing or reading figurative language and, because this process is under conscious control, it can be summoned actively to make sense of metaphors.

Strategy When an author's word choice feels surprising, or loaded, or biased in some way, pause to consider a deeper meaning beyond the most obvious or basic meaning. Think about other words that mean something similar (synonyms). Then think, "Why would the author have chosen *this* word?"

Lesson Language *Words that authors use may have a* denotative *meaning and a* connotative *meaning. That is, when we look up a word in a dictionary, we can find the denotative meaning (the technical definition of the word). But, the word may also carry connotative meanings (additional layers or associations that attach to a word over time). In stories, connotations can impact the mood, the tone, or your feelings about a character, place, or action. In expository texts, connotations can influence how you sift between facts and opinion, help you consider author bias, or deepen your understanding of the content. We can be alert when reading to notice descriptive language that might communicate something deeper than what the word literally means. For example, the words* youthful *and* juvenile *both mean young, but carry different layered meanings.* Youthful *is often positive and communicates a "full of life" kind of feeling. On the other hand,* juvenile *can be used in a negative way to communicate someone who acts young and immature when they should act more mature. You can stop to think about why the author chose a precise word and what that word choice helps you to understand about what's being described.*

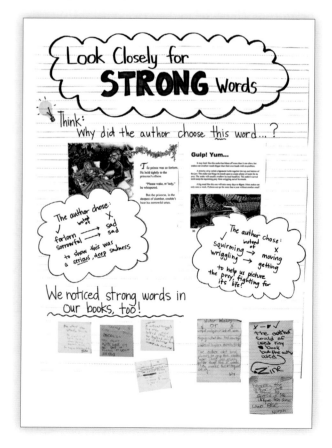

Prompts

- Based on how the word is used, do you feel it has a positive or negative connotation?
- Why do you think the author chose this word?
- What other words would work here? Think about why the author chose this one instead.
- That's an accurate definition. What other layers of meaning are in this word, based on how it's used in this context?

Vocabulary knowledge
helps students access background
knowledge, express ideas,
communicate effectively, and
learn about new concepts.

—Jennifer Serravallo

Goal
12

Conversation

◎ Why is this goal important?

Conversation about books can support student comprehension (Cazden, 2005; Wilkinson, Murphy, & Binici, 2015) and make the reading process engaging and social (e.g., Kelley & Clausen-Grace, 2013). When kids truly engage in talk about books, their conversations can be invigorating and enlightening. However, without strong conversational skills, readers may become bored or off task, wasting precious class time. Often, students benefit from instruction in general speaking and listening skills (Zwiers, 2019; Zwiers & Crawford, 2011), and also how to talk *about books* specifically (Kong & Fitch, 2002; Raphael, Pardo, & Highfield, 2013).

There is a reciprocal relationship, of course, between conversation and comprehension (McKeown & Beck, 2015). Readers need to be actively thinking about and beyond the text so they come prepared to conversation time with thoughts, questions, and ideas worth talking about. And then, once they are fully engaged in talk about their books, their comprehension will deepen, laying a foundation for even better conversation.

Active listening
Listening with respect and interest to understand another's point of view and responding appropriately and in turn.

Staying on topic
Determining the main topic under discussion and contributing thoughts, ideas, and details from the texts that relate to that topic.

Questioning
Asking questions to invite elaboration from a speaker, clarify someone's points, express a tentative thought, or invite in a quieter voice.

Skills a reader might work on as part of this goal

Being accountable
Staying accountable to both the book (citing places or parts that fit with your thinking) and to peers (referencing comments already shared).

Preparing for conversation
Thinking ahead about ideas that will make for good conversation.

Balancing conversation
Being aware when you are dominating the conversation and intentionally inviting quieter voices to contribute.

Elaborating
Adding on, defending, and explaining thinking.

Keeping conversation growing
Deepening ideas so that staying on topic doesn't feel redundant or knowing when it's time to move on to a new idea.

Thinking flexibly
Approaching conversation open to having your mind changed or to learn something new.

Debating
Identifying sides to an issue, idea, or topic and using relevant information to discuss each side.

◎ How do I know if this goal is right for my student?

Listen to your students' conversations about books—whether in a whole-class conversation, literature circles or book clubs, or with a partner. Take notes on what students say and what skills you notice they are using or could use additional support with.

When you determine that the *content* of the conversation seems to be causing it to fall flat or stall, then you will want to identify the strategies students need to support comprehension in Chapters 5 through 11. If you feel like conversational strategies would be the best help, you'll find plenty of ideas within this chapter.

One way to take notes during conversation by dividing a page in half—one side for notes about conversational skills (strengths and needs) and the other side for comprehension skills (strengths and needs). This type of note taking requires more in-the-moment thinking and processing on the part of the notetaker, as you'll need to name the strategies and skills students are using in real time.

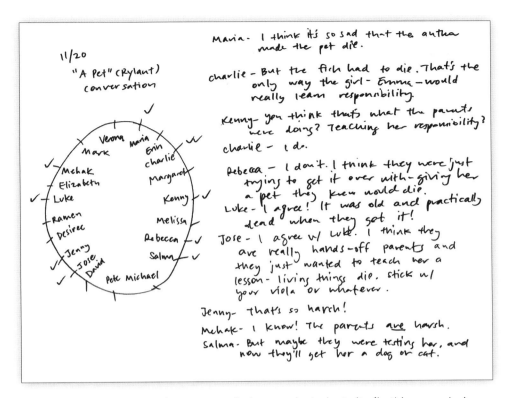

You can also take notes to draw a map of where each student sits (in this example, in a circle for a whole-class conversation). Put a check mark next to each student's name to keep track of how many times each student has spoken, and record their comments on the same page. Later, you can go back and analyze it to think about comprehension and conversational skills. In this example, notice that the conversation stays on topic, children are disagreeing respectfully, and they are agreeing and elaborating when warranted. They are taking risks and considering new ideas. However, several students haven't participated, and those who have spoken tend to speak their ideas rather than invite others into the conversation with questions, so some suggestions to work on those skills may help them all (see Strategies 12.12–12.16).

What Texts Might Students Use When Practicing Strategies from This Chapter?

The strategies in this chapter can be used when students are talking about any type of text, in any genre or format.

◎ How do I support students' conversations about reading?

After listening to your students' conversation about their reading, select strategies that you can model, that they can practice with you, and that they can use independently to increase their skills.

Although development is rarely perfectly linear, skill progressions can help us pinpoint where a student is now and what might come next. Use the if-then chart on page 391 to evaluate your students' reading and find strategies that will support their growth.

A Progression of Skills: *Conversation*

If a student . . .

Needs support to listen actively, stay on topic, and take turns.

Is able to stay on topic and listen. Is ready to come prepared with ideas that will lead to strong conversation, stay accountable to the book under discussion, and elaborate on ideas.

Elaborates on own ideas and is ready to ask questions, invite in quieter speakers, and keep conversation growing—sometimes to a new topic.

Has developed good conversational skills and stamina and is ready to take risks, debate, and think flexibly when encountering new opinions, ideas, and/or information.

Then you might teach . . .

12.1	Set Yourself Up to Listen
12.2	Say Back What You Heard
12.3	Listen and Connect
12.4	Jot, Follow, Fit
12.5	Use a Conversation Playing Board
12.6	Take Turns Without Raising Hands

12.7	Come Prepared to Talk
12.8	Choose from Your Talk Menu
12.9	Keep the Book in the Book Talk
12.10	Listen for Key Ideas
12.11	Reflect and Set Goals for a Conversation

12.12	Prompt Yourself with Sentence Starters
12.13	Invite Quieter Voices
12.14	Ask Power Questions
12.15	Extend the Line of Thinking
12.16	Move On to a New Idea

12.17	Take Risks with *Maybe*
12.18	Try an Idea on for Size
12.19	Challenge Ideas
12.20	Consider the Other Hand
12.21	Bring On the Debate

Strategy Think about how you position your body when you're doing your best listening. Will you turn your shoulders and head toward the speaker? Will you sit still or hold a fidget? Will you make eye contact or focus your eyes on something else?

Teaching Tip Some children may listen best when they face the speaker, make eye contact, and nod as they listen. Others concentrate best when they have something in their hands to work with (such as a squeeze ball). Still other children can become distracted or uncomfortable when forced to make eye contact. Also keep in mind cultural variations that may cause misunderstandings based on different expectations: cultures differ when it comes to length of wait times between turns of talk, amount of eye contact (if any), distance between speakers, among other norms. Use your judgment, and your knowledge of your children and their needs, to (re)define what "listening" looks like for your students.

Prompts
- How will you set your body up to listen?
- Show your book club you're listening.
- Check your body.
- How can you change your body to show you're listening?

SHOW YOU'RE LISTENING
Set up your body.

| What will your body do? | Will you make eye contact or focus on something else? | Will you sit still or hold a fidget? |

Skill
- **active listening**

Progression

Needs support to listen actively, stay on topic, and take turns.

Research Link

To coordinate and self-monitor not only words, but also body language, during a conversation, participants need communicative competence. Since many nonverbal cues are unconscious, learners need to be made aware of them so that they can actively manage their bodies to signal their engagement with what others are saying (e.g., Hennings, 1977; Jalongo, 1995).

Skills

- **active listening**
- **staying on topic**
- **being accountable**

Progression

Needs support to listen actively, stay on topic, and take turns.

● ○ ○ ○

Research Link

In a study with college students (Weger, Castle, & Emmett, 2010), researchers examined different components of active listening to determine their impact on the relationship between conversation partners. In experimental interviews, participants who received paraphrased reflections rated their conversation partners as more likeable than those who received a simple verbal acknowledgement ("OK," "That's great," etc.).

Strategy Listen to what the person before you said. Paraphrase their comments. Give them a chance to OK your understanding, or revise it. Then add to the conversation.

Lesson Language *Active listening is so important to good conversation. As you listen carefully, think about what the other person is saying. Then, say back what you thought you heard: "I heard you say . . ." or "Are you saying . . ." or "So what I think I heard is . . ." Watch for a smile or a nod, or verbal comment, that communicates, "Yes, that's what I meant" before you connect your thought to their comment. If it seems like you haven't represented your classmate's thinking exactly right, give them a chance to clear up what you misunderstood before you add your thought.*

Teaching Tip You might invite students to try taking notes to see if it helps them remember and tune in to the conversation better, jotting key words as they listen to each other talk.

Prompts
- Say back what you heard in your own words.
- Say, "I think you said . . ."
- Now that you paraphrased the person before you, try to add your own thoughts.
- If you're not sure, you can ask them to repeat themselves.

Strategy Listen to what the person before you said. Pause and think, "What do I think about that?" Then, share thoughts that connect to their idea.

Lesson Language *Make sure you're really taking in what others say, and respond in a way that connects. You might agree and extend their idea, give another example, ask them a question, disagree—just be sure your response connects to their thinking. For example, imagine we're talking about* We Are Water Protectors *(Lindstrom, 2020) and someone shares the thought, "I think that protecting water is not just a Native American issue. We all need access to clean water, and it also matters for animals and plants. We should all do more to protect it." I would then think, "What do I think about that?" and rather than share an idea I'd already planned, I'd try to say something that connects. I might, for example, talk about my ideas about what people can do to protect the water or about what I understand about the impacts of polluted water on wildlife.*

Prompts
- Does what you want to say connect to what the person before you said?
- Make sure your thought connects.
- Think, "What do I think about that?"
- You have a thought that connects? Good, go ahead and share it.

Skills
- **active listening**
- **staying on topic**
- **being accountable**

Progression

Needs support to listen actively, stay on topic, and take turns.

● ○ ○ ○

Research Link

Accountable talk emphasizes being accountable to the community, to knowledge, and to reasoning. Accountability to the community means truly listening to other speakers and building upon their contributions. Researchers have found that introducing conversation prompts that lead to this type of accountability can transform classroom discussions within a few weeks (Michaels, O'Connor, & Resnick, 2008).

12.4 Jot, Follow, Fit

Skills

- **active listening**
- **staying on topic**
- **being accountable**

Progression

Needs support to listen actively, stay on topic, and take turns.

Strategy As ideas come to you during a conversation, jot them down. Then, turn your attention back to listening and following the conversation. Share your idea (that you jotted) when it fits with the discussion. If the idea is off topic, wait to share until it's time for the conversation to shift.

Lesson Language *When a conversation is going well, your mind will be racing along with it and you'll have ideas you want to share, but you have to wait your turn to speak. Thinking of the idea you're excited about also makes it hard to listen. Instead of holding the idea in your mind so it blocks your ability to listen, jot it down. Then, go back to listening carefully to your friends.*

Teaching Tip For a more advanced version of this strategy, you can point out to children that while they may sometimes find the perfect moment to share exactly what they wrote down, other times they may want to revise their idea based on what they are hearing. This might include forming new conclusions or even scratching their note in favor of a whole new idea.

Prompts

- Do you have an idea? Jot it down to hold on to it.
- Listen for when what you jotted fits with the conversation.
- Are you having a hard time listening because you have something you want to share?
- It's helpful to have it jotted down so you can refer to it, but still be able to focus and listen.

Research Link

According to a classic study by Sacks, Schegloff, & Jefferson (1974), conversations follow a simple set of turn-taking rules, wherein the space between comments is minimized. Neuroimaging studies (Bögels & Levinson, 2017) have shown that listeners begin planning their response while the speaker is still speaking, so that their reply can be produced immediately. Jotting notes allows listeners to "reply" without interrupting the flow of conversation.

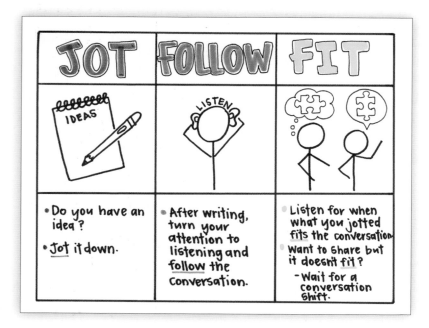

THE READING STRATEGIES BOOK 2.0

Use a Conversation Playing Board

Strategy Place your best thoughts (captured on sticky notes) in a stack on your individual square of the playing board. Choose someone to start the conversation by selecting one note, placing it in the center and reading it. All members of the group think about, focus on, and talk about the idea in the center. When there is nothing left to say about the one in the center, choose a new sticky note to move to the center.

Teaching Tip I learned about creating a playing board to visually represent taking turns and sticking to a topic from educator and author Donna Santman. As students become more practiced, the need for the playing board will fade away; think of it as a temporary scaffold.

Prompts

- Check the center of the board to see what topic is under discussion.
- (*Tap or point to sticky note in center.*) Does what you just said connect to this?
- You each took turns and shared thoughts about what's in the center. That's staying on topic!
- Do you think we can keep going with this topic or is it time to switch to another one?

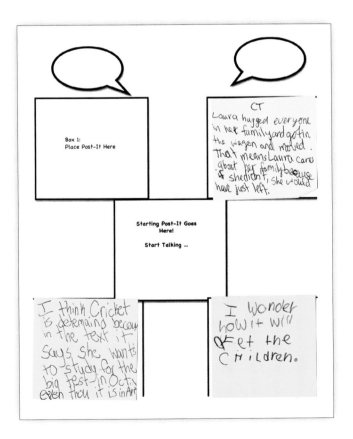

Skills

- **staying on topic**
- **elaborating**
- **being accountable**
- **keep conversation growing**

Progression

Needs support to listen actively, stay on topic, and take turns.

Research Link

In an extensive review of research on collaborative dialogue in small groups, Webb (2009) found that intentionally structuring interactions, or providing specific activities, had positive effects on group collaboration, task performance, and, often, on academic achievement.

Skill

• **active listening**

Progression

Needs support to listen actively, stay on topic, and take turns.

Strategy Make eye contact with the others in the group (to discern if they are about to speak or are listening). Notice when a voice fades—listen for the quiet moment when it's time for you to speak up. When you notice someone is trying to interject, or more than one person is trying to speak, you may decide to let your voice fade.

Lesson Language _When adults are in a conversation, it's unusual for them to raise their hands before they speak or to take turns speaking around a circle. Instead, everyone in the group is responsible to watch, listen, and then speak when it's appropriate. I think we're ready to try this kind of communicating that involves our eyes (point to your eyes) and our bodies (point to your shoulders) and our ears (point to your ears). Let's listen for the quiet spaces between our talk, make eye contact to know when it's our turn, and be ready with good ideas in our minds. And if it happens that more than one person has an idea at the same time and they both try to speak, one voice should get quieter. You might say, "You go ahead" or "I'll go after you" or "You first."_

Prompts

• Make eye contact.
• You'll know it's your turn when you hear quiet.
• Right there—did you notice how someone paused and looked your way? That's your cue to start talking.
• It sounds like there are a few people trying to talk at once. Let's hear one voice, then move to another.

Research Link

In conversation, turn yielding involves a complex set of aural and visual signals. Studies examining grammatical completion and intonation have found that either a rising pitch or using low intonation at the bottom of the speaker's range are both fairly consistent cues that a speaker is signaling that they have completed their statement (Ford & Thompson, 1996; Wennerstrom & Siegel, 2003).

Strategy Review the notes you took while reading. Look for any that would invite good conversation and those that go beyond the obvious or literal facts of the text. Bring them with you and have them ready.

Lesson Language *A good conversation has a lot of back-and-forth where each speaker listens, learns something new, gets new ideas, and/or changes their mind. When you're prepared for a conversation like this, you come with interesting ideas or provocative questions that you think will spur talk, and you're ready to be genuinely interested in what others have to say by keeping an open mind. For example, if I reviewed my notes from reading* Art of Protest *(Nichols, 2021), which of these would I have ready to share? (See chart below.)*

I think the one that is most likely to start a great conversation is the one about the Ai Weiwei quote because there are so many ways to think about it. Several parts in the book relate to art and politics, so we'd have many pages to reference to spark even more discussion.

Teaching Tip Students who try to discuss very literal facts may benefit from additional comprehension strategy instruction geared at supporting inferences and interpretation. See strategies in Chapters 6 and 7 (for narrative texts) and Chapters 8, 9, and 10 (for expository texts) for more support.

Prompts

- Look over the notes you took while reading. What ideas seem conversation-worthy?
- Do you think that will invite your book club members to share different ideas?
- Look for a question you jotted that feels open-ended.
- Some might really disagree with that statement! That should provoke some good conversation.

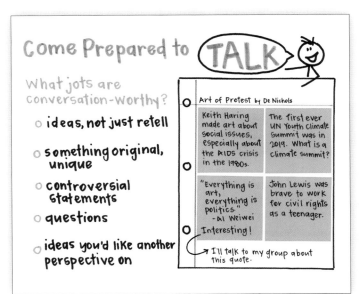

Skill

- **preparing for conversation**

Progression

Is able to stay on topic and listen. Is ready to come prepared with ideas that will lead to strong conversation, stay accountable to the book under discussion, and elaborate on ideas.

● ● ○ ○

Research Link

In a large study, researchers observed classroom talk and its relationship to the academic rigor of reading comprehension lessons (Wolf, Crosson, & Resnick, 2005). One finding was that the quality of student responses during conversation depended on the ideas and questions that began the conversation, showing that taking time to plan and prepare for conversation can yield higher quality talk.

Skills

- **preparing for conversation**
- **keeping conversation growing**

Progression

Is able to stay on topic and listen. Is ready to come prepared with ideas that will lead to strong conversation, stay accountable to the book under discussion, and elaborate on ideas.

Research Link

In a review of research on structuring group interactions, Webb (2009) cites a number of studies that found that explanation prompts support higher-level conversations by helping students construct explanations, justify answers, activate prior knowledge, and highlight the differences between everyday language and academic talk.

Strategy Take a look at your talk menu to set yourself up to work together. Decide what you'll do as you read your book. Read and then do as the menu says. When you've finished, pick a new purpose and read again.

Lesson Language *I'm going to give you a card to share that is going to be your "talk menu." Like a menu at a restaurant, you're going to choose one of the options on it for what to talk about or how your conversation can go. The first item on your menu is that you can work together to summarize to make sure you both understood the book you read. The second item is that you can talk about your ideas about what you read: what you thought was interesting, funny, surprising; what thoughts you have about the characters or theme or setting; and so on. The third item is to talk about what was confusing to you—you can use your partner to help you figure out answers to your questions. So, let's start. Take a look at your menu and let me hear you decide what one thing you'll do with your first book. Now, let me watch you read and work together.*

Teaching Tip A talk menu is a scaffold, and the goal is for students to outgrow the need for it. These menus should be tailored to each partnership (or book group) to align to what they're working on as readers. Also, just like in the best restaurants, the menu should change to give students new options for talk.

Prompts

- Which item will you choose from the menu?
- You said you wanted to ___. Go ahead and start!
- You worked together with one focus. What will you do next?
- Talk about how the menu helped your partner (or group) time work well today.

> 1-Prepare for partner time with post-its in your book.
> 2-Retell what you've read so far-your partner will rate it!
> 3-Choose from your Reading Menu

> **Act Out a Part That's:**
> -Dramatic
> -Important
> -Well-written
> Then, talk back and forth

> **Talk About Confusing Parts:**
> -Was it a **tricky word**? Use all your strategies together!
> -Did your **mental movie get blurry**? Reread it together and talk about it!

> **Share your sticky note entries!**
> -Talk long back and forth about one idea
> -Use the "Talking Map" to make a plan!

Strategy When you state an outside-the-text connection, make sure to bring the conversation back to the book you are discussing. Explain how the connection you made helps you understand this book.

Teaching Tip A reader's reactions and responses are all crucial to the meaning they construct (Rosenblatt, 1978). This strategy honors the natural outside-of-the-text connections children make based on their own prior experiences (life, other books, the world) and also keeps them connected to the text under discussion. You can offer a sentence frame such as, "This reminds me of __ and that helps me understand __ in this book."

Prompts
- Explain how that connection helps you understand this book.
- Bring the connection back to the book.
- And that helps me understand . . .
- So in this book . . .

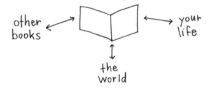

Skills
- **being accountable**
- **elaborating**
- **staying on topic**

Progression

Is able to stay on topic and listen. Is ready to come prepared with ideas that will lead to strong conversation, stay accountable to the book under discussion, and elaborate on ideas.

Research Link

In a large study of text-based discussions in middle and high schools (Alvermann et al., 1996), students acknowledged that they were thinking about many things other than the text and that words or ideas automatically triggered connections to those other thoughts. Although those real-world connections could be generative, straying too far from the topic of the conversation made it difficult to remember.

Skills

• **active listening**
• **staying on topic**
• **elaborating**

Progression

Is able to stay on topic and listen. Is ready to come prepared with ideas that will lead to strong conversation, stay accountable to the book under discussion, and elaborate on ideas.

Research Link

Working with a small group of students with learning disabilities participating in a book club, Paxton-Buursma and Walker (2008) provided students with direct instruction about how to listen for and find opportunities to link to another's idea in a discussion ("piggybacking"). After this instruction, the total number of instances of piggybacking increased, as well as the length of extended conversation.

Strategy Listen carefully for key ideas when one of your classmates is speaking (perhaps jotting notes to help you remember). Think about which of those ideas you'd like to respond to. Say, "When you said __, it made me think __."

Lesson Language *Sometimes when a friend is talking, they will elaborate on their thinking for a few sentences and it can be hard to know which of the things they said you should connect to. For example, suppose my friend said: "I think the author is trying to say that even when you spend a long time apart from someone else, there is a way you can have a relationship. I mean, the girl in the book hadn't seen her dad in a long time, but since they went out together to call crows, they found something they can do together. And also when they got the flannel shirt. And the pie. So I think there is some way they can still be together after all this time."*

After listening to my friend talk, there are a few key ideas that stand out:

- *relationships*
- *effects of time*
- *finding ways to connect*
- *symbolism of things in the story: crow call, flannel, pie.*

So when I speak up next, I can choose from a number of different ideas to connect to what my friend was talking about and stay on topic.

Prompts

- What are some key ideas from what your friend said that are staying with you?
- Think about what was important to you.
- Can you say back what you heard? Start with, "When you said . . ."
- Give your response to one of those key ideas.

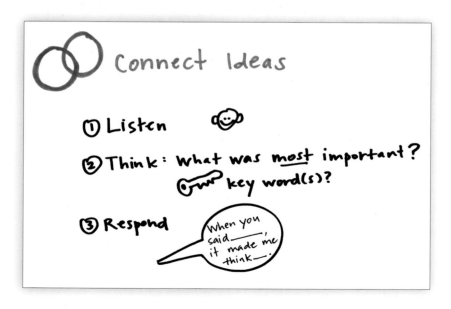

Reflect and Set Goals for a Conversation

Strategy At the end of a conversation, reflect together as a club or partnership. List what went well. Then, set goals for next time.

Teaching Tip Students new to book clubs or partner conversations will benefit from guidance about how to set up and prepare for conversation, including planning out how many pages/chapters they'll read before each meeting, how to troubleshoot if someone is unprepared or doesn't participate, how to follow the conventions for conversation you've taught, and so on. Make reflection and goal setting a routine, and support students with strategies aligned to their goals.

Prompts
- Talk about how your conversation went today. What worked?
- If you were to change one thing about your conversation today, what would it be?
- Let's name some goals you have as a group for your next conversation.
- Name an individual goal you each have for how you'll participate next time.

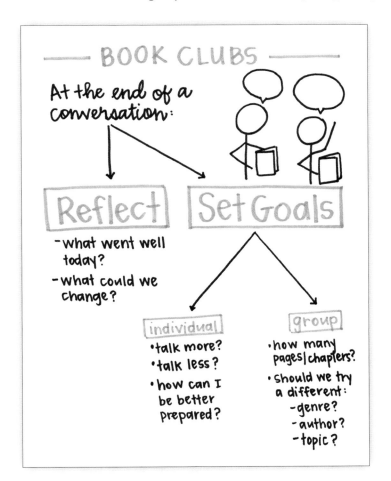

Skill

- **preparing for conversation**

Progression

Is able to stay on topic and listen. Is ready to come prepared with ideas that will lead to strong conversation, stay accountable to the book under discussion, and elaborate on ideas.

Research Link

Using the *Self-Determined Learning Model of Instruction,* Palmer and Wehmeyer (2003) found that students as young as 5 years old can be supported to set learning goals, to reflect, and to self-monitor their progress.

Strategy If the conversation in your group has stalled and no one can think of anything to say, have someone select a sentence-starter-on-a-stick. Read the phrase, then finish the sentence. Make sure what you say connects to what the person before you said.

Lesson Language *Sentence starters can prompt you to move from one thought to the next to keep the conversation moving. Some sentence starters you might use are:*

- *In addition . . .*
- *On the other hand . . .*
- *I agree with you because . . .*
- *I disagree because . . .*
- *I'd like to add on to what __ said . . .*
- *This might not be right, but maybe . . .*
- *Why do you think . . . ?*
- *What do you think about . . . ?*

I've put these sentence starters on popsicle sticks in a cup. If your conversation is stuck, try pulling a sentence starter stick and using the starting phrase to get the conversation going again.

Prompts

- Read the phrase. Finish the sentence.
- Read the sentence starter. Think about what you can say that completes the sentence.
- Think what you can say that connects to what the person before you said.
- Should you be saying something similar to what the person before you said or something different, based on that sentence starter?

Strategy Pay attention to who is talking a lot and who is not talking much. Invite a quieter voice to speak. For example, you might say: "[Name] . . . What do you think about __?"

Lesson Language *One responsibility you have as a book club member is to make sure that there is balance to the conversation. That doesn't mean that everyone needs to take the exact same number of turns talking—that would feel fake. Instead, we want to make sure that there aren't people who seem to talk a lot while others' thoughts go unspoken. Pay attention to "air time," and if you see someone who could use an invitation. Then, try to ask a specific question to draw out their thinking. You might say, "What do you think about __?" and pose a specific question, or ask, "[Name], do you have anything to share?" to leave it more open-ended.*

Teaching Tip Sometimes students can benefit from having visuals such as coins or tickets to help them "see" who is talking a lot. Each person in the group gets a predetermined number of coins (or tickets). Then, every time a student adds their "two cents," they put their coin (or ticket) in front of them. At a glance, children can see who is talking a lot (because they have many coins in front of them) and who has been quieter.

Prompts

- Pay attention to who is speaking a lot, and who isn't speaking much.
- How can you invite someone in?
- Say, "[Name], what are you thinking about this?"
- Let's take a break, think a moment. Now, who hasn't spoken in a while? Can someone invite them to speak?

Skill

- **balancing conversation**

Progression

Elaborates on own ideas and is ready to ask questions, invite in quieter speakers, and keep conversation growing—sometimes to a new topic.

Research Link

In a large survey study of university classrooms (Fritschner, 2000), researchers found that, on average in any given class, about 20% of students contributed about 80% of the comments. Interviews revealed that, within a few class sessions, students had identified classmates who were likely to participate and those who were not. As a result, specific and intentional invitations are needed to break these patterns.

Skills

- **questioning**
- **keeping conversation growing**

Progression

Elaborates on own ideas and is ready to ask questions, invite in quieter speakers, and keep conversation growing—sometimes to a new topic.

Research Link

Researchers have found that students generated the highest-quality questions when they ask "why" questions to construct a basic understanding of the topic, and "wondering" questions in a bid for making connections (Scardamalia & Bereiter, 1992).

Strategy Think about what you wonder—about the book or about another person's ideas about the book. Ask a question without an obvious answer.

Lesson Language *The questions that keep a conversation going and growing are ones that don't really have a single, straightforward answer. For example, if we are talking about* Can We Save the Tiger? *(Jenkins, 2011) and someone asks, "What's the difference between* extinct *and* endangered *animals?" we can just say, "Extinct means they are totally gone and* endangered *means they are close to being gone." Then there's not really anything else to talk about. Now, it's fine to ask a question like that to clear up some confusion, but we need a question that can't be answered quite so directly to really get us talking. So if we ask, "Do you think people are doing more harm or good to protect animal species?" then we have to think about information from across the book and apply some deep thinking to respond.*

Teaching Tip Powerful questions keep conversations going strong. You may extend this strategy to be a series of four or more lessons where you introduce different types of question stems (see chart), and the different sorts of information each one probes. The point is not for students to check off each type of question each time they talk, but rather to be aware of how their questions can keep the ideas in the conversation growing.

Prompts

- Think about what you're wondering.
- Think about what she just said. What can you ask to keep the conversation going?
- Start with "Why . . . ?" or "How . . . ?"
- That's a statement. If you were to ask a question, what would it be?

Strategy Think about the topic your group is talking about. Consider how you can respond—by adding on, agreeing, disagreeing, providing support, or asking a question. Then, say something that extends the line of your group's thinking.

Lesson Language *When we have a conversation, we're not just trying to say another thing about a topic, the goal is to extend our thinking about it—to think new things, to come to new understandings. When someone starts on a topic, that's the beginning of the line of thinking. When we add on, we want to make sure what we say helps us move toward new thinking. We listen to each new comment, then consider if we could add on, agree, disagree, offer some other evidence, or ask a really good question. The thing is, we want to keep stretching and extending our ideas until it feels like there is nothing left to say about the topic. Then we know it's time to start in on a new line of thinking.*

Teaching Tip Some children benefit from being able to see this visually. You could get Unifix cubes—commonplace math manipulatives—to use as a temporary scaffold. When someone begins to talk about a topic or "line of thinking," place a first block to represent the beginning of the vertical line. Each time someone adds a thought that extends the idea, add another cube. When the topic shifts to a completely new line of thinking, start a new line of blocks.

Prompts
- Make sure you heard what the person said.
- Think about the topic we're talking about.
- What can you add on that *extends* this line of thinking?
- Does that extend this line or is that a new topic?

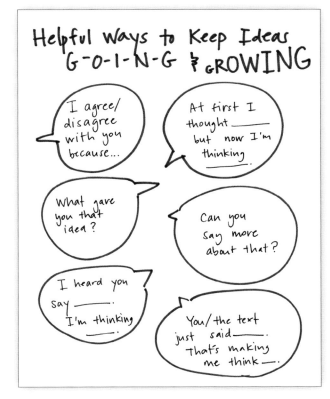

Skills
- **elaborating**
- **staying on topic**
- **being accountable**
- **keeping conversation growing**

Progression

Elaborates on own ideas and is ready to ask questions, invite in quieter speakers, and keep conversation growing—sometimes to a new topic.

Hat Tip

Comprehension Through Conversation: The Power of Purposeful Talk in the Reading Workshop (Nichols, 2006)

Research Link

Working with fourth-grade English language learners, Zwiers and Crawford (2009) noticed that the short verbal responses typical of classroom talk did not provide students the opportunity to substantively develop language or vocabulary. After a year of teaching students strategies for academic conversation that prompted them to extend, support, build on/challenge, or connect ideas contributed by previous speakers, they were successfully participating in extended conversations.

Skill

- **keeping conversation growing**

Progression

Elaborates on own ideas and is ready to ask questions, invite in quieter speakers, and keep conversation growing—sometimes to a new topic.

Research Link

Reporting work conducted in their own second- and third-grade classrooms, Jewell and Pratt (1999) explained how they were able to support their students to conduct student-led literature discussions by intentionally shifting the teacher's role from questioner to facilitator. From their observations, even these young children were able to discuss a topic to the group's satisfaction, then they were able to move on to a new idea.

Strategy It's good to stick to one topic, but when you notice you're all repeating the same idea about the topic, it's time to move on. You might begin by saying, "It seems like we're starting to repeat ourselves. Who has a new idea we can shift to?"

Lesson Language *We have to make sure we are moving the conversation forward. That means we are adding on to an idea, challenging an idea, or reconsidering something. If we aren't going deeper with the topic we're talking about, it's time to shift gears to another topic. For example, if we're talking about Mia from* Front Desk *(Yang, 2018) and someone says, "It seems like she's keeping things from her mom. She should trust her mom to help her." And someone else says, "I agree, she should talk to her mom." And then a third person says, "Yes, she should talk to her mom about her problems; her mom might be able to help her." And then a fourth person chimes in, "Yeah, I bet her mom would help her." You might notice that it sounds like we're sort of saying the same thing in different words. We need to move past that idea and into new territory—talk about another character, the role of parents, the specifics of her problem, or something else entirely.*

Prompts

- Think about if you're adding on to the idea or if you're repeating it.
- Do you feel like you have more to say about the topic?
- It seems like you're repeating ideas.
- Let's move off this topic. Who's got a new one?

Strategy If you feel like you're not totally committed to an idea but want to put it out there, try starting your statement with "I am not sure, but maybe __." It makes the risk feel less risky!

Lesson Language *Conversations often move in new directions when someone takes a risk, speaks up, and offers a new perspective on a topic. Even if it's not an idea you're fully committed to, it's still something you can share with the group to discuss, debate, and decide about. You can separate yourself a bit from the comment by using language that shows you aren't 100% behind the idea, but you think it's one worth discussing.*

Teaching Tip *Maybe* is a very powerful word when used as a tool for conversation. Teaching students that it's OK to share a *tentative* idea can bring a whole new level of complexity to their conversations.

Prompts
- What do you want to say that you're uncertain about?
- You can just put it out there with, "Maybe . . ."
- If you're not sure, you can get your friends' thoughts about the idea.
- Be brave! Share what you're thinking.

Skills
- **elaborating**
- **thinking flexibly**
- **questioning**

Progression

Has developed good conversational skills and stamina and is ready to take risks, debate, and think flexibly when encountering new opinions, ideas, and/or information.

Research Link

Power dynamics—race, class, gender, social status, and other identities—are always at play when people are in groups and may interfere with productive conversations. Supporting students to get to know one another, using visual cues to encourage equal talk time, and practice in giving compliments are just a few ways to develop a classroom community where students are willing to share emergent ideas and take risks (Clarke & Holwadel, 2007).

Skills

- **thinking flexibly**
- **questioning**
- **being accountable**

Progression

Has developed good conversational skills and stamina and is ready to take risks, debate, and think flexibly when encountering new opinions, ideas, and/or information.

Research Link

Even when presented with, and citing, the same evidence, readers may come to different conclusions based upon personal interpretations of ambiguous information (Aukerman & Schuldt, 2016). With multiple meanings possible, it is also possible for any given reader to abandon a previously held position in favor of a different interpretation.

Strategy When you hear an idea that is very different from a thought you had, ask your group, "Can we pause to consider this?" Think together, "What evidence is there from the text to support that idea?" Decide if you want to agree with this new perspective or challenge it.

Lesson Language *When we were talking about* After the Fall *(Santat, 2017), you all shared some differing opinions about Humpty. A few of you agreed that Humpty's fear of falling again kept him from doing the things he loved and that he should do more to overcome his worries. Others thought that his fears were completely justified. He'd had a terrible accident, and he should take the time he needed to get back to doing what he used to do. Let's take one of those ideas and, even if it's one that feels very different from what you believe, try it on for size. I'm going to reread and challenge you to see if there is any evidence you can pull that would support the idea—even if it's not an idea you originally thought up.*

Prompts

- Think about how what you just heard goes with your idea(s) and/or the book.
- Say, "One place in the book that goes with that idea is . . ."
- Say, "That idea is similar to mine because . . ."
- Say, "What do you mean by that?"

Strategy Notice when you disagree during a conversation and begin a challenge. Ask a question or make a statement to get the speaker to say more about their idea and/or to defend their thinking and/or defend something from the book.

Lesson Language *When someone you're in conversation with makes a statement you disagree with, you can challenge them to explain why they think what they do or how they came to that idea or ask them to share evidence from the text that supports their thinking. You can frame your challenge as a request, "Please provide some evidence from the text that supports your thinking," or a question, "Can you explain your thinking, please?" After you challenge, listen carefully to the response. Sometimes, you'll find that after more explanation, you actually understand their logic and agree. Other times, when you challenge them to say more, their explanation will come up short and they will come to agree with your idea. Remember that as you challenge, your focus is on the* idea *not the* person *who had the idea.*

Prompts
- What in their statement do you disagree with?
- Say, "I disagree because . . . "
- Ask them to defend their thinking. Say, "What makes you say that?"
- Say, "What part of the text helped you come up with that idea?"

Skills
- **questioning**
- **being accountable**
- **debating**
- **thinking flexibly**

Progression

Has developed good conversational skills and stamina and is ready to take risks, debate, and think flexibly when encountering new opinions, ideas, and/or information.

Research Link

The back-and-forth of trying to convince peers about a position, even if it is not their own, is mentally stimulating and an exciting shift from the ways reading is usually talked about in school (Clark et al., 2003). In a review of research on *constructive controversy* (Johnson, Johnson, & Tjosvold, 2014), the authors contend that disagreement can be productive in a structured situation where participants are supported to think more deeply about their own positions and to consider additional evidence on both sides of an issue.

Skills

- **thinking flexibly**
- **keeping conversation growing**
- **debating**

Progression

Has developed good conversational skills and stamina and is ready to take risks, debate, and think flexibly when encountering new opinions, ideas, and/or information.

Research Link

Collaborative Reasoning (CR) is a literature-based discussion format that includes discussing an issue with multiple perspectives or positions, leveraging both textual and personal evidence, and focusing on students' reasoning in how they arrived at positions rather than the position itself. Observations of upper elementary classrooms engaged in CR revealed that some students took longer than others to become comfortable with changing positions (Waggoner et al., 1995).

Strategy Listen to understand an idea a speaker in your group shared. Think, "What's another (perhaps *opposite*) way of looking at that?" Propose an alternate viewpoint, whether or not you believe it yet, to explore it in conversation. You can start with, "Well, on the other hand, we could think about . . ."

Lesson Language *Sometimes, when we give ourselves the space to explore different ideas and different perspectives, we can come to new understandings. You might try sharing a completely opposite idea—whether you believe it or not—and discuss it with your group. Let's practice. After reading* Climate Change and How We'll Fix It *(Harman, 2020), let's say someone in your book club said, "Companies shouldn't be forced to change how they operate because it's going to end up costing consumers a lot more." Think, "What's an opposite way of looking at this?" Someone might share, "Well, on the other hand, maybe the goods and materials will cost a bit more, but not taking action impacts our health, which has its own costs." Then, you could explore each of those ideas to see which has more support from the text.*

Teaching Tip This strategy must be used with sensitivity to challenge ideas, not individuals, and never to debate anyone's lived experiences.

Prompts

- Can you think of an *opposite* to that opinion?
- Say, "On the other hand . . ."
- You don't necessarily have to believe it, just share a totally different idea.
- Yes, you're just exploring this other viewpoint. You may end up seeing things a new way, or you may further prove your original idea.

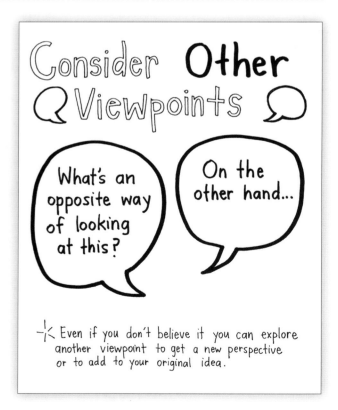

Strategy Identify two opposing ideas (about a character, a main idea, a theme or idea, and so on). Split up into two groups, each taking one of the opposing ideas. Look for proof, decide on explanations, and practice what you'll say. Get together with the other side to debate!

Teaching Tip You can decide how structured (or not) to make the debates. In most cases, having children simply prepare arguments and evidence for "their side" and getting together with peers on the "opposing side" will lead to an interesting back-and-forth conversation, without any added structure. Alternatively, you could choose to introduce a more formal debate protocol that follows a predictable structure, such as beginning with timed opening statements, proceeding with timed rebuttals from each side, and ending with timed closing remarks. These more structured debates are typically regulated for fairness because they are judged, and they include a moderator and audience.

Prompts
- Clarify what the two opposing ideas are.
- Start with, "On the other hand . . ."
- Consider what evidence you have that backs up your side of the debate.
- How can you refute what the "other side" has said?

Bring on the Debate!

Find 2 opposing ideas.
(about a character, theme, or idea)
Split into groups and discuss.
☀ Find evidence to support your idea.
☀ How can you refute the other position?

Skills
- **being accountable**
- **debating**
- **preparing for conversation**

Progression

Has developed good conversational skills and stamina and is ready to take risks, debate, and think flexibly when encountering new opinions, ideas, and/or information.

●●●●

Research Link

A meta-analysis looking at structured classroom debates found large effect sizes for cognitive reasoning, social support, and attitudes toward the task (Johnson & Johnson, 2007).

Goal 13

Writing About Reading

◎ Why is this goal important?

Whether a reader is taking notes to revisit, review, and remember what they have read, or to explore ideas, writing about reading can be a great support for student comprehension (Graham & Harris, 2017). Students may also use writing as a tool to prepare for conversation with peers or with their teacher (see Chapter 12).

However, writing well about reading isn't a simple goal. It begins with teaching students that their thinking about books matters enough to write it down, then incorporates both the thinking readers do as they read and the ability to write so they both capture and further that thinking (e.g., Graham & Hebert, 2011; Wilson, 1989).

Some students who are working to write better about their reading may need a comprehension goal as well. That is, not only do they need to practice writing, but they'll also need to know what it is they are writing about. You could easily use most of the strategies in Chapters 5 through 11 to help students monitor their comprehension, explore deeper thinking, *and* write well about their reading. For example, a reader could "see more than one side" (Strategy 6.14) and create a T-chart in their reading notebook to keep track of the different traits and feelings they infer about the character; "ask questions and form ideas" (Strategy 8.7) and jot those questions and ideas in the margins of an article; or notice figurative language, "picture it" (Strategy 11.23), and then sketch what they visualize in a notebook.

As useful as writing about reading can be, there are also some caveats. First, it's generally not that helpful for very young readers (those in kindergarten and early in first grade) to focus time, energy, and attention to writing about simple books. We also need to be careful that the writing we suggest students try doesn't overtake the aesthetic experience of joyful, engaged reading (Ivey & Johnston, 2013; Rosenblatt, 1978). One way to balance this is to ask students to reflect on the impact writing has on their comprehension and their reading experience, then allow them to make choices about when and how they write about reading. Some will embrace it and write a lot, and others will find that writing helps in certain circumstances but isn't something they want to do all the time.

Note that the focus of the strategies in this chapter are on annotating, note taking, writing to think, and organizing short jots, rather than longer, more structured forms of writing about reading (such as literary essays or book reviews). To learn about more formal types of writing about reading, students will benefit from explicit teaching about the genre, strategies for how to write well in the genre, as well as time to work through a writing process (if you have *The Writing Strategies Book* [Serravallo, 2017] you will find plenty of strategies to teach children how to write well in those genres).

Skills a reader might work on as part of this goal

Note taking
Recording information (on sticky notes, in a notebook, and so on) from the text that you want to remember.

Annotating
Marking key spots in a text with original thinking.

Elaborating
Starting with information, or an inference, from the text and adding on additional thinking to develop an idea or come to new understandings.

Determining importance
Marking or flagging spots worth returning to for rereading or conversation, deciding which parts of the text are most worth writing about.

Organizing and categorizing notes
Finding patterns, similarities, connections, and so on in a collection of notes.

◎ How do I know if this goal is right for my student?

To choose from the strategies in this chapter, take a look at a variety of your students' work—the short jots they write in the margins of articles they read or the sticky notes stuck inside their books, as well as the longer, informal responses to reading they may keep in a reading notebook or journal. If a student isn't jotting at all, or is writing too much in margins (indicating they aren't determining what's most important to jot or aren't jotting with a focus or purpose in mind), take a look at Strategies 13.1–13.5. If the majority of what children write is for the purpose of recording literal information, and you want to teach them to use writing as a tool to think, take a look at Strategies 13.6–13.12.

What Texts Might Students Use When Practicing Strategies from This Chapter?

The strategies in this chapter can be used when students are reading any type of text, in any genre or format.

◎ How do I support students as they write about their reading?

After evaluating samples of your students' writing about reading (annotations, notes, reading responses), select strategies that you can model, that they can practice with you, and that they can use independently to increase their skills.

Although development is rarely perfectly linear, skill progressions can help us pinpoint where a student is now and what might come next. Use the if-then chart on page 417 to evaluate your students' reading and find strategies that will support their growth.

A Progression of Skills: *Writing About Reading*

If a student . . .

Needs support to begin recording important information from the text and/or ideas they have about the text while reading.

Is recording some information or inferences while reading and is ready to use writing as a tool to deepen or expand thinking.

Then you might teach . . .

13.1	Hold On to a Thought with a Symbol
13.2	Take Notes to Remember Text Details
13.3	Consider If an Idea Is Worth Writing Down
13.4	Take Notes Based on Structure
13.5	Pair the Text with Your Thinking

13.6	Organize Your Jots
13.7	Lift a Line and Freewrite
13.8	Draw a Web to Find Relationships
13.9	Extend Your Thinking
13.10	Prompt Your Thinking with Transitions
13.11	Write, Talk, Write
13.12	Write More by Breaking Down a Big Idea

Strategy When you find yourself reacting to something in a text, but don't want to take long to stop and jot, mark the spot with a symbol, then keep reading. Later, when you want to revisit your thinking, you can look at the symbol to remember.

Teaching Tip This strategy is an age-appropriate way to teach young readers to plan for conversation or reading time with a partner. It takes just a moment to quickly jot a symbol on a sticky note. I have seen some kindergarten teachers use a variation of this strategy by making sticky notes with symbols ahead of time, or paper bookmarks with different symbols, and giving them out to children to place in their books (some get nervous with writing implements out at the same time as books—understandably!). For older readers, this strategy might be a way for them to remember a spot where they had a thought or reaction, but where they don't want to stop to write a few sentences. They can quickly flag the spot with a symbol and return to it later at the end of reading time. This will help them maintain their engaged reading state.

Prompts
• What are you thinking here?
• What symbol could you use? Check the chart.
• Jot a quick symbol and keep going.
• Let's go back to your jots. Use them to explain what you're thinking.

Skills
• **determining importance**
• **annotating**

Progression

Needs support to begin recording important information from the text and/ or ideas they have about the text while reading.

Research Link

A number of scholars suggest students use symbols as a shorthand when annotating texts. Porter-O'Donnell (2004) recommends a simple set of circles, boxes, and wavy lines to quickly mark characters, settings, and vocabulary. Diaz (2014) advocates for a more elaborate system of eleven meaning-based symbols, including check marks, arrows, and stars, to quickly code a text for further analysis during rereadings.

Skills

- determining importance
- note taking

Progression

Needs support to begin recording important information from the text and/ or ideas they have about the text while reading.

Research Link

According to cognitive psychology, note taking involves some comprehension of the source material, as well as metacognitive decision making about what to include and how to record the selected information. In a study with fourth graders (Hebert et al., 2014), students who took notes showed greater gains on an inferencing measure than their peers who did not write about the text.

Strategy When you come to a detail in the text that you want to remember, either to think more about or to share with others, pause and take notes.

Lesson Language *Writing can help you hold on to important details that you may want to return to later to help you review or remember or share. What's worth taking notes on might change depending on your purpose—perhaps you're reading an informational text with a specific research question in mind. In that case, information that helps you answer your question is important to note. Perhaps you're reading a novel and working on remembering the key events to be able to summarize it with your book club. In that case, you'll need to note key moments in the story that connect to the main problem or conflict. You can keep a bulleted list of these bits of information or moments, organize your notes into charts or tables, or use sticky notes for short jots that can stay next to the spot in the text where you stopped to write.*

Teaching Tip Keep in mind that, although this strategy can support students with note taking when their goal is to research and record what they've read for a purpose—either to write or talk about a topic—not all reading of informational texts should be connected to writing and/or research. Children should have plenty of opportunities to read whole, continuous texts and apply comprehension strategies without using writing to record their learning and sometimes purely for the joy of reading!

Prompts

- After reading that section, does anything stand out as important?
- What do you think you can jot that will help you hold on to what you read?
- Tell me what you'll write after that part.
- I noticed you thought about what would help you when you stopped to jot.

Strategy When you realize you have a thought while reading, stop and think, "Will writing this thought down help me? Do I need to hold on to this thought to share with my partner/club? Do I need to write it down to share with my teacher? Do I need to jot to help myself remember my ideas?" If yes, quickly jot (on a sticky note next to where you got the idea or in your notebook with a page number reference), and keep reading.

Teaching Tip When readers use sticky notes in books they've borrowed, they can capture their thinking right alongside the text that sparked it, and this has a number of benefits. For one, when you confer with the student you can easily see their thinking, reference their evidence, and assess their comprehension. Second, when students share their ideas in conversation, they can easily reference the text, too. When children return their books, they may need support with organizing the notes they've collected. See Strategy 13.4 for more.

Prompts

- Pause and think: "Will I need to hold on to this thought to share it later?"
- Jot quickly so you can get back to reading.
- Is it a thought you want to hold on to? If so, jot it quickly.
- Tell me why you jotted: to share with a friend or a teacher or to keep a record of your thinking for yourself?

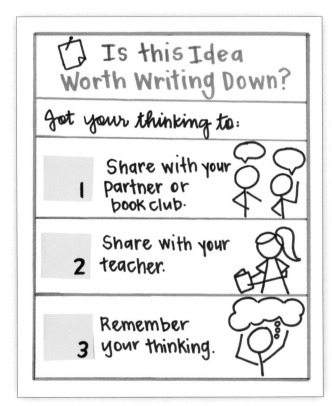

Skills

- **determining importance**
- **annotating**
- **note taking**

Progression

Needs support to begin recording important information from the text and/or ideas they have about the text while reading.

Research Link

Making informed decisions about what information to write down during note taking is critical, as the lag in time between writing and reading may result in comprehension breakdown. As a result, successful note taking involves coordinating the attention and working memory demands of both reading and writing (Baddeley, 2000; Piolat, Olive, & Kellogg, 2005).

Take Notes Based on Structure

Skills

- **determining importance**
- **note taking**

Progression

Needs support to begin recording important information from the text and/or ideas they have about the text while reading.

● ○

Research Link

In a study with seventh graders reading social studies texts (Reynolds & Perin, 2009), one group of students received additional instruction in text structure and were provided with a text structure graphic organizer for taking notes. Compared with the control group, students who received the text structure intervention showed gains in measures of identifying main ideas, writing quality, and content knowledge.

Strategy After reading a section, ask yourself, "How is the text organized or structured?" Think about how you might record notes to capture that structure. Reread or skim as necessary to complete your notes.

Teaching Tip Notes that show how information, ideas, or plot events are related (something inherent in the text's structure) are more helpful than random notes. Before students will be able to use this strategy, they will need to have learned about different text structures (see, for example, Strategy 5.16 or 5.25 for story, and Strategies 8.13–8.17 for informational texts).

Prompts

- How do you think you'll take notes?
- Think about the structure of the text.
- How do you know what the text structure is?
- Now that you know the structure and how you'll take notes, reread.

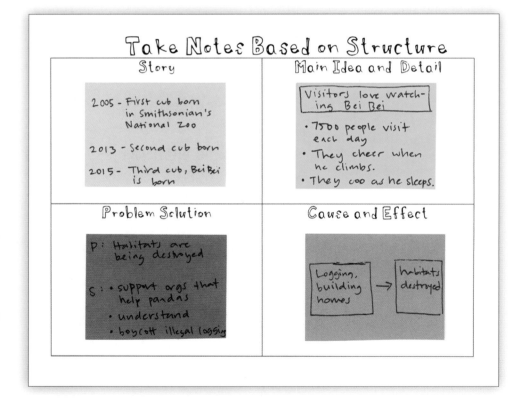

Strategy Create a two-column T-chart on a page in your notebook. On the left side, stop and jot an important idea or event from the text. On the right side, write what you think about it.

Lesson Language *It can help to distinguish between what's in the text* (point to the book) *and ideas from your mind* (point to forehead). *When you keep a double-entry journal, you're capturing both, side by side, to review your own thinking, to share ideas with a peer or with me, and to have the textual evidence that helped you come up with the idea right there. Let's try a few entries in our shared class reading notebook using the book* Where the Mountain Meets the Moon *(Lin, 2009). One important event is in the beginning, when Minli decides to leave her family. So on the left, we can write down what happened, paraphrasing the event described in the text. On the right, we can jot an idea about that detail. I'll do this one for you. "I can't believe she's so brave at such a young age. Or maybe she's foolish!" Notice that nowhere in the text does it say that exactly; those are my own thoughts. OK, your turn. What's the next event that we should jot about on the left, and what ideas do you have? Turn and talk to your partner.*

Prompts

- What do you want to jot about from the text?
- That's from the text. Jot it on the left.
- What made you write that down? What's your response?
- What are your thoughts about that? Jot it on the right.

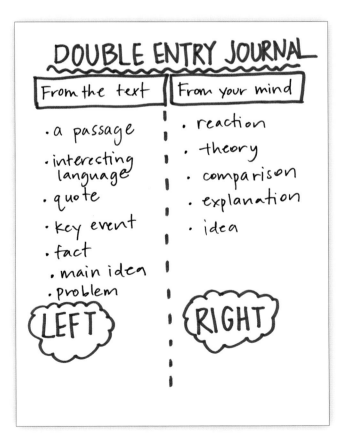

Skills

- **determining importance**
- **note taking**
- **elaborating**

Progression

Needs support to begin recording important information from the text and/ or ideas they have about the text while reading.

Research Link

In a study with engineering students enrolled in writing and humanities courses, the instructors assigned two-column notes as a way to encourage STEM-minded college students to think more critically about their reading (Ives, Mitchell, & Hübl, 2020). The majority of students reported that they found the note-taking strategy useful, and an analysis of their notes revealed that participants did indeed read more critically when using the two-column format.

Skills

- **determining importance**
- **organizing and categorizing notes**

Progression

Is recording some information or inferences while reading and is ready to use writing as a tool to deepen or expand thinking.

● ●

Research Link

According to Mayer (1996), the three cognitive processes that result in meaningful learning from texts include: *Selecting* relevant information, *Organizing* that information into meaningful categories, and *Integrating* that knowledge with existing knowledge (SOI), and the most effective method of implementing the SOI Model is within authentic academic tasks, such as sorting and organizing notes.

Strategy Reread your sticky notes, considering which are worth keeping. Think about how they can be organized or categorized to be filed away or how you might use them to do further thinking. Be sure to jot the book title as a heading on the page for reference.

Lesson Language *I just finished* Nano *(Wade, 2021) and have a stack of sticky notes. Can you help me figure out how to organize them to keep them in my notebook? My notes say:*

- *It's amazing that so many different materials are all made up of the same thing—atoms.*
- *Since atoms are so small, I wonder how scientists first discovered them.*
- *How do scientists change* graphite *to* graphene*?*
- *Nanomaterials are amazing and seem futuristic! I can't believe they're real.*
- *The super-sieve sounds really important to making sure people always have clean water.*

I could organize them by topic—the ones that have to do with atoms *together, the ones that have to do with* nanomaterials *together. Or I could put questions together and ideas together. Maybe I could put the ones I want to share with my partner in one stack, and the ones I just want to remember in another. Do you see all the options? What I decide really depends on what I want to do with the sticky notes later.*

Teaching Tip Digital tools may serve as an alternative, or a supplement, to physical sticky notes. Note-taking apps not only allow for notes to be rearranged and categorized, they also support multimedia information, such as links, embedded photos/audio/videos, or digital drawings, in addition to words.

Prompts

- Reread what you've jotted down. Discard any that don't feel worth keeping.
- What categories do you see?
- How do you plan to use what's on the sticky notes?

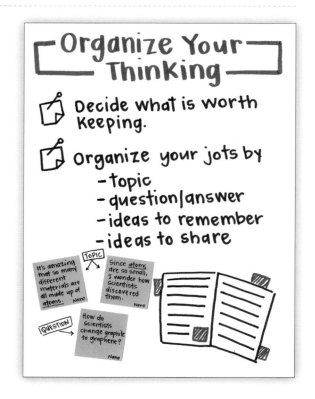

Strategy Find a powerful line from the text you're reading. Copy the line into your notebook and write your thoughts, comments, and reactions that spring from that line. Try not to censor your thinking; write fast and without a filter.

Lesson Language *Authors sometimes have this way of capturing so much in just a few words. These lines—you know them when you come across them—just tug at your heart or say something in such a unique way that it makes you pause, reread, and think. When I write about these one-liners, I sometimes find deeper ideas that help me better understand the story—or life! Take this one, for instance, from* Islandborn *(Díaz, 2018). Toward the end of the book, Lola says, "[E]ven if I'd never set foot on the Island it doesn't matter: The Island is me." When I first read that, I paused and thought about it: it's true. The places we live, the places we're from, they become a part of us. So I jotted that line down, just as it's written in the book, and then wrote my starting thought, which then brought me to writing about the places I've lived and how part of who I am is from those places. That one starting line from the book ended up sparking a whole page of thinking.*

Prompts
- Find a line that stuck with you.
- Start writing your thoughts.
- Try to keep going, write more. Try a prompt like, "In addition . . ." or "On the other hand . . ." or "For example . . ." or "This makes me think . . ."
- Is there a line you find is beautifully crafted, profound, or that caused an emotional reaction?

Red white and whole
by Rajani LaRocca

Page 4. "So I'm caught between the life I want to lead and the one she thinks I should"

I know exactly what Reha means, I want to live my own life, not the life my Mom says. My Mom is always telling me what to do = Brush your teeth, clean your room, pick up your clothes, put down that phone and pick up a book.
I know she loves me and all, but she has her own life. It's not like I'm being bad.

Page 77. "You live in only one world and that is the world in which we love you"

Wow! Her parents actually told her that. Reha feels like she lives in two worlds, but her parents don't want that for her. They just want her to feel loved. Maybe they don't realize the pressure they put on her, or maybe this is their way of letting that go and focusing just on the the love. This makes me think that when my Mom says she me that maybe it means more than just saying "I love you," like she wants me to know that deep down inside she does really really see me and understands.

Skills
- **determining importance**
- **elaborating**

Progression
Is recording some information or inferences while reading and is ready to use writing as a tool to deepen or expand thinking.

Research Link
During a long-term observation of eleventh-grade English instruction, Wilson (1989) reported on one teacher's extensive use of reading journals where students wrote about novels in flexible, informal, and passionate ways. Without the pressure of judgment or an audience, students admitted to confusion, asked themselves questions, and made their own connections and surprising discoveries.

Skills
- **organizing and categorizing notes**
- **elaborating**

Progression

Is recording some information or inferences while reading and is ready to use writing as a tool to deepen or expand thinking.

Research Link

In a review of visualization formats, Eppler (2006) compared concept maps, mind maps, conceptual diagrams, and visual metaphors for displaying relationships between and among pieces of information. Each format has its own strengths, with a combination of techniques most effective for facilitating recall and understanding. Organizing the information and thinking about the ways the bits of information are related is important intellectual work.

Strategy Take a few jots (with character names, ideas, or information) and spread them out on a notebook page. Draw arrows or lines between them. Along those lines, write about how each jot is connected or what new ideas you have from looking for a connection.

Lesson Language *A web is a tool you can use to help you see connections. When you find connections, you can write about them to deepen your thinking and come to new ideas. If you're reading a story, you might put the names of the characters on your page and draw lines between them. Think: "How does one character affect another? In what ways are the characters connected? What's their relationship?" Or, you might be reading a book about science and have three jots with information. You can take those sticky notes, spread them out on your page, and draw lines between them. Does something* cause *something else to happen? Are they different ways of looking at the same topic? Is there something two jots have in common? Writing between and across these topics and ideas grows and deepens your thinking in ways that might surprise you!*

Prompts

- What's the relationship between these two pieces of information?
- Think about how one of these impacts the other.
- Look across these two—what's the same and what's different?
- Write what you're thinking on the line.

---

freedom summer (Deborah Wiles)

The narrator seems to really admire John Henry

It's interesting to notice how the adults in this book react to the friendship btwn John Henry + the narrator. So many seemed shocked, surprised, worried. I think adults need to learn from the kids!

I wonder, how does someone learn respect in an environment of disrespect?

It takes a lot of guts, a lot of courage, to go against the grain. I wonder if the narrator realizes what a trend-setter he is.

I think the spongy tar their feet get stuck in is a symbol.

Seems like so much of this time period is dark, sticky, tar-like. The narrator + John Henry, though, are like the crystal-clear water of the swimming hole.

13.9 *Extend Your Thinking*

Strategy Take a sticky note with a thought that you previously jotted. Place it on the corner of your page. Think: "What else can I say about this? How can I explain my thinking? How can I add on, perhaps moving to a new idea?"

Lesson Language *We hold on to our ideas as we read by stopping and jotting quickly on a sticky note, but we know that these in-the-moment thoughts are just the beginning. We can return to our ideas and use writing to think more about them to see if they grow into something bigger and deeper. For example, I have an idea on a sticky note from* Front Desk *(Yang, 2018) that says, "Mia should tell the truth about how she's feeling." I already know I have more to say: "She should talk to her parents" and "Being honest is better than hiding or stuffing your feelings." But here's what's exciting: many times, as I freewrite and have a sort of conversation with myself on the page, I find that the act of writing itself will cause me to put something unexpected on the page. I actually surprise myself with new thinking, and I grow and deepen my thinking because I'm writing.*

Prompts

- What's your starting idea? Now start writing more.
- Don't let your pencil stop moving.
- Don't worry about perfection. Write freely to get your ideas down and see where they take you.
- Keep exploring the idea and see if you come to some new thinking.

Skill
- elaborating

Progression

Is recording some information or inferences while reading and is ready to use writing as a tool to deepen or expand thinking.

● ●

Research Link

In schooling, writing is often described as writing *about* something—merely an act of recording something that is already out there in the world. However, a number of scholars (e.g., Menary, 2007) describe writing as "thinking in action"; the cognitive work happens *during* the act of composing.

Skill
- **elaborating**

Progression

Is recording some information or inferences while reading and is ready to use writing as a tool to deepen or expand thinking.

Research Link

Although any writer who is stuck may benefit from using transition words to help extend their writing, English language learners may particularly benefit from this type of support. Sentence stems, sentence frames, and other sorts of formulaic sequences are often effective in supporting ELLs to not only use the supplied phrase, but to incorporate previously learned phrases (AlHassan & Wood, 2015).

Strategy When you're writing but get stuck, choose a transition word or phrase to keep going. Reference the chart for help if you can't think of one on your own.

Teaching Tip On the one hand, words like those in the chart make us think of very formal writing because we're used to seeing them in polished essays and arguments. On the other hand, when you look at them just as isolated phrases, they seem sort of empty and not very meaningful. But these functional words and phrases are key transitions and they signify important relationships *between* ideas. When students use them to prompt their thinking, the transitions can help them organize their thinking or even lead them to ideas they wouldn't otherwise have had. This strategy is to help students elaborate beyond a first in-the-moment idea and do some longer-form writing to explore their thinking. Younger readers may write just a couple of sentences, and older readers may fill pages and pages in their notebooks. Adapt the language in the strategy and the sorts of transition words and phrases you introduce to the age and ability level of the readers you're teaching.

Prompts
- See how that sentence starter got you thinking further, beyond your first thought?
- This prompt gets you thinking about ___. Try it and see if it pushes you forward.
- Which prompt do you want to try next?

Purpose/Meaning	Examples	Purpose/Meaning	Examples
Agreement Similarity	not only . . . but also in addition first, second, third equally important and also as well as	Examples Support	in other words another thing to realize including surely especially· surprisingly in fact
Opposition Contradiction	in contrast despite/in spite of even so/though then again but and yet/still besides although	Effect Consequence	as a result in that case then therefore
		Conclusion Summary Restatement	generally speaking after all in summary in conclusion to sum it up
Cause Purpose	with this in mind in order to if-then whenever because of given that	Time Sequence	to begin with after later eventually meanwhile until now

Strategy Start with an idea. Write more to elaborate on your thinking. Then, get together with your book club, partnership, or the class to discuss your thinking. After discussing, come back to your notebook and write about your new thinking. In particular, think about how your ideas have changed or shifted or how you've gotten a new perspective because of the conversation.

Prompts

- Now that you have some initial thoughts down, meet with your friends to discuss.
- What did you think before, and what are you thinking now?
- You can say, "Before, I thought . . . but after talking I'm thinking . . ."
- Think about ideas your partner or club members shared. What's new from what you had written down before?

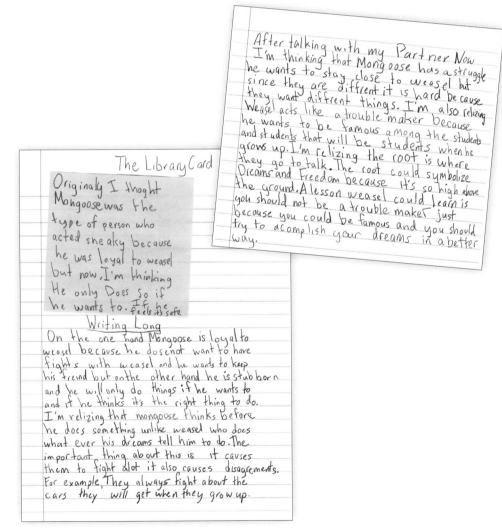

Skill

- elaborating

Progression

Is recording some information or inferences while reading and is ready to use writing as a tool to deepen or expand thinking.

Hat Tip

Talk About Understanding: Rethinking Classroom Talk to Enhance Comprehension (Keene, 2012)

Research Link

In an observation study in a lower elementary classroom, Barone (2013) discovered that responses to a single book over time moved from literal to inferential and that responses to key scenes were highly varied and personal.

Write More by Breaking Down a Big Idea

Skills

- **elaborating**
- **determining importance**

Progression

Is recording some information or inferences while reading and is ready to use writing as a tool to deepen or expand thinking.

Research Link

Using higher-order thinking in written responses is not just for older students. Peterson and Taylor (2012) provide examples from second- and third-grade classrooms where students write about theme, character interpretations, and text-to-self connections, which led to deeper thinking about texts and improved conversation.

Strategy Choose a big idea you had that represents thinking across the text and that you feel is worthy of exploring. Think: "How could I break this big idea down into parts, kinds, or reasons?" Make a list. Write for a while about one, then choose another, then choose another.

Lesson Language *When you have a big idea you want to think more about, it's helpful to break it down. You can make a list to plan what you'll then explore with writing. For example, if you were to write about an idea you had about a character that you developed across a book, you could think about it in time parts: what the character was like at the beginning, middle, and end of the story. If you wanted to write about a theme such as "good versus evil," you might list some ways that good and evil show up in the story. In an expository text, you might list out reasons that support a main idea. A list is a great tool to help you elaborate, to say more. When you move from one item to another, you will inevitably draw on examples and details from different points in the text and can explore them to develop new thinking.*

Prompts

- Start with your big idea—what are you writing about?
- What parts, kinds, or reasons will you explore?
- You wrote about one part, so now it's time for the next—what will this paragraph be mostly about?
- Which details from the text go with that part/kind/reason?

Contents

Research References

Adams, M. J. (1990). *Beginning to read: Thinking and learning about print*. MIT Press.

Adams, M., & Bruce, B. (1982). Background knowledge and reading comprehension. In J. A. Langer & M. T. Smith-Burke (Eds.), *Reader meets author/Bridging the gap: A psycholinguistic and sociolinguistic perspective* (pp. 2–25). International Reading Association.

Afflerbach, P. P. (1990). The influence of prior knowledge on expert readers' main idea construction strategies. *Reading Research Quarterly*, *25*(1), 31–46.

Afflerbach, P., Pearson, P. D., & Paris, S. G. (2008). Clarifying differences between reading skills and reading strategies. *The Reading Teacher*, *61*(5), 364–373.

Alexander, P. A., Graham, S., & Harris, K. (1998). A perspective on strategy research: Progress and prospects. *Educational Psychology Review*, *10*(2), 129–154.

Algozzine, B., & Douville, P. (2004). Use mental imagery across the curriculum. *Preventing School Failure: Alternative Education for Children and Youth*, *49*(1), 36–39.

AlHassan, L., & Wood, D. (2015). The effectiveness of focused instruction of formulaic sequences in augmenting L2 learners' academic writing skills: A quantitative research study. *Journal of English for Academic Purposes*, *17*, 51–62.

Allen, K. D., & Hancock, T. E. (2008). Reading comprehension improvement with individualized cognitive profiles and metacognition. *Literacy Research and Instruction*, *47*(2), 124–139.

Allington, R. L. (2014). How reading volume affects both reading fluency and reading achievement. *International Electronic Journal of Elementary Education*, *7*(1), 13–26.

Allington, R. L., & McGill-Franzen, A. M. (2021). Reading volume and reading achievement: A review of recent research. *Reading Research Quarterly*, *56*(S1), S231–S238.

Alvermann, D. E., Smith, L. C., & Readence, J. E. (1985). Prior knowledge activation and the comprehension of compatible and incompatible text. *Reading Research Quarterly*, *20*(4), 420–436.

Alvermann, D. E., Young, J. P., Weaver, D., Hinchman, K. A., Moore, D. W., Phelps, S. F., Thrash, E. C., & Zalewski, P. (1996). Middle and high school students' perceptions of how they experience text-based discussions: A multicase study. *Reading Research Quarterly*, *31*(3), 244–267.

Anderson, G., Higgins, D., & Wurster, S. R. (1985). Differences in the free-reading books selected by high, average, and low achievers. *The Reading Teacher*, *39*(3), 326–330.

Anderson, N. L., & Kaye, E. L. (2017). Finding versus fixing: Self-monitoring for readers who struggle. *The Reading Teacher*, *70*(5), 543–550.

Anderson, R. C., Wilson, P. T., & Fielding, L. G. (1988). Growth in reading and how children spend their time outside of school. *Reading Research Quarterly*, *23*(3), 285–303.

Anderson, T. H., & Armbruster, B. A. (1984). Content area textbooks. In R. C. Anderson, J. Osborn, & R. J. Tierney (Eds.), *Learning to read in American schools* (pp. 193–226). Erlbaum.

Applebee, A. N., Langer, J. A., & Mullis, I. V. S. (1987). *Learning to be literate in America: Reading, writing, and reasoning*. National Assessment of Educational Progress, Educational Testing Service.

Applegate, M. D., Applegate, A. J., & Modla, V. B. (2009). "She's my best reader; she just can't comprehend": Studying the relationship between fluency and comprehension. *The Reading Teacher*, *62*(6), 512–521.

Archer, A. L., Gleason, M. M., & Vachon, V. L. (2003). Decoding and fluency: Foundation skills for struggling older readers. *Learning Disability Quarterly*, *26*(2), 89–101.

Ardoin, S. P., Morena, L. S., Binder, K. S., & Foster, T. E. (2013). Examining the impact of feedback and repeated readings on oral reading fluency: Let's not forget prosody. *School Psychology Quarterly*, *28*(4), 391–404.

Arizpe, E. (2013). Meaning-making from wordless (or nearly wordless) picturebooks: What educational research expects and what readers have to say. *Cambridge Journal of Education*, *43*(2), 163–176.

Arizpe, E., & Styles, M. (2016). *Children reading picturebooks: Interpreting visual texts* (2nd ed.). Routledge.

Armbruster, B. B. (1984). The problem of "inconsiderate text." In G. G. Duffy, L. R. Roehler, & J. Mason (Eds.), *Comprehension instruction: Perspectives and suggestions* (pp. 202-217). Longman.

Armbruster, B. B., & Armstrong, J. O. (1993). Locating information in text: A focus on children in the elementary grades. *Contemporary Educational Psychology, 18*(2), 139-161.

Armbruster, B. B., Anderson, T. H., & Ostertag, J. (1987). Does text structure/summarization instruction facilitate learning from expository text? *Reading Research Quarterly, 22*(3), 331-346.

Arzubiaga, A., Rueda, R., & Monzó, L. (2002). Family matters related to the reading engagement of Latino children. *Journal of Latinos and Education, 1*(4), 231-243.

Ashby, J. (2006). Prosody in skilled silent reading: Evidence from eye movements. *Journal of Research in Reading, 29*(3), 318-333.

Aukerman, M., & Schuldt, L. C. (2016). Closely reading "reading closely." *Language Arts, 93*(4), 286-299.

Baddeley, A. (2000). The episodic buffer: A new component of working memory? *Trends in Cognitive Sciences, 4*(11), 417-423.

Baker, L., & Wigfield, A. (1999). Dimensions of children's motivation for reading and their relations to reading activity and reading achievement. *Reading Research Quarterly, 34*(4), 452-477.

Barnes, J. A., Ginther, D. W., & Cochran, S. (1989). Schema and purpose in reading comprehension and learning vocabulary from context. *Reading Research and Instruction, 28*(2), 16-28.

Barnes, M. A., Dennis, M., & Haefele-Kalvaitis, J. (1996). The effects of knowledge availability and knowledge accessibility on coherence and elaborative inferencing in children from six to fifteen years of age. *Journal of Experimental Child Psychology, 61*(3), 216-241.

Barone, D. (2013). Making meaning: Individual and group response within a book club structure. *Journal of Early Childhood Literacy, 13*(1), 3-25.

Barone, D., & Barone, R. (2019). Fourth-grade gifted students' participation in literature circles. *Gifted Education International, 35*(2), 121-135.

Barrio, P. J., Goldstein, D. G., & Hofman, J. M. (2016). Improving comprehension of numbers in the news. In *Proceedings of the 2016 Chi Conference on Human Factors in Computing Systems* (pp. 2729-2739).

Barsalou, L. W. (2008). Grounded cognition. *Annual Review of Psychology, 59*(1), 617-645.

Baumann, J. F., & Bergeron, B. S. (1993). Story map instruction using children's literature: Effects on first graders' comprehension of central narrative elements. *Journal of Reading Behavior, 25*(4), 407-437.

Baumann, J. F., Edwards, E. C., Font, G., Tereshinski, C. A., Kame'enui, E. J., & Olejnik, S. (2002). Teaching morphemic and contextual analysis to fifth-grade students. *Reading Research Quarterly, 37*(2), 150-176.

Baumann, J. F., Kame'enui, E. J., & Ash, G. E. (2003). Research on vocabulary instruction: Voltaire redux. In J. Flood, D. Lapp, & J. R. Squire (Eds.), *Handbook of research on teaching the English language arts* (2nd ed., pp. 752-785). Lawrence Erlbaum.

Beach, R., & Wendler, L. (1987). Developmental differences in response to a story. *Research in the Teaching of English, 21*(3), 286-297.

Bean, T. W., & Moni, K. (2003). Developing students' critical literacy: Exploring identity construction in young adult fiction. *Journal of Adolescent & Adult Literacy, 46*(8), 638-648.

Beck, I. (1989). *Reading today and tomorrow: Teachers' editions for grades 1 and 2.* Holt.

Beck, I., & Hamilton, R. (2000). *Beginning reading module.* American Federation of Teachers. (Original work published 1996)

Beck, I. L., Perfetti, C. A., & McKeown, M. G. (1982). Effects of long-term vocabulary instruction on lexical access and reading comprehension. *Journal of Educational Psychology, 74*(4), 506-521.

Beeferman, D., Berger, A., & Lafferty, J. (1999). Statistical models for text segmentation. *Machine Learning, 34*(1), 177-210.

Benjamin, R. G., & Schwanenflugel, P. J. (2010). Text complexity and oral reading prosody in young readers. *Reading Research Quarterly, 45*(4), 388-404.

Berkeley, S., Scruggs, T. E., & Mastropieri, M. A. (2010). Reading comprehension instruction for students with learning disabilities, 1995-2006: A meta-analysis. *Remedial and Special Education, 31*(6), 423-436.

Best, R. M., Floyd, R. G., & McNamara, D. S. (2008). Differential competencies contributing to children's comprehension of narrative and expository texts. *Reading Psychology, 29*(2), 137-164.

Bhattacharya, A. (2006). Syllable-based reading strategy for mastery of scientific information. *Remedial and Special Education, 27*(2), 116–123.

Bhattacharya, A., & Ehri, L. C. (2004). Graphosyllabic analysis helps struggling readers read and spell words. *Journal of Learning Disabilities, 7*(4), 331–348.

Bishop, D. V., & Adams, C. (1992). Comprehension problems in children with specific language impairment: Literal and inferential meaning. *Journal of Speech, Language, and Hearing Research, 35*(1), 119–129.

Bishop, R. S. (1990). Mirrors, windows, and sliding glass doors. *Perspectives: Choosing and using books for the classroom, 6*(3), ix–xi.

Blevins, J. P. (2016). *Word and paradigm morphology.* Oxford University Press.

Block, M. K., & Duke, N. K. (2015). Letter names can cause confusion. *Young Children, 70*(1), 84–91.

Bloome, D., & Egan-Robertson, A. (1993). The social construction of intertextuality in classroom reading and writing lessons. *Reading Research Quarterly, 28*(4), 305–333.

Bloome, D., Kim, M., Hong, H., & Brady, J. (2018). Multiple source use when reading and writing in literature and language arts classrooms. In J. L. G. Braasch, I. Braten, & M. T. McCrudden (Eds.), *Handbook of multiple source use* (pp. 254–266). Routledge.

Boekaerts, M. (1997). Self-regulated learning: A new concept embraced by researchers, policy makers, educators, teachers, and students. *Learning and Instruction, 7*(2), 161–186.

Bögels, S., & Levinson, S. C. (2017). The brain behind the response: Insights into turn-taking in conversation from neuroimaging. *Research on Language and Social Interaction, 50*(1), 71–89.

Bonacina, S., Huang, S., White-Schwoch, T., Krizman, J., Nicol, T., & Kraus, N. (2021). Rhythm, reading, and sound processing in the brain in preschool children. *npj Science of Learning, 6*(1), 1–11.

Bourg, T. (1996). The role of emotion, empathy, and text structure in children's and adults' narrative text comprehension. In R. J. Kreuz & M. S. MacNealy (Eds.), *Empirical approaches to literature and aesthetics* (pp. 241–260). Ablex.

Bourg, T., Risden, K., Thompson, S., & Davis, E. C. (1993). The effects of an empathy-building strategy on 6th graders' causal inferencing in narrative text comprehension. *Poetics, 22*(1–2), 117–133.

Bower, G. H. (1976). Experiments on story understanding and recall. *The Quarterly Journal of Experimental Psychology, 28*(4), 511–534.

Bower, G. H., & Rinck, M. (1999). Goal as generators of narrative understanding. In S. R. Goldman, A. C. Graesser, & P. van den Broek (Eds.), *Narrative comprehension, causality, and coherence: Essays in honor of Tom Trabasso* (pp. 111–134). Erlbaum.

Britt, M. A., Richter, T., & Rouet, J. F. (2014). Scientific literacy: The role of goal-directed reading and evaluation in understanding scientific information. *Educational Psychologist, 49*(2), 104–122.

Brown, A. L., & Day, J. D. (1983). Macrorules for summarizing texts: The development of expertise. *Journal of Verbal Learning and Verbal Behavior, 22*(1), 1–14.

Brown, A. L., & Palincsar, A. S. (1989). Guided, cooperative learning and individual knowledge acquisition. In L. B. Resnick (Ed.). *Knowing, learning and instruction: Essays in honor of Robert Glaser* (pp. 393–451). Lawrence Erlbaum.

Brown, S., & Kappes, L. (2012). *Implementing the Common Core State Standards: A primer on "close reading of text."* Aspen Institute.

Brownell, C. J., & Rashid, A. (2020). Building bridges instead of walls: Engaging young children in critical literacy read alouds. *Journal of Curriculum Studies Research, 2*(1), 76–94.

Brown-Wood, J. E., & Solari, E. J. (2021). Judging books by covers: Exploring antiblackness and Asian and Hispanic children preferences. *The Journal of Educational Research, 114*(1), 13–28.

Bruce, B. (1981). A social interaction model of reading. *Discourse Processes, 4*(4), 273–311.

Brugar, K. A., & Roberts, K. L. (2017). Seeing is believing: Promoting visual literacy in elementary social studies. *Journal of Teacher Education, 68*(3), 262–279.

Brusnighan, S. M., & Folk, J. R. (2012). Combining contextual and morphemic cues is beneficial during incidental vocabulary acquisition: Semantic transparency in novel compound word processing. *Reading Research Quarterly, 47*(2), 172–190.

Burns, M. K. (2007). Reading at the instructional level with children identified as learning disabled: Potential implications for response-to-intervention. *School Psychology Quarterly, 22*(3), 297–313.

Cain, K., Oakhill, J. V., & Bryant, P. E. (2004). Children's reading comprehension ability: Concurrent prediction by working memory, verbal ability, and component skills. *Journal of Educational Psychology, 96*(1), 671–681.

Cain, K., Patson, N., & Andrews, L. (2005). Age- and ability-related differences in young readers' use of conjunctions. *Journal of Child Language, 32*(4), 877–892.

Caldwell, E. C., Roth, S. R., & Turner, R. R. (1978). A reconsideration of phonic generalizations. *Journal of Reading Behavior, 10*(1), 91–96.

Carlisle, J. F. (2010). Effects of instruction in morphological awareness on literacy achievement: An integrative review. *Reading Research Quarterly, 45*(4), 464–487.

Carlson, K., Dickey, M. W., Frazier, L., & Clifton, C., Jr. (2009). Information structure expectations in sentence comprehension. *Quarterly Journal of Experimental Psychology, 62*(1), 114–139.

Carnine, D., Stevens, C., Clements, J., & Kameenui, E. J. (1982). Effects of facultative questions and practice on intermediate students' understanding of character motives. *Journal of Reading Behavior, 14*(2), 179–190.

Carroll, J. B., Davies, P., & Richman, B. (1971). *The American Heritage word frequency book.* Houghton Mifflin.

Carston, R. (2018). Figurative language, mental imagery, and pragmatics. *Metaphor and Symbol, 33*(3), 198–217.

Cartwright, K. B. (2006). Fostering flexibility and comprehension in elementary students. *The Reading Teacher, 59*(7), 628–634.

Cartwright, K. B (2015). *Executive skills and reading comprehension.* Guilford.

Carver, R. P. (1992). Reading rate: Theory, research, and practical implications. *Journal of Reading, 36*(2), 84–95.

Carver, R. P. (1994). Percentage of unknown vocabulary words in text as a function of the relative difficulty of the text: Implications for instruction. *Journal of Reading Behavior, 26*(4), 413–437.

Castles, A., Rastle, K., & Nation, K. (2018). Ending the reading wars: Reading acquisition from novice to expert. *Psychological Science in the Public Interest, 19*(1), 5–51.

Cazden, C. B. (2005). The value of conversations for language development and reading comprehension. *Literacy Teaching and Learning, 9*(1), 1–6.

Cervetti, G. N., Barber, J., Dorph, R., Pearson, P. D., & Goldschmidt, P. G. (2012). The impact of an integrated approach to science and literacy in elementary school classrooms. *Journal of Research in Science Teaching, 49*(5), 631–658.

Cervetti, G. N., & Hiebert, E. H. (2015). The sixth pillar of reading instruction: Knowledge development. *The Reading Teacher, 68*(7), 548–551.

Cervetti, G. N., & Wright, T. S. (2020). The role of knowledge in understanding and learning from text. In E. B. Moje, P. Afflerbach, P. Enciso, & N. K. Lesaux (Eds.), *Handbook of reading research* (Vol. 5, pp. 237–260). Routledge.

Cervetti, G. N., Wright, T. S., & Hwang, H. (2016). Conceptual coherence, comprehension, and vocabulary acquisition: A knowledge effect? *Reading and Writing, 29*(4), 761–779.

Chafel, J. A., & Neitzel, C. (2005). Young children's ideas about the nature, causes, justification, and alleviation of poverty. *Early Childhood Research Quarterly, 20*(4), 433–450.

Chafel, J. A., & Neitzel, C. (2012). "I would like to see how they got poor and see what it's like to be poor": An analysis of young children's responses to a critical literacy text about poverty. *Journal of Poverty, 16*(2), 147–170.

Chandler, M. J. (1973). Egocentrism and antisocial behavior: The assessment and training of social perspective-taking skills. *Developmental Psychology, 9*(3), 326–332.

Chandler, P., & Sweller, J. (1991). Cognitive load theory and the format of instruction. *Cognition and Instruction, 8*(4), 293–332.

Chard, D. J., Vaughn, S., & Tyler, B. J. (2002). A synthesis of research on effective interventions for building reading fluency with elementary students with learning disabilities. *Journal of Learning Disabilities, 35*(5), 386–406.

Chiu, C. W. T. (1998). *Synthesizing metacognitive interventions: What training characteristics can improve reading performance?* [Paper presentation]. American Educational Research Association Annual Meeting, San Diego, CA, United States.

Cipparone, P. (2014). Reading *Pancho Rabbit and the Coyote:* An allegory of immigration sparks rich discussions. *Social Studies and the Young Learner, 27*(2), 9–13.

Clark, A. M., Anderson, R. C., Kuo, L. J., Kim, I. H., Archodidou, A., & Nguyen-Jahiel, K. (2003). Collaborative reasoning: Expanding ways for children to talk and think in school. *Educational Psychology Review, 15*(2), 181–198.

Clark, R., Morrison, T. G., & Wilcox, B. (2009). Readers' theater: A process of developing fourth-graders' reading fluency. *Reading Psychology, 30*(4), 359–385.

Clarke, L. W., & Holwadel, J. (2007). Help! What is wrong with these literature circles and how can we fix them? *The Reading Teacher, 61*(1), 20–29.

Cohen, L., Krustedt, R. L., & May, M. (2009). Fluency, text structure, and retelling: A complex relationship. *Reading Horizons: A Journal of Literacy and Language Arts, 49*(2), 101–124.

Cole, K., Schroeder, K., Bataineh, M., & Al-Bataineh, A. (2021). Flexible seating impact on classroom environment. *Turkish Online Journal of Educational Technology-TOJET, 20*(2), 62–74.

Coleman, J. M., Bradley, L. G., & Donovan, C. A. (2012). Visual representations in second graders' information book compositions. *The Reading Teacher, 66*(1), 31–45.

Connelly, V., Johnston, R., & Thompson, G. B. (2001). The effect of phonics instruction on the reading comprehension of beginning readers. *Reading and Writing, 14*(5), 423–457.

Connor, C. M., Morrison, F. J., & Katch, L. E. (2004). Beyond the reading wars: Exploring the effect of child-instruction interactions on growth in early reading. *Scientific Studies of Reading, 8*(4), 305–336.

Cook, K. E., Earles-Vollrath, T., & Ganz, J. B. (2006). Bibliotherapy. *Intervention in School and Clinic, 42*(2), 91–100.

Corcoran, C. A., & Davis, A. D. (2005). A study of the effects of readers' theater on second and third grade special education students' fluency growth. *Reading Improvement, 42*(2), 105–111.

Council of Chief State School Officers. (2010). *Common core state standards for English language arts.* National Governors Association Center for Best Practices.

Craddock, S. (1981). An investigation of physical setting in narrative discourse, and its influence on the reading comprehension and reading interest of elementary students [Doctoral dissertation, University of British Columbia]. University of British Columbia Library. https://dx.doi.org/10.14288/1.0078340

Cromley, J. G., & Azevedo, R. (2007). Testing and refining the direct and inferential mediation model of reading comprehension. *Journal of Educational Psychology, 99*(2), 311.

Crosson, A. C., & McKeown, M. G. (2016). Middle school learners' use of Latin roots to infer the meaning of unfamiliar words. *Cognition and Instruction, 34*(2), 148–171.

Csikszentmihalyi, M. (1990). *Flow: The psychology of optimal experience.* HarperCollins.

Culatta, B., Hall-Kenyon, K., & Black, S. (2010). Teaching expository comprehension skills in early childhood classrooms. *Topics in Language Disorders, 30*(4), 323–338.

Culpeper, J. (1996). Inferring character from texts: Attribution theory and foregrounding theory. *Poetics, 23*(5), 335–361.

Culpeper, J. (2014). *Language and characterisation: People in plays and other texts.* Routledge.

Cunningham, A. E., & Stanovich, K. E. (1991). Tracking the unique effects of print exposure in children: Associations with vocabulary, general knowledge, and spelling. *Journal of Educational Psychology, 83*(2), 264–274.

Cunningham, J. W., & Foster, E. O. (1978). The ivory tower connection: A case study. *The Reading Teacher, 31*(4), 365–369.

David, D., Wade-Woolley, L., Kirby, J. R., & Smithrim, K. (2007). Rhythm and reading development in school-age children: A longitudinal study. *Journal of Research in Reading, 30*(2), 169–183.

Davis, Z. T., & McPherson, M. D. (1989). Story map instruction: A road map for reading comprehension. *The Reading Teacher, 43*(3), 232–240.

de Boer, H., Donker, A. S., Kostons, D. D., & van der Werf, G. P. (2018). Long-term effects of metacognitive strategy instruction on student academic performance: A meta-analysis. *Educational Research Review, 24*, 98–115.

De Koning, B. B., & van der Schoot, M. (2013). Becoming part of the story! Refueling the interest in visualization strategies for reading comprehension. *Educational Psychology Review, 25*(2), 261–287.

Dean, R. S., & Enemoh, P. A. C. (1983). Pictorial organization in prose learning. *Contemporary Educational Psychology, 8*(1), 20-27.

Deane, P. (2020). *Building and justifying interpretations of texts: A key practice in the English language arts* (Research Report No. RR-20-20). Educational Testing Service.

Denton, C. A., Tolar, T. D., Fletcher, J. M., Barth, A. E., Vaughn, S., & Francis, D. J. (2013). Effects of tier 3 intervention for students with persistent reading difficulties and characteristics of inadequate responders. *Journal of Educational Psychology, 105*(3), 633-648.

Diaz, T. (2014). A notable process: Teaching critical reading via notetaking (making). *Library Media Connection, 32*(4), 18-20.

Dickson, S. V., Simmons, D. C., & Kameenui, E. J. (1998). Text organization: Instructional and curricular basics and implications. In D. C. Simmons & E. J. Kameenui (Eds.), *What reading research tells us about children with diverse learning needs* (pp. 279-294). Routledge.

Dignath, C., & Büttner, G. (2008). Components of fostering self-regulated learning among students. A meta-analysis on intervention studies at primary and secondary school level. *Metacognition and Learning, 3*(3), 231-264.

Dimino, J., Gersten, R., Carnine, D., & Blake, G. (1990). Story grammar: An approach for promoting at-risk secondary students' comprehension of literature. *The Elementary School Journal, 91*(1), 19-32.

Dochy, F., Segers, M., & Buehl, M. M. (1999). The relation between assessment practices and outcomes of studies: The case of research on prior knowledge. *Review of Educational Research, 69*(2), 145-186.

Dole, J. A., Valencia, S. W., Greer, E. A., & Wardrop, J. L. (1991). Effects of two types of prereading instruction on the comprehension of narrative and expository text. *Reading Research Quarterly, 26*(2) 142-159.

Donker, A. S., De Boer, H., Kostons, D., Van Ewijk, C. D., & van der Werf, M. P. (2014). Effectiveness of learning strategy instruction on academic performance: A meta-analysis. *Educational Research Review, 11*, 1-26.

Donovan, A. M., & Rapp, D. N. (2018). Updating of character information when reading multiple texts for pleasure. In J. L. G. Braasch, I. Braten, & M. T. McCrudden (Eds.), *Handbook of multiple source use* (pp. 303-319). Routledge.

Donovan, C. A., Smolkin, L. B., & Lomax, R. G. (2000). Beyond the independent-level text: Considering the reader-text match in first graders' self-selections during recreational reading. *Reading Psychology, 21*(4), 309-33.

Dorfman, M. H. (1988). *A model for understanding the points of stories: Evidence from adult and child readers* (Publication No. 8908668) [Doctoral dissertation, University of Illinois at Urbana-Champaign]. ProQuest Dissertations Publishing.

Dorfman, M. H., & Brewer, W. F. (1994). Understanding the points of fables. *Discourse Processes, 17*(1), 105-129.

Dowhower, S. (1997). Wordless books: Promise and possibilities, a genre comes of age. In K. Camperell, B. L. Hayes, & R. Telfer (Eds.), *Yearbook of American Reading Forums 17* (pp. 57-79). Springer.

Downey, M. T., & Long, K. A. (2015). *Teaching for historical literacy: Building knowledge in the history classroom.* Routledge.

Drake, D. A., & Ehri, L. C. (1984). Spelling acquisition: Effects of pronouncing words on memory for their spellings. *Cognition and Instruction, 1*(3), 297-320.

Dreher, M. J., & Sammons, R. B. (1994). Fifth graders' search for information in a textbook. *Journal of Reading Behavior, 26*(3), 301-314.

Drill, R. B., & Bellini, S. (2022). Combining readers theater, story mapping and video self-modeling interventions to improve narrative reading comprehension in children with autism spectrum disorder. *Journal of Autism and Developmental Disorders, 52*(1), 1-15.

Dufrene, B. A., Reisener, C. D., Olmi, D. J., Zoder-Martell, K., McNutt, M. R., & Horn, D. R. (2010). Peer tutoring for reading fluency as a feasible and effective alternative in response to intervention systems. *Journal of Behavioral Education, 19*(3), 239-256.

Duke, N. K. (2014a, April 16). *Limitations of Broad Phonics Generalizations: When two vowels go walking, the first one doesn't necessarily do the talking!* Literacy Now. https://www.literacyworldwide.org/blog/literacy-now/2014/04/16/limitations-of-broad-phonics-generalizations-when-two-vowels-go-walking-the-first-one-doesn-t-necessarily-do-the-talking

Duke, N. K. (2014b). *Inside information: Developing powerful readers and writers of informational text through project-based instruction.* Scholastic.

Duke, N. K. (2020, November 1). *When young readers get stuck*. ASCD. https://www.ascd.org/el/articles/when-young-readers-get-stuck

Duke, N. K., & Cartwright, K. B. (2021). The science of reading progresses: Communicating advances beyond the simple view of reading. *Reading Research Quarterly*, *56*(S1), S25–S44.

Duke, N. K., & Kays, J. (1998). "Can I say 'Once upon a time'?": Kindergarten children developing knowledge of information book language. *Early Childhood Research Quarterly*, *13*(2), 295–318.

Duke, N. K., Pearson, P. D., Strachan, S. L., & Billman, A. K. (2011). Essential elements of fostering and teaching reading comprehension. In S. J. Samuels & A. E. Farstrup (Eds.), *What research has to say about reading instruction* (4th ed., pp. 51–93). International Reading Association.

Duke, N. K., & Purcell-Gates, V. (2003). Genres at home and at school: Bridging the known to the new. *The Reading Teacher*, *57*(1), 30–37.

Duke, N. K., & Roberts, K. M. (2010). The genre-specific nature of reading comprehension. In D. Wyse, R. Andrews, & J. Hoffman (Eds.), *The Routledge international handbook of English, language and literacy teaching* (pp. 74–86). Routledge.

Duke, N. K., Ward, A. E., & Pearson, P. D. (2021). The science of reading comprehension instruction. *The Reading Teacher*, *74*(6), 663–672.

Dunning, D. B. (1992). *Instructional questions that clarify story characters' feelings and motivations: Their effect on student's narrative comprehension* (Report No. CSR-TR-563). Center for the Study of Reading. (ERIC Document Reproduction Service No. ED 350 597)

Dymock, S. (2007). Comprehension strategy instruction: Teaching narrative text structure awareness. *The Reading Teacher*, *61*(2), 161–167.

Ebarvia, T., Germán, L., Parker, K. N., & Torres, J. (2020). #DISRUPTTEXTS. *English Journal*, *110*(1), 100–102.

Edmunds, K. M., & Bauserman, K. L. (2006). What teachers can learn about reading motivation through conversations with children. *The Reading Teacher*, *59*(5), 414–424.

Ehri, L. C. (1995). Phases of development in learning to read by sight. *Journal of Research in Reading*, *18*(2), 116–125.

Ehri, L. C. (2002). Phases of acquisition in learning to read words and implications for teaching. In *BJEP Monograph Series II, Number 1-Learning and Teaching Reading* (Vol. 7, No. 28, pp. 7–28). British Psychological Society.

Ehri, L. C. (2005). Learning to read words: Theory, findings, and issues. *Scientific Studies of Reading*, *9*(2), 167–188.

Ehri, L. C. (2014). Orthographic mapping in the acquisition of sight word reading, spelling memory, and vocabulary learning. *Scientific Studies of Reading*, *18*(1), 5–21.

Ehri, L. C. (2017). Orthographic mapping and literacy development revisited. In K. Cain, D. L. Compton, & R. K. Parrila (Eds.), *Theories of reading development* (pp. 127–146). John Benjamins.

Ehri, L. C. (2020). The science of learning to read words: A case for systematic phonics instruction. *Reading Research Quarterly*, *55*(S1), S45–S60.

Ehri, L. C., & McCormick, S. (1998). Phases of word learning: Implications for instruction with delayed and disabled readers. *Reading & Writing Quarterly: Overcoming Learning Difficulties*, *14*(2), 135–163.

Ehri, L. C., Nunes, S. R., Stahl, S. A., & Willows, D. M. (2001). Systematic phonics instruction helps students learn to read: Evidence from the National Reading Panel's meta-analysis. *Review of Educational Research*, *71*(3), 393–447.

Ehri, L. C., Nunes, S. R., Willows, D. M., Schuster, B. V., Yaghoub-Zadeh, Z., & Shanahan, T. (2001). Phonemic awareness instruction helps children learn to read: Evidence from the National Reading Panel's meta-analysis. *Reading Research Quarterly*, *36*(3), 250–287.

Ehri, L. C., & Robbins, C. (1992). Beginners need some decoding skill to read words by analogy. *Reading Research Quarterly*, *27*(1), 13–26.

Eitel, A., Bender, L., & Renkl, A. (2019). Are seductive details seductive only when you think they are relevant? An experimental test of the moderating role of perceived relevance. *Applied Cognitive Psychology*, *33*(1), 20–30.

Elardo, P. T., & Caldwell, B. M. (1979). The effects of an experimental social development program on children in the middle childhood period. *Psychology in the Schools*, *16*(1), 93–100.

Ellis, E. S., & Graves, A. W. (1990). Teaching rural students with learning disabilities: A paraphrasing strategy to increase comprehension of main ideas. *Rural Special Education Quarterly, 10*(2), 2–10.

Emery, D. W. (1996). Helping readers comprehend stories from the characters' perspectives. *The Reading Teacher, 49*(7), 534–541.

Emery, D. W., & Milhalevich, C. (1992). Directed discussion of character perspectives. *Literacy Research and Instruction, 31*(4), 51–59.

Eppler, M. J. (2006). A comparison between concept maps, mind maps, conceptual diagrams, and visual metaphors as complementary tools for knowledge construction and sharing. *Information Visualization, 5*(3), 202–210.

Ericsson, K. A., & Kintsch, W. (1995). Long-term working memory. *Psychological Review, 102*(2), 211–245.

Feathers, K. M. (2002). Young children's thinking in relation to texts: A comparison with older children. *Journal of Research in Childhood Education, 17*(1), 69–83.

Fielding, L. G., & Pearson, P. D. (1994). Synthesis of research reading comprehension: What works. *Educational leadership, 51*(5), 62–68.

Fisher, D., & Frey, N. (2012). *Engaging the adolescent learner: Text-dependent questions.* International Reading Association.

Fisher, D., & Frey, N. (2014). Close reading as an intervention for struggling middle school readers. *Journal of Adolescent & Adult Literacy, 57*(5), 367–376.

Fisher, D., Frey, N., & Lapp, D. (2008). Shared readings: Modeling comprehension, vocabulary, text structures, and text features for older readers. *The Reading Teacher, 61*(7), 548–556.

Fitzgerald, J., & Teasley, A. B. (1986). Effects of instruction in narrative structure on children's writing. *Journal of Educational Psychology, 78*(6), 424–432.

Fitzgerald, P. (2016). Differentiation for all literacy levels in mainstream classrooms. *Literacy Learning: The Middle Years, 24*(2), 17–25.

Flanigan, K. (2007). A concept of word in text: A pivotal event in early reading acquisition. *Journal of Literacy Research, 39*(1), 37–70.

Flood, J. E. (1978). The influence of first sentences on reader expectations within prose passages. *Literacy Research and Instruction, 17*(4), 306–315.

Foorman, B., Beyler, N., Borradaile, K., Coyne, M., Denton, C. A., Dimino, J., Furgeson, J., Hayes, L., Henke, J., Justice, L., Keating, B., Lewis, W., Sattar, S., Streke, A., Wagner, R., & Wissel, S. (2016). *Foundational skills to support reading for understanding in kindergarten through 3rd grade* (NCEE 2016-4008). National Center for Education Evaluation and Regional Assistance (NCEE), Institute of Education Sciences, U.S. Department of Education. http://whatworks.ed.gov

Ford, C., & Thompson, S. (1996). Interactional units in conversation: Syntactic, intonational, and pragmatic resources for the management of turns. In E. Ochs, E. Schegloff, & S. Thompson (Eds.), *Interaction and grammar* (pp. 134–184). Cambridge University Press.

Forgan, J. (2002). Using bibliotherapy to teach problem-solving. *Intervention in School and Clinic, 38*(2), 75–82.

Freire, P. (1970). *Pedagogy of the oppressed.* Continuum International Publishing Group.

Freire, P. (2005). *Education for critical consciousness.* Continuum International Publishing Group.

Freire, P., & Macedo, D. (2001). *Literacy: Reading the word and the world.* Routledge.

French, R. (2012). Learning the grammatics of quoted speech: Benefits for punctuation and expressive reading. *The Australian Journal of Language and Literacy, 35*(2), 206–222.

Fresch, M. J. (1995). Self-selection of early literacy learners. *The Reading Teacher, 49*(3), 220–227.

Friel, S. N., Curcio, F. R., & Bright, G. W. (2001). Making sense of graphs: Critical factors influencing comprehension and instructional implications. *Journal for Research in Mathematics Education, 32*(2), 124–158.

Fritschner, L. M. (2000). Inside the undergraduate college classroom: Faculty and students differ on the meaning of student participation. *The Journal of Higher Education, 71*(3), 342–362.

Fuchs, L. S., Fuchs, D., & Deno, S. L. (1985). Importance of goal ambitiousness and goal mastery to student achievement. *Exceptional Children, 52*(1), 63–71.

Fuchs, D., Fuchs, L. S., Thompson, A., Svenson, E., Yen, L., Al Otaiba, S., Yang, N., McMaster, K. N., Prentice, K., Kardan, S., & Saenz, L. (2001). Peer-assisted learning strategies in reading: Extensions for kindergarten, first grade, and high school. *Remedial and Special Education, 22*(1), 15–21.

Gajria, M., Jitendra, A. K., Sood, S., & Sacks, G. (2007). Improving comprehension of expository text in students with LD: A research synthesis. *Journal of Learning Disabilities, 40*(3), 210–225.

Garner, R., Gillingham, M. G., & White, C. S. (1989). Effects of "seductive details" on macroprocessing and microprocessing in adults and children. *Cognition and Instruction, 6*(1), 41–57.

Gaskins, I. W., Downer, M. A., Anderson, R. C., Cunningham, P. M., Gaskins, R. W., & Schommer, M. (1988). A metacognitive approach to phonics: Using what you know to decode what you don't know. *Remedial and Special Education, 9*(1), 36–41.

Gates, L., & Yale, I. (2011). A logical letter-sound system in five phonic generalizations. *The Reading Teacher, 64*(5), 330–339.

Gentry, J. R., & Graham, S. (2010). *Creating better readers and writers.* Saperstein Associates. https://www.zaner-bloser.com/products/pdfs/Creating_Better_Readers_and_Writers_White_Paper.pdf

Georgiou, G. K., & Das, J. P. (2018). Direct and indirect effects of executive function on reading comprehension in young adults. *Journal of Research in Reading, 41*(2), 243–258.

Gerlach, J. M., & Rinehart, S. D. (1992). Can you tell a book by its cover? *Reading Horizons: A Journal of Literacy and Language Arts, 32*(4), 289–298.

Gibson, E. J., & Levin, H. (1975). *The psychology of reading.* MIT Press.

Glaser, R. (1984). Education and thinking: The role of knowledge. *American Psychologist, 39*(2), 93–104.

Glover, J. A., Dinnel, D. L., Halpain, D. R., McKee, T. K., Corkill, A. J., & Wise, S. L. (1988). Effects of across-chapter signals on recall of text. *Journal of Educational Psychology, 80*(1), 3–15.

Glynn, S. M., & Takahashi, T. (1998). Learning from analogy-enhanced science text. *Journal of Research in Science Teaching, 35*(10), 1129–1149.

Gnaedinger, E. K., Hund, A. M., & Hesson-McInnis, M. S. (2016). Reading-specific flexibility moderates the relation between reading strategy use and reading comprehension during the elementary years. *Mind, Brain, and Education, 10*(4), 233–246.

Goldman, S. R., McCarthy, K. S., & Burkett, C. (2014). Interpretive inferences in literature. In E. J. O'Brien, A. E. Cook, & R. F. Lorch, Jr. (Eds.), *Inferences during reading* (pp. 386–415). Cambridge University Press.

Goldman, S. R., & Varnhagen, C. K. (1986). Memory for embedded and sequential story structures. *Journal of Memory and Language, 25*(4), 401–418.

Gonzalez-Frey, S. M., & Ehri, L. C. (2021). Connected phonation is more effective than segmented phonation for teaching beginning readers to decode unfamiliar words, *Scientific Studies of Reading, 25*(3), 272–285.

Goodwin, A. P., & Ahn, S. (2013). A meta-analysis of morphological interventions in English: Effects on literacy outcomes for school-age children. *Scientific Studies of Reading, 17*(4), 257–285.

Goswami, U. (1986). Children's use of analogy in learning to read: A developmental study. *Journal of Experimental Child Psychology, 42*(1), 73–83.

Goswami, U. (1998). The role of analogies in the development of word recognition. In J. L. Metsala & L. C. Ehri (Eds.), *Word recognition in beginning literacy* (pp. 41–63). Lawrence Erlbaum.

Goswami, U., & Bryant, P. (2016). *Phonological skills and learning to read: Classic edition.* Routledge. (Original work published 1990)

Goswami, U., Mead, N., Fosker, T., Huss, M., Barnes, L., & Leong, V. (2013). Impaired perception of syllable stress in children with dyslexia: A longitudinal study. *Journal of Memory and Language, 69*(1), 1–17.

Gough, P. B. (1983). Context, form, and interaction. In K. Rayner (Ed.), *Eye movements in reading: Perceptual and language processes* (pp. 203–211). Academic.

Gough, P. B. (1993). The beginning of decoding. *Reading and Writing: An Interdisciplinary Journal, 5,* 181–192.

Gough, P. B., & Juel, C. (1991). The first stages of word recognition. In L. Rieben & C. A. Perfetti (Eds.), *Learning to read: Basic research and its implications* (pp. 47–56). Erlbaum.

Gough, P. B., & Tunmer, W. E. (1986). Decoding, reading, and reading disability. *Remedial and Special Education, 7*(1), 6–10.

Grabe, W. (2002). Narrative and expository macro-genres. In A. M. Johns (Ed.), *Genre in the classroom: Multiple perspectives* (pp. 249–267). Erlbaum.

Graesser, A. C., Bowers, C. A., Bayen, U. J., & Hu, X. (2001). Who said what? Who knows what? Tracking speakers and knowledge in narratives. In W. van Peer and S. Chatman (Eds.), *New perspectives on narrative perspective* (pp. 255–274). SUNY University Press.

Graesser, A. C., Bowers, C., Olde, B., & Pomeroy, V. (1999). Who said what? Source memory for narrator and character agents in literary short stories. *Journal of Educational Psychology, 91*(2), 284–300.

Graesser, A. C., & Klettke, B. (2001). Agency, plot, and a structural affect theory of literary story comprehension. In D. Schram & G. Steen (Eds.), *The psychology and sociology of literature: In honor of Elrud Ibsch* (pp. 57–69). John Benjamins.

Graesser, A. C., Singer, M., & Trabasso, T. (1994). Constructing inferences during narrative text comprehension. *Psychological Review, 101*(3), 371–395.

Graham, J. (1998). Turning the visual into the verbal: Children reading wordless picture books. In J. Evans (Ed.), *What's in the picture? Responding to illustrations in picture books* (pp. 25–43). Paul Chapman.

Graham, S., & Harris, K. R. (2017). Reading and writing connections: How writing can build better readers (and vice versa). In C. Ng & B. Bartlett (Eds.), *Improving reading and reading engagement in the 21st century: International research and innovation* (pp. 333–350). Springer.

Graham, S., & Hebert, M. (2011). Writing-to-read: A meta-analysis of the impact of writing and writing instruction on reading. *Harvard Educational Review, 81*(4), 710–744.

Greenlee, A. A., Monson, D. L., & Taylor, B. M. (1996). The lure of series books: Does it affect appreciation for recommended literature? *The Reading Teacher, 50*(3), 216–225.

Grimes, J. E. (1975). *The thread of discourse.* Mouton.

Gross, M., Latham, D., Underhill, J., & Bak, H. (2016). The peritext book club: Reading to foster critical thinking about STEAM texts. *School Library Research, 19*, 1–17.

Guéraud, S., Harmon, M. E., & Peracchi, K. A. (2005). Updating situation models: The memory-based contribution. *Discourse Processes, 39*(2–3), 243–263.

Guo, D., Zhang, S., Wright, K. L., & McTigue, E. M. (2020). Do you get the picture? A meta-analysis of the effect of graphics on reading comprehension. *AERA Open, 6*(1). https://doi.org/10.1177/2332858420901696

Gurney, D., Gersten, R., Dimino, J., & Carnine, D. (1990). Story grammar: Effective literature instruction for high school students with learning disabilities. *Journal of Learning Disabilities, 23*(6), 335–342.

Guthrie, J. T. (1977). Research views: Story comprehension. *The Reading Teacher, 30*(5), 574–577.

Guthrie, J. T. (2004). Differentiating instruction for struggling readers within the CORI classroom. In J. T. Guthrie, A. Wigfield, & K. C. Perencevich (Eds.), *Motivating reading comprehension: Concept-oriented reading instruction* (pp. 1–24). Erlbaum.

Guthrie, J. T., Wigfield, A., & You, W. (2012). Instructional contexts for engagement and achievement in reading. In S. L. Christenson, A. L. Rescgly, & C. Wylie (Eds.), *Handbook of research on student engagement* (pp. 601–634). Springer.

Guzman, G., Goldberg, T. S., & Swanson, H. L. (2018). A meta-analysis of self-monitoring on reading performance of K-12 students. *School Psychology Quarterly, 33*(1), 160–168.

Guzzetti, B. J. (2000). Learning counter-intuitive science concepts: What have we learned from over a decade of research? *Reading & Writing Quarterly, 16*(2), 89–98.

Hagaman, J. L., Luschen, K., & Reid, R. (2010). The "RAP" on reading comprehension. *Teaching Exceptional Children, 43*(1), 22–29.

Hagaman, J., & Reid, R. (2008). The effects of the paraphrasing strategy on the reading comprehension of middle school students at risk of failure in reading. *Remedial and Special Education, 29*, 222–234.

Hall, K. M., Sabey, B. L., & McClellan, M. (2005). Expository text comprehension: Helping primary-grade teachers use expository texts to full advantage. *Reading Psychology, 26*(3), 211–234.

Hall, K. W., Hedrick, W. B., & Williams, L. M. (2014). Every day we're shufflin': Empowering students during in-school independent reading. *Childhood Education, 90*(2), 91–98.

Haller, E. P., Child, D. A., & Walberg, H. J. (1988). Can comprehension be taught? A quantitative synthesis of "metacognitive" studies. *Educational Researcher, 17*(9), 5–8.

Hammann, L. A., & Stevens, R. J. (2003). Instructional approaches to improving students' writing of compare-contrast essays: An experimental study. *Journal of Literacy Research, 35*(2), 731–756.

Hancock, M. R. (1993a). Exploring the meaning-making process through the content of literature response journals: A case study investigation. *Research in the Teaching of English, 27*(4), 335–368.

Hancock, M. R. (1993b). Exploring and extending personal response through literature journals. *The Reading Teacher*, *46*(6), 466–474.

Hanno, E. C., Jones, S. M., & McCoy, D. C. (2020). The joint development of literacy and self-regulation in early childhood: Implications for research and practice. In E. B. Moje, P. Afflerbach, P. Enciso, & N. K. Lesaux (Eds.), *Handbook of reading research* (Vol. 5, pp. 279–306). Routledge.

Hansen, J. (1981). The effects of inference training and practice on young children's reading comprehension. *Reading Research Quarterly*, *16*(3), 391–417.

Hardy, J. K., Pennington, R., Griffin, R., & Jacobi-Vessels, J. (2020). Comparing the effects of protagonist race on preschoolers' engagement in book reading. *Early Childhood Education Journal*, *48*(6), 781–791.

Harris, P. L., Mandias, F., Terwogt, M. M., & Tjintjelaar, J. (1980). The influence of context on story recall and feelings of comprehension. *International Journal of Behavioral Development*, *3*(2), 159–172.

Harris, T. L., & Hodges, R. E. (Eds.). (1995). *The literacy dictionary: The vocabulary of reading and writing*. International Reading Association.

Hartley, J., Kenely, J., Owen, G., & Trueman, M. (1980). The effect of headings on children's recall from prose text. *British Journal of Educational Psychology*, *50*(3), 304–307.

Hartley, J., & Trueman, M. (1982). The effects of summaries on the recall of information from prose: Five experimental studies. *Human Learning*, *1*(1), 63–82.

Hartley, J., & Trueman, M. (1985). A research strategy for text designers: The role of headings. *Instructional Science*, *14*(2), 99–155.

Hasan, R. (1996). Literacy, everyday talk and society. In R. Hasan & G. Williams (Eds.), *Literacy in society* (pp. 377–424). Addison Wesley Longman.

Hattie, J., Biggs, J., & Purdie, N. (1996). Effects of learning skills interventions on student learning: A meta-analysis. *Review of Educational Research*, *66*(2), 99–136.

Hattie, J., & Clarke, S. (2019). *Visible learning: Feedback*. Routledge.

Hattie, J., & Timperley, H. (2008). The power of feedback. *Review of Educational Research*, *77*, 81–112.

Hattie, J. A. C. (2009). *Visible learning: A synthesis of over 800 meta-analyses relating to achievement*. Routledge.

Hearst, M. A. (1997). TextTiling: Segmenting text into multi-paragraph subtopic passages. *Computational Linguistics*, *23*(1), 33–64.

Hebert, M., Graham, S., Rigby-Wills, H., & Ganson, K. (2014). Effects of note-taking and extended writing on expository text comprehension: Who benefits? *Learning Disabilities: A Contemporary Journal*, *12*(1), 43-68.

Hedin, L. R., Mason, L. H., & Gaffney, J. S. (2011). Comprehension strategy instruction for two students with attention-related disabilities. *Preventing School Failure*, *55*(3), 148-157.

Henderson, G. (1999). Learning with diagrams. *Australian Science Teachers' Journal*, *45*(2), 17-25.

Hennings, D. G. (1977). Learning to listen and speak. *Theory into Practice*, *16*(3), 183-188.

Herman, P. A., Anderson, R. C., Pearson, P. D., & Nagy, W. E. (1987). Incidental acquisition of word meaning from expositions with varied text features. *Reading Research Quarterly*, *22*(3), 263-284.

Hibbing, A. N., & Rankin-Erickson, J. L. (2003). A picture is worth a thousand words: Using visual images to improve comprehension for middle school struggling readers. *The Reading Teacher*, *56*(8), 758-770.

Hidi, S. (2001). Interest, reading, and learning: Theoretical and practical considerations. *Educational Psychology Review*, *13*(3), 191-209.

Hiebert, E. H. (1981). Developmental patterns and inter-relationships of preschool children's print awareness. *Reading Research Quarterly*, *16*(2), 236-260.

Hiebert, E. H. (Ed.). (2015). *Teaching stamina and silent reading in the digital-global age*. TextProject.

Hiebert, E. H., & Reutzel, D. R. (2010). *Revisiting silent reading: New directions for teachers and researchers*. TextProject.

Ho, E. S. C., & Lau, K. L. (2018). Reading engagement and reading literacy performance: Effective policy and practices at home and in school. *Journal of Research in Reading*, *41*(4), 657-679.

Hodges, T. S., McTigue, E., Wright, K. L., Franks, A. D., & Matthews, S. D. (2018). Transacting with characters: Teaching children perspective taking with authentic literature. *Journal of Research in Childhood Education*, *32*(3), 343-362.

Hoffman, J. V. (2017). What if "just right" is just wrong? The unintended consequences of leveling readers. *The Reading Teacher*, *71*(3), 265–273.

Hofstadter-Duke, K. L., & Daly, E. J., III (2011). Improving oral reading fluency with a peer-mediated intervention. *Journal of Applied Behavior Analysis*, *44*(3), 641–646.

Holliman, A. J., Wood, C., & Sheehy, K. (2010). Does speech rhythm sensitivity predict children's reading ability 1 year later? *Journal of Educational Psychology*, *102*(2), 356–366.

Honig, A. (2001). *Teaching our children to read*. Corwin Press.

Howard, J. R., Milner-McCall, T., & Howard, T. C. (2020). *No more teaching without positive relationships*. Heinemann.

Hudson, A., Koh, P. W., Moore, K. A., & Binks-Cantrell, E. (2020). Fluency interventions for elementary students with reading difficulties: A synthesis of research from 2000–2019. *Education Sciences*, *10*(3), 52.

Hyönä, J. (1994). Processing of topic shifts by adults and children. *Reading Research Quarterly*, *29*(1), 77–90.

Hyönä, J., Lorch, R. F., Jr., & Kaakinen, J. K. (2002). Individual differences in reading to summarize expository text: Evidence from eye fixation patterns. *Journal of Educational Psychology*, *94*(1), 44–55.

Idol-Maestas, L. (1985). Getting ready to read: Guided probing for poor comprehenders. *Learning Disability Quarterly*, *8*(4), 243–254.

Iran-Nejad, A. (1987). Cognitive and affective causes of interest and liking. *Journal of Educational Psychology*, *79*(2), 120–130.

Irvine, E. (2021). The role of replication studies in theory building. *Perspectives on Psychological Science*, *16*(4), 844–853.

Ives, L., Mitchell, T. J., & Hübl, H. (2020). Promoting critical reading with double-entry notes: A pilot study. *InSight: A Journal of Scholarly Teaching*, *15*, 13–32.

Ivey, G., & Broaddus, K. (2007). A formative experiment investigating literacy engagement among adolescent Latina/o students just beginning to read, write, and speak English. *Reading Research Quarterly*, *42*(4), 512–545.

Ivey, G., & Johnston, P. H. (2013). Engagement with young adult literature: Outcomes and processes. *Reading Research Quarterly*, *48*(3), 255–275.

Iwasaki, B., Rasinski, T., Yildirim, K., & Zimmerman, B. S. (2013). Let's bring back the magic of song for teaching reading. *The Reading Teacher*, *67*(2), 137–141.

Jacobs, J. E., & Paris, S. G. (1987). Children's metacognition about reading: Issues in definition, measurement, and instruction. *Educational Psychologist*, *22*(3–4), 255–278.

Jacobson, J., Lapp, D., & Flood, J. (2007). A seven-step instructional plan for teaching English-language learners to comprehend and use homonyms, homophones, and homographs. *Journal of Adolescent & Adult Literacy*, *51*(2), 98–111.

Jacoby, J. W., & Edlefsen, K. (2020). "I love Paw Patrol!": Book selection and the allure of popular media characters among preschoolers. *Journal of Research in Childhood Education*, *34*(2), 208–222.

Jalongo, M. R. (1995). Promoting active listening in the classroom. *Childhood Education*, *72*(1), 13–18.

Jenkins, J. R., Stein, M. L., & Wysocki, K. (1984). Learning vocabulary through reading. *American Educational Research Journal*, *21*(4), 767–787.

Jewell, T. A., & Pratt, D. (1999). Literature discussions in the primary grades: Children's thoughtful discourse about books and what teachers can do to make it happen. *The Reading Teacher*, *52*(8), 842–850.

Johnson, D. W., & Johnson, R. (2007). *Creative controversy: Intellectual conflict in the classroom*. Interaction Book Company.

Johnson, D. W., & Johnson, R. T. (1989). Cooperative learning: What special education teachers need to know. *The Pointer*, *33*(2), 5–11.

Johnson, D. W., Johnson, R. T., & Tjosvold, D. (2014). Constructive controversy: The value of intellectual opposition. In P. T. Coleman, M. Deutsch, & E. C. Marcus (Eds.), *The handbook of conflict resolution: Theory and practice* (3rd ed., pp. 76–103). Routledge.

Johnston, F. P. (2001). The utility of phonic generalizations: Let's take another look at Clymer's conclusions. *The Reading Teacher*, *55*(2), 132–143.

Johnston, F. R. (1999). The timing and teaching of word families. *The Reading Teacher*, *53*(1), 64–75.

Joseph, L. M., Alber-Morgan, S., Cullen, J., & Rouse, C. (2016). The effects of self-questioning on reading comprehension: A literature review. *Reading & Writing Quarterly*, *32*(2), 152–173.

Josephs, N. L., & Jolivette, K. (2016). Effects of peer mediated instruction on the oral reading fluency skills of high school aged struggling readers. *Insights into Learning Disabilities, 13*(1), 39–59.

Jung, C. (1959). *The archetypes and the collective unconscious.* Princeton University Press.

Just, M. A., & Carpenter, P. A. (1980). A theory of reading: From eye fixations to comprehension. *Psychological Review, 87*(4), 329–354.

Justice, L. M., Skibbe, L., Canning, A., & Lankford, C. (2005). Pre-schoolers, print and storybooks: An observational study using eye movement analysis. *Journal of Research in Reading, 28*(3), 229–243.

Kachorsky, D., Moses, L., Serafini, F., & Hoelting, M. (2017). Meaning making with picturebooks: Young children's use of semiotic resources. *Literacy Research and Instruction, 56*(3), 231–249.

Kaefer, T., Neuman, S. B., & Pinkham, A. M. (2015). Pre-existing background knowledge influences socioeconomic differences in preschoolers' word learning and comprehension. *Reading Psychology, 36*(3), 203–231.

Kamberelis, G. (1999). Genre development and learning: Children writing stories, science reports, and poems. *Research in the Teaching of English, 33*(4), 403–460.

Kamberelis, G., & Bovino, T. D. (1999). Cultural artifacts as scaffolds for genre development. *Reading Research Quarterly, 34*(2), 138–170.

Katims, D. S., & Harris, S. (1997). Improving the reading comprehension of middle school students in inclusive classrooms. *Journal of Adolescent & Adult Literacy, 41*(2), 116–123.

Keehn, S., Harmon, J., & Shoho, A. (2008). A study of readers theater in eighth grade: Issues of fluency, comprehension, and vocabulary. *Reading & Writing Quarterly, 24*(4), 335–362.

Kelley, M., & Clausen-Grace, N. (2008). From picture walk to text feature walk: Guiding students to strategically preview informational text. *Journal of Content Area Reading, 7*(1), 5–28.

Kelley, M. J., & Clausen-Grace, N. (2010). Guiding students through expository text with text feature walks. *The Reading Teacher, 64*(3), 191–195.

Kelley, M. J., & Clausen-Grace, N. (2013). *Comprehension shouldn't be silent: From strategy instruction to student independence* (2nd ed.). International Reading Association.

Khataee, E. (2019). The effect of THIEVES strategy on EFL learners' reading comprehension. *International Journal of Instruction, 12*(2), 667–682.

Kieras, D. E. (1981). Component processes in the comprehension of simple prose. *Journal of Verbal Learning and Verbal Behavior, 20*(1), 1–23.

Kim, J. S., Burkhauser, M. A., Mesite, L. M., Asher, C. A., Relyea, J. E., Fitzgerald, J., & Elmore, J. (2021). Improving reading comprehension, science domain knowledge, and reading engagement through a first-grade content literacy intervention. *Journal of Educational Psychology, 113*(1), 3–26.

Kim, S. (1999) The effects of storytelling and pretend play on cognitive processes, short-term and long-term narrative recall, *Child Study Journal, 29*(3), 175–191.

Kintsch, W. (1986). Learning from text. *Cognition and Instruction, 3*(2), 87–108.

Kintsch, W. (1988). The role of knowledge in discourse comprehension: A construction-integration model. *Psychological Review, 95*(2), 163–182.

Kintsch, W., & Mangalath, P. (2011). The construction of meaning. *Topics in Cognitive Science, 3*(2), 346–370.

Klauda, S. L., & Guthrie, J. T. (2008). Relationships of three components of reading fluency to reading comprehension. *Journal of Educational Psychology, 100*(2), 310–321.

Klein, D. E., & Murphy, G. L. (2001). The representation of polysemous words. *Journal of Memory and Language, 45*(2), 259–282.

Klingner, J. K., & Vaughn, S. (1998). Using collaborative strategic reading. *Teaching Exceptional Children, 30*(6), 32–37.

Klingner, J. K., Vaughn, S., & Schumm, J. S. (1998). Collaborative strategic reading during social studies in heterogeneous fourth-grade classrooms. *The Elementary School Journal, 99*(1), 3–22.

Kluger, A. N., & DeNisi, A. (1996). The effects of feedback interventions on performance: A historical review, a meta-analysis, and a preliminary feedback intervention theory. *Psychological Bulletin, 119*(2), 254–284.

Knight-McKenna, M. (2008). Syllable types: A strategy for reading multisyllabic words. *Teaching Exceptional Children, 40*(3), 18–24.

Knight, L. N., & Hargis, C. H. (1977). Math language ability: Its relationship to reading in math. *Language Arts, 54*(4), 423–428.

Kong, A., & Fitch, E. (2002). Using book club to engage culturally and linguistically diverse learners in reading, writing, and talking about books. *The Reading Teacher*, *56*(4), 352–362.

Krashen, S. D. (2004). *The power of reading: Insights from the research* (2nd ed.). Libraries Unlimited.

Kress, G. (2009). *Multimodality: A social semiotic approach to contemporary communication*. Routledge.

Krug, D., George, B., Hannon, S. A., & Glover, J. A. (1989). The effect of outlines and headings on readers' recall of text. *Contemporary Educational Psychology*, *14*(2), 111–123.

Kucan, L. (2012). What is most important to know about vocabulary? *The Reading Teacher*, *65*(6), 360–366.

Kucan, L., & Palincsar, A. S. (2018). Text analysis: Critical component of planning for text-based discussion focused on comprehension of informational texts. *Literacy Research and Instruction*, *57*(2), 100–116.

Kucer, S. B. (2017). The monitoring and responding behaviours of proficient fourth grade readers to miscues on a complex scientific text. *Literacy*, *51*(3), 154–161.

Kuhn, M. R., Schwanenflugel, P. J., & Meisinger, E. B. (2010). Aligning theory and assessment of reading fluency: Automaticity, prosody, and definitions of fluency. *Reading Research Quarterly*, *45*(2), 230–251.

Lai, S. A., George Benjamin, R., Schwanenflugel, P. J., & Kuhn, M. R. (2014). The longitudinal relationship between reading fluency and reading comprehension skills in second-grade children. *Reading & Writing Quarterly*, *30*(2), 116–138.

Landry, S. H., & Smith, K. E. (2006). The influence of parenting on emerging literacy skills. In D. K. Dickinson & S. B. Neuman (Eds.), *Handbook of early literacy research* (Vol. 2, pp. 135–148). Guilford.

Landy, D., Silbert, N., & Goldin, A. (2013). Estimating large numbers. *Cognitive Science*, *37*(5), 775–799.

Langer, J. A. (1984). Examining background knowledge and text comprehension. *Reading Research Quarterly*, *19*(4), 468–481.

Lauterbach, S. L., & Bender, W. N. (1995). Cognitive strategy instruction for reading comprehension: A success for high school freshmen. *The High School Journal*, *79*(1), 58–64.

Leal, D. J., Glascock, C. H., Mitchell, D., & Wasserman, D. (2000). Reading character in children's literature: A character trait study of Newbery Medal books. *Ohio Reading Teacher*, *34*(1), 49–56.

Lee, S. H. (2017). Learning vocabulary through e-book reading of young children with various reading abilities. *Reading and Writing*, *30*(7), 1595–1616.

Lehr, S. (1988). The child's developing sense of theme as a response to literature. *Reading Research Quarterly*, *23*(3), 337–357.

Lehr, S. S. (1991). *The child's developing sense of theme: Responses to literature*. Teachers College Press.

Lekwilai, P. (2014). Reader's theater: An alternative tool to develop reading fluency among Thai EFL learners. *PASAA: Journal of Language Teaching and Learning in Thailand*, *48*, 89–111.

Leopold, C., & Leutner, D. (2012). Science text comprehension: Drawing, main idea selection, and summarizing as learning strategies. *Learning and Instruction*, *22*(1), 16–26.

LeVasseur, V. M., Macaruso, P., Palumbo, L. C., & Shankweiler, D. (2006). Syntactically cued text facilitates oral reading fluency in developing readers. *Applied Psycholinguistics*, *27*(3), 423–445.

LeVasseur, V. M., Macaruso, P., & Shankweiler, D. (2008). Promoting gains in reading fluency: A comparison of three approaches. *Reading and Writing*, *21*(3), 205–230.

Liang, L. A., & Lowe, A. (2018). "Really reading" and really responding. In D. A. Wooten, L. A. Liang, & B. E. Cullinan (Eds.), *Children's literature in the reading program: Engaging young readers in the 21st Century* (5th ed., pp. 125–139). Guilford.

Lindeman, B., & Kling, M. (1968–1969). Bibliotherapy: Definitions, uses, and studies. *Journal of School Psychology*, *7*(2), 36–41.

Lipson, M. Y. (1982). Learning new information from text: The role of prior knowledge and reading ability. *Journal of Reading Behavior*, *14*(3), 243–261.

Liu, J. (2000). The power of readers theater: From reading to writing. *ELT Journal*, *54*(4), 354–361.

Logan, J. K., & Kieffer, M. J. (2017). Academic vocabulary instruction: Building knowledge about the world and how words work. In D. Lapp & D. Fisher (Eds.), *Handbook of research on teaching the English language arts* (4th ed., pp. 162–182). Routledge.

Lorch, R., Lemarié, J., & Grant, R. (2011). Signaling hierarchical and sequential organization in expository text. *Scientific Studies of Reading*, *15*(3), 267–284.

Lorch, R. F. (1989). Text-signaling devices and their effects on reading and memory processes. *Educational Psychology Review*, *1*(3), 209–234.

Lorch, R. F., Jr., Lorch E. P., & Matthews, P. D. (1985). On-line processing of the topic structure of a text. *Journal of Memory and Language, 24*(3), 350–362.

Lorch, R. F., Jr., Lorch E. P., & Morgan, A. M. (1987). Task effects and individual differences in on-line processing of the topic structure of a text. *Discourse Processes, 10*(1), 63–80.

Lovett, M. W., Lacerenza, L., Borden, S. L., Frijters, J. C., Steinbach, K. A., & De Palma, M. (2000). Components of effective remediation for developmental reading disabilities: Combining phonological and strategy-based instruction to improve outcomes. *Journal of Educational Psychology, 92*(2), 263–283.

Lubliner, S., & Smetana, L. (2005). The effects of comprehensive vocabulary instruction on Title I students' metacognitive word-learning skills and reading comprehension. *Journal of Literacy Research, 37*(2), 163–200.

Luke, A. (2012). Critical literacy: Foundational notes. *Theory into Practice, 51*(1), 4–11.

Lupo, S. M., Strong, J. Z., Lewis, W., Walpole, S., & McKenna, M. C. (2018). Building background knowledge through reading: Rethinking text sets. *Journal of Adolescent & Adult Literacy, 61*(4), 433–444.

Lysaker, J. T., Tonge, C., Gauson, D., & Miller, A. (2011). Reading and social imagination: What relationally oriented reading instruction can do for children. *Reading Psychology, 32*(6), 520–566.

Maloch, B. (2008). Beyond exposure: The uses of informational texts in a second grade classroom. *Research in the Teaching of English, 42*(3), 315–362.

Mancilla-Martinez, J., & McClain, J. B. (2020). What do we know today about the complexity of vocabulary gaps and what do we not know? In E. B. Moje, P. Afflerbach, P Enciso, & N. K. Lesaux (Eds.), *Handbook of reading research* (Vol. 5, pp. 216–236). Routledge.

Mandler, J. M., & Johnson, N. S. (1977). Remembrance of things parsed: Story structure and recall. *Cognitive Psychology, 9*(1), 111–151.

Manoli, P., & Papadopoulou, M. (2012). Reading strategies versus reading skills: Two faces of the same coin. *Procedia-Social and Behavioral Sciences, 46*, 817–821.

Manz, S. L. (2002). A strategy for previewing textbooks: Teaching readers to become THIEVES. *The Reading Teacher, 55*(5), 434–436.

Marr, M. B., Algozzine, B., Nicholson, K., & Keller Dugan, K. (2011). Building oral reading fluency with peer coaching. *Remedial and Special Education, 32*(3), 256–264.

Martin, L. E., & Kragler, S. (2011). Becoming a self-regulated reader: A study of primary-grade students' reading strategies. *Literacy Research and Instruction, 50*(2), 89–104.

Martin, N. M. (2011). *Exploring informational text comprehension: Reading biography, persuasive text, and procedural text in the elementary grades* (Publication No. 3465046) [Doctoral dissertation, Michigan State University]. ProQuest Dissertations Publishing.

Mason, J. M., & Allen, J. (1986). A review of emergent literacy with implications for research and practice in reading. *Review of Research in Education, 13*(1), 3–47.

Mason, L. H. (2004). Explicit self-regulated strategy development versus reciprocal questioning: Effects on expository reading comprehension among struggling readers. *Journal of Educational Psychology, 96*(2), 283–296.

Mason, L. H. (2013). Teaching students who struggle with learning to think before, while, and after reading: Effects of self-regulated strategy development instruction. *Reading & Writing Quarterly, 29*(2), 124–144.

Mason, L. H., Meadan-Kaplansky, H., Hedin, L., & Taft, R. (2013). Self-regulating informational text reading comprehension: Perceptions of low-achieving students. *Exceptionality, 21*(2), 69–86.

Mason, L. H., Snyder, K. H., Sukhram, D. P., & Kedem, Y. (2006) TWA + PLANS strategies for expository reading and writing: Effects for nine fourth-grade students, *Exceptional Children, 73*(1), 69–89.

Matthews, M. W., & Cobb, M. B. (2005). Broadening the interpretive lens: Considering individual development along with sociocultural views of learning to understand young children's interactions during socially mediated literacy events. *Journal of Literacy Research, 37*(3), 325–364.

Mayer, R. E. (1996). Learning strategies for making sense out of expository text: The SOI model for guiding three cognitive processes in knowledge construction. *Educational Psychology Review, 8*(4), 357–371.

Mayer, R. E. (2005). *Cognitive theory of multimedia learning.* In R. E. Mayed (Ed.), *The Cambridge handbook of multimedia learning* (pp. 31–38). *Cambridge University Press.*

Mayer, R. E. (2008). *Learning and instruction* (2nd ed.). Pearson Merrill Prentice Hall.

Mayer, R. E., Steinhoff, K., Bower, G., & Mars, R. (1995). A generative theory of textbook design: Using annotated illustrations to foster meaningful learning of science text. *Educational Technology Research and Development, 43*(1), 31–41.

McBreen, M., & Savage, R. (2021). The impact of motivational reading instruction on the reading achievement and motivation of students: A systematic review and meta-analysis. *Educational Psychology Review, 33*(3), 1125–1163.

McBride-Chang, C. (1999). The ABCs of the ABCs: The development of letter-name and letter-sound knowledge. *Merrill-Palmer Quarterly 45*(2), 285–308.

McCandliss, B., Beck, I. L., Sandak, R., & Perfetti, C. (2003). Focusing attention on decoding for children with poor reading skills: Design and preliminary tests of the word building intervention. *Scientific Studies of Reading, 7*(1), 75–104.

McCarthy, K. S., & Goldman, S. R. (2015). Comprehension of short stories: Effects of task instructions on literary interpretation. *Discourse Processes, 52*(7), 585–608.

McConaughy, S., Fitzhenry-Coor, I., & Howell, D. (1983). Developmental differences in story schemata. In K. E. Nelson (Ed.), *Children's language* (Vol. 4, pp. 421–427). Erlbaum.

McGeown, S. P. (2012). Sex or gender identity? Understanding children's reading choices and motivation. *Journal of Research in Reading, 38*(1), 35–46.

McGill-Franzen, A., & Ward, N. (2018). To develop proficiency and engagement, give series books to novice readers! In D. A. Wooten, L. A. Liang, & B. E. Cullinan (Eds.), *Children's literature in the reading program: Engaging young readers in the 21st Century* (5th ed., pp. 125–139). Guilford.

McGrew, S., Breakstone, J., Ortega, T., Smith, M., & Wineburg, S. (2018). Can students evaluate online sources? Learning from assessments of civic online reasoning. *Theory & Research in Social Education, 46*(2), 165–193.

McKeown, M. G., & Beck, I. L. (2015). Effective classroom talk *is* reading comprehension instruction. In L. B. Resnick, C. S. C. Asterhan, & S. N. Clarke (Eds.), *Socializing intelligence through academic talk and dialogue* (pp. 51–62). American Educational Research Association.

McTigue, E., Douglass, A., Wright, K. L., Hodges, T. S., & Franks, A. D. (2015). Beyond the story map: Inferential comprehension via character perspective. *The Reading Teacher, 69*(1), 91–101.

McTigue, E. M. (2010). Teaching young readers imagery in storytelling: What color is the monkey? *The Reading Teacher, 64*(1), 53–56.

McTigue, E. M., & Flowers, A. C. (2011). Science visual literacy: Learners' perceptions and knowledge of diagrams. *The Reading Teacher, 64*(8), 578–589.

Meese, R. L. (2016). We're not in Kansas anymore: The TOTO strategy for decoding vowel pairs. *The Reading Teacher, 69*(5), 549–552.

Menary, R. (2007). Writing as thinking. *Language Sciences, 29*(5), 621–632.

Merga, M. K. (2017). Becoming a reader: Significant social influences on avid book readers. *School Library Research: Research Journal of the American Association of School Librarians, 20*, 1–21.

Merga, M. K., & Roni, S. M. (2017). Choosing strategies of children and the impact of age and gender on library use: Insights for librarians. *Journal of Library Administration, 57*(6), 607–630.

Mesmer, H. A., & Kambach, A. (2022). Beyond labels and agendas: Research teachers need to know about phonics and phonological awareness. *The Reading Teacher, 76*(1), 62–72. https://doi-org.proxy.lib.umich.edu/10.1002/trtr.2102

Meyer, B. J., Brandt, D. M., & Bluth, G. J. (1980). Use of top-level structure in text: Key for reading comprehension of ninth-grade students. *Reading Research Quarterly, 16*(1), 72–103.

Meyer, B. J., & Poon, L. W. (2001). Effects of structure strategy training and signaling on recall of text. *Journal of Educational Psychology, 93*(1), 141–159.

Meyer, B. J., & Ray, M. N. (2011). Structure strategy interventions: Increasing reading comprehension of expository text. *International Electronic Journal of Elementary Education, 4*(1), 127–152.

Meyer, B. J. F. (1975). *The organization of prose and its effects on memory*. North-Holland.

Meyer, B. J. F. (1981). Basic research on prose comprehension: A critical review. In D. F. Fisher & C. W. Peters (Eds.), *Comprehension and the competent reader: Inter-specialty perspectives* (pp. 8–35). Praeger.

Meyer, B. J. F. (1985). Prose analysis: Purposes, procedures, and problems. In B. K. Britton & J. Black (Eds.), *Analyzing and understanding expository text* (pp. 11–64). Erlbaum.

Michaels, S., O'Connor, C., & Resnick, L. B. (2008). Deliberative discourse idealized and realized: Accountable talk in the classroom and in civic life. *Studies in Philosophy and Education*, *27*(4), 283–297.

Miller, G. A. (1999). On knowing a word. *Annual Review of Psychology*, *50*(1), 1–19.

Miller, J., & Schwanenflugel, P. J. (2006). Prosody of syntactically complex sentences in the oral reading of young children. *Journal of Educational Psychology*, *98*(4), 839–843.

Miller, J., & Schwanenflugel, P. J. (2008). A longitudinal study of the development of reading prosody as a dimension of oral reading fluency in early elementary school children. *Reading Research Quarterly*, *43*(4), 336–354.

Montag, J. L., Jones, M. N., & Smith, L. B. (2015). The words children hear: Picture books and the statistics for language learning. *Psychological Science*, *26*(9), 1489–1496.

Moran, K. J. K. (2006). Nurturing emergent readers through readers theater. *Early Childhood Education Journal*, *33*(5), 317–323.

Mork, T. A. (1973). The ability of children to select reading materials at their own instructional level. In W. H. MacGinitie (Ed.), *Assessment problems in reading* (pp. 87–95). International Reading Association.

Morris, D. (1993). The relationship between children's concept of word in text and phoneme awareness in learning to read: A longitudinal study. *Research in the Teaching of English*, *27*(2), 133–154.

Morrow, L. M. (1985). Retelling stories: A strategy for improving young children's comprehension, concept of story structure, and oral language complexity. *The Elementary School Journal*, *85*(5), 647–661.

Motha, S. (2014). *Race, empire, and English language teaching: Creating responsible and ethical anti-racist practice*. Teachers College Press.

Moyer, J. E. (2011). What does it really mean to "read" a text? *Journal of Adolescent & Adult Literacy*, *55*(3), 253–256.

Mraz, M., Nichols, W., Caldwell, S., Beisley, R., Sargent, S., & Rupley, W. (2013). Improving oral reading fluency through readers theatre. *Reading Horizons: A Journal of Literacy and Language Arts*, *52*(2), 163–180.

Nagy, W. E., Anderson, R. C., & Herman, P. A. (1987). Learning word meanings from context during normal reading. *American Educational Research Journal*, *24*(2), 237–270.

Nagy, W. E., Herman, P. A., & Anderson, R. C. (1985). Learning words from context. *Reading Research Quarterly*, *20*(2), 233–253.

Naiditch, F. (2010). Critical pedagogy and the teaching of reading for social action. *Critical Questions in Education*, *1*(2), 94–107.

Nation, K., & Cocksey, J. (2009). The relationship between knowing a word and reading it aloud in children's word reading development. *Journal of Experimental Child Psychology*, *103*(3), 296–308.

National Endowment for the Arts. (2007). *To read or not to read: A question of national consequence. Research Report #47.* https://www.arts.gov/impact/research/publications/read-or-not-read-question-national-consequence

National Reading Panel. (2000). *Report of the National Reading Panel. Teaching children to read: An evidence-based assessment of the scientific research literature on reading and its implications for reading instruction* (00-4769). National Institute of Child Health & Human Development.

National Research Council. (1998). *Preventing reading difficulties in young children.* The National Academies Press.

Nelson, J. R., Smith, D. J., & Dodd, J. M. (1992). The effects of teaching a summary skills strategy to students identified as learning disabled on their comprehension of science text. *Education and Treatment of Children*, *15*(3)228–243.

Neumann, D., Gilbertson, N., & Hutton, L. (2014). Context: The foundation of close reading of primary source texts. *Social Studies Research and Practice*, *9*(2), 68–76.

Nichols, W. D., Rasinski, T. V., Rupley, W. H., Kellogg, R. A., & Paige, D. D. (2018). Why poetry for reading instruction? Because it works! *The Reading Teacher*, *72*(3), 389–397.

Nikolajeva, M. (2013). Picturebooks and emotional literacy. *The Reading Teacher*, *67*(4), 249–254.

Nikolajeva, M. (2017). Emotions in picturebooks. In B. Kümmerling-Meibauer (Ed.), *The Routledge companion to picturebooks* (pp. 110–118). Routledge.

Nippold, M. A. (1985). Comprehension of figurative language in youth. *Topics in Language Disorders*, *5*(3), 1–20.

Nodelman, P. (1988). *Words about pictures: The narrative art of children's picture books*. University of Georgia Press.

Nolan, T. E. (1991). Self-questioning and prediction: Combining metacognitive strategies. *Journal of Reading, 35*(2), 132–138.

Nomvete, P., & Easterbrooks, S. R. (2020). Phrase-reading mediates between words and syntax in struggling adolescent readers. *Communication Disorders Quarterly, 41*(3), 162–175.

Norman, R. R. (2012). Reading the graphics: What is the relationship between graphical reading processes and student comprehension? *Reading and Writing, 25*(3), 739–774.

Norman, R. R., & Roberts, K. L. (2015). Getting the bigger picture: Children's utilization of graphics and text. *Journal of Visual Literacy, 34*(1), 35–56.

O'Brien, E. J., Rizzella, M. L., Albrecht, J. E., & Halleran, J. G. (1998). Updating a situation model: A memory-based text processing view. *Journal of Experimental Psychology: Learning, Memory, and Cognition, 24*(5), 1200–1210.

O'Brien, B. A., Van Orden, G. C., & Pennington, B. F. (2013). Do dyslexics misread a ROWS for a ROSE? *Reading and Writing, 26*(3), 381–402.

O'Hallaron, C. L., Palincsar, A. S., & Schleppegrell, M. J. (2015). Reading science: Using systemic functional linguistics to support critical language awareness. *Linguistics and Education, 32*, 55–67.

Okkinga, M., van Steensel, R., van Gelderen, A. J., van Schooten, E., Sleegers, P. J., & Arends, L. R. (2018). Effectiveness of reading-strategy interventions in whole classrooms: A meta-analysis. *Educational Psychology Review, 30*(4), 1215–1239.

Olson, C. B., Land, R., Anselmi, T., & AuBuchon, C. (2010). Teaching secondary English learners to understand, analyze, and write interpretive essays about theme. *Journal of Adolescent & Adult Literacy, 54*(4), 245–256.

Padeliadu, S., & Giazitzidou, S. (2018). A synthesis of research on reading fluency development: Study of eight meta-analyses. *European Journal of Special Education Research, 3*(4), 232–256.

Palincsar, A. S., & Brown, A. L. (1984). Reciprocal teaching of comprehension-fostering and comprehension-monitoring activities. *Cognition and Instruction, 1*(2), 117–175.

Palmer, S. B., & Wehmeyer, M. L. (2003). Promoting self-determination in early elementary school: Teaching self-regulated problem-solving and goal-setting skills. *Remedial and Special Education, 24*(2), 115–126.

Pappas, C. C. (1993). Is narrative "primary"? Some insights from kindergarteners' pretend readings of stories and information books. *Journal of Reading Behavior, 25*(1), 97–129.

Paratore, J. R., Cassano, C. M., & Schickedanz, J. A. (2011). Supporting early (and later) literacy development at home and at school: The long view. In M. L. Kamil, P. D. Pearson, E. B. Moje, & P. Afflerbach (Eds.), *Handbook of reading research* (Vol. 4, pp. 133–161). Routledge.

Pardeck, J. T., & Markward, M. J. (1995). Bibliotherapy: Using books to help children deal with problems. *Early Child Development and Care, 106*(1), 75–90.

Paris, S. G., & Cross, D. R. (1983). Ordinary learning: Pragmatic connections among children's beliefs, motives, and actions. In J. Bisanz, G. L. Bisanz & R. Kail (Eds.). *Learning in children*. Springer.

Paris, S. G., Lipson, M. Y., & Wixson, K. K. (1983). Becoming a strategic reader. *Contemporary Educational Psychology, 8*(3), 293–316.

Paxton-Buursma, D., & Walker, M. (2008). Piggybacking: A strategy to increase participation in classroom discussions by students with learning disabilities. *Teaching Exceptional Children, 40*(3), 28–34.

Pearson, P. D., & Fielding, L. (1991). Comprehension instruction. In R. Barr, M. L. Kamil, P. Mosenthal, & P. D. Pearson (Eds.), *Handbook of reading research* (Vol. 2, pp. 815–860). Routledge.

Pearson, P. D., Moje, E., & Greenleaf, C. (2010). Literacy and science: Each in the service of the other. *Science, 328*(5977), 459–463.

Peck, S. M., & Virkler, A. J. (2006). Reading in the shadows: Extending literacy skills through shadow-puppet theater. *The Reading Teacher, 59*(8), 786–795.

Pennington, L. K., & Tackett, M. E. (2021). Using text sets to teach elementary learners about Japanese-American incarceration. *Ohio Social Studies Review, 57*(1), 1–14.

Peracchi, K. A., & O'Brien, E. J. (2004). Character profiles and the activation of predictive inferences. *Memory & Cognition, 32*(7), 1044–1052.

Pérez, A. M., Peña, E. D., & Bedore, L. M. (2010). Cognates facilitate word recognition in young Spanish-English bilinguals' test performance. *Early Childhood Services, 4*(1), 55–67.

Perfetti, C. A. (1994). Psycholinguistics and reading ability. In M. A. Gernsbacher (Ed.), *Handbook of psycholinguistics* (pp. 849–894). Academic Press.

Peskin, J., & Wells-Jopling, R. (2012). Fostering symbolic interpretation during adolescence. *Journal of Applied Developmental Psychology*, *33*(1), 13–23.

Peterson, D. S. (2019). Engaging elementary students in higher order talk and writing about text. *Journal of Early Childhood Literacy*, *19*(1), 34–54.

Peterson, D. S., & Taylor, B. M. (2012). Using higher order questioning to accelerate students' growth in reading. *The Reading Teacher*, *65*(5), 295–304.

Peterson, M. E., & Haines, L. P. (1992). Orthographic analogy training with kindergarten children: Effects on analogy use, phonemic segmentation, and letter-sound knowledge. *Journal of Reading Behavior*, *24*(1), 109–127.

Pfaff, K. L., & Gibbs, R. W., Jr. (1997). Authorial intentions in understanding satirical texts. *Poetics*, *25*(1), 45–70.

Phillips, L. M. (1988). Young readers' inference strategies in reading comprehension. *Cognition and Instruction*, *5*(3), 193–222.

Pintrich, P. R. (2000). The role of goal orientation in self-regulated learning. In M. Boekaerts, P. R. Pintrich, & M. Zeidner (Eds.). *Handbook of self-regulation* (pp. 451–502). Academic Press.

Pintrich, P. R., Smith, D. A. F., Garcia, T., & McKeachie, W. J. (1991). *A manual for the use of the Motivated Strategies for Learning Questionnaire (MSLQ)*. National Center for Research to Improve Postsecondary Teaching and Learning.

Piolat, A., Olive, T., & Kellogg, R. T. (2005). Cognitive effort during note taking. *Applied Cognitive Psychology*, *19*(3), 291–312.

Plucker, J. A., & Makel, M. C. (2021). Replication is important for educational psychology: Recent developments and key issues. *Educational Psychologist*, *56*(2), 90–100.

Porter-O'Donnell, C. (2004). Beyond the yellow highlighter: Teaching annotation skills to improve reading comprehension. *English Journal*, *93*(5), 82–89.

Powell, R., McIntyre, E., & Rightmyer, E. (2006). Johnny won't read, and Susie won't either: Reading instruction and student resistance. *Journal of Early Childhood Literacy*, *6*(1), 5–31.

Pressley, M. (2002a). Comprehension strategies instruction: A turn-of-the-century status report. In C. C. Block & M. Pressley (Eds.). *Comprehension instruction: Research-based best practices* (pp. 11–27). Guilford.

Pressley, M. (2002b). Metacognition and self-regulated comprehension. In A. E. Farstrup & S. J. Samuels (Eds.), *What research has to say about reading instruction* (3rd ed., pp. 291–309). International Reading Association.

Pressley, M., & Afflerbach, P. (1995). *Verbal protocols of reading: The nature of constructively reading*. Erlbaum.

Pressley, M., & Allington, R. L. (2014). *Reading instruction that works: The case for balanced teaching*. (4th ed.). Guilford.

Pressley, M., Wharton-McDonald, R., Allington, R., Block, C. C., Morrow, L., Tracey, D., Baker, K., Brooks, G., Cronin, J., Nelson, E., & Woo, D. (2001). A study of effective first-grade literacy instruction. *Scientific Studies of Reading*, *5*(1), 35–58.

Prichard, C., & Atkins, A. (2021). Evaluating the vocabulary coping strategies of L2 readers: An eye tracking study. *TESOL Quarterly*, *55*(2), 593–620.

Priebe, S. J., Keenan, J. M., & Miller, A. C. (2012). How prior knowledge affects word identification and comprehension. *Reading and Writing*, *25*(1), 131–149.

Proctor, C. P., Dalton, B., & Grisham, D. L. (2007). Scaffolding English language learners and struggling readers in a universal literacy environment with embedded strategy instruction and vocabulary support. *Journal of Literacy Research*, *39*(1), 71–93.

Prouty, J. H. L. (1986). *Third grade readers' comprehension of a flashback in a narrative* (Publication No. 8625432) [Doctoral dissertation, Texas A&M University]. ProQuest Dissertations Publishing.

Puranik, C. S., Lonigan, C. J., & Kim, Y. S. (2011). Contributions of emergent literacy skills to name writing, letter writing, and spelling in preschool children. *Early Childhood Research Quarterly*, *26*(4), 465–474.

Purcell-Gates, V. (1988). Lexical and syntactic knowledge of written narrative held by well-read-to kindergartners and second graders. *Research in the Teaching of English*, *22*(2), 128–160.

Purcell-Gates, V., Duke, N. K., & Martineau, J. A. (2007). Learning to read and write genre-specific text: Roles of authentic experience and explicit teaching. *Reading Research Quarterly*, *42*(1), 8–45.

Raphael, T. E., Pardo, L. S., & Highfield, K. (2013). *Book club: A literature-based curriculum* (2nd ed.). Small Planet Communications.

Rapp, D. N., Gerrig, R. J., & Prentice, D. A. (2001). Readers' trait-based models of characters in narrative comprehension. *Journal of Memory and Language, 45*(4), 737-750.

Rapp, D. N., & Kendeou, P. (2007). Revising what readers know: Updating text representations during narrative comprehension. *Memory & Cognition, 35*(8), 2019-2032.

Rapp, D. N., & Kendeou, P. (2009). Noticing and revising discrepancies as texts unfold. *Discourse Processes, 46*(1), 1-24.

Rapp, D. N., van den Broek, P., McMaster, K. L., Kendeou, P., & Espin, C. A. (2007). Higher-order comprehension processes in struggling readers: A perspective for research and intervention. *Scientific Studies of Reading, 11*(4), 289-312.

Rasinski, T., Samuels, S. J., Hiebert, E., Petscher, Y., & Feller, K. (2011). The relationship between a silent reading fluency instructional protocol on students' reading comprehension and achievement in an urban school setting. *Reading Psychology, 32*(1), 75-97.

Rasinski, T. V. (1990). *The effects of cued phrase boundaries on reading performance: A review.* Kent State University. (ERIC Document Reproduction Service No. ED313689).

Rayner, K. (1998). Eye movements in reading and information processing: 20 years of research. *Psychological Bulletin, 124*(3), 372-422.

Rayner, K. (1988). Word recognition cues in children: The relative use of graphemic cues, orthographic cues, and grapheme-phoneme correspondence rules. *Journal of Educational Psychology, 80*(4), 473-479.

Rayner, K., Foorman, B. R., Perfetti, C. A., Pesetsky, D., & Seidenberg, M. S. (2001). How psychological science informs the teaching of reading. *Psychological Science in the Public Interest, 2*(2), 31-74.

Recht, D. R., & Leslie, L. (1988). Effect of prior knowledge on good and poor readers' memory of text. *Journal of Educational Psychology, 80*(1), 16-20.

Reed, D. K., & Vaughn, S. (2012). Retell as an indicator of reading comprehension. *Scientific Studies of Reading, 16*(3), 187-217.

Reese, C., & Wells, T. (2007). Teaching academic discussion skills with a card game. *Simulation & Gaming, 38*(4), 546-555.

Reinking, D., & Watkins, J. (2000). A formative experiment investigating the use of multimedia book reviews to increase elementary students' independent reading. *Reading Research Quarterly, 35*(3), 384-419.

Renga, I. P., & Lewis, M. A. (2018). Wisdom, mystery, and dangerous knowledge: Exploring depictions of the archetypal sage in young adult literature. *Study and Scrutiny: Research on Young Adult Literature, 3*(1), 25-50.

Renz, K., Lorch, E. P., Milich, R., Lemberger, C., Bodner, A., & Welsh, R. (2003). On-line story representation in boys with Attention Deficit Hyperactivity Disorder. *Journal of Abnormal Child Psychology, 31*(1), 93-104.

Resnick, L., & Beck, I. L. (1976). Designing Instruction in reading: Interaction of theory and practice. In J. T. Guthrie (Ed.), *Aspects of reading acquisition.* Johns Hopkins University Press.

Reutzel, D. R. (1985). Story maps improve comprehension. *The Reading Teacher, 38*(4), 400-404.

Reutzel, D. R., Jones, C. D., & Newman, T. H. (2010). Scaffolded silent reading: Improving the practice of silent reading practice in classrooms. In E. H. Hiebert & D. R. Reutzel (Eds.), *Revisiting silent reading: New directions for teachers and researchers* (pp. 129-150). International Reading Association.

Reutzel, D. R., & Morgan, B. C. (1990). Effects of prior knowledge, explicitness, and clause order on children's comprehension of causal relationships. *Reading Psychology: An International Quarterly, 11*(2), 93-114.

Reynolds, G. A., & Perin, D. (2009). A comparison of text structure and self-regulated writing strategies for composing from sources by middle school students. *Reading Psychology, 30*(3), 265-300.

Richards, E., & Singer, M. (2001). Representation of complex goal structures in narrative comprehension. *Discourse Processes, 31*(2), 111-135.

Rinehart, S. D., Gerlach, J. M., Wisell, D. L., & Welker, W. A. (1998). Would I like to read this book? Eighth graders' use of book cover clues to help choose recreational reading. *Literacy Research and Instruction, 37*(4), 263-280.

Roberts, K. L., & Brugar, K. A. (2017). The view from here: Emergence of graphical literacy. *Reading Psychology, 38*(8), 733-777.

Robinson, H. M., & Weintraub, S. (1973). Research related to children's interests and to developmental values of reading. *Library Trends*, *22*(2), 81–108.

Rodríguez, T. A. (2001). From the known to the unknown: Using cognates to teach English to Spanish-speaking literates. *The Reading Teacher*, *54*(8), 744–746.

Romance, N. R., & Vitale, M. R. (2001). Implementing an in-depth expanded science model in elementary schools: Multi-year findings, research issues, and policy implications. *International Journal of Science Education*, *23*(4), 373–404.

Rosenblatt, L. (1978). *The reader, the text, the poem: The transactional theory of the literary work*. Southern Illinois University Press.

Rosenshine, B., Meister, C., & Chapman, S. (1996). Teaching students to generate questions: A review of the intervention studies. *Review of Educational Research*, *66*(2), 181–221.

Roser, N., Martinez, M., Fuhrken, C., & McDonnold, K. (2007). Characters as guides to meaning. *The Reading Teacher*, *60*(6), 548–559.

Rupley, W. H., Logan, J. W., & Nichols, W. D. (1998). Vocabulary instruction in a balanced reading program. *The Reading Teacher*, *52*(4), 336–346.

Ryan, M.-L. (2020). Narrative cartography. In D. Richardson, N. Castree, M. F. Goodchild, A. Kobayashi, W. Liu, & R. A. Marston (Eds.), *The International Encyclopedia of Geography*. John Wiley & Sons. https://doi.org/10.1002/9781118786352.wbieg2024

Sacks, H., Schegloff, E. A., & Jefferson, G. (1974). A simplest systematics for the organization of turn-taking for conversation. *Language*, *50*(4), 696–735.

Sadler, D. R. (1989). Formative assessment and the design of instructional systems. *Instructional Science*, *18*(2), 119–144.

Sadoski, M., & Paivio, A. (2012). *Imagery and text: A Dual Coding Theory of reading and writing* (2nd ed.). Routledge.

Sadoski, M., & Quast, Z. (1990). Reader response and long-term recall for journalistic text: The roles of imagery, affect, and importance. *Reading Research Quarterly*, *25*(4), 256–272.

Sampson, M. R., Valmont, W. J., & Van Allen, R. (1982). The effects of instructional cloze on the comprehension, vocabulary, and divergent production of third-grade students. *Reading Research Quarterly*, *17*(3), 389–399.

Samuelstuen, M. S., & Bråten, I. (2005). Decoding, knowledge, and strategies in comprehension of expository text. *Scandinavian Journal of Psychology*, *46*(2), 107–117.

Sanders, S., Rollins, L. H., Mason, L. H., Shaw, A., & Jolivette, K. (2021). Intensification and individualization of self-regulation components within self-regulated strategy development. *Intervention in School and Clinic*, *56*(3), 131–140.

Scanlon, D. M., Anderson, K. L., & Sweeney, J. M. (2010). *Early intervention for reading difficulties: The interactive strategies approach*. Guilford.

Scarborough, H. S. (2001). Connecting early language and literacy to later reading (dis)abilities: Evidence, theory, and practice. In S. B. Neuman & D. K. Dickinson (Eds.), *Handbook of early literacy research* (pp. 97–110). Guilford.

Scardamalia, M., & Bereiter, C. (1992). Text-based and knowledge-based questioning by children. *Cognition and Instruction*, *9*(3), 177–199.

Schmitt, N., Jiang, X., & Grabe, W. (2011). The percentage of words known in a text and reading comprehension. *The Modern Language*, *95*(1).

Schooler, J. W., Reichle, E. D., & Halpern, D. V. (2004). Zoning Out while Reading: Evidence for Dissociations between Experience and Metaconsciousness. In D. T. Levin (Ed.), *Thinking and seeing: Visual metacognition in adults and children* (pp. 203–226). MIT Press.

Schraw, G., & Dennison, R. S. (1994). Assessing metacognitive awareness. *Contemporary Educational Psychology*, *19*(4), 460–475.

Schraw, G., & Lehman, S. (2001). Situational interest: A review of the literature and directions for future research. *Educational Psychology Review*, *13*(1), 23–52.

Schreiber, P. A. (1991). Understanding prosody's role in reading acquisition. *Theory into Practice*, *30*(3), 158–164.

Schumaker, J. B., Denton, P. H., & Deshler, D. D. (1984). *The Paraphrasing Strategy: Instructor's manual*. University of Kansas Institute for Research in Learning Disabilities.

Schunk, D. H., & Rice, J. M. (1989). Learning goals and children's reading comprehension. *Journal of Reading Behavior*, *21*(3), 279–293.

Schunk, D. H., & Rice, J. M. (1991). Learning goals and progress feedback during reading comprehension instruction. *Journal of Reading Behavior*, *23*(3), 351–364.

Schwamborn, A., Mayer, R. E., Thillmann, H., Leopold, C., & Leutner, D. (2010). Drawing as a generative activity and drawing as a prognostic activity. *Journal of Educational Psychology, 102*(4), 872–879.

Schwanenflugel, P. J., Westmoreland, M. R., & Benjamin, R. G. (2015). Reading fluency skill and the prosodic marking of linguistic focus. *Reading and Writing, 28*(1), 9–30.

Scott, J. A., Miller, T. F., & Flinspach, S. L. (2012). Developing word consciousness: Lessons from highly diverse fourth-grade classrooms. In E. J. Kame'enui & J. F. Baumann (Eds.), *Vocabulary instruction: Research to practice* (2nd ed., pp. 169–188). Guildford.

Seidenberg, P. L. (1989). Relating text-processing research to reading and writing instruction for learning disabled students. *Learning Disabilities Focus, 5*(1), 4–12.

Seifert, C. M., Dyer, M. G., & Black, J. B. (1986). Thematic knowledge in story understanding. *Text: Interdisciplinary Journal for the Study of Discourse, 6*(4), 393–426.

Shanahan, T. (2019, February 9). *Which texts for teaching reading: Decodable, predictable, or controlled vocabulary?* Shanahan on Literacy. https://www.shanahanonliteracy.com/blog/which-texts-for-teaching-reading-decodable-predictable-or-controlled-vocabulary#sthash.vLrOY4Ac.dpbs

Shanahan, T., Callison, K., Carriere, C., Duke, N. K., Pearson, P. D., Schatschneider, C., & Torgesen, J. (2010). *Improving reading comprehension in kindergarten through 3rd grade: IES practice guide* (NCEE 2010-4038). National Center for Education Evaluation and Regional Assistance, Institute of Education Sciences, U.S. Department of Education. Retrieved from the NCEE website: https://ies.ed.gov/ncee/wwc/practiceguide/14

Shanahan, T., & Shanahan, C. (2012). What is disciplinary literacy and why does it matter? *Topics in Language Disorders, 32*(1), 7–18.

Shannon, P., Kame'enui, E. J., & Baumann, J. F. (1988). An investigation of children's ability to comprehend character motives. *American Educational Research Journal, 25*(3), 441–462.

Share, D. L. (1995). Phonological recoding and self-teaching: *Sine qua non* of reading acquisition. *Cognition, 55*(2), 151–218.

Share, D. L. (2008). Orthographic learning, phonology, and self-teaching. In R. V. Kail (Ed.), *Advances in child development and behavior* (pp. 31–82). Elsevier.

Shattuck-Hufnagel, S., Ostendorf, M., & Ross, K. (1994). Stress shift and early pitch accent placement in lexical items in American English. *Journal of Phonetics, 22*(4), 357–388.

Shine, S., & Roser, N. L. (1999). The role of genre in preschoolers' response to picture books. *Research in the Teaching of English, 34*(2), 197–254.

Short, E. J., & Ryan, E. B. (1984). Metacognitive differences between skilled and less skilled readers: Remediating deficits through story grammar and attribution training. *Journal of Educational Psychology, 76*(2), 225.

Simons, D. J. (2014). The value of direct replication. *Perspectives on Psychological Science, 9*(1), 76–80.

Sinatra, G. M., Brown, K., J., & Reynolds, R. E. (2002). Implications of cognitive resource allocation for comprehension strategy instruction. In C. C. Block & M. Pressley (Eds.), *Comprehension instruction: Research-based best practices* (pp. 62–76). Guilford.

Slough, S. W., McTigue, E. M., Kim, S., & Jennings, S. K. (2010). Science textbooks' use of graphical representation: A descriptive analysis of four sixth grade science texts. *Reading Psychology, 31*(3), 301–325.

Smallwood, J. (2011). Mind-wandering while reading: Attentional decoupling, mindless reading, and the cascade model of inattention. *Language and Linguistics Compass, 5*(2), 63–77.

Smallwood, J., Fishman, D. J., & Schooler, J. W. (2007). Counting the cost of an absent mind: Mind wandering as an underrecognized influence on educational performance. *Psychonomic Bulletin & Review, 14*(2), 230–236.

Snow, C. (2002). *Reading for understanding: Toward an R&D program in reading comprehension.* Rand Corporation. https://www.rand.org/pubs/monograph_reports/MR1465.html

Snow, C. E., Burns, M. S., & Griffin, P. (Eds.) (1998). *Preventing reading difficulties in young children.* National Academy Press.

Sorenson Duncan, T., Mimeau, C., Crowell, N., & Deacon, S. H. (2021). Not all sentences are created equal: Evaluating the relation between children's understanding of basic and difficult sentences and their reading comprehension. *Journal of Educational Psychology, 113*(2), 268–278.

Sosa, T., Hall, A. H., Goldman, S. R., & Lee, C. D. (2016). Developing symbolic interpretation through literary argumentation. *Journal of the Learning Sciences*, *25*(1), 93–132.

Souto-Manning, M., Llerena, C. I. L., Martell, J., Maguire, A. S., & Arce-Boardman, A. (2018). *No more culturally irrelevant teaching*. Heinemann.

Stanfield, R. A., & Zwaan, R. A. (2001). The effect of implied orientation derived from verbal context on picture recognition. *Psychological Science*, *12*(2), 153–156.

Stanovich, K. E. (1986). Matthew effects in reading: Some consequences of individual differences in the acquisition of literacy. *Reading Research Quarterly*, *21*(4), 360–407.

Stanovich, K. E., & Cunningham, A. E. (1993). Where does knowledge come from? Specific associations between print exposure and information acquisition. *Journal of Educational Psychology*, *85*(2), 211–229.

Stanovich, K. E., West, R. F., Cunningham, A. E., Cipielewski, J., & Siddiqui, S. (1996). The role of inadequate print exposure as a determinant of reading comprehension problems. In C. Cornoldi & J. V. Oakhill (Eds.), *Reading comprehension difficulties: Processes and intervention* (pp. 15–32). Lawrence Erlbaum.

Stapp, A. C. (2019). Reconceptualizing the learning space through flexible seating: A qualitative analysis of select third-grade students' and teacher perceptions. *Research in the Schools*, *26*(2), 32–44.

Steacy, L. M., Elleman, A. M., Lovett, M. W., & Compton, D. L. (2016). Exploring differential effects across two decoding treatments on item-level transfer in children with significant word reading difficulties: A new approach for testing intervention elements. *Scientific Studies of Reading*, *20*(4), 283–295.

Stein, N. L. (1978). The comprehension and appreciation of stories: A developmental analysis. In S. S. Madeja (Ed.), *The arts, cognition, and basic skills* (pp. 231–249). Central Midwestern Regional Educational Laboratory.

Stein, N., & Glenn, C. (1979). An analysis of story comprehension in elementary school children. In R. Freedle (Ed.), *New directions in discourse processing* (Vol. 2, pp. 53–120). Ablex.

Stein, N., & Levine, L. (1990). Making sense out of emotion: A goal-directed analysis of action. In N. Stein, B. Leventhal, & T. Trabasso (Eds.), *Psychological and biological approaches to emotion* (pp. 45–73). Erlbaum.

Stein, N., & Trabasso, T. (1982). The child's understanding of story. In R. Glasser (Ed.), *Advances in instructional psychology* (pp. 97–102). Academic Press.

Stevens, E. A., Walker, M. A., & Vaughn, S. (2017). The effects of reading fluency interventions on the reading fluency and reading comprehension performance of elementary students with learning disabilities: A synthesis of the research from 2001 to 2014. *Journal of Learning Disabilities*, *50*(5), 576–590.

Stevens, R. J. (1988). Effects of strategy training on the identification of the main idea of expository passages. *Journal of Educational Psychology*, *80*(1), 21–26.

Stouffer, J. (2011). Listening to yourself reading: Exploring the influence of auditory input in literacy processing. *Journal of Reading Recovery*, *11*(1), 15–28.

Sulzby, E. (1985). Children's emergent reading of favorite storybooks: A developmental study. *Reading Research Quarterly*, *20*(4), 458–481.

Sulzby, E. (1991). Assessment of emergent literacy: Storybook reading. *The Reading Teacher*, *44*(7), 498–500.

Sulzby, E. (1996). Roles of oral and written language as children approach conventional literacy. In C. Pontecorvo, M. Orsolini, B. Burge, & L. B. Resnick (Eds.), *Early text construction in children* (pp. 25–46). Erlbaum.

Sulzby, E., & Teale, W. (1991). Emergent literacy. In R. Barr, M. L. Kamil, P. B. Mosenthal, & P. D. Pearson (Eds.), *Handbook of reading research* (Vol. 2, pp. 727–758). Lawrence Erlbaum.

Sweet, A. P., & Snow, C. E. (Eds.). (2003). *Rethinking reading comprehension*. Guilford.

Sychterz, T. (2002). Rethinking childhood innocence. *The New Advocate*, *15*(3), 183–195.

Taft, M. L., & Leslie, L. (1985). The effects of prior knowledge and oral reading accuracy on miscues and comprehension. *Journal of Reading Behavior*, *17*(2), 163–179.

Tarchi, C. (2010). Reading comprehension of informative texts in secondary school: A focus on direct and indirect effects of reader's prior knowledge. *Learning and Individual Differences*, *20*(5), 415–420.

Taylor, B. M., Frye, B. J., & Maruyama, G. M. (1990). Time spent reading and reading growth. *American Educational Research Journal*, *27*(2), 351–362.

Teale, W. H. (1987). Emergent literacy: Reading and writing development in early childhood. *National Reading Conference Yearbook*, *36*, 45–74.

Teale, W. H., & Sulzby, E. (1986). *Emergent literacy: Writing and reading.* Ablex.

Thein, A. H., Beach, R., & Parks, D. (2007). Perspective-taking as transformative practice in teaching multicultural literature to white students. *The English Journal, 97*(2), 54–60.

Thomas, J. (1986). Woods and castles, towers and huts: Aspects of setting in the fairy tale. *Children's Literature in Education, 17*(2), 126–134.

Tierney, R. J., & Cunningham, J. W. (1984). Research on teaching reading comprehension. In M. Kamil, P. Mosenthal, P. D. Pearson, & R. Barr (Eds.), *Handbook of reading research* (Vol. 1, pp. 609–655). Longman.

Tippett, C. D. (2010). Refutation text in science education: A review of two decades of research. *International Journal of Science and Mathematics Education, 8*(6), 951–970.

Tobin, R. (2008). Conundrums in the differentiated literacy classroom. *Reading Improvement, 45*(4), 159–170.

Torr, J., & Scott, C. (2006). Learning "special words": Technical vocabulary in the talk of adults and preschoolers during shared reading. *Journal of Early Childhood Research, 4*(2), 153–167.

Tracy, K. N., Menickelli, K., & Scales, R. Q. (2017). Courageous voices: Using text sets to inspire change. *Journal of Adolescent & Adult Literacy, 60*(5), 527–536.

Treiman, R., Cohen, J., Mulqueeny, K., Kessler, B., & Schechtman, S. (2007). Young children's knowledge about printed names. *Child Development, 78*(5), 1458–1471.

Tyler, B.-J., & Chard, D. J. (2000). Using readers theatre to foster fluency in struggling readers: A twist on the repeated reading strategy. *Reading & Writing Quarterly, 16*(2), 163–168.

Vadasy, P. F., & Sanders, E. A. (2008). Code-oriented instruction for kindergarten students at risk for reading difficulties: A replication and comparison of instructional groupings. *Reading and Writing, 21*(9), 929–963.

Vadasy, P. F., Sanders, E. A., & Peyton, J. A. (2006). Code-oriented instruction for kindergarten students at risk for reading difficulties: A randomized field trial with paraeducator implementers. *Journal of Educational Psychology, 98* (3), 508–528.

van den Broek, P. (1989). Causal reasoning and inference making in judging the importance of story statements. *Child Development, 60*(2), 286–297.

van den Broek, P., Lynch, J. S., Naslund, J., Ievers-Landis, C. E., & Verduin, K. (2003). The development of comprehension of main ideas in narratives: Evidence from the selection of titles. *Journal of Educational Psychology, 95*(4), 707–718.

van den Broek, P., & Trabasso, T. (1986). Causal networks versus goal hierarchies in summarizing text. *Discourse Processes, 9*, 1–15.

Van Dijk, T. A. (1979). Relevance assignment in discourse comprehension. *Discourse Processes, 2*(2), 113–126.

Varelas, M., Pappas, C. C., Kokkino, S., & Ortiz, I. (2008). Students as authors. *Science & Children, 45*(7), 58–62.

Vaughn, S., Klingner, J. K., Swanson, E. A., Boardman, A. G., Roberts, G., Mohammed, S. S., & Stillman-Spisak, S. J. (2011). Efficacy of collaborative strategic reading with middle school students. *American Educational Research Journal, 48*(4), 938–964.

Veenman, M. V., Van Hout-Wolters, B. H. A. M., & Afflerbach, P. (2006). Metacognition and learning: Conceptual and methodological considerations. *Metacognition and Learning, 1*(1), 3–14.

Venezky, R. L. 1999. *The American way of spelling: The structure and origins of American English orthography.* Guilford.

Von Sprecken, D., Kim, J., & Krashen, S. (2000). The home run book: Can one positive reading experience create a reader. *California School Library Journal, 23*(2), 8–9.

Waggoner, M., Chinn, C., Yi, H., & Anderson, R. C. (1995). Collaborative reasoning about stories. *Language Arts, 72*(8), 582–589.

Walczyk, J. J., & Griffith-Ross, D. A. (2007). How important is reading skill fluency for comprehension? *The Reading Teacher, 60*(6), 560–569.

Walton, P. (2014). Using singing and movement to teach pre-reading skills and word reading to kindergarten children: An exploratory study. *Language and Literacy, 16*(3), 54–77.

Ward, A. E., Duke, N. K., & Klingelhofer, R. (2020, October 27). *Observing young readers and writers: A tool for informing instruction.* Literacy Now. https://www.literacyworldwide.org/blog/literacy-now/2020/10/27/observing-young-readers-and-writers-a-tool-for-informing-instruction

Watts-Taffe, S., Fisher, P., & Blachowicz, C. (2017). Vocabulary instruction: Research and practice. In D. Lapp & D. Fisher (Eds.), *Handbook of research on teaching the English language arts* (4th ed., pp. 130-161). Routledge.

Webb, N. M. (2009). The teacher's role in promoting collaborative dialogue in the classroom. *British Journal of Educational Psychology, 79*(1), 1-28.

Weber, R.-M. (2018). Listening for schwa in academic vocabulary. *Reading Psychology, 39*(5), 468-491.

Weger, H., Jr., Castle, G. R., & Emmett, M. C. (2010). Active listening in peer interviews: The influence of message paraphrasing on perceptions of listening skill. *The International Journal of Listening, 24*(1), 34-49.

Weinstein, C. E., & Mayer, R. E. (1986). The teaching of learning strategies. In M. Wittrock (Ed.). *Handbook of research on teaching* (3rd ed., pp. 315-327). Macmillan.

Weinstein, C., Husman, J., & Dierking, D. (2000). Self-regulation interventions with a focus on learning strategies. In M. Boekaerts, P. R. Pintrich, & M. Zeidner (Eds.), *Handbook of self-regulation: Theory, research, and applications* (pp. 727-747). Academic Press.

Wennerstrom, A., & Siegel, A. F. (2003). Keeping the floor in multiparty conversations: Intonation, syntax, and pause. *Discourse Processes, 36*(2), 77-107.

Wiggins, G. (2013, March 4). *On so-called "reading strategies"—the utter mess that is the literature and advice to teachers.* https://grantwiggins.wordpress.com/2013/03/04/on-so-called-reading-strategies-the-utter-mess-that-is-the-literature-and-advice-to-teachers/

Wilder, A. A., & Williams, J. P. (2001). Students with severe learning disabilities can learn higher order comprehension skills. *Journal of Educational Psychology, 93*(2), 268-278.

Wilkie-Stibbs, C. (2006). Intertextuality and the child reader. In P. Hunt (Ed.), *Understanding children's literature* (2nd ed., pp. 168-179). Routledge.

Wilkinson, I. A. G., Murphy, P. K., & Binici, S. (2015). Dialogue-intensive pedagogies for promoting reading comprehension: What we know, what we need to know. In L. B. Resnick, C. S. C. Asterhan, & S. N. Clarke (Eds.), *Socializing intelligence through academic talk and dialogue* (pp. 37-50). American Educational Research Association.

Williams, J. P. (1988). Identifying main ideas: A basic aspect of reading comprehension. *Topics in Language Disorders, 8*(3), 1-13.

Williams, J. P. (1993). Comprehension of students with and without learning disabilities: Identification of narrative themes and idiosyncratic text representations. *Journal of Educational Psychology, 85*(4), 631-641.

Williams, J. P. (2005). Instruction in reading comprehension for primary-grade students: A focus on text structure. *The Journal of Special Education, 39*(1), 6-18.

Williams, J. P., Brown, L. G., Silverstein, A. K., & de Cani, J. S. (1994). An instructional program in comprehension of narrative themes for adolescents with learning disabilities. *Learning Disability Quarterly, 17*(3), 205-221.

Williams, J. P., Lauer, K. D., Hall, K. M., Lord, K. M., Gugga, S. S., Bak, S.-J., Jacobs, P. R., & deCani, J. S. (2002). Teaching elementary school students to identify story themes. *Journal of Educational Psychology, 94*(2), 235-248.

Williams, L. M. (2008). Book selections of economically disadvantaged black elementary students. *The Journal of Educational Research, 102*(1), 51-64.

Williamson, P., Carnahan, C. R., Birri, N., & Swoboda, C. (2015). Improving comprehension of narrative using character event maps for high school students with autism spectrum disorder. *The Journal of Special Education, 49*(1), 28-38.

Willson, A., Falcon, L., & Martinez, M. (2014). Second graders' interpretation of character in picturebook illustrations. *Reading Horizons: A Journal of Literacy and Language Arts, 53*(2), 41-61.

Willson, V. L., & Rupley, W. H. (1993). Structural components of single word recognition: Activation of orthographic, meaning, and phonological processors. *Literacy Research and Instruction, 32*(4), 33-45.

Wilson, N. (1989). Learning from confusion: Questions and change in reading logs. *The English Journal, 78*(7), 62-69.

Winograd, P. N. (1984). Strategic difficulties in summarizing texts. *Reading Research Quarterly, 19*(4), 404-425.

Winograd, P., & Bridge, C. (1986). The comprehension of important information in written prose. In J. F. Baumann (Ed.), *Teaching main idea comprehension* (pp. 18-48). International Reading Association.

Wise, C. N. (2019). *Assessment and instruction for developing second graders' skill in ascertaining word meanings from context* (Publication No. 27614419) [Doctoral dissertation, University of Michigan]. ProQuest Dissertations Publishing.

Wolf, M. (2007). *Proust and the squid: The story and science of the reading brain.* Harper Perennial.

Wolf, M. K., Crosson, A. C., & Resnick, L. B. (2005). Classroom talk for rigorous reading comprehension instruction. *Reading Psychology, 26*(1), 27-53.

Wong, B. Y. L. (1985). Self-questioning instructional research: A review. *Review of Educational Research, 55*(2), 227-268.

Wong, B. Y. L., & Jones, W. (1982). Increasing metacomprehension in learning disabled and normally achieving students through self-questioning training. *Learning Disability Quarterly, 5*(3), 228-240.

Woolley, G. (2010). Developing reading comprehension: Combining visual and verbal cognitive processes. *The Australian Journal of Language and Literacy, 33*(2), 108-125.

Wright, T. S., & Cervetti, G. N. (2017). A systematic review of the research on vocabulary instruction that impacts text comprehension. *Reading Research Quarterly, 52*(2), 203-226.

Wright, T. S., Cervetti, G. N., Wise, C., & McClung, N. A. (2022). The impact of knowledge-building through conceptually-coherent read alouds on vocabulary and comprehension. *Reading Psychology, 43*(1), 70-84.

Yaden, D. B., Jr., Rowe, D. W., & MacGillivray, L. (2000). Emergent literacy: A matter (polyphony) of perspectives. In M. L. Kamil, P. B. Mosenthal, P. D. Pearson, & R. Barr (Eds.), *Handbook of reading research* (Vol. 3, pp. 425-454). Routledge.

Yang, Y. H., Chu, H. C., & Tseng, W. T. (2021). Text difficulty in extensive reading: Reading comprehension and reading motivation. *Reading in a Foreign Language, 33*(1), 78-102.

Young, C., & Rasinski, T. (2018). Readers theatre: Effects on word recognition automaticity and reading prosody. *Journal of Research in Reading, 41*(3), 475-485.

Young, C., Valadez, C., & Gandara, C. (2016). Using performance methods to enhance students' reading fluency. *The Journal of Educational Research, 109*(6), 624-630.

Yuill, N., & Joscelyne, T. (1988). Effect of organizational cues and strategies on good and poor comprehenders' story understanding. *Journal of Educational Psychology, 80*(2), 152-158.

Zengilowski, A., Schuetze, B. A., Nash, B. L., & Schallert, D. L. (2021). A critical review of the refutation text literature: Methodological confounds, theoretical problems, and possible solutions. *Educational Psychologist, 56*(3), 175-195.

Zimmerman, B. J. (1986). Becoming a self-regulated learner: Which are the key subprocesses? *Contemporary Educational Psychology, 11*(4), 307-313.

Zimmerman, B. J. (2002). Becoming a self-regulated learner: An overview. *Theory into Practice, 41*(2), 64-70.

Zuljevic, V. (2005). Puppets: A great addition to everyday teaching. *Thinking Classroom, 6*(1), 37-44.

Zutell, J., & Rasinski, T. V. (1991). Training teachers to attend to their students' oral reading fluency. *Theory into Practice, 30*(3), 211-217.

Zwaan, R. A. (1999). Embodied cognition, perceptual symbols, and situation models. *Discourse Processes, 28*(1), 81-88.

Zwiers, J. (2019). *Next steps with academic conversations: New ideas for improving learning through classroom talk.* Stenhouse.

Zwiers, J., & Crawford, M. (2009). How to start academic conversations. *Educational Leadership, 66*(6), 70-73.

Zwiers, J., & Crawford, M. (2011). *Academic conversations: Classroom talk that fosters critical thinking and content understandings.* Stenhouse.

Professional Text References

Ahmed, S. K. (2019). *Being the change: Lessons and strategies to teach social comprehension.* Heinemann.

Allington, R. L. (2011). *What really matters for struggling readers: Designing research-based programs.* Pearson.

Atwell, N. (2007). *The reading zone: How to help kids become skilled, passionate, habitual, critical readers.* Scholastic.

Beck, I. L., & Beck, M. E. (2013). *Making sense of phonics: The hows and whys* (2nd ed.). Guilford.

Beck, I. L., McKeown, M. G., & Kucan, L. (2013). *Bringing words to life: Robust vocabulary instruction* (2nd ed.). Guilford.

Beers, K. (2002). *When kids can't read—what teachers can do: A guide for teachers 6–12.* Heinemann.

Beers, K., & Probst, R. E. (2012). *Notice and note: Strategies for close reading.* Heinemann.

Bomer, R., & Bomer, K. (2001). *For a better world: Reading and writing for social action.* Heinemann.

Blevins, W. (2016). *A fresh look at phonics: Common causes of failure and 7 ingredients for success.* Corwin.

Burroway, J. (2003). *Imaginative writing; The elements of craft.* Longman.

Cartwright, K. B. (2010). *Word callers: Small-group and one-to-one interventions for children who "read" but don't comprehend.* Heinemann.

Cherry-Paul, S., & Johansen, D. (2014). *Teaching interpretation: Using text-based evidence to construct meaning.* Heinemann.

Clay, M. (2017). *Concepts about print* (2nd ed.). Heinemann.

Cobb, C., & Blachowicz, C. (2014). *No more "look up the list" vocabulary instruction.* Heinemann.

Collins, K. (2004). *Growing readers: Units of study in the primary classroom.* Stenhouse.

Collins, K. (2008). *Reading for real: Teach students to read with power, intention, and joy in K–3 classrooms.* Stenhouse.

Collins, K., & Glover, M. (2015). *I am reading: Nurturing young children's meaning making and joyful engagement with any book.* Heinemann.

Curwood, J. S. (2013). Redefining normal: A critical analysis of (dis)ability in young adult literature. *Children's Literature in Education, 44*(1), 15–28.

Duke, N. K. (2014). *Inside information: Developing powerful readers and writers of informational text through project-based instruction.* Scholastic.

Duke, N. K., & Bennett-Armistead, S. V. (2003). *Reading & writing informational text in the primary grades.* Scholastic.

España, C., & Herrera, L. Y. (2020). *En comunidad: Lessons for centering the voices and experiences of bilingual Latinx students.* Heinemann.

Gibbons, P. (1993). *Learning to learn in a second language.* Heinemann.

Hammond, Z. (2015). *Culturally responsive teaching and the brain: Promoting authentic engagement and rigor among culturally and linguistically diverse students.* Corwin.

Harvey, S., & Goudvis, A. (2007). *Strategies that work: Teaching comprehension for understanding and engagement* (2nd ed.). Stenhouse.

Keene, E. O. (2012). *Talk about understanding: Rethinking classroom talk to enhance comprehension.* Heinemann.

Keene, E. O., & Zimmerman, S. (2007). *Mosaic of thought: The power of comprehension strategy instruction* (2nd ed.). Heinemann.

Kilpatrick, D. A. (2015). *Essentials of assessing, preventing, and overcoming reading difficulties.* John Wiley & Sons.

Kintsch, W. (1988). The role of knowledge in discourse comprehension: A construction-integration model. *Psychological Review, 95*(2), 163–182.

Kuhn, M. R. (2008). *The hows and whys of fluency instruction.* Pearson.

Lesesne, T. (2010). *Reading ladders: Leading students from where they are to where we'd like them to be.* Heinemann.

Lubliner, S. (2001). *A practical guide to reciprocal teaching.* Wright Group/McGraw-Hill.

Martinelli, M., & Mraz, K. (2012). *Smarter charts K–2: Optimizing an instructional staple to create independent readers and writers.* Heinemann.

Mesmer, H. A. (2019). *Letter lessons and first words: Phonics foundations that work.* Heinemann.

Miller, D. (2009). *The book whisperer: Awakening the inner reader in every child.* Jossey-Bass.

Miller, D. (2012). *Reading with meaning: Teaching comprehension in the primary grades* (2nd ed.). Stenhouse.

Miller, D. (2013). *Reading in the wild.* Jossey Bass.

Miller, D., & Moss, B. (2013). *No more independent reading without support.* Heinemann.

Minor, C. (2018). *We got this: Equity, access, and the quest to be who our students need us to be.* Heinemann.

Mraz, K., & Martinelli, M. (2014). *Smarter charts for math, science, and social studies: Making learning visible in the content areas.* Heinemann.

Nichols, M. (2006). *Comprehension through conversation: The power of purposeful talk in the reading workshop.* Heinemann.

Owocki, G. (2012). *The common core lesson book, K–5: Working with increasingly complex literature, informational text, and foundational reading skills.* Heinemann.

Porcelli, A., & Tyler, C. (2008). *Quick guide to boosting English acquisition in choice time, K–2.* Heinemann.

Rasinski, T. V. (2010). *The fluent reader: Oral and silent reading strategies for building fluency, word recognition, and comprehension* (2nd ed.). Scholastic.

Ray, K. W., & Glover, M. (2008). *Already ready: Nurturing writers in preschool and kindergarten.* Heinemann.

Santman, D. (2005). *Shades of meaning: Comprehension and interpretation in middle school.* Heinemann.

Serravallo, J. (2010). *Teaching reading in small groups: Differentiated instruction for building strategic, independent readers.* Heinemann.

Serravallo, J. (2015). *The reading strategies book: Your everything guide to developing skilled readers.* Heinemann.

Serravallo, J. (2017). *The writing strategies book: Your everything guide to developing skilled writers.* Heinemann.

Serravallo, J. (2018). *Understanding texts & readers: Responsive comprehension instruction with leveled texts.* Heinemann.

Smith, M. W., & Wilhelm, J. D. (2010). *Fresh takes on teaching literary elements: How to teach what really matters about character, setting, point of view, and theme.* Scholastic.

Snowball, D., & Bolton, F. (1999). *Spelling K–8: Planning and teaching.* Stenhouse.

Taberski, S. (2000). *On solid ground: Strategies for teaching reading, K–3.* Heinemann.

Taberski, S. (2011). *Comprehension from the ground up: Simplified, sensible instruction for the K–3 reading workshop.* Heinemann.

Teale, W. H. (1987). Emergent literacy: Reading and writing development in early childhood. *National Reading Conference Yearbook, 36,* 45–74.

Willingham, D. T. (2015). *Raising kids who read: What parents and teachers can do.* Jossey-Bass.

Willingham, D. T. (2017). *The reading mind: A cognitive approach to understanding how the mind reads.* John Wiley & Sons.

Children's and Young Adult Literature References

Aesop. (n.d.). *Aesop's fables.*

Ajmera, M., & Browning, D. (2016). *Every breath we take: A book about air.* Charlesbridge.

Arlon, P. (2012). *Farm.* Scholastic.

Arlon, P., & Gordon-Harris, T. (2012). *Penguins.* Scholastic.

Atinuke. (2019). *Africa, amazing Africa.* Walker Books.

Bardoe, C. (2021). *Bei Bei goes home: A panda story.* Candlewick Entertainment.

Baum, F. (1990). *The Wonderful Wizard of Oz.* George M Hill Company.

Becker, B. (2012). *A visitor for bear.* Candlewick.

Bishop, N. (2008). *Frogs.* Scholastic.

Browning, D., & Ajmera, M. (2016). *Every breath we take: A book about air.* Charlesbridge.

Buyea, R. (2015). *Saving Mr. Terupt.* Yearling Books.

Cazet, D. (1998–2007). Minnie and Moo series. Scholastic.

Coerr, E. (1977). *Sadako and the thousand paper cranes.* G.P. Putnam's Sons.

Collard, S. B., III (2022). *Little killers: The ferocious lives of puny predators.* Millbrook Press.

Craft, J. (2019). *New kid.* Quill Tree Books.

Davies, N. (2015). *One tiny turtle.* Candlewick.

Díaz, J. (2018). *Islandborn.* Dial Press.

Dillard, J. (2021). *J.D. and the great barber battle.* Kokila.

Ehlert, L. (1989). *Eating the alphabet.* Harcourt Brace Jovanovich.

Erdrich, L. (1999). *The birchbark house.* Hyperion.

Faruqi, S. (2018–2022). Yasmin series. Picture Window Books.

Florence, D. M. (2019–2020). My Furry Foster Family series. Picture Window Books.

Gantos, J. (1998). *Joey Pigza swallowed the key.* Square Fish Books.

Gratz, A. (2021). *Ground zero.* Scholastic.

Greenfield, E. (n.d.). Rope rhyme. In *Honey, I love and other love poems.* HarperCollins.

Grimes, N. (2009–2012). Dyamonde Daniel series. G.P. Putnam's Sons Books for Young Readers.

Harman, A. (2020). *Climate change and how we'll fix it.* QED Publishing.

Hughes, L. (1994). April rain song. *The collected poems of Langston Hughes.* Vintage Books.

Jackson, S. (1948). "The lottery." *The New Yorker.*

Jay, A. (2003). *ABC: A child's first alphabet book.* Templar Books.

Jenkins, M. (2011). *Can we save the tiger?* Candlewick Press.

Jennings, T. C. (2021). Definitely Dominguita series. Aladdin Books.

Kalman, B. (1999). *What is a primate?* Crabtree Publishing Company.

Keating, J. (2016). *Pink is for blobfish.* Knopf Books for Young Readers.

Kramer, S. (1993). *To the top! Climbing the world's highest mountain.* Random House Children's Books.

Lai, T. (2011). *Inside out and back again.* HarperCollins.

LaRocca, R. (2021). *Red, White, and Whole.* Quill Tree Books.

Lee, S. (2008). *Wave.* Chronicle Books.

Libenson, T. (2017). *Invisible Emmie.* Balzer + Bray.

Lin, G. (2009). *Where the mountain meets the moon.* Little, Brown and Company.

Lindstrom, C. (2020). *We are water protectors.* Roaring Brook Press.

Lobel, A. (1970–1979). Frog and Toad series. Harper and Row.

Lyons, K. S. (2022). *Ty's travels: Lab magic.* HarperCollins.

Medina, M. (2018). *Merci Suárez changes gears.* Candlewick Press.

Mora, O. (2018). *Thank you, Omu!* Little, Brown Books for Young Readers.

Mora, O. (2019). *Saturday.* Little, Brown Books for Young Readers.

Nichols, D. (2021). *Art of protest: Creating, discovering, and activating art for your revolution.* Big Picture Press.

Novak, B. J. (2014). *The book with no pictures.* Rocky Pond Books.

Nye, N. (2008). There was no wind. *Honeybee: Poems and short prose.* Greenwillow Books.

Orwell, G. (1945). *Animal farm.* Secker and Warburg.

Park, L. S. (2010). *A long walk to water.* Clarion Books.

Phi, B. (2019). *My footprints.* Capstone Editions.

Poe, E. A. (1843). "The tell-tale heart." *The Pioneer.*

Quigley, D. (2021). *Jo Jo Makoons: The used-to-be best friend*. Heartdrum.

Quintero, I. (2019). *My papi has a motorcycle*. Kokila.

Raschka, C. (1993). *Yo! Yes?* Orchard Books.

Rathmann, P. (1996). *Good Night, Gorilla*. G.P. Putnam's Sons.

Reynolds, J. (2016). *Ghost*. Simon and Schuster.

Riley, S. (2021). *The floating field*. Millbrook Press.

Rocco, J. (2011). *Blackout*. Little, Brown Books for Young Readers.

Rodríguez, A. M. (2018). *The secret of the scuba diving spider . . . and more!* Enslow Publishing.

Rotner, S., & Woodhull, A. L. (2020). *Shapes*. Holiday House.

Ryan, P. M. (2000). *Esperanza rising*. Scholastic.

Rylant, C. (1987–2007). Henry and Mudge series. Simon Spotlight.

Rylant, C. (1994–2016). Mr. Putter and Tabby series. HMH Books for Young Readers.

Rylant, C. (1997–2001). Poppleton series. Blue Sky Press.

Santat, D. (2017). *After the fall*. Roaring Brook Press.

Silverstein, S. (1964). *The giving tree*. Harper and Row.

Singh, S. J. (2020). *Fauja Singh keeps going*. Kokila.

Soontornvat, C. (2020). *All thirteen*. Candlewick Press.

Soundar, C. (2021). *Sona Sharma, very best big sister?* Candlewick Press.

Truss, L. (2006). *Eats, shoots & leaves*. G.P. Putnam's Sons Books for Young Readers.

Wade, J. (2021). *Nano: The spectacular science of the very (very) small*. Candlewick Press.

Wang, A. (2015). *The science of an oil spill*. Cherry Lake Publishing.

Willems, M. (2004). *Knuffle bunny: A cautionary tale*. Hyperion.

Willems, M. (2007–2016). Elephant and Piggie series. Hyperion Books.

Yang, G. L. (2006). *American born Chinese*. First Second Books.

Yang, K. (2018). *Front desk*. Arthur A. Levine Books.

Zuckerman, A. (2009). *Creature ABC*. Chronicle Books.

Image credits